SOCIAL STUDIES FOR CHILDREN
A Guide to Basic Instruction

John U. Michaelis

University of California, Berkeley

Prentice-Hall, Inc., Englewood Cliffs, New Jersey 07632

SOCIAL STUDIES FOR CHILDREN

A GUIDE TO BASIC INSTRUCTION

7TH EDITION

Library of Congress Cataloging in Publication Data

MICHAELIS, JOHN UDELL (date)
  Social studies for children

  First–6th ed. published under title: Social studies
for children in a democracy.
  Includes bibliographies and index.
  1. Social sciences—Study and teaching (Elementary)
2. Career education. 3. Mainstreaming in education.
I. Title.
LB1584.M43 1980   372.8'3'044   79-21628
ISBN 0-13-818880-7

SOCIAL STUDIES FOR CHILDREN
A Guide to Basic Instruction
seventh edition
John U. Michaelis

Editorial/production supervision by Lynda Heideman/Marianne Baltzell
Cover and interior design by Judith Winthrop
Manufacturing buyer: John Hall

Printed in the United States of America
10 9 8 7 6 5 4 3 2 1

Prentice-Hall International, Inc., *London*
Prentice-Hall of Australia Pty. Limited, *Sydney*
Prentice-Hall of Canada, Ltd., *Toronto*
Prentice-Hall of India Private Limited, *New Delhi*
Prentice-Hall of Japan, Inc., *Tokyo*
Prentice-Hall of Southeast Asia Pte. Ltd., *Singapore*
Whitehall Books Limited, *Wellington, New Zealand*

To
Elizabeth Ann Michaelis
John Barry Michaelis
Susan Ann Michaelis

CONTENTS

IDENTIFYING AND USING
INSTRUCTIONAL MEDIA   68

PLANNING AND GUIDING
GROUP WORK   108

PLANNING AND PROVIDING
FOR INDIVIDUAL DIFFERENCES   137

INCORPORATING CONCEPTUAL
AND PROCESS COMPONENTS
FROM THE SOCIAL SCIENCES   165

PREFACE

This volume has been written to serve as a guide for those who teach basic social studies in elementary and middle schools. It incorporates the best ideas from the past and critically reviews promising current developments and projected future trends. New material has been included in each chapter of this seventh edition. New charts and photographs provide concrete and practical examples of basic aspects of social studies instruction.

The chapters have been specifically designed and organized to aid study. Each begins with focusing questions that give an overview of the material and serve as study guides. Guidelines, teaching strategies, examples of applications, charts, checklists, and photographs are included to provide practical approaches to instruction. The questions and activities at the end of each chapter facilitate discussion, evaluation, and application of ideas. The list of references should be scanned to note further reading and checked to find answers to individual questions and concerns. Instructors and students in competency-based programs will find the focusing questions and activities to be helpful in preassessment and postassessment, as well as in developing basic competencies.

The opening chapter gives an overview of effective, up-to-date social studies programs. It defines the social studies, discusses goals and objectives, reviews the curriculum, and points out other matters that concern today's teachers.

Chapter 2 discusses the planning of units of instruction, with emphasis on establishing objectives and bringing together appropriate learning materials and activities to achieve these objectives—an essential teacher competency. This chapter provides examples of different models of unit planning and shows how to sequence learning from intake and organizing activities through summarizing activities and on to applicative and creative activities. Chapter 3 discusses a closely related and equally essential task: identifying and planning to incorporate a variety of instructional media. It provides checklists for identifying materials, suggestions for teacher-prepared materials, and guidelines for using various media.

Chapters 4 and 5 discuss two other basic teacher competencies: planning and guiding group work and meeting individual differences. Chapter 4 examines group discussion and questioning techniques, committee work, and other small-group activities. It provides charts and checklists for guiding and assessing group work; it gives examples of questions for directing discussion and model study guides for improving group work. Chapter 5 gives guidelines and provides checklists for meeting individual differences; it suggests ways to individualize reading, to use learning contracts and activity cards, and to tailor instruction to those with special educational needs.

The next three chapters contain suggestions and guidelines for incorporating basic content, processes, and activities from three basic sources. Conceptual and process elements from the social sciences are treated in chapter 6; conceptual elements and learning activities for multicultural, global, law-focused, environmental, and career education—areas of basic social concern—are discussed in chapter 7. Both chapters 6 and 7 emphasize concepts, themes, and generalizations; they show how focusing questions are used to link concepts to thinking processes. Chapter 8 presents procedures for including current affairs, issues, and special events and gives guidelines and activities for doing so.

Because teaching strategies and techniques are so important to effective social studies instruction, five chapters have been devoted to them. The development of concepts, generalizations, and thinking processes is presented in chapter 9; the development of creative thinking through expressive activities, in chapter 10. Reading and study skills are discussed in chapter 11, and globe and map concepts and skills are reviewed in chapter 12. The development of attitudes, values, and democratic behavior—basic long-term outcomes of instruction—are discussed in chapter 13. Each chapter on teaching strategies provides questions, activities, and models that teachers can adapt and use in instructional units at all levels.

The last chapter is devoted to evaluation of students' learning. Featured in this chapter are charts, checklists, test items, and other evaluative devices that may be adapted to assess both cognitive and affective learning.

The order in which the chapters are presented has been suggested by several instructors and their students. It is the sequence used by the author. Some instructors prefer, however, to move from the first two chapters to those dealing with incorporating content from the social sciences, areas of social concern, and current affairs, in this way clarifying basic sources of content of the social studies. Others prefer to move from the first two chapters to those dealing with teaching strategies for developing concepts, thinking processes, skills, and attitudes and values, thus clarifying procedures to include in teaching units. Whatever sequence is used, each chapter should be viewed as a source of ideas to meet special needs and solve problems, just as materials in the social studies program are used as data sources and not necessarily followed in a fixed order.

Special acknowledgment is made to the following individuals who contributed ideas, charts, and photographs or suggested changes: Ruth H. Grossman, Nina Gabelko, Val Arnsdorf, Haig Rushdoonny, Lewis C. Vinson, Pat Harvey, Robert Griffin, Emma Wiley, Fred Wilson, Donald Bye, Mrs. Benjamin F. Benson, Thomas A. Sinks, Leonard F. Dalton, Sandra Crosby, Roy Harris, Gerald Hunter, Gerald Olson, Eileen McNab, Douglas Superka, Douglas MacDonald, David Wright, Herb Wong, Richard Endsley, and Carolyn Hall. Special acknowledgment is also made to the many instructors of social studies courses and their students for practical suggestions that have been incorporated in this edition.

BASIC FEATURES OF THE SOCIAL STUDIES

How is the social studies program defined?
What are its central goals and objectives?
How should instructional objectives be stated?
What is included in the curriculum?
What are other special features of the social studies?

The central purpose of this volume is to set forth basic features of the social studies as a developmental area of the curriculum. The changes and innovations of the past two decades, current movements, and projected future developments have created a need to clarify those features that need emphasis now and in the years ahead. The view is taken in this volume that social studies education is of basic importance for children growing up in a democracy. The unique contributions that may be made to the development of democratic citizenship must be clearly identified. Teachers must take a comprehensive view of what is basic so that all dimensions of democratic citizenship will be nurtured.

This chapter gives an overview of the basic features that form an effective and up-to-date social studies program. It presents definitions of the social studies and discusses goals and objectives. It then focuses on key aspects of the curriculum. The final section previews the basic features to be treated in depth in subsequent chapters.

Definitions of the Social Studies

Before proceeding, ask yourself these questions: How should the social studies be defined? What elements should be included in a definition? Make a mental note of your answers, then see whether or not your definition resembles any of those that follow.

Each of the brief definitions below reflects an orientation toward the best approach to the development of citizenship. The first two emphasize the use of content to develop citizenship: a subject matter orientation. The next two emphasize the abilities needed to deal with the conditions, changes, and problems of society: a society-centered orientation. The last emphasizes optimum development of the individual: a student-centered orientation. Each definition is rooted in a philosophical point of view of long standing in American education.

social studies as citizenship transmission	Those who adhere to this definition hold that social studies should transmit basic aspects of our history and our cultural heritage. They feel that responsible citizenship grows from a thorough understanding of the best of our cultural heritage.
social studies as social science education	This definition is favored by those exponents of realism and positivism who believe that the social studies content and methods of study should be drawn from the social sciences. Effective citizens know basic concepts and can use methods drawn from the social sciences to handle issues and problems.
social studies as reflective thinking	This definition is emphasized by those pragmatists who believe that the central aim of the social studies is to develop thinking and decision-making ability. Effective citizens can use models and processes of thinking and decision making to solve problems and resolve issues.
social studies as social criticism and action	This is the emphasis of reconstructionists who believe that the central aim of the social studies is to develop the knowledge and skills needed to improve society. Responsible citizens can make critical analyses of current issues and problems and take appropriate action.
social studies as personal development of the individual	This is stressed by proponents of progressivism and existentialism who believe that the program should be student-centered and should develop the whole child—socially, emotionally, intellectually, and physically. Self-understanding and self-direction are essential to responsible citizenship.

A COMPREHENSIVE DEFINITION

Although some teachers may lean toward one point of view, most find some merit in each definition. In fact, all social studies programs teach critically selected aspects of our cultural heritage; all draw content and methods from the social sciences. Effective and up-to-date programs invariably develop thinking processes and decision-making abilities. Varying amounts of social criticism and action may be found in environmental, ethnic, law-focused, and other phases of instruction. Individual development is nurtured in the context of a balanced program that includes attention to content, societal needs, and students' needs.

Instead of defining the social studies in terms of a single emphasis, this volume takes the position that it is better to include several components in a comprehensive definition tailored to current realities.

Viewing social studies programs in action, it is possible to identify the previously-noted emphases plus other elements. The dimensions noted in chart 1-1 are clearly evident in well-designed programs that focus on relationships between people and their social and physical environments.

The social studies program includes the study of those human relation-

The Social Studies

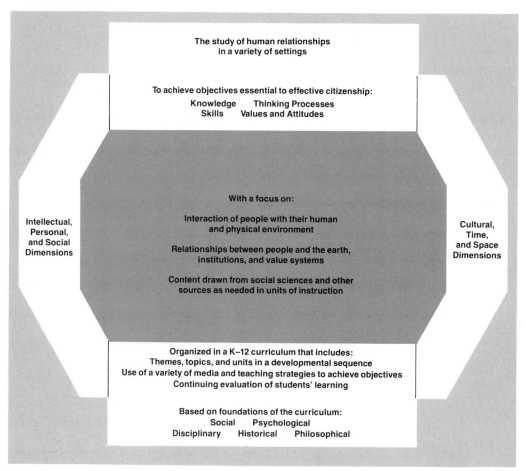

The study of human relationships
in a variety of settings

To achieve objectives essential to effective citizenship:
Knowledge   Thinking Processes
Skills   Values and Attitudes

Intellectual,
Personal,
and Social
Dimensions

With a focus on:

Interaction of people with their human
and physical environment

Relationships between people and the earth,
institutions, and value systems

Content drawn from social sciences and other
sources as needed in units of instruction

Cultural,
Time,
and Space
Dimensions

Organized in a K–12 curriculum that includes:
Themes, topics, and units in a developmental sequence
Use of a variety of media and teaching strategies to achieve objectives
Continuing evaluation of students' learning

Based on foundations of the curriculum:
Social   Psychological
Disciplinary   Historical   Philosophical

Chart 1–1

ships believed to be most important in the general education of students. Its central aim is to develop responsible citizenship. This aim is broken down into goals and objectives that include knowledge, thinking processes, skills, and attitudes and values. Instruction focuses on the interaction of people with their human and physical environment. Students investigate human interaction to identify relationships between people and the earth, people and institutions, and people and value systems. Content, which includes subject matter and methods of study, is drawn from the social sciences and other sources as needed to study selected topics, issues, and problems.

All programs include intellectual, personal, and social dimensions. The intellectual dimension includes the thinking processes and the concepts, themes, and generalizations that are tools of thinking. The personal dimension includes the conceptions, values, learning styles, and background of experience that students bring to the classroom. The social dimension includes interaction among students. As students study human relationships and participate in classroom, school, and community activities, they also discover for themselves processes of interaction.

Cultural, time, and space dimensions are also important. The cultural dimension includes the diverse ways of living among peoples of the world, as evidenced in those portions of the cultural heritage selected for study. The time dimension includes the past, present, and future; the emphasis varies depending on the topic under study, the maturity of students, and the need to place a topic in time perspective. The space dimension is critical as students study particular areas or regions, clarify distance and areal relationships, and analyze the interaction of people in one place with people in other places.

The program of instruction is organized in a kindergarten through twelfth grade curriculum that includes defined topics, themes, and units of study. To develop responsible citizenship, a developmental program of instruction must be provided. It includes the study of human relationships in a variety of settings, ranging from the local neighborhood and community to our nation and to other lands and peoples. It presents comparative studies of selected cultures and gives attention to the cultural roots of various groups in our society. A variety of media and teaching strategies help achieve objectives and tailor the program to individual differences among students. Ongoing evaluation is conducted as an integral part of instruction.

The entire social studies program is grounded in social, psychological, disciplinary, historical, and philosophical foundations. From these foundations are drawn the ideas and implications that are useful in program planning, development, and evaluation. From the social foundations are drawn the values, beliefs, trends, local demands, and legal requirements that must be considered in planning programs designed to develop democratic citizenship. From the psychological foundations are drawn findings about learning and development and about implications for curriculum and instructional planning. From the social sciences and other fields that serve as disciplinary foundations are drawn concepts, generalizations, and methods of inquiry that are related to units of instruction. From the historical foundations are drawn traditions, goals, patterns of organization, content, and procedures that have been used in the past. From the philosophical foundations are drawn the point of view, values, goals, and objectives that guide the planning, teaching and evaluating of the program.

Social studies should not be confused with social competence, social learning, or social education. *Social competence* is the ability to engage in group enterprises both in and out of school. *Social learning* encompasses all the experiences that help one to become oriented to society. *Social education* takes place in the school, family, church, and other institutions. Although the social studies program contributes to all of these, it is first and foremost a developmental area of the curriculum, as are the language arts, science education, and humanities education.

Goals and Objectives

Goals are the long-range desired outcomes of instruction; objectives are the specific and measurable outcomes of instruction. Goals and objectives of the social studies are related directly to our society's expectations, concerns, and mandates. Legislatures across the country have set down requirements for the social studies; they have established accountability programs to assure that students attain what is believed to be essential, or basic, learning. Over and above such requirements are goals and objectives related to our democratic heritage in general and our view of human rights and dignity in particular.

This chapter considers goals and objectives in several contexts. First, contributions of the social studies to goals of education are noted. Second, examples are given of goals in four major categories emphasized in programs throughout the country. Third, procedures for stating instructional or performance objectives are identified and examples of different types of objectives are given.

CONTRIBUTIONS TO GOALS OF EDUCATION

Social studies contribute to goals of education in several fundamental ways. Students gain *self-realization* through experiences that foster each individual's growth in knowledge, skills, and personal values. Students better understand *human relationships* through multicultural and ethnic studies, the study of various cultures, the development of interpersonal skills, and analysis of intergroup problems. Students develop *civic responsibility* through learning activities in and out of school; they learn the concepts and main ideas of government and the legal rights of individuals; and they develop thinking and valuing processes that help them to deal with issues and make decisions. Students gain in *economic competence* as they explore concepts, attitudes, and skills related to good workmanship, career awareness, contributions of different workers, and use of resources. The social studies sharpen *thinking ability* through learning activities that involve students in critical and creative thinking and in decision-making activities. Students *learn how to learn* as they apply reading, study, and other skills; as they engage in independent study activities that emphasize self-direction and self-evaluation; and as they progressively develop the ability to use models of inquiry and processes of thinking. Still more examples of social studies' contributions to education are found in the following section on social studies goals.

GOALS OF THE SOCIAL STUDIES

Goal statements serve as overall guides to the planning, development, and evaluation of the social studies program. They provide teachers at each level of instruction with a sense of direction. Goal statements can be organized into two categories, cognitive and affective goals; three categories, knowledge, skills, and values and attitudes; or a larger number of categories. Regardless of the number of categories used, analysis of goal statements consistently reveals four basic categories singled out for emphasis: knowledge; thinking processes; skills; and attitudes, values, and behavior patterns. Goals in each category are aimed at developing democratic citizenship.

knowledge The knowledge needed by citizens in a pluralistic society is given high priority, with emphasis on information, concepts, understandings, main ideas, and generalizations related to the following:

> How people meet basic needs and are interdependent in families, neighborhoods, communities, states, and nations, both here and now and in other times and places
>
> The history, geography, and government of the community, state, and nation
>
> Economic, political, and legal systems of the community, state, and nation
>
> Selected countries and regions of the world, their cultures, their relations with our country and with other countries, and how their ways of living are like and different from ours
>
> Multicultural studies of the common needs and diverse backgrounds of the ethnic groups in our pluralistic society
>
> Topics, issues, and problems of social concern, including the environment, energy, equality for women and ethnic groups, law-focused studies, global studies, career education, and values education
>
> Social functions in our society and in other societies, including transportation, communication, production, distribution, consumption, conservation, government, education, recreation, and religious and aesthetic expression

thinking processes Thinking processes may be referred to as cognitive processes, inquiry processes, or intellectual abilities or processes. Whatever the label, goals in this category give attention to developing ability to use models of critical and creative thinking, to problem solving and decision making, and to the specific processes included within them:

To develop critical thinking by identifying the object or activity to evaluate or critique, clarifying standards of appraisal, classifying and interpreting related information, applying the standards, and making a judgment

To develop creative thinking by clarifying the focus of the creative activity, identifying elements to be expressed in a new way, exploring and comparing forms of presentation, and synthesizing the elements in a new way

To develop problem-solving ability by defining the problem, analyzing available data to state a hypothesis or possible solution, collecting and interpreting new evidence to test the hypothesis or solution, and stating a conclusion

To develop decision-making ability by defining the decision to be made, identifying viable alternatives, evaluating alternatives and predicting the consequences of each one, selecting an alternative, taking and evaluating action, and recycling the process

To develop the processes involved in the above, including observing, remembering, interpreting, comparing, classifying, generalizing, inferring, hypothesizing, predicting, analyzing, synthesizing, and evaluating

To develop competence in applying thinking processes to achieve such objectives as detecting bias in persuasive materials, distinguishing facts from opinions, appraising points of view, and identifying cause-effect, part-whole, and other relationships

skills Reading, study, and language skills are given special attention so that students will adapt, refine, and apply them as they encounter the vocabulary, concepts, varying styles of presentation, and other distinctive aspects of social studies materials. Participation skills are brought to a high level of development as students take part in various large- and small-group activities. Among the skills that fall within the province of social studies instruction are map and globe skills, the ability to interpret time and chronology, and skill in making maps and models. Basic goals are

To develop the ability to apply reading skills to achieve such objectives as finding the main idea, forming a sensory impression, proving a point, noting directions for an activity, or predicting outcomes

To apply and refine study skills, including the ability to locate, gather, appraise, and organize information found in books, references, the library, and other sources

To develop participation skills, including the ability to work in large and small groups, share ideas and materials, respect others, work on committees, engage in role-taking activities, participate in discussion, preside over a meeting, take the roles of leader and follower, and help make and abide by group decisions

> To develop the ability to interpret maps and globes and to interpret time and chronology as presented in time charts, time lines, and reading materials
>
> To develop the ability to interpret pictures, charts, diagrams, tables, graphs, and cartoons
>
> To develop the ability to make maps, murals, models, charts, graphs, and other items needed in units of instruction

attitudes, values,
and behavior
patterns

Goals in this category are aimed at shaping democratic ideals and behavior believed essential to effective citizenship in a pluralistic society. Values expressed in the Declaration of Independence and the Constitution, positive attitudes toward others, and appreciations of present and past contributions of individuals and groups to our way of life are emphasized. Because students need to develop ability to handle value-laden issues, the development of valuing processes is a goal in many programs. Key goals are

> To develop positive attitudes toward and appreciation of the diverse individuals, groups, and cultures encountered in and out of school and studied in multicultural units of instruction
>
> To develop appreciation of strength through diversity, unity through democratic values and processes, progress through teamwork, and reasoned loyalty to the values underlying the American way of life
>
> To develop valuing processes, including the ability to clarify personal and societal values, analyze issues in terms of defined values, engage in moral reasoning, and participate in decision-making and action projects
>
> To develop understanding and appreciation of the core values of our society and related patterns of democratic behavior, including respect for human dignity, individual rights, freedom, and property; equality, justice, due process of law, and the general welfare; consent of the governed and faith in the ability of people to use intelligence to solve problems; consideration of the views and rights of others regardless of class, sex, ethnicity, national origin, or religion; responsibility, concern for others, open-mindedness, creativity, and cooperation

INSTRUCTIONAL OBJECTIVES

Goals such as those noted above are translated into instructional (performance, or behavioral) objectives by selecting a dimension of a goal and writing a statement that is useful in planning, guiding, and evaluating learning (see reference by Hannah and Michaelis, listed under Sources of Objectives at end of chapter, for an exhaustive treatment and a variety of examples). One may take an aspect of knowledge, a thinking process, a skill, or a value and prepare a statement that describes a desired learning outcome for a unit, a series of lessons, or a single lesson. Statements of objective should indicate what students will learn and how they will reveal what they learn—how they will perform and what they will be able to do, say, write, make, demonstrate. Four

Sojourner Truth
1797-1883

HINMATON YALATKIT
CHIEF JOSEPH

What achievements did these Americans make?

What achievements have members of other ethnic groups made?

elements usually included are object, behavior (performance), performance level (criterion), and conditions, as shown in these examples:

Knowledge: To write [behavior] a definition of stereotype [object] similar to the one in the textbook [performance level], without referring to the textbook or a dictionary [conditions].

Thinking: Using information in the textbook [conditions], students will generalize [object] by writing [behavior] one [performance level] main idea about the role of governors.

Skill: To make [behavior] a map of trails westward [object], using crayons and an outline map of the United States [conditions] to show three trails in different colors [performance level].

Value: To state [behavior] the extent to which the value justice was upheld [object] in a story read by the teacher [conditions], giving one [performance level] reason for the judgment.

Two other elements may be added when detailed statements are needed for accountability programs, specification of details for a competence-based assessment program, or clear communication of details to others. These two elements are *time* of attainment and *who* (which students) will attain the objective, as shown in these examples:

> At the end of the unit [time] students without learning disabilities [who] will state [behavior] from memory [conditions] at least five [performance level] public services provided by cities [object].
>
> By the end of the year [time] students reading at the fifth-grade level [who] will list [behavior] five or more [performance level] contributions of black Americans to science [object] without referring to reading materials [conditions].

Notice that all of the preceding examples focus on what students will learn, not on what the teacher will do. A mistake to be on guard against is the writing of such statements as the following:

> The teacher will demonstrate interviewing techniques.
>
> Contributions of members of minority groups will be presented.
>
> The teacher's objective is to show how justice can be upheld.

These statements focus on the teacher, not on students. To change any of them into an objective for students, the teacher must state what students will be able to do after instruction. For example, if ability to interview is the object, the teacher may select a key aspect and state an objective in this manner:

> After a demonstration of interviewing [condition] students will write [behavior] a plan for an interview [object] that includes an introduction and five questions [performance level].

Both open and closed objectives should be used in the social studies. Open objectives are useful to individualize instruction, provide choices, and tap students' creativity. Divergent thinking is emphasized, as shown in this example designed to elicit differing responses from students:

> To develop creative thinking by finding and describing three or more new ways to save energy at home.

Closed objectives are useful in making plans to develop key concepts, thinking processes, skills, and values that all students should achieve. Convergent thinking is emphasized, as shown in this example designed to elicit similar responses from students:

> To demonstrate respect for others in group work by helping to set and by adhering to group work standards.

When writing objectives, include only those elements necessary to make the objective clear. In no instance should the writing of objectives become a ritual in which all six elements are included, whether or not they add to understanding. Conditions need not be stated when they are obvious. One need not state "given an outline map" as part of an objective that includes "to complete an outline map." Who will attain the objective need not be specified when it is obvious that all students should, as in the objective "to show respect for others during discussion."

Objectives can be kept to reasonable length by not repeating certain terms or phrases. For example, one may write "to describe" instead of "to be able to describe." As one teacher put it, "Why write to *be able to* over and over when we know it is implied." When listing objectives to be attained by the end of a unit, it is not necessary to repeat "at the end of the unit" for each objective. Nor is it necessary to repeat "by the end of the year" for objectives to be used in an accountability program. Do not include "after instruction" when instruction obviously will be provided. In short, include only that information necessary to make the intent clear. Keep in mind the following special points.

object State the knowledge, thinking process, skill, or value that is the intended object of instruction. This is a basic step to make one's intent clear, to provide a focus for instruction, and to indicate the desired student learning. For example, the intent may be to develop such concepts as stereotype, justice, or public services; the ability to interpret or generalize; skill in reporting; or positive attitudes toward members of various ethnic groups.

behavior State what a student will be able to do after the objective is achieved, for example, to *explain* the meaning of stereotype, to *state* a generalization, to *write* a report, to *list* or *describe* contributions of ethnic groups. Use such verbs as

> Point to, group, sort, arrange, match, put in order, select, choose
> Describe, state, explain, tell, present, report, name
> Write, list, label, mark, circle, underline, outline
> Demonstrate, act out, show, role play, pantomime
> Make, draw, construct, prepare, produce, assemble, compose

Verbs expressing nonobservable (covert) behavior are sometimes used in statements of objectives. These verbs include *understand, know, appreciate, believe, develop insight into, enjoy,* and the like. Using such terms can create difficulties, as the following examples illustrate. The comment below each example shows how the objective can be clarified by using terms that express observable (overt) behavior.

12

To *know* the zones of a city [How will the student demonstrate a knowledge of the zones? The objective will be clear if *describe, draw on a map* or *list* is substituted for *know.*]

To *understand* the basic services provided by government [How will the student reveal understanding? It is better to use *describe, state, outline,* or *name.*]

To *appreciate* the achievements of black Americans in literature, art, science, medicine, education, and sports [How will students show appreciation? It is better to use *describe, report,* or *list.*]

If *understand, appreciate,* and other abstract terms are used, they may be clarified by adding a phrase indicative of observable behavior:

To develop appreciation of the achievements of native Americans by choosing five examples from materials in the learning center and *presenting* them to the class

To demonstrate understanding of the rights guaranteed in the First Amendment to the Constitution by *explaining* the meaning of each one

To develop the ability to synthesize by *preparing* a written report that includes ideas from at least three sources on a career of the student's choice

performance level   When an acceptable standard of performance is to be established and is not obvious, state a criterion, or desired level of achievement. For such an objective as "to describe achievements of native Americans," the standard may be "five or more." or other criterion depending on the capabilities of students and the available sources of information. Other examples of phrases to use are "at least eight out of ten," "according to standards in the textbook," or "similar in quality to [a map, report, or other model used as a standard.]"

conditions   Note any special conditions that should be provided and are not obvious, such as materials, equipment, or restrictions. If special materials are needed or if students may not use references to demonstrate achievement of the objective, state these conditions. Use phrases like "given a dictionary," "using notes," "without the aid of references" or "working in groups of three."

other elements   Indicate who (which students) should achieve an objective with such phrases as "students reading at grade level," "students in the advanced reading group," or "students needing help on map skills." When required to do so for an accountability program, you may indicate the percentage of students who should achieve an objective by such phrases as "all students," "90 percent of the students," or "students reading at or above grade level." Established procedures for making estimates should be followed.

Indicate time limitations with such phrases as "by the end of the week," "by the end of the unit," or "by the end of the year." When it is obvious that objectives are being stated for a unit or an accountability program, such phrases are not needed.

Several sources of objectives are available for reference (see references by Bloom, Krathwohl, and others listed under Sources of Objectives at the end of this chapter). Many of them are organized into the categories suggested by Bloom and Krathwohl in taxonomies for the cognitive and affective domains. The cognitive domain includes six categories: knowledge, comprehension, application, analysis, synthesis, and evaluation. The affective domain includes five categories: receiving, responding, valuing, organization, and characterization.

A recent source includes a skill domain as well as the cognitive and affective domains (see reference by Hannah and Michaelis listed under Sources of Objectives at the end of this chapter). The cognitive domain in this reference includes the categories noted above plus others that are widely used in the social studies: observing, remembering, interpreting, comparing, classifying, generalizing, inferring, analyzing, synthesizing, hypothesizing, predicting, and evaluating. The affective domain includes responding, complying, accepting, preferring, and integrating. The skill domain includes imitating, patterning, mastering, applying, and improvising. Sample objectives, questions, and test items are given for each category within each domain.

The Curriculum

PATTERNS OF ORGANIZATION

Patterns of unit and course organization range from interdisciplinary approaches, in which disciplines are indistinguishable, to separate subject approaches, in which geography, history, and other disciplines are given primary emphasis. Interdisciplinary patterns are used, for example, in units on family life, community workers, communities around the world, improving the environment, and ethnic studies; in middle and high schools they are also found in such courses as career exploration, youth and the law, current problems, and international relations.

The separate subject approach is used in units such as those on history of our community, geography of our state, and local government. Separate subject instruction is predominant in such secondary school courses as United States history, American government, and economics.

In between the interdisciplinary and separate subject approaches are multidisciplinary studies that bring the perspectives of different disciplines to bear on topics and problems in units on such topics as our state, the New England states, changing Japan, Latin America, and the Middle East. In multidisciplinary approaches the geographic, historical, economic, political, and sociocultural features of the area under study are considered and relationships among them highlighted. Each discipline is clearly visible, and the content is not brought together into an amalgam that renders the disciplines indistinguishable.

The trend is clearly toward using interdisciplinary approaches; other approaches are brought in when appropriate, depending on the focus of study. For example, when relationships are to be emphasized and when topics, issues, and problems call for the use of a mix of concepts, as in the study of families, communities, and world cultures, interdisciplinary approaches may be used. When the focus is on economic, political, geographic, or historical factors, there is good reason to use the concepts and processes that are directly relevant.

CONCEPTUAL STRUCTURE

The conceptual structure of the social studies includes content drawn from the social sciences and other sources, contemporary affairs, and the experiences of students. Instruction may be structured around main ideas or generalizations, concepts and concept clusters, and themes. Terms critical to the conceptual structure of the social studies are defined below. Later chapters on incorporating elements from the social sciences and areas of special concern, such as environmental education, include key concepts and generalizations that are used to structure units of study.

Vocabulary, or words such as *wagon, Civil War, brave,* and *communication,* encompasses the terms, names, or labels given to objects, events, qualities, or processes. Vocabulary can be used meaningfully by students only if they understand the concepts represented.

Concepts, represented by such terms as *family, urban,* and *ethnic group,* are abstractions that apply to a class or category of objects or activities that have certain characteristics in common. Vocabulary development is related to concepts through activities that build meaning.

Concept clusters, such as *natural resources* (water, soil, plants, animals, minerals), are sets of concepts subsumed under a major concept. All concepts within a cluster must be developed in a way that brings students to associate them with the major concept.

Themes, such as growth of the community, the westward movement, and industrial growth in the South, contain concepts in a phrase that indicates a topic, issue, or trend. Themes can be used to highlight an emphasis in a unit or part of a unit. Broad themes, such as studies of the immediate environment, families around the world, and world culture regions, are used to designate the focus of instruction at various grades.

Facts, such as "The capital of New York is in Albany," are statements of information that include concepts, but they apply only to a specific situation. A set of related facts can form a generalization, such as "All states have a capital."

Generalizations, such as "People use resources to meet basic needs," are statements of broad applicability that contain two or more concepts and show the relationship between them. Generalizations are stated as main ideas, basic understandings, principles, laws, rules, and conclusions. *Descriptive* generalizations are based on what is, for example, "Members of minority groups have not had equality of opportunity.'' *Prescriptive* generalizations are based on what ought to be, for example, ''Steps must be taken to extend equality of opportunity to minority groups.'' Additional examples are given in chapter 7.

SEQUENCE OF THEMES, TOPICS, AND UNITS

The content of the curriculum is often organized around themes for each grade and within units designated for each grade. There is great diversity among school systems in different states in the grade placement of units. The local course of study must be checked to determine the particular units that are included at each level. Some topics and units are included in most programs. Units on families, schools, communities, and cities are common in primary grades. State and United States history and geography, countries in the Western and Eastern hemispheres, and historical backgrounds of our cultural heritage are included in virtually all programs. Study of the Constitution and American government, along with United States history, is required in most secondary schools.

In most school systems several topics recur throughout the program. These include current affairs, holidays, commemorations, and the roles and contributions of significant men and women. Ethnic, environmental, law-focused, and career education are often included, either as a part of the regular units or in separate units at various levels. Consumer education, conservation and energy education, and the American free enterprise system also recur at various levels. Future studies may be incorporated into units at all levels to highlight the importance of planning for the future rather than ''letting it just happen.''

Presented below is a summary of typical themes for each grade followed by illustrative units and topics. Those topics that recur throughout the levels have not been included. A short note on required and elective courses in the ninth through twelfth grades is given to round out this overview of the kindergarten through twelfth-grade program.

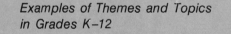

Examples of Themes and Topics
in Grades K–12

KINDERGARTEN:
LEARNING TOGETHER IN SCHOOL,
LOCAL ENVIRONMENT STUDIES

How to work and play with others, adjustment to school, and exploring the neighborhood around the school are typical themes. Short-term and informal learning activities are provided.

Learning in School
Rules for Work and Play
Myself
Our Families
Helping at Home

Places in our Neighborhood
Workers in Our Neighborhood
Where Families Buy Things
The Fire Station
Working and Playing Safely

GRADE 1:
FAMILY, SCHOOL, AND NEIGHBORHOOD

Studies of children's own families, school, and neighborhood followed by comparative studies of others are provided to highlight common basic needs and to nurture respect for differences.

Myself and Others
Our Families and Other Families
Our School and Other Schools
Workers in the Neighborhood
Families around the World

The Shopping Center
The Supermarket
The Diary Farm
Why We Need Rules
Schools around the World

GRADE 2: LIVING IN COMMUNITIES

Ways of living in the neighborhood provide a base for studying community life here and now and in other places with consideration of ways in which basic human needs are met.

Roles of Community Workers
Producing Food, Shelter, and
    Clothing
Rural and Urban Communities
Comparative Community Studies

Producers of Goods and Services
Working and Living on Farms
Transportation and Communication
How Communities Are Interdependent

GRADE 3: CITY LIFE, TOWNS AND CITIES,
CITIES AROUND THE WORLD

The nature of urban life and extension of the concept of community to include cities and metropolitan areas are provided through comparative studies of selected urban centers.

What Is a City?
Services Provided in Cities
Transportation and Communication
How Cities Have Changed
Careers in Cities

How Our City Grew from a Town
How Our City Is Governed
City Laws That Affect Us
Urban Planning and Renewal
Cities of the Future

GRADE 4: LIVING IN OUR STATE,
REGIONS AROUND THE WORLD,
REGIONS OF THE UNITED STATES

Some programs include study of the home state; others include selected geographic regions of the world or regions of the United States.

History of Our State
Our State Today
How Our State Is Governed
Roles of State Workers
Transportation and Communication
Conserving Resources and Energy
State Laws That Affect Us

Living in Desert Regions
Living in Wet Tropical Regions
Living in Mediterranean-Type Regions
Living in Other Regions
Changing Japan
Living in India
Living in Regions of Our Country

GRADE 5: LIVING IN THE AMERICAS, LIVING IN EARLY AND MODERN AMERICA

The most common theme is early development and history of the United States. Some programs include Canada and Latin America and emphasize geography of the Americas or the Western Hemisphere.

The First Americans
Exploration and Colonization
Colonial and Pioneer Life
The Westward Movement
Living in Different Regions
Contributions of Ethnic Groups

Our Neighbor to the North
Regions of Canada
Relationships with Canada
Relationships with Latin America
Interdependence in the Americas
Man, A Course of Study

GRADE 6: WORLD CULTURES, WESTERN (OR EASTERN) HEMISPHERE

Some programs follow the study of the United States in grade 5 with a study of Latin America. Others emphasize geography of the Western Hemisphere, global geography, or our heritage from Europe.

Living in Mexico
Central American Countries
The ABC Countries
Urban Centers in Latin America
Latin American Cultures

Geography of North America
Geography of South America
Historical Backgrounds
Economic and Social Problems
Early Cultures in Latin America

GRADE 7: WORLD CULTURES, STATE HISTORY, EASTERN (OR WESTERN) HEMISPHERE

Studies of world cultures initiated in grade 6 are rounded out in many programs at this level. Diversity is great among school districts, with some including state history, others world geography or world history, and others geography of the Eastern Hemisphere.

Old World Backgrounds
Rise of Civilizations
Greece and Rome
The Middle Ages
Beginning of Modern Times

The Middle East
North Africa
Africa, South of the Sahara
India and Pakistan
Changes in China

Western Europe   Third World Countries
Eastern Europe and the USSR   Australia and New Zealand

GRADE 8:
UNITED STATES HISTORY; THE CONSTITUTION;
LOCAL, STATE, AND NATIONAL GOVERNMENT

History of the United States is commonplace, with emphasis on events up to the period of Reconstruction. Some programs include the Constitution and aspects of local, state, and national government along with law-related studies.

Interaction with Native Americans   The Constitution
The Colonial Period   Rights Guaranteed All Citizens
Winning Independence   Relationships between Levels of
Building a Government   Government
Early Patterns of Living   Our Legal Rights and Responsibilities
Civil War and Reconstruction   Justice and Order through Law
Emergence as a World Power   Justice for Minority Groups
Contributions of Ethnic Groups   Equal Rights for Women
Our Democratic Heritage

GRADES 9–12:
REQUIRED COURSES AND ELECTIVES

The most frequently required courses are United States history and government. Some schools also require other courses, such as introduction to the social sciences or world history. The variety of electives is vast in large secondary schools, ranging from world history and geography, psychology, sociology, and economics to ethnic studies, international relations, criminal and civil law, the changing role of women, and Asian or other area studies.

GENERALIZING, PARTICULARIZING,
AND DECISION-MAKING STUDIES

Within the framework of themes and topics noted in the preceding section, three types of studies may be identified: generalizing, particularizing, and decision-making studies. Classroom instruction should provide for all three; a single type of study is not adequate when one is learning about human affairs. Chart 1-2 gives examples of the three types.

generalizing   Generalizing studies are designed to help the student to develop generalizations
studies   of broad applicability, to sharpen the process of generalizing, and to recognize
                sound generalizations. For example, if the objective is to develop a generaliza-
                tion about the public services that cities provide, then services in several cities
                should be identified and a general statement should be made about commonly

19

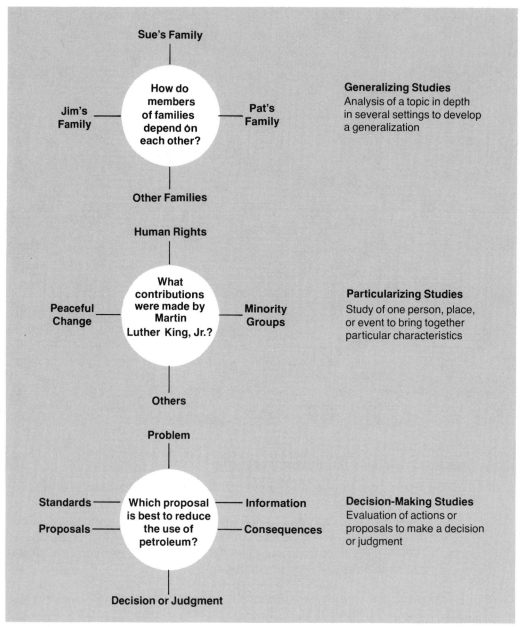

Sue's Family

Jim's Family — **How do members of families depend on each other?** — Pat's Family

Other Families

Generalizing Studies
Analysis of a topic in depth in several settings to develop a generalization

Human Rights

Peaceful Change — **What contributions were made by Martin Luther King, Jr.?** — Minority Groups

Others

Particularizing Studies
Study of one person, place, or event to bring together particular characteristics

Problem

Standards — **Which proposal is best to reduce the use of petroleum?** — Information

Proposals — — Consequences

Decision or Judgment

Decision-Making Studies
Evaluation of actions or proposals to make a decision or judgment

Chart 1–2

provided services. Other examples of studies in which a single topic is analyzed in several settings are illustrated by these questions:

What are the basic needs of all families?
What is the primary role of mayors in large cities?
How is the price of an item related to supply and demand?
How does the culture of people affect their ways of living?

Students should learn that an adequate number of cases or situations must be studied to make a good generalization. They should also learn that it is sometimes wise to put limits on generalizations; for example, a generalization about the main role of mayors may be limited to "the mayor of our town." Then, as the role of mayors in other places is studied, students can extend their generalizations accordingly. This kind of learning helps students to avoid generalizing from a single instance or a few cases, and to avoid generalizing beyond the reasonable limits of the data they have collected. Furthermore, it helps them to identify faulty generalizations and to recognize prejudices, which are usually based on a lack of information that leads to biased judgments.

particularizing studies   Particularizing studies bring together (integrate or synthesize) particular characteristics of a person, place, or event, such as the distinctive characteristics of Chicago, the contributions of Harriet Tubman, or the events that occurred at the Boston Tea Party. Other examples of studies that integrate particular characteristics are illustrated by these questions:

What is special about the families of members of our class?
How did our community grow from a few homes to a large city?
What were the main periods in the development of our state?
What were the special contributions of Susan B. Anthony?

A key learning for students is that every person, city, region, country, culture, or historical event has distinctive characteristics that set it apart from others—there is only one Abraham Lincoln, one New York, one New England, and one Brazil; no other school, community, or state is just like our own; the American Revolution differs from other revolutions; and no two countries have identical histories (though some similarities in development may be identified). Therefore, to investigate a particular setting thoroughly it is necessary to do a comprehensive study that integrates key elements. A second key learning is that generalizations made in one situation do not necessarily hold up in others. To find out if they do, an adequate number of analytic multisetting studies must be made. A third key learning is that some concepts have special meanings and that terms such as the *Loop* in Chicago, the *French Quarter* in New Orleans, *carpetbaggers* and *muckrakers* in American history, the *caste system* in India, and *democracy* in China must often be defined in specific contexts. Finally,

Social Studies Workshop, University of California, Berkeley

Touring Club do Brasil

What is special about each of these cities? Why are they different?

students should develop an appreciation of how art, music, literature, and other material from the humanities contribute to one's understanding of the particular features of the setting under study.

decision-making studies

Decision-making studies are designed to develop students' ability to evaluate proposals and actions so that sound decisions or judgments can be made. For example, if the problem is to improve safety on the playground, the problem is defined, standards are considered, proposals are made, consequences of each proposal are pondered, and a decision is made about the proposal(s) that best meets the defined standards. Other examples of decision-making studies to develop evaluative abilities are illustrated by these questions:

Which plan is best to stop waste pollution at school?
Which proposal for urban renewal is best?

What should each of us do to eliminate prejudice against members of minority groups?

How fair is the city council's position on adding women to the police force?

Two key learnings for students are, first, that the issue or problem must be clearly defined and, second, that related values must also be clarified. When students have different notions about an issue and use different values to appraise it, they make little progress. They must learn to interpret and analyze situations in which individuals arrived at different conclusions or decisions because of differing views of the problem and differing values. After clarifying the issue and the related values, students proceed to evaluate proposals, project consequences, and make a judgment, as noted in the section on evaluation in chapter 9 and the sections on valuing strategies in chapter 13.

UNIFIED INQUIRY, CONCEPTUAL,
AND TOPICAL APPROACHES

Some programs emphasize inquiry or conceptual approaches; others stress a topical approach. The advantages of all three approaches may be combined into an inquiry-conceptual approach to the study of topics. The procedure for doing so is simple and straightforward. Thinking processes and concepts are linked together and used to guide the study of topics, as shown in chart 1–3.

The Inquiry-Conceptual Model

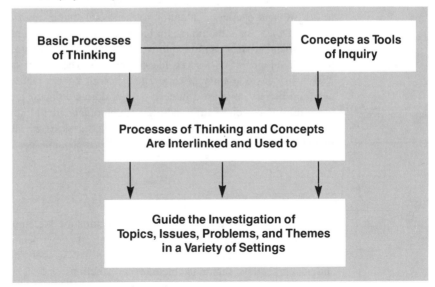

Chart 1–3

A practical use of the model is to generate questions to guide study. The procedure is simply one of framing questions that include one or more concepts and that call for the use of interpreting, generalizing, or other thinking processes. These questions drawn from a teaching unit on Japan illustrate the procedure:

What *natural resources* for industries are shown in this film on Japan [observing]?

What is meant by "Japan must import *raw materials*" [interpreting]?

Is Japan more or less *dependent* on other countries for *raw materials* than we are [comparing]?

Why do you think that Japan has been able to become an *industrialized* country with such limited *natural resources*? What data do we need to test your idea [hypothesizing]?

Other examples of questions that link concepts and thinking processes are presented in the following chapters and in the appendix.

BASIC SKILLS

The public has been demanding "a return to the basics," but few can agree on what is basic. Many define the basics as the 3Rs. Some go beyond and stress tougher discipline, more stringent grading and promotion standards, systematic testing, more attention to geography and history, an emphasis on patriotism, and tighter control of students by teachers. Still others argue that nothing is more basic than developing each child's potentialities to the fullest—intellectually, socially, emotionally, and physically.

In response to the critics, some schools have increased the time devoted to the 3Rs and decreased attention to the social studies, particularly in the early grades. Others have maintained a balanced curriculum, pointing out the contribution social studies can make to reading, language, and study skills as well as to the development of responsible citizenship. They point out that qualities of citizenship develop early in children. It is well known that basic attitudes, values, and beliefs developed in early and middle childhood are of critical importance throughout one's life, and their development should not be left to chance. A balanced curriculum gives attention to basic skills in all subjects but also includes other learnings that are essential to responsible participation in a democratic society.

ROLES OF MALES AND FEMALES

Equality, independence, and nondiscrimination are emphasized in units of study and in learning materials. Deliberate efforts have been made to eliminate stereotyped sex roles and to show both men and women in a variety of roles and careers. New materials include contributions and achievements of both sexes, and invidious comparisons have been removed. Teachers should provide instruction that portrays men and women in coequal roles, develops positive attitudes, and roots out any lingering vestiges of sexism. Equality should be evident in contexts ranging from family life and community activities to careers, sports, education, politics—the full range of human activities.

FUTURE STUDIES

The study of alternative futures may be a part of units on families, schools, communities, our state, our country, and other topics. Underlying future studies is the key idea that the future can be planned; it need not just happen. Because traditional attitudes, values, technology, and institutions are changing constantly, students need to develop an orientation toward change so that instead of experiencing ''future shock'' they can guide and evaluate change and plan for alternative futures.

Many topics in the social studies invite a consideration of future developments—population growth, food and energy problems, conservation of resources, human relations, transportation, communication, urbanization, changing roles of men and women, and the impact of scientific discoveries on human affairs. Students can compare their projections and predictions to those made by others. Ways of influencing change through individual and group action and through organizations established to advance the interests and concerns of various groups may be examined. The full range of valuing and decision-making processes may be put to use as students consider alternative proposals and weigh the consequences of various courses of action. Charts 1–4 through 1–6 present examples of questions that could be used in future studies.

Projecting Basic Trends	The Year 2000	Ways to Influence Change
What is the future for these?	What will be most important?	Know what we and others value
Freedom and equality for all	Community life Jobs for	Consider causes and effects
Changes in the family and other institutions	Conservation everyone	Consider alternative proposals
Scientific developments and new inventions	Education Justice	Consider consequences of actions
Careers for women and men	The environment Leisure	Join with others to take action
	Family life Recreation	Make plans for the future now
	Health Wealth	Can you add other ways?
	Housing	

Chart 1–4   Chart 1–5   Chart 1–6

The stages of the child's intellectual and moral development have broad implications for the curriculum and instruction. Using Piaget's stages of intellectual growth to provide general guidelines, the program would provide for sensorimotor activities in early childhood education, an emphasis on concrete operations between the ages of seven to eleven, and the nurturing of formal operations from age twelve and on.* Using Kohlberg's stages and levels of moral development as broad guidelines for values education, the program would begin with obedience and self-benefit orientations at the preconventional level characteristic of most elementary students; it would emphasize acceptance by others and maintenance of the social order orientations at the conventional level characteristic of many secondary students; and it would explore the social contract and ethical principle orientations at the postconventional level characteristic of mature adults.†

Studies of human learning offer guidelines that can help establish a favorable learning environment. Each student can be helped to develop a positive self-concept by setting realistic and achievable objectives and by providing feedback during and after instruction. Providing a variety of learning activities and materials stimulates interest, motivates learning, and meets individual differences. Teachers guide learning toward stated objectives, give help when needed, and encourage each student to participate actively in individual and group work. The classroom atmosphere is marked by mutual respect, concern for others, self-discipline, and high regard for individual differences.

Students in the typical classroom show a broad range of distinctive learning styles. These must be recognized, and appropriate adjustments in instruction must be made to help students improve their learning skills.‡ Some students need help in identifying and analyzing key concepts embedded in reading and other materials and in breaking topics and problems into manageable parts. Other more independent students tend to move ahead on their own, but they may need help in developing group participation skills. Some students are reflective and systematic in their approach; others plunge ahead haphazardly. Some students are uncomfortable with ambiguity; others ponder conflicting information and try to make sense out of it. Effective teachers are sensitive to differences in learning styles and utilize the techniques for meeting individual differences discussed in chapter 5.

Other Basic Features

The following are features that make social studies instruction dynamic, exciting, and challenging. They are drawn from the foundations of the social studies and from promising developments of the past decade. They are mentioned briefly below and treated in detail in the chapters that follow.

*Barry J. Wadsworth, *Piaget for the Classroom Teacher* (New York: Longman, 1978).

†Lawrence Kohlberg, "Moral Issues and Moralization," in *Moral Development and Behavior,* ed. Thomas Lickona (New York: Holt, Rinehart & Winston, 1976), pp. 31–83.

‡H. A. Witkin and others, "Educational Implications of Cognitive Style," *Review of Educational Research,* 47 (Winter 1977), 1–64.

PLANNING OF INSTRUCTION

Systematic planning is the backbone of effective instruction. Various models of unit planning may be used. Daily lesson plans are most effective when set in the context of a teaching unit. Challenging learning activities and materials should be included in a sequence that moves from initiating to intake activities and then to organizing, applicative, and creative activities, as noted in chapter 2.

MULTIMEDIA APPROACHES

Planning is based on the available learning materials. Effective programs provide print and nonprint materials in three categories: reading materials, audiovisual (AV) materials, and community resources. In many schools, multimedia kits, television instruction, computer-assisted instruction, simulation games, data banks, and resources for creating materials are available. Both group and individual instruction may be improved by incorporating a variety of media, as discussed in chapter 3.

GROUP AND INDIVIDUAL ACTIVITIES

In well-planned programs learning takes place in whole-class, small-group, and individual activities. The whole class benefits from planning sessions, discussions, case study analyses, demonstrations, field trips, presentations by the teacher and resource visitors, films and other audiovisual materials, and group evaluation of learning activities. Small groups are often more appropriate for role playing, construction, committee research, interviewing experts, brainstorming, team learning, conducting field studies, and planning debates, panel presentations, and other activities. Individual activities range from reading, preparing reports, practicing skills, and completing learning contracts and task cards to creating poems, stories and songs, planning and giving demonstrations, constructing objects, interviewing an expert, and engaging in art activities. Guidelines for group activities are presented in chapter 4. Guidelines for individualizing instruction are presented in chapter 5.

EMPHASIS ON BASIC CONTENT

Conceptual and process elements drawn from the social sciences and from areas of social concern are kept in central focus. Concepts, concept clusters, themes, and generalizations are identified and incorporated into instruction, as noted in chapters 6 and 7. Various methods of inquiry and values of inquiry are included, as noted in chapter 6. Social concerns, such as multicultural, global, law-focused, environmental and career education add new dimensions to learning, as noted in chapter 7. Current affairs and special events are critically selected to keep the program up-to-date and to include significant daily happenings, as noted in chapter 8.

VARIETY OF TEACHING STRATEGIES

Of basic importance are teaching strategies for developing concepts, generalizations, and thinking processes. Concepts as tools of thinking are put to use interpreting, classifying, generalizing, analyzing, and evaluating. Concepts and thinking processes are linked together to generate focusing questions that move students from first-level to higher-level thinking. Appropriate teaching strategies for sharpening thinking processes are outlined in chapter 9.

The development of creative thinking is continually encouraged by providing expressive activities, as noted in chapter 10. Creative thinking is emphasized throughout instruction and brought to high levels in such expressive activities as role taking, creative writing, arts and crafts, music, and construction and processing of materials. Students can bring their own learning styles into full use as they express their thoughts and feelings in original ways.

Systematic attention is given to developing the skills essential to productive learning. Chapters 3 through 5 include a discussion of skills used in group work and individual activities and use of instructional media. Chapter 11 includes a detailed treatment of reading and study skills, and chapter 12 covers globe and map concepts and skills.

Strategies for developing attitudes, values, valuing processes, and democratic behavior are presented in chapter 13. They are of vital importance in achieving fundamental and lasting affective outcomes of instruction. As a thoughtful teacher put it, "What have we gained if students do not develop the attitudes, values, valuing processes, and democratic behavior that are basic in our society?" Indeed, it is difficult to think of more basic learning.

EVALUATION OF LEARNING

Evaluation is an ongoing process throughout all phases of instruction. It begins at the planning stage with diagnostic assessment. Formative assessment guides instruction and replanning. Summative assessment appraises outcomes of units of study. Formal devices, such as tests, and informal devices, such as charts and checklists, are used along with observation by the teacher. Systematic attention is given to concepts and generalizations, thinking processes, basic skills, and attitudes, values, and behavior patterns. Criterion-referenced tests are used to assess performance in well-defined domains of learning, such as map concepts and skills; norm-referenced tests are used to assess and compare progress on commonly emphasized concepts and basic skills. Evaluation information is used in accountability systems designed to report students' achievements and to make improvements in the program of instruction. Guiding principles and techniques of evaluation are presented in chapter 14.

 Questions, Activities, and Evaluation

1. Obtain a local curriculum guide and check it for the following:
   a. How are the social studies defined? How does the definition differ from the one presented in this chapter?

    b. What goals and objectives are identified? What suggestions are given for writing instructional objectives?

    c. What position is taken on the following: basic skills, career education, environment and energy education, future studies, global education, law-focused education, multicultural education, roles of males and females, and values education?

    d. What themes, topics, and units are recommended for each grade?

    e. What suggestions are made for using a variety of instructional media?

    f. What suggestions are made regarding teaching strategies?

    g. What suggestions are made for evaluating learning?

2. Write a set of instructional objectives for a unit of your choice, using the guidelines presented in this chapter. Do at least one objective for each of these four categories: (a) knowledge, (b) thinking processes, (c) skills, and (d) attitudes, values, and behavior patterns. Refer to one of the references listed below under Sources of Objectives for examples.

3. Check one of the guides to current materials listed below and identify three or four items that you might use to plan a unit of your choice.

4. Check each of the periodicals listed below and note articles that are related to social studies topics of special interest to you.

references

BARR, ROBERT D., JAMES L. BARTH, AND S. SAMUELS SHERMIS, *Defining the Social Studies*. Washington, D.C.: National Council for the Social Studies, 1977. Section on social studies as citizenship transmission, social science, and reflective inquiry.

BRUBAKER, DALE L., LAWRENCE H. SIMON, AND JO WATTS WILLIAMS, "A Conceptual Framework for Social Studies Curriculum and Instruction," *Social Education*, 41 (March 1977), 201–05. Five definitions of the social studies.

BROWN, FRANK B., "Report of the National Task Force on Citizenship Education," in *Education for Responsible Citizenship*. New York: McGraw-Hill, 1977. Review of issues and needs; recommendations for improvement.

FITCH, ROBERT M., AND CORDELL M. SVENGALIS, *Futures Unlimited*. Washington, D.C.: National Council for the Social Studies, 1979. Chapters on methods, values, and instructional resources.

JOYCE, WILLIAM W., AND FRANK L. RYAN, eds., *Social Studies and the Elementary Teacher: Promises and Practices*. Washington, D.C.: National Council for the Social Studies, 1977. Articles on recent trends and developments.

KALTSOUNIS, THEODORE, *Teaching Social Studies in the Elementary School: The Basics for Citizenship*. Englewood Cliffs, N.J.: Prentice-Hall, 1979. Chapter on accountability.

MUESSIG, RAYMOND H., ed., *Social Studies Curriculum Improvement*. Washington, D.C.: National Council for the Social Studies, 1978. Guidelines and examples for curriculum improvement.

"Revision of the NCSS Social Studies Curriculum Guidelines," *Social Education*, 43 (April 1979), 261–73. Rationale, goals, and nine guidelines; followed by an example of how to use the guidelines for program assessment.

SCHOMBURG, CARL E., "Integrating the Social Studies Component in a CBTE Model," in *Competency-Based Teacher Education: Professionalizing Social*

Studies Teaching, ed. Dell Felder. Washington, D.C.: National Council for the Social Studies, 1978. Statement of teacher competencies.

STAKE, ROBERT E., AND JACK A. EASLEY, *Case Studies in Science Education,* Center for Instructional Research, University of Illinois, Urbana. Washington, D.C.: Superintendent of Documents, Government Printing Office, 1978. Eleven ethnographic case studies of science, mathematics, and social studies education in selected schools; views of current problems, practices, strengths, and weaknesses.

WEISS, IRIS R., *Report of the 1977 National Survey of Science, Mathematics, and Social Studies Education,* Center for Education Research and Evaluation, Research Triangle Park, North Carolina. Washington, D.C.: Superintendent of Documents, Government Printing Office, 1978. Status of current requirements, problems, uses of instructional materials, teaching techniques, teacher characteristics, and factors influencing instruction.

WILEY, KAREN B., WITH JEANNE RACE, *The Status of Pre-College Science, Mathematics, and Social Science Education: 1995–1975, Volume III: Social Science Education.* Washington, D.C.: Superintendent of Documents, Government Printing Office, 1978. Review of literature and research on trends, effectiveness of practices, and teacher education.

Sources of Objectives

BLOOM, BENJAMIN S., ed., *Taxonomy of Educational Objectives. Cognitive Domain.* New York: David McKay Co., 1956. Objectives arranged by levels of complexity.

HANNAH, LARRY S., AND JOHN U. MICHAELIS, *A Comprehensive Framework of Objectives.* Reading, Mass.: Addison-Wesley Publishing Co., 1977. Examples of objectives, questions, and test items for interpreting, classifying, generalizing, and other thinking processes.

INSTRUCTIONAL OBJECTIVES EXCHANGE, P.O. Box 24095, Los Angeles, California. Booklets of objectives and related test items.

KRATHWOHL, DAVID R., BENJAMIN S. BLOOM, AND BERTRAM B. MASIA, *Taxonomy of Educational Objectives: Affective Domain.* New York: David McKay Co., 1964. Objectives arranged by degree of internalization.

SCORE, *School Curriculum Objective-Referenced Evaluation.* Iowa City, Iowa: Westinghouse Learning Corporation, 1974. Instructional objectives and related test items.

TRI-COUNTY GOAL DEVELOPMENT PROJECT, *Course Goals for K–12 Social Science.* Portland, Oreg.: Commercial-Educational Distribution Services, 1977. Goals and objectives for all levels of instruction.

Guides to Current Materials

The following sources should be checked for current materials in the social studies and other areas:

Current Index to Journals in Education. Guide to articles.

Education Index. Guide to articles and other publications.

Resources in Education (until 1975, *Research in Education*). Guide to articles, research, units, teaching guides and other materials available in microfiche and reproduced form from ERIC Document Reproduction Service, P.O. Box 190, Arlington, Virginia 22210. ERIC microfiche available in many college and school district professional libraries.

Social Studies Curriculum Materials Data Book. Boulder, Colo.: Social Science Education Corsortium. Reviews of project materials, media, games; annual supplements on new media.

Periodicals

Use the following to keep abreast of new developments and materials:

Social Education and *The Social Studies Professional* (journal and newsletter of the National Council for the Social Studies).

Journal of Geography and *Perspective* (journal and newsletter of the National Council for Geographic Education).

The Link (Newsletter from Social Science Education Consortium).

The Social Studies (journal, McKinley Publishing Co.).

Progress in Economic Education and *Checklist* (bulletin of the Joint Council on Economic Education).

PLANNING UNITS OF INSTRUCTION

What is included in a plan for a unit of instruction?
What models are used to organize units of instruction?
What guidelines are used to plan various parts of a unit?
What learning activities may be used and how should they be sequenced?
What provisions should be made for the evaluation of learning?
Where can examples of units be obtained?

Planning for the social studies program takes place at the national, state, and local levels. The federal government funds special programs to stimulate state and local educators to add or improve instruction in such areas as environmental education, energy conservation, career education, and multicultural education. The state establishes legal requirements, legislative mandates, board of education regulations, frameworks for various areas of the curriculum, and other provisions that influence local planning. Planning at the local level, while it includes attention to the foregoing, goes beyond them to indicate themes, topics, and units of instruction to be taught in various grades. The local school system's course of study and the available instructional materials serve as the basis for planning by teachers.

Of critical importance to the total program is the instructional planning of the classroom teacher. It ranges from planning long-term units of several weeks duration, such as a study of colonial life or living in Mexico, to planning miniunits of a few days duration, such as the fire station or saving energy at home. The teacher also plans independent study modules and lessons that students can complete in a day or two.

This chapter provides guidelines and examples for planning classroom units of instruction. It emphasizes specific teaching plans for daily instruction. Models and guidelines suggest ways to incorporate pertinent ideas from subsequent chapters into the teaching units.

A teaching unit differs from a resource unit in that a teaching unit is prepared for a particular class and is often in the form of plans for daily instruction. As one teacher put it, ''I think of a teaching unit as a sequence of interrelated lesson plans.'' Resource units are usually prepared by a group, and individual teachers select and adapt objectives, content, questions, materials, and evaluation techniques from the resource units to fit their classes. An example of a resource unit is presented in the appendix.

Main Sections of Units

A typical unit contains the sections listed below:

1. *Title:* the theme, topic, or problem, such as ''Improving the Environment'' or ''Development of Our Community''
2. *Background information:* rationale for unit; overview of content of the unit or in appropriate sections within the unit
3. *Objectives:* the expected outcomes; the understandings, concepts, processes, skills, and attitudes, values, and appreciations to be developed
4. *Initiation, introduction, or approach:* suggestions for beginning the unit in an interesting and productive manner
5. *A sequence of learning activities:*
   a. *Opening activities* to focus attention on specific questions, issues, or problems to investigate
   b. *Developmental activities* to provide for intake, organization, application, and expression of content
   c. *Concluding activities* to stimulate stating main ideas, drawing conclusions, making judgments, and culminating the unit
6. *Evaluation:* suggestions for assessment of learning during the unit and at the end of the unit
7. *Bibliography:* for students and teachers

Models for Unit Plans

The unit models in this section have been selected to illustrate ways of organizing units. They range from models based on main ideas to miniunits designed to develop specific competencies. With the exception of the independent study module, which can be completed in one session, the learning activities in each example take place over several instructional sessions.

MAIN IDEA MODEL

This model is built around main ideas or generalizations to be developed. Each main idea may be viewed as a subunit or miniunit that is part of the topic of study. In planning the unit the main idea is stated first, but teachers are not expected to begin by presenting it directly to the students. Rather, teachers begin with a focusing question or hypothesis for the students, then develop the main idea through a sequence of learning activities that involve gathering information; these are followed by organizing the information and then stating the main idea. With a focusing question to guide data processing activities, students may develop the main idea inductively–moving from information and concepts to the main idea.

The following example illustrates one way of organizing units around main ideas. All of the main ideas and related focusing questions are presented first to show the scope of the unit. A teaching plan for one of the main ideas follows.

Workers in Cities

BACKGROUND INFORMATION

This unit is part of a social studies program that integrates career education within designated units. Career awareness is developed as students learn to understand and appreciate the goods and services that people need and the workers who produce them. The first part of the unit focuses on the goods and services that people need and want. The second part focuses on two major groups of workers: those who produce goods and those who produce services. Subsequent units more fully explore particular groups of workers, such as those in health, education, or construction.

In each section of the unit, content and notes related to questions and activities are presented to show relationships to learning experiences. The unit is organized around the main ideas listed in the next section. The supporting ideas and focusing questions indicate the concepts that are emphasized.

MAIN IDEAS

People in cities consume many goods and services to meet their needs and wants.

Supporting ideas: Food, shelter, clothing, and other goods are needed. Education, government, protection, and other services are needed.

Focusing question: What goods and services do people in cities need?

Two major groups of workers are needed to meet people's needs.

Supporting ideas: Producers of goods provide food, shelter, clothing, and other goods to meet human needs and wants. Service workers provide education, health care, protection, and other services.

Focusing question: What goods and services do these workers produce to meet people's needs?

GOALS

To develop understanding of the variety of goods and services people need to meet basic human needs

To develop understanding and appreciation of the many different workers that are needed to produce goods and services

To develop awareness of the different types of careers in a city and the personal satisfactions to be gained from them

To develop concepts, related vocabulary, and reading skills essential to learning in the social studies and in career education

TEACHING PLAN

Main idea: Many kinds of workers are needed in cities to meet human needs.

INSTRUCTIONAL OBJECTIVES

To describe and classify producers of goods and service workers

To increase vocabulary by using the following words in discussion and in reading: *producers of goods, service workers, production*

To state the main idea and supporting idea in one's own words

INSTRUCTIONAL MATERIALS

Books: Brandwein, *The Social Sciences, Concepts and Values* (Red); and Grossman, *Working, Playing, Learning; People, Places, Products*

Filmstrip: Community Workers

Kit: Pictures, booklets, and other materials from media center

(Supplementary materials to meet special needs or to subtitute for the above are listed at the end of this unit along with teacher references.)

INITIATION

Arrange a bulletin board display that includes pictures of producers of goods and service workers. Print this question on a strip of paper and place it above the pictures: *What goods and services do these workers produce to meet people's needs?* On a table or in a learning center near the display place books and pamphlets that include material on producers of goods and services.

SEQUENCE OF LEARNING EXPERIENCES

Notes and Content

Questions, Activities, Materials

OPENER

This introductory activity links the unit to preceding learning activities, which developed concepts of goods, services, producers, and consumers. Ways in which people depend on others have been introduced. The stage is set to find the variety of workers

1. Review the goods and services that people must have to meet their needs and wants by asking: What are some goods that members of your family produce at home? What are some services they provide? What are some goods they

needed in a community and to place them in two major groups.

pay for? What are some services they pay for? Why do they depend on others for them?

2. Pose a question such as What different workers are needed to produce the goods and services that people need?

DEVELOPMENT
Data Collection, Intake Activities

Elicit a variety of examples by following such responses as "builds houses, drives a truck, sells shoes, or is a nurse" by such questions as Are there others who make things? Deliver or sell things? Do things to serve people? Ask students if the pictures make them think of other workers.

Direct attention to workers in each picture to help students identify the doctor, salesperson, sewing machine operator, street cleaner, police, bus driver, truck driver, shoemaker, firefighter, and so on.

Take time to discuss any workers that may not be familiar to students.

1. Ask children to tell the jobs that members of their family have. List responses on the chalkboard or on a chart.

2. Call attention to the pictures on the bulletin board. Have students identify the workers that are shown.

3. Ask if there are workers in the pictures that have not been listed, adding them as they are identified.

4. Have students look for other workers in these books: Grossman, *Working, Playing, Learning,* pp. 94–105 (low reading level); and Brandwein, *Concepts and Values,* pp. 108–9. Ask students what different workers they found to add to the list.

5. Show filmstrip *Community Workers* and ask students to find still more workers to add to the list.

Organizing, Summarizing Activities

Direct attention to the first sentence, "Some people make goods." Ask students to find the sentence that means the same, "Some people produce goods." Discuss *produce* as a synonym for *make.*

To build vocabulary, write *produce, producer,* and *production* on the chalkboard and discuss how all three words are based on the same root. Encourage students to use the words in discussion.

6. After discussing the need to group workers, ask students to turn to page 108 in Brandwein, *Concepts and Values.* Ask them what name is given to the workers that are listed.

7. Explain that producers of goods make things that people buy. Print *producers of goods* on a chart (or the chalkboard). Ask students to look at the list of workers made during the preceding activities and

37

Point out that service workers do things for people. They may use goods made by others as they provide services. The key concept is that they do things for people but do not produce goods.

Producers of Goods	Service Workers

Explain roles of workers that may not be clear to students, such as builders, printers, spinners, weavers, potters, and artists (*producers of goods*); and repairers of various items, train conductors, and police radio operators (*service workers*).

find those that make things. List them as they are identified.

8. Ask students to turn to page 109 in Brandwein, *Concepts and Values*, to find a second group of workers. Ask the following questions: What workers do things for people? How are they different from producers of goods? Why is *service workers* a good name for them?

9. Print *Service Workers* on the chart. Ask students to find examples on the list of workers to place in this group.

10. Extend and enrich concepts of goods producers and service workers by asking students to find examples of each kind of worker in the following: Brandwein, *Concepts and Values*, pp. 110–19 and 134–39; and Grossman, *People, Places, Products*, pp. 18–29, 36–49, 70–73, 86–101, and 124–27. As students report different workers, ask them in which group they should be placed.

11. List workers that are found by students under *Producers of Goods* or *Service Workers*.

Applicative, Demonstrative, and Creative Activities

Alternative activities that may be used are making a roller movie that shows producers of goods and services selected by students and asking each student to choose a worker and describe the activities of the worker chosen; inviting resource visitors to describe their jobs and to answer questions posed by students; and having students interview parents or neighbors to find out about other workers.

12. Have students take turns pantomiming particular occupations. Have the class guess the worker and state whether the worker produces goods or provides services.

13. Ask students to prepare and share an oral report on a worker of their choice, including what the worker does, why the work is needed, what materials are used, what the personal satisfactions are, and what education is needed.

14. Play "What's My Line." Four

children at a time act as a panel to guess the job of the mystery worker and the group in which the worker belongs.

Conclusion

1. Elicit statements of the main idea by asking, What two kinds of workers are needed to meet people's needs?
2. Elicit statements of the supporting ideas by asking, What are the kinds of things goods producers make? and What are the main kinds of services provided by other workers?
3. Have a quiz program in which one student describes a worker, a second student names the worker, and a third student states the group in which the worker should be placed.
4. Have students make a montage or scrapbook with sections on *goods producers* and *service workers*, using pictures from discarded magazines.

EVALUATION

1. Show a set of pictures numbered from 1 to 10. Ask students to write the number of each picture as it is shown and after it write *production* or *service* to indicate the type of worker in the picture.
2. Write a list of workers on the chalkboard, some that have been discussed and some that have not. Distribute worksheets with the headings of *producers of goods* and *service workers*, and ask students to list the workers under the proper heading.
3. Give students a ditto on which names of workers and job descriptions are scrambled. Have students match workers with the job descriptions. Next have them label each worker as *goods* or *service*.

Note: A transition to the next unit may be made by discussing a particular group of workers (health, telephone, construction, delivery, and so on) in which children have shown interest or by showing a film or filmstrip that introduces special workers.

SUPPLEMENTARY MATERIALS

Books: Fugate, *Neighbors and Neighborhoods;* King, *Communities and Social Needs;* Munson, *Groups and Communities;* and Senesh, *Our Working World* (volumes on *Neighborhoods* and *Cities*)

Films: Our Community Services; Jobs in the City: Construction Jobs in the City: Distribution, and *Jobs in the City: Manufacturing*
Filmstrips: Our Community Utilities and *Health Workers*

Teacher references: Hoyt, *Career Education and the Elementary Teacher,* and Marland, *Career Education*

The inquiry-conceptual model includes regular components of a unit and also identifies thinking processes and concepts to be emphasized in each learning activity. Thinking processes are sequenced from lower- to higher-level processes as needed during intake, organizing, applicative, and expressive activities. Concepts are used as tools of thinking as needed to interpret, classify, generalize, or use other processes. In the following model, processes appear in brackets and concepts in boldface.

The Environment

MAJOR UNDERSTANDINGS

The natural environment includes living and nonliving things.
The cultural environment includes things made by people.
The environment includes natural things and things made by people—all of our surroundings.

OBJECTIVE

To define environment by describing living and nonliving things in the natural environment and things made by people in the cultural environment

MATERIALS

Books: Planet Earth
Kit: materials on different reading levels from instructional media center
Soundstrips: Our Environment and *Our Land: Uses and Values*
Pictures: Magazine cutouts of things in the natural and cultural environment
Teacher references: Slate, *Earthwalk,* and Watson, *Our World Tomorrow*

INITIATION

Arrange a display of pictures that show natural and cultural features of the environment. Place a caption such as *things in our environment* above them.

QUESTIONS AND ACTIVITIES

opener   1. Look at the pictures of things in our **environment** on the bulletin board [observing]. Which ones can you name [recalling]?
2. Let's see if we can add to our list. If we took an imaginary trip what other things would we see? Around the school? In the community? Out in the country? Other places [recalling]?

Intake Activities

1. Look at the pictures and read the text on pages 14–19 in *Planet Earth*. What things are noted as part of the **environment** [interpreting]? Which ones should be added to our list?
2. A distinction is made between **natural** things and things made by people–**cultural** things. What are some examples of things in the **natural environment** [interpreting]? What are examples of things in the **cultural environment** [interpreting]? What is the main difference between **natural** and **cultural** things? Between the **natural environment** and **cultural environment** [comparing]?
3. Did you notice the two kinds of things (living and nonliving) in the **natural environment** [interpreting]? What are some examples of **living** things? **Nonliving** things [interpreting]?
4. Look at the pictures on the bulletin board [observing]. Which show **living** things? **Nonliving** things [interpreting]?
5. Let's find more examples of things in the **natural environment** and **cultural environment** [observing]. Here are reading materials from the media center. Will group A look for **living** things in the **natural environment** [low reading-level materials]? Will group B look for **nonliving** things in the **natural environment** [grade-level materials]? Will group C look for things in the **cultural environment** [high reading-level materials]?
6. Look at the list of things in the **environment** on the chalkboard. Check your notes against the list [comparing]. What can group A add to the list? Group B? Group C [recalling]?

Organizing Activities

7. The items on our list are not grouped together. Place them in the following groups [classifying]: living things, nonliving things, and things made by people.
8. Look at the list of **living** things. Three major kinds of living things are listed (people, plants, and animals). What are they [interpreting]? Why is each one important in a study of the **environment** [inferring]?
9. Look at the list of **nonliving** things (air, water, soil, and so on). Why are they important [inferring]?
10. Look at the list of things made by people (buildings, roads, cars, and so on). Why are they important in a study of the environment [inferring]?

Applicative Activities

11. Let's apply what we have learned about things in the environment. Watch the soundstrip *Our Environment* [observing]. As each frame is shown state whether each thing in the picture is a living thing, nonliving thing, or thing made by people [interpreting].
12. Watch the soundstrip *Our Land: Uses and Values*. This time you are to list items that are shown under the headings **natural environment** (living things

and nonliving things), and **cultural environment** (things made by people) [interpreting].

13. Now, in your own words state a definition of **natural environment** [interpreting]. Do the same for **cultural environment** [interpreting]. Who can state the main difference between the **natural environment** and the **cultural environment** [contrasting]?

14. Find the definitions of **natural environment** and **cultural** environment in the glossary of our textbook. Should any changes be made in our definitions [interpreting]?

15. Now, in your own words state a definition of **environment** [interpreting].

16. Check your definition against the one in our textbook. Should any change be made [interpreting]?

conclusion *Expressive Activities*

17. In general, what can we say is included in the **environment** [generalizing]?

18. Make a picture album on the environment, including pictures of things in both the **natural environment** and **cultural environment** [synthesizing]. Placed in the library corner are magazines from which pictures may be cut.

19. Make a mural that shows things in the **natural environment** and **cultural environment** around our school [synthesizing].

20. What things do you value the most [evaluating]? Make a list of three things you value the most in the **natural environment**. Make a list of three things you value the most in the **cultural environment**. Give reasons for your choices [evaluating].

EVALUATION

1. Complete the following by listing five or more things in each column:

Major Things in the Natural and Cultural Environments

Natural Environment		Cultural Environment
Living Things	Nonliving Things	Things Made by People

What things in this photograph are part of the cultural environment?

2. Listed below are items in the natural and cultural environments. Write an *N* next to those in the natural environment; write a *C* next to those in the cultural environment.

____ Bottles	____ Rocks	____ Cans	____ Concrete
____ Wool	____ Sheep	____ Metal wheels	____ Steel
____ Iron ore	____ Plants	____ People	____ Animals
____ Tree farm	____ Forest	____ Air	____ Soil

3. Complete this sentence:
   Our environment includes _____.
4. Provide for self-evaluation by having each student choose a concept such as environment, resources, or pollution and keeping a record of everything that is done to learn about the concept. Self-evaluative questions are How can I improve? In what other ways can I learn about the concept? How can meaning be enriched and extended? Let the students share ways they find to improve.
5. (Note: The following activity may be used as a transition to the next unit, thus bringing immediate past learning to bear on a new unit on the changing community environment.) Which aspects of the environment change the most? How might we find out about changes in the environment of our community [hypothesizing]?

MODELS FOR MODULES

Modules are referred to as instructional packages, learning activity packages, or individualized learning packages. They are designed to provide instruction on a single topic, are self-contained or complete within themselves, and may be used alone or in connection with other units, the textbook, and other instructional materials. A module may vary in length from one that can be completed in a few minutes to one that requires several hours. Some use a single source, such as a reading or a filmstrip; others require students to use a variety of materials.

Two examples are given in this section. The first is a performance-based competency module designed as part of a map skills development program. This module uses preassessment and postassessment of students' learning. Students who do well on the preassessment move to other learning activities. Postassessment identifies any students who need additional instruction. The second example is designed to be used with all students as an independent study activity with no time limit. It is part of a module on Africa that includes geography, history, traditions, changes, past and present leaders, and current problems.

performance-based competency module

Modules designed to develop specific competencies contain such components as an introduction, objectives stated as competencies, preassessment, learning activities and materials, postassessment, and related reteaching (recycling) to clinch learning for those who have not mastered the stated competencies. The example that follows is the first part of a module designed to develop the ability to interpret physical-political maps. It is part of a map skills program for grade 5.

44

Interpreting Physical-Political Maps

INTRODUCTION

A physical-political map shows physical features and political areas. For example, the map of the United States on pages 226–27 of our basic textbook shows such physical features as mountain ranges, rivers, and lakes; it also shows the boundaries of each state, state capitals, and major cities. This type of map is used to answer such questions as these: In what states are mountain ranges located? What part of our country has the largest mountains? What areas are drained by different river systems? How are boundaries related to physical features? What are the relationships between surface features and land and water transportation systems?

OBJECTIVES

This module is part of the map skills program for grade 5. Two skills are to be developed that will enable you (a) to locate major mountain ranges in the United States and write the names of the states in which they are located and (b) to use the scale to measure the distance across the mountain ranges at various places. Other skills that are needed to find areas drained by rivers, land and water transportation routes, and similar topics will be presented later.

INSTRUCTIONS

You will need a pencil and a ruler or strip of paper. Complete the items listed in the preassessment. Raise your hand when finished, and the teacher or a monitor will bring an answer sheet to check your responses. If your answers are correct, do the next lesson. If not, complete this one.

PREASSESSMENT

Directions: Examine the map on pp. 226–27 of our textbook. Complete the following items:

1. Find Tennessee on the map. Write the name of the range of mountains in the eastern part of this state.

   _____

2. Find Pennsylvania on the map. What mountains are in the eastern part of this state?

   _____

3. Find Idaho. What mountains are in this state?

   _____

4. Determine the miles to inch or kilometers to centimeter with your ruler, or mark the scale on a strip of paper, then measure these distances:

   Across the range near Salem, Oregon _____

Across the range along Georgia's northern border   _____

Across the range along New Mexico's northern border   _____

OBJECTIVES AND LEARNING ACTIVITIES

A. To identify the location of the Appalachian, Rocky, Cascade, and Sierra Nevada mountain ranges by writing the names of the states in which they are located

Directions: Use the map on pp. 226–27 of the textbook and complete the following:

1. Write the name of the mountains that are in the eastern part of the United States.

   _____

   Beginning with Alabama and moving north, write the names of six states that have these mountains within their borders.

   _____   _____

   _____   _____

   _____   _____

2. What is the name of the mountains that are west of Kansas and Nebraska?

   _____

   Starting with Montana and moving south, write the names of six states that have these mountains within their borders.

   _____   _____

   _____   _____

   _____   _____

3. What is the name of the large mountain range in California?

   _____

4. What mountain range is in Oregon and Washington?

   _____

B. To use the scale to measure the distance across mountain ranges at designated points.

1. Determine the miles to inch or kilometers to centimeter with your ruler, or mark the scale on a strip of paper, and measure these distances:

   Across the mountains west of Richmond, Virginia _____

   Across the mountains east of Salt Lake City _____

   Across the mountains west of Carson City _____

   Across the mountains east of Olympia _____

POSTASSESSMENT

1. Find West Virginia on the map. What mountains are in this state?

   _____

2. Find Wyoming. What mountains are in this state?

_____

3. Find Washington. What mountains are in this state?

_____

4. Determine the miles to inch or kilometers to centimeter with your ruler, or mark the scale on a strip of paper, then measure these distances:

Across the range near Sacramento _____

Across the range near Denver _____

Across the range near Harrisburg _____

independent study modules The example below is a plan designed for students to use at their desks or in a learning center. Students are given a specific objective, a statement of materials to use, and procedures to follow. Self-evaluation procedures are built into each plan. Plans of this type may be included in an overall unit to individualize instruction and to extend learning through the use of a variety of materials.

Mansa Musa and the Mali Empire

OBJECTIVES

You are to answer the questions and complete the statements on Activity Sheet 1.

MATERIALS

You will need a pencil, a sheet of paper, and the booklet *Africa*, by Stephen Marvin.

PROCEDURES

1. Look at the picture map on page 100 that shows Mansa Musa holding a gold nugget. Find other items that show Mansa Musa's great wealth.
2. Mansa Musa was a ruler of Mali. It was a great empire, 1000 miles from one end to the other. There were poets, artists, scholars, and architects. During its golden age, Mali had a level of civilization that was higher than many others during the 1300s.
3. Look at the map of the Mali Empire on page 102. Find the location of Mali today on the map on page 31.
4. Read the story about the trader from England who visits Mansa Musa in his palace, pages 99–101. How do you think a person from England will react

to what he sees? How do you think Mansa Musa will react to what the trader tells him about England?

5. After you have read the story, answer the questions on Activity Sheet 1.
6. Reread the story and correct your answers after you have completed Activity Sheet 1. See the teacher if you have questions.

ACTIVITY SHEET 1:
WORKING ON YOUR OWN

Directions: After you have read the story, answer the questions below. Find the best answer and make an X on the line next to the answer you choose.

1. In what year did Sadin, the trader from England, come to the palace of Mansa Musa?
   ___ 1300   ___ 1327   ___ 1350   ___ 1377
2. As Mansa Musa entered the courtyard, he was followed by
   ___ 100 slaves   ___ 200 slaves   ___ 300 slaves   ___ 400 slaves
3. Sadin was invited to sit by Mansa Musa on
   ___ the throne   ___ cushions   ___ chairs   ___ a bench
4. Never before had Sadin seen a man of such
   ___ strength   ___ size   ___ dignity   ___ aloofness
5. Mansa Musa traveled to Mecca because
   ___ he wanted gold   ___ he wanted to be safe   ___ he was an explorer
   ___ he was religious
6. To Mansa Musa, England seemed to be a
   ___ backward country   ___ a great empire   ___ a safe country
   ___ a large country
7. Your rating of Mansa Musa's empire is
   ___ one of the greatest   ___ great   ___ just fair   ___ not so great
8. Your rating of England as described by the trader is
   ___ one of the greatest places   ___ great   ___ just fair   ___ not so great
9. Your interest in this story was
   ___ very high   ___ high   ___ fair   ___ low
10. In one sentence, write the main idea you got from this story.

OBJECTIVE-REFERENCED MODEL
FOR ACCOUNTABILITY PROGRAM

The example below is adapted from an ethnic studies unit that was designed to facilitate accountability (San Diego City Schools, "The People in our Community," 1973). It is presented in a three-column arrangement to show how performance objectives are related to activities and to evaluation. The part of the unit selected for this example begins with one of the unit objectives and a note on the materials that are needed. The performance objectives are related to the unit objective, and the materials are used with the learning activities as noted. Teacher observation is used during evaluation to note students who have achieved each performance objective and to identify those in need of further instruction.

People in Our Community

UNIT OBJECTIVE

To develop understanding of the need to accept differences in people in a positive way and to avoid appraising people on superficial characteristics.

MATERIALS

Soundstrip: ''Acceptance of Differences''
Film: ''King of the Hill''

Performance Objective	Learning Activities	Evaluation
1. Identify both physical and cultural differences to be accepted by all students.	See Soundstrip *Acceptance of Differences* to answer these questions: What differences between people should we accept? Why?	Each student lists two or more differences to accept and gives reasons.
2. Identify responsibilities of everyone to accept differences and to avoid prejudice.	Make list of responsibilities as shown on the soundstrip, plus others suggested by students.	Each student states orally or in writing two responsibilities.
3. Identify problems that may arise and propose ways to handle them.	Groups of 4 to 5 students note intergroup problems, propose solutions, and present them to the class.	Each student sticks to the group task and participates.
4. Discourage name calling, ethnic jokes, stereotyping, and discrimination.	Role play situations in which students refuse to tell jokes or engage in other negative behavior.	Students refuse to engage in negative behavior.
5. Make positive statements about one's own and other ethnic groups.	Groups of 4 to 5 students make lists of good things about their own and one other group.	Students describe three or more good things about their own and one other group.
6. State rules and actions that reflect positive attitudes toward others.	See *King of the Hill* to get ideas for human relations rules and actions.	Students describe what can be done to act by the ''Golden Rule.''

Other Formats

The preceding examples of models for units are illustrative of formats that may be used to write a unit plan. The following examples show other formats with multicolumn arrangements that may be used.

Objectives	Learning Activities	Materials

Objectives	Content	Teaching Procedures	Materials	Evaluation

Generalizations (and other content)	Learning Activities and Materials	Evaluation

Objectives	Content	Learning Activities and Evaluation	Materials

Daily Planning

Daily planning in the form of lesson plans must be done to assure optimum learning each day. Lesson planning is what brings units to life in the classroom. If a resource unit is being used, suggested activities and materials must be selected. If a teaching unit is being used it may contain appropriate lesson plans, such as those included in the examples in the first part of this chapter; if it does not, adaptations must be made to tailor it to the needs of students. Manuals that accompany textbooks and other materials usually contain plans that can readily be modified to the needs of a particular class.

Whatever their format, most daily plans include objectives, activities, evaluation, and needed materials. A new development, the inquiry-conceptual model, links thinking processes and concepts together, as shown in this example.

50

Where Is Our Country?

MAJOR UNDERSTANDINGS

Location of the United States: We live on a certain part of the earth. The name of our part of the earth is the United States.

OBJECTIVES

The students should develop the ability to

Recognize the name *United States of America* and state that it is the name of our country

Point to the location of the United States, including Alaska and Hawaii, on a pictorial map of the United States and on the classroom globe

State the colors used to show land and water in textbook picture maps and on the classroom globe

TEACHING STRATEGY

Thinking Processes	Questions and Activities	Data, Concepts, and Generalizations
	Introduction	
Observing	Look at the large picture map on page 5 of our textbook. What does this picture map show? Where would you have to be to make a picture like this?	*Map:* Pictorial map that shows United States borders and Hawaii.
Interpreting	What does the blue color show? Which colors show land? Point to a part that shows water; that shows land.	*Color Symbols:* Blue is used for water; various earth tones, for land.
	Development	
Observing	Something special is marked on this drawing of the earth. What is it?	*Line Symbols:* Lines are used on globes to show the borders between countries.
Interpreting	Point to the two white lines that go across part of the land. What is shown between the two white lines? What is the name of our country? Point to this part of our country.	*Boundary Lines:* The area between the white lines is the largest part of the United States.

Observing, Interpreting	Other places on the earth are part of our country too. What can you see on this picture that marks off another part of our country? Point to that part. What is that part called?	*Line Symbol*: The white line in the north area marks off the state of Alaska.
Observing, Interpreting	Look at the part that shows an ocean. What do you see there that shows another part of our country? What is that part called?	*Line Symbol*: Arrows are used to point out specific, small areas. The state of Hawaii is shown in the Pacific Ocean.

Conclusion

Synthesizing	Our country, the United States, is shown in different places. Who can point to all of them to show us our whole country?	*Location*: States and communities in the United States can be located on the globe.
Classifying	Which part of our country is the largest? Which part has water all around it? Which part is closer to the North Pole? Which parts are separate from the largest part of our country?	*Parts of the United States*: Hawaii is surrounded by water; Alaska is to the north. Both of these states are separate from the largest part of our country.

Guidelines for Unit Planning

SELECTING A UNIT

The most widely used procedure for selecting units is to refer to the course of study, note the units proposed for each grade, and select a unit that matches the backgrounds and capabilities of students in a given class. This procedure avoids repetition, promotes the use of appropriate instructional materials for each unit, and prevents the selection of insignificant units. Basic or required units are usually listed in the course of study, and one or more optional units may be suggested. To select optional units or any of special interest to the teacher or students, ask yourself the following questions:

Will it contribute to basic goals—knowledge, thinking processes, skills, attitudes and values?

Does it fit into the program and provide for continuity—not disruption—of learning?

Is it feasible in terms of available time and learning materials?

Can a variety of learning activities be provided to meet individual differences?

Give special attention to the educational backgrounds and growth characteristics of those for whom the unit is intended. Specifically, determine which units were studied in previous grades, the children's reading level, oral and written language skills, independent study and group work skills, special talents and interests, home study and library skills, cultural background, socioeconomic level, home background, and the like. A teacher can make a profile of the class by reviewing cumulative records, observing children in class, and conferring with the former teacher. When planning is done before school opens, teachers should plan resource units in terms of general growth characteristics of children in the grade to be taught. The resource unit may be converted into a teaching unit after specific information on students is obtained. A review of available materials for a unit helps to clarify the level and nature of instruction that should be provided.

BUILDING A BACKGROUND AND REVIEWING INSTRUCTIONAL MEDIA

An essential step in preparing to teach a unit is to build a background of knowledge, including the concepts, main ideas, and related content to be emphasized. Teachers should first review textbooks, supplementary books, other resources available for children, and background materials. Most teachers review adopted textbooks first, then check other materials as time permits. They then make an outline of content that can be refined as audiovisual and other resources are reviewed.

Appropriate learning materials may be more easily identified by noting items listed in the school system's media catalog and in the school and neighborhood or community libraries. A search should be made for the following:

Reading materials, including textbooks, unit booklets, reference, pamphlets, children's weekly news publications, articles in newspapers and magazines, literary materials, source materials, and programmed materials

Audiovisual materials, including filmstrips, soundstrips, slides, films, realia, models, maps, posters, transparencies, pictures, and post cards

Community resources, including study trips, resource visitors, local publications, people to interview, service organizations, museums, and historical associations

Detailed checklists for identifying instructional media and guidelines for using them are presented in chapter 3.

Depending on the time available, teachers can take several steps to enrich their background and identify learning materials. Audiovisual materials may be previewed and notes made about how they might be used to develop concepts and achieve other objectives. Community resources can be checked by interviewing potential class visitors and investigating field trip possibilities. Pictures, maps, source materials, and other items may be collected and filed with notes about their possible uses. Materials for art, music, construction, and other expressive activities may be gathered, and notes may be made for their use, using the guidelines suggested in chapter 10.

STATING GOALS AND OBJECTIVES

At the beginning of a unit state the goals briefly under such headings as knowledge (concepts and main ideas), thinking processes (generalizing and synthesizing), skills (reading, map and globe), and attitudes, values, and appreciations (respect for others, cultural values, contributions). The goals should be related to overall goals of the social studies and the statement should indicate how the unit contributes to their achievement.

Instructional objectives spell out the goals in terms of observable behavior, or products of behavior, as noted in chapter 1. They may be listed after each goal, be presented in a separate section, or be placed at appropriate points within the unit to show how they are related to learning activities. The models for units, presented earlier, show ways of stating goals and objectives.

Main ideas, generalizations, or major understandings to be developed require special attention. Two procedures to employ are identifying main ideas in various materials and generating main ideas when sources of them are not available.

identifying main ideas The first step in identifying main ideas is to check the instructional materials. This procedure helps to ensure that the necessary content is available in students' learning materials. Teacher's manuals for class textbooks include main ideas for different chapters and units under such headings as major understandings or generalizations. Manuals for films, filmstrips, and other media should also be checked.

Main ideas are also found in teaching and resource units available in school district offices. Charts 2–1 through 2–9 show main ideas in units that are typically found in the basic social studies program.

generating main ideas One of the best ways to generate main ideas is to outline the content of a unit, then state generalizations that can be made from the content. Why is this so effective? Because if effective learning is to take place, students must have sufficient content to be able to make a generalization—to state the main idea in their own words. They may try to verbalize a main idea the teacher is forcing on them, but they will not really understand it. To be truly learned main ideas must be earned! They can be earned only by processing the information on which they are based. Keep this principle in mind as the following additional ways of generating main ideas are presented.

Families
Around The World

Families differ in size and composition.

Everyone at home has work to do.

Changes take place in homes and families.

Money may be earned by one or more members of the family.

Some members of the family produce goods and services.

Chart 2–1

Living on Farms

Our country has many different kinds of farms.

Different kinds of work are done as seasons change.

Water, soil, and weather are important to the farmer.

New machines have changed the work of farmers.

People depend on farmers, and farmers depend on other workers.

Chart 2–2

Living
in Our Community

People work at many different jobs to provide goods and services.

People depend on one another for food, clothes, and other goods.

Many goods that we need are made in other communities.

Many changes have taken place since our community was founded.

Chart 2–3

Communities
around The World

Weather, climate, and landforms vary from place to place.

People work for food, shelter, and clothing.

Changes take place as new ideas are put to use.

Some communities are like ours in some ways but different in other ways.

Chart 2–4

Growth
of Our State

Industries have been set up to use capital, resources, and labor supply.

Some ways of living brought by early settlers are still evident.

Many people have contributed to the growth of our state.

Changes have taken place faster in recent years.

Chart 2–5

Colonists
in Early America

Many settlers came in search of a better life.

The reasons for coming to America differed among settlers from different countries.

Ways of living in the colonies were related to beliefs, past experiences, and new problems.

The idea of self-government was expressed in many ways.

Chart 2–6

Achievements
of Minority Groups

Many achievements have been made in response to critical problems.

Achievements have been made in science, medicine, and the social sciences.

Achievements have been made in law, education, and other professions.

Achievements have been made in art, music, literature, and sports.

Chart 2–7

Developing Countries
in Latin America

The countries of South America attained freedom from European nations after a long struggle.

Countries in the Americas are interdependent in many ways.

Economic development projects are designed to improve living conditions.

Many nations have a single major industry.

Chart 2–8

Growth
of Democracy

Democratic concepts of government began to emerge early in America.

The Constitution provided the basic framework of government.

Principles of democracy were extended as frontiers were opened.

Many individuals and groups have contributed to the growth of democracy.

Chart 2–9

Main ideas may also be generated by using key or core concepts that are stressed across grade levels as a basis for stating the main ideas of a particular unit. For example, the concept of *interdependence,* which is stressed in all programs, may be used to generate such main ideas as the following:

Members of the family depend on each other for many things.

Community workers depend on each other for many goods and services.

We depend on other countries for some goods and they depend on us for goods they need.

The growing interdependence between our country and other countries is evident in trade and international relations.

Countries around the world have formed organizations to handle problems created by increasing interdependence.

The usefulness of key concepts to generate main ideas may be further illustrated by chart 2–10. It includes concepts and related generalizations from which main ideas for a unit on food production are derived. Notice that the main ideas suggest the nature of the content to be used in the unit.

A third way to generate main ideas is to begin with generalizations from the social sciences, such as those presented in chapter 6. For example, the following generalization may be used to derive main ideas for various units:

Main Ideas in a Unit on Food Production

Core Concepts and Generalizations		*Main Ideas to Be Developed*
Basic needs: People work to satisfy needs for food, clothing, and shelter.	→	Workers who provide food are needed in all communities.
Group action: The work of society is carried on through groups.	→	Many groups work to produce and distribute food.
Culture: Individual behavior is influenced by the culture.	→	People eat different foods to obtain the nourishment they need.
Interdependence: People depend on others in all societies.	→	Families depend on workers in food stores.
Rules: Societies make laws and regulations for group welfare.	→	Laws and regulations apply to the production and distribution of food.
Technology: Level of technology limits production.	→	Use of machines aids food production in our society.
Contributions: Others have contributed to our cultural heritage.	→	Some foods have been brought from other lands.
Change: Change takes place in the cultural and physical environment.	→	Ways of producing food have brought desirable and undesirable changes.

Chart 2–10

Societies require a system of social control in order to survive.
All families have rules that members are expected to follow.
Communities have rules and regulations to provide for the safety and welfare of children and adults.
State and federal laws protect individual rights and promote the general welfare.
Both democratic and totalitarian systems of social control exist in various countries of Latin America.

Some main ideas should be broken down into subideas (also referred to as organizing, supporting, or contributing ideas) to indicate the emphasis in a unit and the content provided in instructional materials. For example, the following main idea may be broken down into subideas:

Communities have rules and regulations to provide for the safety and welfare of children and adults.
Traffic laws provide for the safety of children and adults.
Foods laws set standards for the production, distribution, and handling of food.
Housing laws provide for the rights of ethnic, racial, and other groups.

Additional examples of generalizations and main ideas are presented in chapters dealing with the social sciences and special areas of study, such as multicultural and law-focused education.

INITIATING A UNIT

A good beginning stimulates interest, arouses curiosity, clarifies the major topic of study, and gives students opportunities to become involved in discussing questions and problems to be investigated in a unit. It also serves to set the scope of the unit, to relate a new unit to past units, and to focus attention on what is to be studied first. Many different approaches, alone or in combination, may be used as described below.

ongoing study Often the most effective way to start is to have a unit grow out of the preceding unit as an ongoing study. For example, a community study may grow out of a study of the neighborhood, a study of the westward movement may grow out of a study of pioneer life, and a study of countries in a region of South America may grow out of a study of neighboring countries. In this approach it is essential that the teacher clarify the relationship between concluding activities in one unit and beginning activities in the next one. Connecting relationships may be made by discussing questions and problems that focus attention on logical next steps to take.

arranged environment An arrangement of pictures, realia, books, maps, and learning centers to initiate a unit is one of the most widely used approaches. Students are given an opportunity to examine the materials, make comments, and raise questions about them. A film, story, set of slides, or other materials may be used to stimulate thinking. During follow-up discussion, students' questions are clarified and listed on the chalkboard or a chart. The teacher may raise other questions to make sure that important points are not overlooked and to guide thinking in profitable directions. Even when an ongoing study is the main approach, arranging of materials helps to make the transition to the next unit more meaningful.

teacher suggestion

Direct teacher suggestions is often used to initiate required units, optional units, or units on current events of special significance. To be effective this approach should be planned to involve students and encourage them to participate. The teacher may raise questions, pose issues or problems, invite students to share related experiences, present pictures or a wall map to provoke discussion, or give reasons for undertaking the unit.

a current event

A unit may be initiated because of a current or upcoming event, such as an election, commemoration, ethnic folk festival, special week, celebration of the founding of the community, or other significant happening. To meet the problem of timing, the teacher may plan certain units to coincide with elections or other scheduled events. A sound procedure is to use events as springboards when possible but to have other plans ready for initiating units.

preassessment

A pretest or inventory may be used to initiate a unit. This approach should be designed to open up questions and problems and to identify particular needs of students. A discussion of the findings would then follow to clarify objectives. Backgrounds of understandings, skills and attitudes and values may be assessed and areas in need of further study may be identified. Preassessment should generally be coupled with an arranged environment or other approach to stimulate interest and suggest questions.

instructional materials

The textbook may be used to initiate a unit by giving specific attention to introductory sections, photo essays, and the pictures that are typically included at the beginning of each unit. The teacher may display supplementary books or books from the library, calling attention to selected sections or reading portions to the class to arouse interest. A film or other audiovisual materials may be shown to introduce a unit. Pitfalls to avoid are failing to open up questions, neglecting to define clearly the focus of the unit, and eliciting passive instead of active student participation. The teacher can avoid these difficulties with careful planning and by formulating questions and comments to guide the students and to direct follow-up discussion.

community resources

A study trip or a resource visitor may be used to initiate a unit. With careful planning, the experience can focus on selected problems and stimulate each child to think. Community resources are effective when the class plans in ad-

Social Studies Workshop, University of California, Berkeley

What questions might be stimulated by a display such as this?

vance to find the answers to specific questions and problems under study. As an approach to a new unit they are most effective when used as an ongoing activity growing out of the preceding unit. For example, in concluding a study of life on the farm, one group planned to visit a wholesale market to find out how farm produce was processed and distributed. The visit to the market initiated the unit on the wholesale market without interrupting the overall emphasis for the year, which was on how people secure food, shelter, and clothing.

Selecting and Sequencing Learning Activities

Whatever model of unit planning is used, the selection and sequencing of a variety of learning activities deserves special attention. For best results activities should be selected and organized in a sequence that begins with opening activities; moves to intake and organizing activities; followed by applicative, demonstrative and creative activities; and ends with concluding activities that wrap up the unit. This sequence parallels the problem-solving process in that it provides for defining the problem; collecting, appraising, and organizing information; and using the information to answer questions, test hypotheses, draw conclusions, and synthesize key learnings. It also gives students opportunities to use thinking processes in a sequence that begins with recalling and observing; brings in interpreting, comparing, classifying, generalizing, and inferring; and extends thinking to include analyzing, synthesizing, hypothesizing, predicting, and evaluating.

The sections that follow contain a detailed listing of learning activities and may be used as a master checklist for planning. They should be supplemented by adding activities from locally available units of instruction and from the teacher's manuals that accompany the social studies textbooks currently in use.

OPENING ACTIVITIES

Openers, or beginning activities, for each main idea or other section of a unit build readiness, create interest, focus attention, open up questions, find out what children know about the topic, recall relevant information, make plans, and set the stage for data-gathering activities. Introductory activities that clarify or define what is to be studied may be followed by group planning and discussion of materials to use. During opening activities the teacher should incorporate well-founded ideas and note any misconceptions that students have.

Introductory Activities

Examine and discuss pictures and photo essays that the textbook uses to introduce the first topic of study.

Examine and discuss bulletin board arrangements, items in learning centers, and other materials set up to stimulate questions and form hypotheses to guide study.

Recall related ideas in response to questions raised by the teacher or presented in the textbook.

View a set of slides, a group of pictures, a filmstrip, or a film selected to introduce the topic.

Start a chart, bulletin board display, map, scrapbook, or other item to be completed by students.

Ask students what they have done or might do if they were in a certain imaginary situation.

Listen to a story or a selection from the textbook or other source read by the teacher to open up questions related to the topic.

Complete unfinished sentences or a story related to the topic. Discuss questions and problems students can expect to encounter in the unit.

Take a pretest or inventory designed to assess students' backgrounds, then discuss results and state objectives.

Planning Activities

List questions, objectives, or hypotheses that can be used to guide study.

Discuss additional sources of information, including specific library materials, pamphlets, and other materials.

Discuss materials available in learning centers and standards and procedures for using them.

Consider individual, small-group, and whole-class activities.

Formulate rules and work standards to guide individual and group work.

Define difficult terms and clarify concepts needed to begin data-gathering activities.

Developmental activities should grow out of opening activities to provide a smooth learning sequence. A complete series of developmental activities should flow from data-gathering or intake activities to data-organizing activities, applicative and demonstrative activities, and on to creative and expressive activities. Data-gathering or intake activities provide the input needed to handle questions and hypotheses. Organizing activities help students structure and summarize information. Applicative and demonstrative activities extend learning and give students opportunities to show that they achieved stated objectives. Creative and expressive activities enrich learning and develop the ability to improvise and apply learning in original ways. Evaluation is an ongoing process throughout the unit, from intake to creative activities, culminating in the final assessment.

Some activities overlap different types of learning activity and can be used to organize information, to demonstrate competence, and to express ideas creatively. For example, a student may complete an outline map to organize information, make a map of an area with a key to demonstrate mapping ability, and create a map to portray information gathered on transportation, resources, or other items. Sketching, drawing, preparing reports, graphing, and other activities can be similarly used. The guiding principle is to use an activity to achieve a given objective, whether it is to organize and summarize information, to demonstrate a capability, or to express thoughts and feelings in new ways.

Data Gathering, or Intake Activities

Review ideas learned in preceding units of study related to the current topic or questions.

Use tables of contents, indexes, study guides, and reading lists to locate needed information.

Read textbooks, references, periodicals, pamphlets, charts, graphs, diagrams, encyclopedias, yearbooks, and almanacs.

Listen to experts, reports of individuals and committees, material read by the teacher, and recordings.

See films, filmstrips, slides, stereographs, pictures, exhibits, displays, television programs, dioramas, panoramas, and demonstrations.

Observe demonstrations, festivals, pageants, people at work, holiday commemorations, seasonal changes, and community activities.

Interview experts in the community, old timers, parents, teachers, members of ethnic groups, and people who have visited places under study.

Examine collections, models, specimens, textiles, instruments, tools, utensils, and costumes.

Collect news articles, pictures, maps, and other items related to questions under study.

Gather information from maps, atlases, graphs, tables, pamphlets, and other sources.

Engage in such activities as operating models and touching, tasting, and smelling various items.

Take notes on specific items of information to answer questions under study.

Keep a diary or log of seasonal changes, an ongoing current event, experiments, and other activities.

Write letters to request information or materials.

Appraise information by checking one source against another, finding proof for statements, asking experts, and double-checking.

Organizing and Summarizing Activities

Compare objects, activities, and behavior to identify similarities and differences and to arrange them by size, shape, color, value, or other attribute.

Classify information, objects, and pictures by function or use, descriptive characteristics, cause-effect or other relationships, time periods, or place of origin.

Select information related to questions, issues, concepts, and the main idea under study.

Make picture charts, pictorial booklets, albums, and minipicture data banks to organize and summarize information.

Place information in a scrapbook, card file, filing system, or data bank.

Record information on tapes, charts, graphs, maps, time lines, diagrams, and tables for later use.

Prepare drawings or sketches of tools, utensils, instruments, or other items that can be best understood through pictorial representation.

Organize notes on a topic or question under headings to break it down into meaningful parts.

Generalize by stating the common or general features of objects, activities, and behavior.

Appraise the adequacy of organization of information in terms of completeness, clarity, and usefulness for other activities.

Applicative and Demonstrative Activities

Describe activities, objects, and events in one's own words.

Present reports, reviews, and other prepared material to the class.

Explain the reasons or causes of events, why ways of living differ among groups with different cultures, and other items under study.

Infer by stating possible feelings, reasons, motives, purposes, or other factors that may be involved in a situation.

Analyze by identifying the main parts of objects, steps in a process, causes of events, alternatives and related consequences, cause-effect, and other relationships.

Predict future developments related to the topic under study.

Demonstrate understanding of a topic by participating in a discussion, a debate, role playing, a simulation, a program, or a panel.

Write reports, reviews, outlines, and descriptive statements that include material from several sources.

Complete an individual learning contract or independent study module.

Give a demonstration of an activity, such as weaving, candle dipping, playing an instrument from another culture, or folk dancing.

Make a map, chart, booklet, movie box roll, diorama, or other item, using information gathered from reading materials and other sources.

Model objects that have been studied, using clay, papier-mâché, or other materials.

Appraise applicative and demonstrative activities by means of charts, checklists, tests, and other devices to find out if students have achieved objectives.

Creative and Expressive Activities

Propose new ways to classify items, new solutions to problems, new explanations of events, and new questions or hypotheses in need of study.

Compose stories, poems, playlets, skits, songs, and rhymes related to topics under study.

Express thoughts and feelings through dramatic play, role playing, rhythmic expression, singing, playing instruments, and folk dances.

Take roles through dramatizing, role playing, story telling, pantomiming, gaming, and engaging in simulations.

Arrange displays, bulletin boards, and exhibits around concepts, themes, and main ideas.

Write letters to the editor, articles, editorials, and position statements on environmental and other issues.

Propose an individual learning activity or committee project, such as a demonstration, an investigation, an individual learning contract, a survey, or an interview.

Draw, paint, and sketch objects and activities under study.

Create murals, posters, cartoons, collages, and montages.

Plan and present a program to culminate a unit.

Make original maps, charts, graphs, dioramas, and other items.

Evaluate expressive and creative activities for originality, achievement of purpose, form of presentation, and expression of thoughts and feelings.

CONCLUDING ACTIVITIES

Closely related to and flowing from expressive activities are concluding activities of two types. The first type are activities related to each main idea in the unit. The second are those culminating activities that encompass the entire unit and bring together the different main ideas. Culminating activities usually result in a presentation to parents or other classes, but care should be taken to see that the emphasis is on educational outcomes rather than "putting on a show."

Share, discuss, and evaluate as a group individual and committee reports with emphasis on key concepts and the main idea under development.

Plan and present a skit, quiz program, round-table discussion, or other activity that synthesizes major unit outcomes.

Select and discuss murals, maps, charts, and other items made by students, emphasizing relationships to the main idea under development.

Complete notebooks, scrapbooks, murals, or other items that are made to synthesize information around the main idea.

Plan, take, and evaluate a field trip designed to highlight relationships among activities, content, and the main idea.

Guide students to phrase the main idea in their own words, drawing on charts, reports, and other materials.

Evaluate students' depth and breadth of understanding through discussion, a test, guided self-evaluation, checklists, and other procedures.

Identify questions and topics in need of further study and new questions that may be considered in the next part of the unit or in a new unit.

Culminating Activities

Present summary reports related to displays, murals, bulletin board arrangements, scrapbooks, and other items prepared by students.

Present a program or pageant in which commentary, songs, folk dances, pictures, and other materials are used to highlight main ideas.

Dramatize major events, episodes, or activities studied during the unit.

Have students report key points related to each main idea with emphasis on interrelationships.

Discuss similarities and differences in the main idea under consideration and main ideas formulated during preceding activities.

Evaluation of Learning

Evaluation is important in all phases of the unit from initiation on through concluding activities. A variety of devices may be used to appraise objectives of the unit. Some devices are prepared as a part of learning activities, for example, charts on work standards, checklists for evaluating discussion and other activities, and standards for using materials. Many devices such as tests and inventories may be constructed ahead of time. The following list is illustrative of devices and procedures that may be used. Specific examples and a more detailed discussion appear in chapter 14.

Anecdotal records	Checking of written work
Attitude and interest inventories	Essay tests
Checking by a partner	Group discussion

Individual self-checking	Reviewing files of each student's work
Keeping individual and group logs or diaries	Student analysis of tape recordings
Objective tests	Teacher analysis of tape recordings
Rating scales and checklists	Teacher observation

KEEPING A LOG TO EVALUATE THE UNIT

An item that needs special comment is the keeping of a log. Teachers who have kept a log report that it is a great help in evaluating the unit and in gathering ideas to use in revising the unit. A satisfactory log is a brief running account of the unit and includes notes on strengths and weaknesses of instructional materials, changes to be made in learning experiences, and other ways in which the unit should be modified. Items are entered during or at the end of the day and kept in a folder. After the culmination of the unit, notes related to all main ideas or problems should be brought together and used as a basis for revising the unit.

Other Aspects of Unit Planning

TEAM PLANNING OF UNITS

Many teachers find it helpful to work with a partner or a committee to prepare unit plans. Special talents of each member of the team can be tapped, responsibilities for reviewing materials can be designated, best ideas drawn from past experience can be shared, work can be divided by each member of the team. After the unit is prepared, each teacher has the responsibility of adapting the unit to educational needs and individual differences of students.

MOVING FROM TEXTBOOK TO UNIT INSTRUCTION

Some new teachers, faced with the multiplicity of problems that typically arise, rely primarily on the adopted textbook for social studies instruction. It is possible to move from textbook to unit teaching in a series of steps as time permits. First, identify other reading materials, on various levels of difficulty, and audiovisual materials that complement textbook units. Note related field trips, resource visitors, and other community resources. In the beginning these materials may be used with chapters in the textbook and learning activities suggested in the accompanying teacher's manual. Next, make plans that are structured around main ideas, key concepts, and guiding questions that are central to the topic of study. Then list learning activities and instructional materials (including the textbook) under the main ideas, concepts, and questions as appropriate. Evaluation activities may also be planned to assess objectives related to all of the instructional materials used.

Another procedure that some teachers use to develop units, particularly in new areas of study, is to begin by making lesson plans related to new filmstrips, reading materials, or other resources. For example, a new filmstrip on energy conservation may be available or a new textbook may be adopted. The accompanying manuals are checked, ideas on needs of students are noted, ideas from past experience are drawn upon, and plans for using the new materials are made. After several plans are made, they are brought together, revised, and put together as a section of a unit clustered around a main idea or generalization. Then plans are made for other parts of the new textbook or other materials, clustering them around another main idea. A practical teaching unit is thus developed inductively by moving from daily planning to an overall plan that is a synthesis of specific plans.

Where to Obtain Units

Preplanned units are available from local and county school districts, state departments, curriculum laboratories and media centers, and libraries in colleges and universities. Many have been placed in ERIC (Educational Resources Information Center) and are listed in *Resources in Education*. Some may be found in magazines such as *Instructor, Teacher,* and the teacher edition of *Scholastic*. Teacher's manuals that accompany social studies textbooks contain unit plans directly related to the text and supplemented by a variety of activities and related materials. Other sources are noted in the references at the end of the chapter.

Questions, Activities, Evaluation

1. Obtain a unit of instruction from one of the sources noted above and do the following:
   a. Note the contents of each major section. Does the unit include the same general sections noted in this chapter?
   b. How are the goals and objectives stated? What changes, if any, might be made to improve them?
   c. Summarize the opening, developmental, and concluding activities that you believe to be most helpful.
   d. Note techniques of evaluation that are suggested.
   e. Note references that may be useful in your own future planning.
2. Plan a short teaching unit similar to one of those presented in this chapter. Review as many related instructional resources as time permits. As you obtain ideas from subsequent chapters, add them to the unit.
3. Prepare a kit or box of materials that can be used with the unit you are planning. Include pictures, maps, free or inexpensive materials, songs, directions for arts and crafts, and other resources.

4. Arrange to visit a classroom where a unit of instruction of interest to you is in progress. Try to visit several times so as to observe the initiation, subsequent activities, and the culmination. Discuss questions that you would ask the teacher in charge.

references

BANKS, JAMES, *Strategies for Teaching Ethnic Studies* (2nd ed.). Boston, Mass.: Allyn & Bacon, 1979. Sections on materials and procedures.

CHASE, LINWOOD W., AND MARTHA TYLER JOHN, *A Guide for the Elementary Social Studies Teacher* (3rd ed.). Boston, Mass.: Allyn & Bacon, 1978. Chapters on unit planning and exemplary units.

Curriculum Materials. Washington, D.C.: Association for Supervision and Curriculum Development, annual. Listing of units available from various school systems.

HANNAH, LARRY S., AND JOHN U. MICHAELIS, *A Comprehensive Framework for Instructional Objectives.* Reading, Mass.: Addison-Wesley Publishing Co., 1977. Sample objectives and how to write them for intellectual processes, knowledge, skills, and values.

JONES, RALPH H., ed., *Social Studies for Young Americans.* Dubuque, Iowa: Kendall/Hunt Publishing Company, 1970. Articles on unit teaching.

McASHAN, H. H., *The Goals Approach to Performance Objectives.* Philadelphia, Pa.: W. B. Saunders Company, 1974. Chapter on performance-based competency modules.

MICHAELIS, JOHN U., RUTH H. GROSSMAN, AND LLOYD SCOTT, *New Designs for Elementary Curriculum and Instruction.* New York: McGraw-Hill, 1975. Sections on objectives, unit planning, teaching strategies, and evaluation.

MICHAELIS, JOHN U., AND EVERETT T. KEACH, JR., eds., *Teaching Strategies for Elementary Social Studies.* Itasca, Ill.: F. E. Peacock Publishers, 1972. Section on sample lessons and units.

OLINER, PEARL M., *Teaching Elementary Social Studies.* New York: Harcourt Brace Jovanovich, 1976. Chapter on unit and lesson plans.

QUIGLEY, CHARLES N., *Law in a Free Society.* 5115 Douglas Fir Avenue, Calabasas, Calif. 91302. Teaching units based on concepts of authority, justice, privacy, responsibility, participation, diversity, property, and freedom.

TABA, HILDA, MARY C. DURKIN, JACK R. FRAENKEL, AND ANTHONY H. McNAUGHTON, *A Teacher's Handbook To Elementary Social Studies.* Reading, Mass.: Addison-Wesley Publishing Co. 1971. Planning units around main ideas; main and organizing ideas in appendix.

IDENTIFYING AND USING INSTRUCTIONAL MEDIA

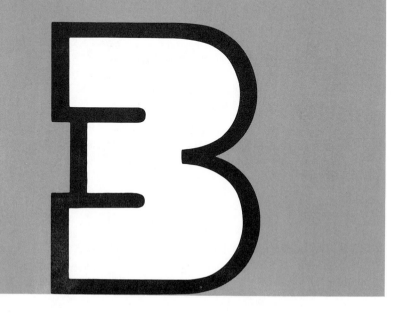

What procedures should be used to improve the use of textbooks, charts, library materials, literary selections, and practice materials?

What types of audiovisual materials should be used? What guidelines should be followed when using films, pictures, and other materials?

What community resources should be identified? What procedures are essential to use them effectively?

What criteria are used to select materials for a unit? To select free or inexpensive materials? To select new materials?

What guidelines are helpful in clarifying the objectives for using materials? Developing readiness for them? Guiding their use? Providing follow-up activities? Evaluating their use?

What sources may be used when special materials not available in a school are needed?

Because multimedia approaches to instruction have demonstrated their value, teachers have an obligation to identify and use a variety of media. The guidelines and procedures given in this chapter will enable the teacher to use effectively both print and nonprint media. Reading materials are discussed first, beginning with a checklist of various types followed by guidelines for using textbooks, charts, and other resources. The most widely used audiovisual materials are discussed next, then community resources are considered. The remainder of the chapter discusses criteria for selecting media, helpful guidelines for using materials, and sources of needed materials.

Other instructional media are treated in later chapters. Chapter 10 includes guidelines for using simulation games, art and music materials, and construction and processing materials. Chapter 12 discusses maps and globes.

Reading Materials

Reading materials are the most widely used of all the instructional media, but because of the vast variety and wide availability of reading materials, great care must be taken to select them carefully and use them well.

Grateful acknowledgement is made to Dr. Ruth Grossman, City University of New York, City College, for suggested revisions in this chapter.

Checklist 3–1 provides a quick way to identify and locate materials related to units of instruction for a particular grade.

Checklist 3–1
Reading Materials

_____ Textbooks, including interdisciplinary ones and ones that focus on geography, history, civics, or other disciplines

_____ Booklets on a variety of topics, ranging from family life and community workers to ethnic groups and other lands

_____ Reference materials, including almanacs, anthologies, atlases, dictionaries, directories, encyclopedias, gazetteers, government bulletins, scrapbooks, yearbooks, and data banks

_____ Fugitive materials, including bulletins, clippings, folders, leaflets, simulation games, pamphlets, and free or inexpensive materials

_____ Current events materials, including children's weekly news publications, children's magazines, daily newspapers, and adult magazines

_____ Literary materials, including biography, fiction, folklore, short stories, and travel books

_____ Source materials, including ballots, diaries, directions, logs, maps, minutes of meetings, recipes, and timetables

_____ Programmed materials, including geographic, historical, and other content arranged in a step-by-step sequence

_____ Self-help materials, including charts, checklists, directions, outlines, study guides, teacher-prepared practice materials, and workbooks

_____ Display materials, including titles, captions, signs, and labels

_____ Teacher-prepared materials, including charts, rewritten material, and scrapbooks

---

TEXTBOOKS

Textbooks serve as the core of instruction in many social studies programs, and they are used in several different ways. Some teachers use the adopted textbook as the basis of instruction, employing teaching procedures similar to those used in the reading program. Other teachers use a basic textbook as a general guide but supplement various chapters of the text with other reading material and audiovisual materials. This approach, a step beyond sole reliance on a single textbook, gives children opportunities to use materials on different readability levels and to gather data from various sources. In schools where unit instruction and multimedia approaches are used, the textbook becomes one component of instruction, along with audiovisual and community resources and a variety of other reading materials. All instructional media, including textbooks, are sources of information that must be geared to the capabilities of students and the nature of the topics under study.

No matter which approach is used, teachers may use social studies textbooks to achieve such objectives as these:

1. To introduce a unit through photo essays and introductory sections that set the stage or give an overview
2. To develop new concepts and related vocabulary as children use picture and context clues, phonics, and structural analysis
3. To find main ideas and details related to topics and problems under study
4. To provide a background of ideas that students can use to make comparisons as they study media that present different information
5. To provide more detailed or extensive information after initial data-gathering activities involving firsthand experiences or visual materials
6. To answer questions and "prove" points by having students locate and report relevant information
7. To improve skill in reading, in interpreting maps, charts, diagrams, illustrations, tables, and graphs, and in using the table of contents, glossary and index
8. To sharpen the ability to draw inferences, derive generalizations, predict outcomes, and use other thinking processes
9. To foster positive feelings and attitudes toward others as children read about other groups and cultures
10. To summarize and bring together key ideas at selected points during a unit and at the end of a unit

TEACHER-PREPARED MATERIAL

One of the most useful types of material is that which has been rewritten by the teacher to fit the levels of reading ability of students. A sound approach is to imagine you are writing a letter or telling an exciting story to a child, keeping in mind that every idea must be expressed as simply and clearly as possible. Choose vocabulary, phrasing, and sentences similar to those used by children, and keep sentences and paragraphs short, as they are in children's periodicals.

Other types of teacher-prepared material are charts, vocabulary lists and card files, practice exercises, and activity cards such as the one that follows.

Map Activity Card

Directions. Look at the map of the city shown on page 69 of our textbook. Write answers to these questions on a separate sheet of paper.

1. What is the name of the city?
2. What are the symbols for the following?
   a. Freeways   b. Railroads   c. Rivers   d. Lakes

3. How far is it across the city from north to south?
4. How far is it across the city from east to west?
5. List three natural features that are shown.
6. List three cultural features that are shown.

Booklets may be made of pictures and articles related to a topic, and folders may be organized to include materials on topics in a unit. Reports and scrapbooks prepared by students may be edited and revised for use by future classes.

making
and using
charts

Charts are useful in units at all levels of instruction. They are especially helpful in developing reading ability in the social studies. For example, as concepts and generalizations and the related vocabulary are developed and used to make charts, children develop the backgrounds of meaning that are essential to effective reading.

The variety of charts that may be used include

Experience charts based on field trips, interviews, and other activities

Question charts to guide individual and group study of topics

Vocabulary charts made up of special terms needed in a unit

Classification charts for recording specific items under such headings as fruits, vegetables, natural resources, and modes of transportation

Retrieval charts for recording data about cities, countries, and other topics

Organization charts that show committees, structure of government, economic or political systems, and organization of other groups

Direction charts to guide field trips, map making, and other activities

Sequence charts that show a series of events, processes or steps in producing various items, and the flow of materials from farm to city

Group standard charts to guide and evaluate discussion, committee work, role-playing, and other activities

Progress charts to record the completion of individual and group work

The format of charts should be similar to the format of those included in this volume. Make the lettering large enough for group use, use standard paragraph form, and leave adequate space between words and lines. Balanced placement of illustrations, consistent use of standard letter forms, and margins similar to those on picture mats are other important elements of good charts.

LITERARY MATERIALS

Literature enriches social learning in the elementary school. As Ernest Horn said many years ago, "Of all the subjects not traditionally included under the social studies, none is more intimately affiliated with them than litera-

Time to read and time to choose. How can materials selected by
students promote learning in the social studies?

ture.''* Literary selections can heighten interest, deepen understanding, create
mood and atmosphere, portray the diversity of ways of living and thinking
among people in various cultures, stimulate imagination, give colorful
backgrounds, promote more complete identification with others, create sym-
pathy for the problems of others, improve attitudes toward others, build appreciations for other cultures, provoke creativity, and give vivid impressions of
ways of living being studied in various units. Factual material rarely kindles a
feeling for the joys, sorrows, and problems of others; hence the importance of
poetry, stories, biography, fiction, letters, legends, and travel literature to take

*Ernest Horn, *Methods of Instruction in the Social Studies* (New York: Scribner's, 1937), p. 265.

children beyond facts to the spiritual and aesthetic qualities and values involved in human relationships. The following examples of the uses of literary selections in various units may serve to clarify the specific ways in which literature can enrich the social studies program.

> In studying pets as a part of a unit on the home, one group was thrilled by the teacher's reading of Hill and Maxwell's *Charlie and His Puppy Bingo* and Gemmill's *Joan Wanted a Kitty*. Selected poems from *Sung Under the Silver Umbrella* (Association for Childhood Education) were also enjoyed.
>
> A primary group learning about the community enjoyed Field's *General Store*, Clymer's *The Big Pile of Dirt*, and Chute's *Rhymes About the City*. Another group studying the farm liked Chute's *Farmers* and Nast's *A Farm Story*. A group studying trains enjoyed Tippett's poem "Trains" and Lenski's *The Little Train*.
>
> In a study of life in the United States, several children read Gate's *Blue Willow* and expressed keenly felt sympathy for the problems of the itinerant worker's child. Others read Buffler's *Rodrigo and Rosalita*, Lenski's *Blue Ridge Sally, Bayou Suzette*, and *Strawberry Girl*, which enriched their understanding of life in different sections of the country, and Kurelek's *A Prairie Boy's Winter*, which portrays the end of autumn, the long cold winter, and finally the beginning of spring. Several were sensitized to the thoughts and feelings of individuals in ethnic groups by reading Jackson's *Call Me Charley*, De Angeli's *Bright April*, Davis's *Americans Everyone*, Eberle's *Very Good Neighbors*, Sommerfelt's *My Name Is Pablo*, and Beim's *Two Is a Team*. These books were also helpful in showing how individuals and groups can work and play together even though differences exist.
>
> A study of the growth of democracy was greatly enriched for upper-grade children who read D'Aulaires's *George Washington*, Daugherty's *Abraham Lincoln*, and Forbes's *America's Paul Revere*, and who listened to recordings such as "Ballad for Americans," "The Lonesome Train," and "Mine Eyes Have Seen the Glory." A greater appreciation of the contributions of famous Americans was developed by those who read Franklin's *Autobiography*, Petry's *Harriet Tubman*, Pace's *Clara Barton*, Gray's *William Penn*, and Holt's *George Washington Carver*.

Care should be taken to distinguish fact from fiction and to discuss deviations from reality. Other guidelines to follow when using a literary selection are these:

1. Emphasize subjective outcomes, such as the enjoyment and excitement that children should experience as they read it or listen to it.
2. Enjoy it with the class; do not dissect it, and analyze it only if analysis increases enjoyment.
3. Share and discuss elements that children like; do not give tests or evaluate it as you evaluate factual materials.
4. Let the children discover moods, meanings, and values; do not moralize or over-emphasize points of keen interest to you.
5. Use a variety of techniques and activities to share and enjoy literary works—book reports, card files of favorite poems and stories, choral reading, creative writing, dramatization, filmstrips, independent reading, films, oral reading by children or the teacher, programs and pageants, puppets and marionettes, radio and television programs, recordings, and storytelling.

Data banks range in size from minibanks kept in the classroom to large ones in the school library and huge ones maintained in instructional media centers. These sources of information can supply materials ranging from pictorial and low-level reading materials for children in the early grades to a variety of more sophisticated materials for students in middle and upper grades. Types of data include pictures, clippings, articles, slides, maps, charts, diagrams, graphs, tables, recordings, photographs, facsimiles, and realia—any useful source of information. They may be obtained from publishers, prepared by teachers and students, or made by a team of school personnel. When the data bank is supplemented with almanacs, encyclopedias, atlases, and other library materials, students have access to an abundance of learning resources.

The making of data banks is a creative activity that contributes to both knowledge and skills. Students enrich concepts as they gather and select information, improve skills in locating and organizing data, and increase their ability to find information for various purposes. They also learn effective ways of recording information and setting up an indexing system that facilitates retrieval. These activities increase the students' appreciation of the value of tables of contents and indexes in books, almanacs, encyclopedias, and other references and their appreciation of the value of the card catalog in libraries.

In the early grades children should be guided to make simple and easy-to-use minibanks that include pictures, drawings, pupil-made charts, neighborhood and community maps, and other items related to units under study. Children should keep the materials in large envelopes or folders clearly labeled with such titles as food, shelter, clothing, goods, services, production workers, service workers, transportation, communication, and recreation.

In the middle and upper grades students can create more refined and detailed banks as they develop greater skill in locating and organizing information. They can prepare a card file system to guide retrieval of materials that they have filed. Indexing and cross-referencing, as used in libraries, take on new meaning as students discover that they can improve their own data bank by specifying where to look to retrieve data on topics and questions of immediate concern.

A practical approach to the building of a data bank is to involve students in making one for a particular unit. To encourage contributions from all students, plan such activities as the following:

Collect or draw pictures that illustrate concepts, activities, or objects under study.

Clip news reports and articles related to a topic.

Prepare data sheets or cards on particular countries under study, for example, geography (physical features, climate, resources), people (population, urban centers, ancestry), economy (agriculture, manufacturing, mining, trade, transportation, communication), culture (education, traditions, customs, festivals, arts, values, religion), and government (national, other levels, branches, form, capital).

Make data sheets or cards that contain information on topics in a unit, such as achievements of members of minority group, the Treaty of Guadalupe Hidalgo, the views of W. E. B. DuBois, and the Freedom March.

Make a chronology of key dates in a period or set of events, such as the exploration of the New World, settlement of the West, Afro-Americans in historical perspective, civil rights acts, and equal rights for women.

Prepare definitions and list examples of terms for concepts in a unit, such as *stereotype, prejudice, racism, ethnic group,* and *minority group.*

Prepare main idea or generalization sheets that contain data supporting a main idea being developed in a unit.

Make a tape recording that answers a question, describes an event, gives differing points of view on an issue, or provides other information.

Prepare biographical sketches of men and women included in a unit.

Prepare book reviews that may be used as guides to supplementary materials.

Make charts, diagrams, graphs, and tables on topics in a unit.

Make reference cards that indicate where to locate information in almanacs, encyclopedias, and other sources.

Select slides, filmstrips, and other materials that focus on questions, issues, and topics under study.

Prepare index and cross-reference cards to guide use of the data bank.

PRACTICE MATERIALS

Practice materials to develop reading and other skills in the social studies should accomplish the following:

1. Provide practice materials for individuals and small groups to eliminate specific difficulties that have arisen.
2. Provide practice to strengthen skills needed in the ongoing program of instruction.
3. Provide multilevel materials that match students' reading levels.
4. Relate practice directly to the reading materials, maps, or other resources that children are using.
5. Provide for immediate feedback on progress and needs for further improvement.

The same care should be taken to provide individualized practice in social studies as is taken in reading, arithmetic, or other subjects.

Listed below are sources of materials on reading skills, study skills, map-reading skills, and the interpretation of pictures, graphs, tables, charts, diagrams, and cartoons.

1. The teacher's manual that accompanies social studies textbooks provides individual activities for pupils, questions to guide the organization of information, test items, vocabulary-building techniques, and other activities that are based on the text. In addition, helpful suggestions for teachers to use in meeting the needs of more able, average, and less able children are usually included.

2. End-of-chapter activities in children's textbooks contain summarizing activities, map-making activities, vocabulary extension activities, study skill suggestions, and other suggested activities that are directly related to the text and are worded in children's language.

3. Children's weekly news periodicals for all grades provide practice materials and tests on reading and study skills and on interpreting graphs, tables, diagrams, and maps. They also contain cartoons and pictures. Editions on different reading levels are available.

4. Social studies units of instruction, or resource units, contain many specific examples of ways in which basic skills can be developed as an inherent part of learning activities.

5. Social studies workbooks that accompany children's textbooks contain practice materials. Some teachers select materials from workbooks for different grades, cut them apart, mount them on tagboard, use them for individualized practice, have children write the responses on sheets of paper, and thus use them over and over again.

6. Supplementary practice materials include the booklets from publishers of children's periodicals (*Weekly Reader* and *Scholastic Magazine*), multilevel kits designed to develop various skills (Science Research Associates), and activities suggested in magazines for teachers (*Teacher* and *Instructor*).

Audiovisual Materials

Audiovisual materials are basic components of multimedia approaches to instruction. Their use is essential to the attainment of unit objectives, the meeting of individual differences, and the achievement of well-rounded learning. The different types are summarized in checklist 3–2, developed to guide the search for materials.

Checklist 3–2
Audiovisual Materials

REALIA AND REPRESENTATIONS OF REALIA

____ Objects	____ Art products	____ Facsimiles
____ Tools	____ Decorative objects	____ Mock-ups
____ Utensils	____ Textiles	____ Models
____ Documents	____ Plant specimens	____ Miniatures
____ Clothing	____ Rock samples	____ Exhibits
____ Costumes	____ Building materials	____ Dioramas
____ Dolls	____ Collections	____ Instruments
____ Other: _____		

SOUND AND FILM RESOURCES

____ Films	____ Cassettes	____ Recordings
____ Radio and television	____ Film loops	____ Sound filmstrips
____ Videotapes		

PICTURES AND PICTORIAL REPRESENTATIONS

____ Photographs	____ Postcards	____ Montages
____ Pictures	____ Prints	____ Murals
____ Drawings	____ Etchings	____ Filmstrips
____ Sketches	____ Albums	____ Silent films
____ Slides	____ Scrapbooks	____ Opaque projections
____ Transparencies	____ Microfilms	____ Storyboards
____ Other: _____		

SYMBOLIC AND GRAPHIC REPRESENTATIONS

____ Maps	____ Cartoons	____ Chalkboard
____ Globes	____ Posters	____ Bulletin board
____ Atlases	____ Diagrams	____ Flannel board
____ Charts	____ Graphs	____ Time lines
____ Other: _____		

PROJECTORS AND VIEWERS

____ Slide	____ Film	____ Opaque
____ Stereoscope	____ Overhead	____ Film loop

PLAYERS AND RECORDERS

____ Record	____ Tape	____ Cassette

SUPPLIES AND MATERIALS FOR PRODUCTION

____ Lettering devices	____ Slide making	____ Bookbinding
____ Map outlines	____ Chart making	____ Map making
____ Transparencies	____ Picture mounting	____ Model making
____ Other: _____		

REALIA

The term *realia* means real things or artifacts, including objects, models, specimens, and items in museums, exhibits, dioramas, and panoramas. Children cannot go back in time and space to early periods and to the many eras and places included in the social studies, but they can have experiences with real things, or replicas of them, related to the unit. Artifacts from a particular culture or time period can be analyzed to learn about the people who made or used them. Examples of comparable objects from different cultures or time periods can be compared to discover similarities, differences, changes, and developments. For example, in a study of colonial living one group studied candle molds, muskets, powder horns, cooking utensils, tableware, a spinning wheel, and clothing of the period. In a study of Mexico, another group ate tortillas, frijoles, chili, and enchiladas. In addition, they examined sombreros, serapes, rebozos, huaraches, and models of furniture and utensils. In a study of communication, one class experimented with a simple crystal radio set, a telegraph key, drums, hollow logs, a whistle, a bone horn, bells, a telephone, and flag signals.

Oakland, California

How can realia such as these be used to develop concepts?

Realia and models can be used most effectively if the following guidelines are observed:

1. Use realia to initiate a unit, to enrich concepts encountered in the unit, and to share experiences during concluding activities.
2. Allow children to handle them and see how they work. If they are fragile, demonstrate them to the class.
3. Be alert to children's questions and comments as they handle objects; you may pick up vital clues to interests and misconceptions.
4. Use questions to guide students as they observe and describe the object and compare it with known objects. Help students suggest hypotheses about an object's use and make inferences about the culture based on the object's materials, construction, and assumed uses. Chart 3–1 suggests questions to use.

Analyzing a Real Object

1. Describe it. What is it made of? How heavy is it?
2. Do we (or a group we've studied) have anything like this? What are the similarities and differences?
3. What might this object be used for? Why do you think so?
4. Who might have made or used it? Why do you think so?
5. If this is what it is used for, what could that tell us about the environment, the work, or values of the people who used it?
6. Do the materials or design suggest a relationship between this culture and any other culture?

Chart 3–1

EXHIBITS

Exhibits are used to display a variety of materials in social studies. In one study of transportation, models and pictures of boats, aircraft, trains, wagons, carts, and other items were arranged in a chronological sequence. The exhibit was set against a time line with explanatory material and related pictures. A group studying China made an exhibit of the processing of silk, starting with the cocoon and ending with a piece of cloth. A class studying industrial America made several exhibits showing the processing of iron, petroleum, and soybeans from raw material to finished product. Other examples of exhibits used successfully in the social studies program are art in the community, growth of democratic institutions, basic documents in American democracy, changes in transportation, the development of communication, ethnic group contributions, uses of energy, and environmental changes. The following guidelines should be used to plan effective exhibits:

1. Select a theme, concept, or main idea for the exhibit.
2. Work out space arrangements using tables, bulletin boards, and other equipment to display materials.
3. Select items that fit the theme, but avoid the cluttered effect of too much detail.
4. Plan the color scheme, background, labeling, and lettering to fit the theme and to appeal to the group.
5. Place the most important objects in strategic positions so that the eyes will naturally move to them.
6. Give attention to eye level in arranging materials; provide effective lighting.
7. Arrange for demonstrations, discussions, and reports to make the exhibit more effective.
8. Use movement and sound if they add to the value of the exhibit.
9. Plan to share the exhibit with other classes and parents.

DIORAMAS AND PANORAMAS

Dioramas are scenes recreated in perspective, using three-dimensional models to depict the activity. They can present such scenes as life in Boonesboro, living in a log cabin in pioneer times, neighborhood helpers at work, or activities at the airport. Careful attention must be given to the setting in which the diorama is placed. Panoramas are broad scenes that use models to depict a topic; they are not necessarily in perspective. Panoramas are used to show industries, activities of the United Nations, ways to conserve energy, recreational opportunities, activities in a lumber camp, and the like. Many teachers have found that children will do a great amount of research to make their dioramas and panoramas realistic.

DEMONSTRATIONS

The social studies program offers many possibilities for demonstrations. In a unit on the home and family, appropriate demonstrations include ways of growing plants and flowers, making things for the playhouse, and arranging the

Social Studies Workshop, University of California, Berkeley

What planning and research are needed to be sure that a diorama such as this is authentic?

playhouse for different uses. In a study of pioneers, carding wool, candle making, operating the spinning wheel, making soap, and processing flax might be demonstrated. Other illustrative demonstrations include proper use of tools, materials, utensils, musical instruments, art media, maps, globes, and models. Objects brought from home can be demonstrated by children as they relate to questions and topics in the unit.

What procedures are involved in effective demonstrations? Consider a demonstration of candle making carried out during a study of colonial life. The objectives were to identify the processes colonists used to make candles, to show early methods of providing illumination in the home, and to develop readiness for candle making by the children. Need for the demonstration had arisen in a discussion of how the colonists provided light and heat in their homes. The class decided to invite a local resident (a resource visitor) who collected colonial candles and candle-making equipment. The resource visitor and the teacher planned the sequence of steps in the process, giving attention to timing, space arrangements, and materials the children should use following the demonstration. During the demonstration the children were seated so that all could see and hear, and the teacher guided questions. Afterward, the steps in candle making were summarized on a chart. This was followed by a candle-dipping activity; the class made several candles with the assistance of the resource visitor and the teacher.

MOTION PICTURES

Because of their effectiveness in portraying action, motion pictures are used extensively in the social studies. They can show a broad sweep of events and can highlight interrelationships. Films can show the development of inventions, the growth of institutions, or the contributions of great men and women. Slow motion and time-lapse photography can slow down or speed up activities in a way that increases a child's understanding. Film loops can be used in individual and small-group study to develop specific concepts. In addition, films are interesting to watch, hold attention, and can change and shape attitudes.

Films can do more than simply portray facts if these guidelines are applied:

1. Concepts and generalizations supported by information should be identified.
2. Aspects of human behavior such as cooperation and concern for others may be identified in many films.
3. Interpreting, analyzing, evaluating, and other thinking processes can be sharpened.
4. Time, space, and size distortions can be detected; and stereotypes, unfair treatment of women and minority groups, and other evidence of bias may be noted.
5. The values, attitudes, and feelings reflected in films may be discussed in response to such questions as the following: How do you think they must have felt? What does this show to be important to them?
6. Vocabulary can be increased as attention is focused on new terms and concepts included in a film.
7. Ideas gleaned from a film may be applied in problem solving as students respond to this question: How can we use these ideas?

The availability of portable videotape cameras enables students to create their own motion pictures. In the early grades the "production" may be a simple portrayal of community workers or events in the growth of the community. In later grades the production would demand research and planning to portray accurately environmental problems, historical events, or other topics. Scenes can be revised and shot again if needed. If a permanent copy is needed, the tape may be kept or the final production can be shot on film with a motion-picture camera. Before production begins a storyboard should be made, as described later in this chapter.

TELEVISION

Educational television programs are designed to contribute directly to instructional objectives. Some commercial programs can also be adapted to social studies instruction. Documentaries, plays, selected movies, forums, round-table discussions, interviews, news reports, editorials, and other programs can enrich and extend learning in authentic and interesting ways. Special feature programs on holidays, use of energy, campaigns, and festivals can give students insight into their significance. Programs are often taped for future use. With a library of videotapes available, programs can be used when they fit into ongoing instruction.

When a program that contributes to a unit is presented in the evening or on a weekend, children should be encouraged to watch it so that the program can be shared and discussed in class. Some teachers successfully employ a simple forum technique in which four or five children are asked to report on a particular program. Other members of the class are urged to be ready to ask questions and suggest additional points, thus encouraging them to watch the same program. By rotating membership in the ''forum,'' the teacher can get the entire class to participate in a direct and challenging manner. As the reports and discussion are carried out in class, relationships to units of instruction and other classroom experiences can be emphasized. Both public and commercial television schedules should be checked and programs assigned as appropriate. Announcements and program notes are available from local educational television stations and from commercial networks. If you have not obtained them, check the weekly program schedule published in the local newspaper.

listening
and viewing
skills

Radio and television programs help children develop and use several skills. Radio programs require listening without the aid of related visual imagery. With both types of program a clear purpose should be stated as a basis for use: to learn the story behind a person or event, to get new ideas on a topic, or to note points related to a question. Many middle- and upper-grade children can achieve skill in critical listening and viewing. Chart 3–2 lists instructions for students that help to develop such skills.

> **Critical Listeners and Viewers**
>
> Be alert from start to finish.
> Remember the most important points.
> Be ready to ask questions at the end.
> Be ready to agree or disagree.
> Note ideas we can use in our unit.
> Note ideas we need to learn more about.

Chart 3–2

RECORDINGS

Recordings are made and used for many different purposes in social studies. They provide excellent background and sound effects for dramatization, pageants, creative work, and choral and individual readings. Recordings may be made of children's work, speeches of famous people, school visitors, travelogs, and radio programs. If recordings are made at various times during the year and compared, growth in planning, discussion, reporting, and group evaluation may be appraised. Stories, rhythms, comments for use with slides or filmstrips, and music for folk dances and accompaniment may be recorded and used as needed.

PICTURES

Of all visual materials, pictures are the most widely used. The photographs and illustrations in textbooks and other reading materials add interest and help to clarify difficult terms and understandings. Postcards, cutouts from magazines and newspapers, and other pictures are used to achieve a variety of instructional objectives. Pictures can introduce major topics and problems. They can raise key questions and stimulate interest. They can make children's reports and scrapbooks more meaningful. Pictures can help correct erroneous ideas and misunderstandings and stir emotions. Symbols on maps can be visualized by pairing them with appropriate pictures. Critical thinking can be sharpened as children use pictures to prove points at issue—for example, how tools such as the adz were used, how a serape should be adorned, or how iron ore is processed. Pictures are especially helpful in developing visual literacy—recognizing and naming objects, interpreting what is seen, analyzing what is portrayed, and inferring feelings, relationships, and other possibilities about the people, objects, or events being observed. When several pictures are shown, students may compare and contrast items, identify a sequence of processes or actions, and evaluate what is shown and how well it is portrayed.

When pictures are used to promote learning, these guidelines should be followed:

1. Select and arrange pictures to initiate a unit so that significant questions are raised as students examine them. Use a few pictures at a time. As new topics arise, related pictures can be brought out, moving students smoothly from one part of a unit to another.
2. Direct the interpretation of pictures, moving discussion from simple identification of objects and descriptions of what is shown to items noted in charts 3–3 and 3–4.
3. Plan for individuals and small groups to use pictures for making scrapbooks, arranging displays and bulletin boards, making reports, and other activities, as shown in charts 3–5 and 3–6.
4. Organize picture collections around main ideas or problems in the unit and place them in a file for easy handling. Mount them to add to their attractiveness and durability. Place them in labeled folders or large envelopes with an index for easy reference. Keep the collection up to date by adding new pictures and replacing old ones.

Interpreting Pictures of Land Scenes

Where is the scene located?
What items stand out? Hills? Valleys? Rivers? Others?
How high, large, or small are they?
Is natural vegetation shown?
Are crops or gardens shown? If so, what is being raised?
Are there indicators of the weather? Temperature? Amount of rainfall? Wind? Snow?
Are there roads? Canals? Railroads? Buildings?

Chart 3–3

Interpreting Pictures of Human Activities

Where is the activity located?
What are the people doing?
Is individual or group work emphasized?
What tools and materials are being used?
Are their ways of working modern or traditional?
What kind of clothing are they wearing?
Are homes or other buildings shown?

Chart 3–4

How We Use Pictures

To explain new words
To prove points
To make reports more interesting
To show difficult ideas
To show places on maps
To arrange bulletin boards

Chart 3–5

The Bulletin Board

Bring pictures that fit the topics.
Use postcards, photographs, and cutout pictures.
Select the very best ones.
Arrange them to show steps in an activity or tell a story.

Chart 3–6

FILMSTRIPS AND SLIDES

Filmstrips and slides are among the most popular audiovisual materials used in social studies. They are easy to project, they are accompanied by helpful manuals, they cover a variety of topics, they are available in both color and black and white, they are relatively inexpensive, and their use enables a teacher to show selected materials when they are needed and to stop at a particular point and discuss an item as long as the situation demands. Some filmstrips are accompanied by recordings and thus require little or no commentary as they are being shown. Slides are easy to make and can be shown in any order. They cost more than filmstrips, however, and must be handled carefully to avoid damage. When sequence is not a fundamental problem or when the sequence of pictures in the filmstrip is satisfactory, the filmstrip is probably more desirable because of lower cost and ease of use and storage.

OVERHEAD PROJECTIONS

Overhead projectors enable teachers to project material while facing the class. A teacher can write on transparent plastic or point to diagrams, sketches, or maps and guide discussion while they are being projected. Overlays (laying one drawing over another) can effectively show relationships. For example, a drawing of the topography of the United States is projected; on this is placed a second one showing forests or some other item. By showing the sketch of topography and then laying the sketch of forests over it, pupils can grasp relationships quickly. One drawing can be taped to another along one edge to achieve a hingelike effect, then the second drawing will fall over the first so that borders line up correctly. By choosing colors carefully, the teacher can obtain dramatic and realistic effects. The technique of making overlays is similar to that of placing sketches made on clear plastic over a relief map to show relationships.

OPAQUE PROJECTIONS

Opaque projections used in the social studies program include a variety of nontransparent materials—pictures, drawings, diagrams, pages in books and encyclopedias, maps, charts, coins and paper money, songs, illustrations from newspapers and magazines, postcards, textiles, and other items that are magnified for class discussion. Since the pictures are projected by means of reflected light, the room must be darkened. Opaque projections are valuable for several reasons. Up-to-date materials can be used in units; maps and graphs can be enlarged easily; picture interpretation can be improved; attention can be focused on significant details in illustrations; children's work can be shared; reports can be made more interesting; and the entire class can examine an item at once, eliminating the need to pass it around the room. By hinging several drawings together or pasting them on a strip, children can make simulated motion pictures to illustrate stories and reports.

STEREOGRAPHS

Stereographic pictures have a realistic three-dimensional effect that ordinary photographs do not possess, and many are available for units commonly used in social studies. Because of their realistic effect, they are a most practical aid for individual use. Inexpensive stereoscopic reels (colored slides in a circular mounting for use in a plastic viewer) are available on places throughout the world. A helpful practice is to select reels related to topics under study and to place them and a viewer in the reading center for individual use.

THE BULLETIN BOARD

The bulletin board is useful for initiating units, stimulating new interests, clarifying problems, posting children's work, and displaying materials. In initiating units, display materials that evoke interest and stimulate questions about those topics that come first in the unit. By changing and rearranging materials to stimulate new interests, the development of the unit can be guided in sound directions. Related materials, such as posters, drawings, charts, maps, or graphs, should be posted as they are needed to solve problems that arise. Children's work may be displayed to share and summarize the various learning experiences. Charts 3–7 and 3–8 give some guidelines.

Bulletin Board Planning		
Blocks	Graphs	Rhythm
Borders	Letters	Signs
Charts	Lines	Space
Circles	Maps	Strips
Clippings	Models	Symbols
Cloth	Objects	Symmetry
Color	Paper	Tape
Contrast	Pictures	Textiles
Diagrams	Posters	Yarn

Chart 3–7

Trying Different Arrangements

Arrange materials on a table or on the floor.
Try different arrangements.
Try different background material.
Try different ways of placing the title and lettering.
Try lines, circles, arrows, and colors to accent ideas.
Try different mountings for pictures.

Chart 3–8

FLANNEL BOARD AND MAGNETIC BOARD

Although the flannel (or felt) board is not used so extensively in social studies as in other subjects, it should not be overlooked. It is especially helpful in presenting events or ideas in sequence as a story unfolds, a report is given, a demonstration is performed, steps in a process are given, or basic concepts are presented in a definite order. It can also be used to show the layout of a farm, to experiment with different arrangements of items for a display or floor layout, to assemble jigsaw maps, to show how a bill becomes a law, and to make circle and bar graphs. An outline map can be sketched on the flannel board and cutouts of areas used to show how territory was added. One of the main advantages of flannel boards is their flexibility, which permits various arrangements to be tried experimentally.

In its uses the magnetic board is similar to the flannel board. Small magnets are attached to objects, pictures, maps, cutouts, and other items to hold them to the thin iron sheeting used to make the board. The magnetic board is used primarily to demonstrate key concepts, although it may occasionally be used as a bulletin board. Some schools have installed magnetic chalkboards, which serve the same purpose.

THE STORYBOARD

A storyboard guides the making of a film, filmstrip, videotape, or photo essay; it consists of sketches or pictures arranged in a sequence to portray a story, theme, or topic. To make a storyboard follow these basic steps: (1) select a topic related to the unit under study, (2) make sketches or select pictures to tell the story, (3) place the sketches or pictures in sequence, (4) add notes for making the photo essay, film, or tape, (5) make the resource, and (6) evaluate. Some teachers find that making a storyboard is itself a rewarding experience because of the contribution it makes to the development of visual literacy.

THE CHALKBOARD

The chalkboard is a basic and versatile visual tool. Use it to list suggestions during group planning, sketch illustrations, list reading materials, note assignments, copy suggestions for charts, note facts under main ideas, summarize a discussion, record group-dictated stories or letters, and so on. Many teachers increase the effectiveness of chalkboard use by adding simple stick figures to illustrate points, using colored chalk to emphasize key ideas and using rulers, compasses, and stencils to obtain neat, artistic effects. Select materials to place on the chalkboard carefully, remembering that slides, charts, and duplicated materials are more effective when large amounts of information or detailed data are to be presented.

SYMBOLIC AND GRAPHIC MATERIALS

Posters convey a single idea in a way that can be grasped at a glance. They are used to sway people to a course of action and are often used in campaigns for safety, energy conservation, or other topics of concern. Space, line, form, and color direct attention to the desired action. Making posters acquaints students with ways of presenting a single idea simply and forcefully.

Tables summarize data on population, resources, products, exports, and other topics in succinct form. The first tables interpreted by students may simply be a list of figures headed by a title—for example, classroom attendance or population growth in our community. Next, tables with two or more headings are introduced, and the teacher directs attention to the title, column headings, comparisons between columns, and changes and trends to be identified. Students can make tables to organize data collected for a unit, using procedures drawn from the mathematics program and applying them to social studies content.

Graphs are visual presentations of data. In the early grades they are used to show such information as daily temperature, enrollment, attendance, books read, and other items familiar to children. In later grades they are used to show population growth, resources, exports, and other items originally organized in tables. In all grades the interpretation and construction of graphs must be related to instruction in the mathematics program. The application of mathematical skills to social studies content enriches learning in both programs.

Cartoons are designed to convey an idea by means of caricature, humor, stereotype, oversimplification, exaggeration, and satire. Such symbols as Uncle Sam, John Bull, and the dove of peace may be used. The meaning of the symbol must be clear and an understanding of the situation, issue, or problem must be developed if students are to interpret cartoons. This is why so many cartoons that amuse adults have little or no impact on children. When cartoons are encountered in reading and other materials they must be analyzed to help students understand the symbols used, the situation or problem portrayed, and the purpose of the cartoonist.

Learning activities and questions that help students learn to interpret symbolic and graphic material are presented in chapter 11, which deals with reading and study skills.

time charts
and time lines

Time charts and time lines are used to clarify time relationships, to relate events to major time periods, and to relate events in one country to those in another. In the early grades charts may be made to show events of the day, major events during the week, events related to the growth of the community, changes in transportation, changes in farming, and changing ways of providing food, shelter, and clothing. In later grades charts and time lines may be used to show events during major periods of the history of the state or nation, the development of transportation or communication and the like.

Children should be guided to develop a time base or frame of reference for interpreting time periods and time relationships. Many teachers have children use their own age for this purpose. For example, the following time periods were charted by a group of ten-year-olds.

> *Decade*—10 years, equal to my age, about one third my parents' age
> *Generation*—33 years, a little more than three times my age, about the same as my parents' age
> *Century*—100 years, ten times my age, about three times my parents' age

In all grades units of time that students understand, a meaningful theme for selecting events to include on time charts, and an appropriate and accurate scale are emphasized.

Time charts and time lines take many different forms, as shown in charts 3–9 through 3–11. The most common form is simply a sequence of events listed on paper with space between the events scaled to show elapsed time. But almost any approach that shows the relationship between events and time can be used. A wire can be strung across the room, and cards representing events hung at appropriate intervals. Large envelopes can be attached to the wall under a line showing time periods, and children can place appropriate pictures or names of events in them. Events in two or more regions or countries can be arranged in parallel form, either vertically or horizontally, to show what occurred in different places at the same time.

Main Events in Our Community	
1950 1960 1970 1980	

Chart 3–9

Major Events in the Western Hemisphere	
1700 1750 1800 1850 1900 1950 1980	
United States	
Canada	
Mexico	

Chart 3–10

Main Events in the United States, 1860–90			
Decade	Social	Political	Economic
1860			
1870			
1880			
1890			

Chart 3–11

Community Resources

The community can be a social studies laboratory where geographic, historical, economic, and other concepts can be developed in a realistic setting. Changing conditions can be studied as they take place, and factors that produce them can be explored. Holidays, special events, and commemorations can be experienced with others. Field trips can be taken, local experts can be interviewed, and historical sites can be visited. Local publications can be used in the classroom. Processes of interaction can be studied directly as students observe various groups and participate in them. Indeed, if we are to have "schools without walls" extensive and critical use must be made of community resources.

The main types of community resources are included in checklist 3–3.

Checklist 3-3
Community Resources

_____ Study (or field) trips (industries, museums): _____
_____

_____ Field studies (housing, pollution, transportation): _____
_____

_____ People to interview (travelers, police): _____
_____

_____ Resource visitors (panel or individuals): _____

_____ Service and other organizations (Red Cross, clubs): _____

_____ Service projects (safety, cleanup): _____

_____ Local current events (campaigns, drives): _____

_____ Recreational resources (parks, marinas): _____

_____ School resources (collections, teachers): _____

_____ Publications, visual media (newspapers, bulletins): _____

_____ Television, radio (travel programs, news): _____

_____ Other: _____

THE COMMUNITY SURVEY

In many social studies programs the community is the focus of study, and the topics chosen for study are determined by the curriculum and the maturity of the students. Topics can include:

Art shows	Health services	Religions
Communication	History	Residences
Concerts	Mass media	Resources
Conservation	Museums, theaters	Safety services
Cultural features	Natural features	Sanitation services
Ecology	Occupations	Social services
Education	Our school	Sports facilities
Ethnic groups	Parks and zoos	Transit system
Future Plans	Pollution	Transportation
Geography	Population	Urban renewal
Government	Recreation	Utilities

There are many diverse educational benefits to be gained from a community survey. As students conduct their survey—perhaps checking safety hazards, type and location of residence, housing conditions, the business and industrial sections, or parks and playgrounds—their observation skills are sharpened. As they talk with old-timers, business people, school workers, public officials, and other community workers, they improve their interviewing techniques. As they examine pictures, letters, newspapers, reports, and other local documents, they develop skill in content analysis.

DAILY EXPERIENCES

The everyday experiences of children in the community constitute one of the student's most valuable resources. As children see buildings under construction, watch changes in the season, see workers in action, observe holidays and celebrations, enjoy radio and television, hear and discuss current events, buy articles in stores, use the transportation system, attend churches, and engage in a host of other activities, they make discoveries and are stimulated to raise questions. Alert teachers capitalize on these experiences and use them in the social studies program.

STUDY TRIPS

In dynamic social studies programs, many different types of study trips are taken. They may be completed in a class period, in a full day, or over a period of several days. At times they may be taken over the weekend, with the children's parents coming along. The following list suggests some of the many opportunities for study trips in social studies.

Airport	Farms	Petroleum company
Aquarium	Firehouse	Police station
Art gallery	Forest service	Post office
Bakery	Greenhouse	Radio station
Bank	Historic homes	Railroad station
Botanical garden	Housing construction	Reservoir
Bottling works	Lake	River
Cannery	Library	Sawmill
City hall	Lumbermill	Shipyard
Construction sites	Mission	Stores
Courtroom	Museum	Telephone exchange
Dairy	Newspaper	Television station
Docks	Observatory	Weather station
Factories	Park	Zoo

Short informal walks taken in the immediate neighborhood can be valuable study trips. Children could see a house being built, changes in the season, operation of a ditch-digging machine, a special garden, soil erosion, a collection of pictures and objects, or a modern bakery. Children may take short walking trips to gather specimens, study architectural changes in the neighborhood, visit an expert to get answers to questions, study safety problems, and the like. Such informal and easy to plan walking trips require a minimum of organization and make children more critical observers of their immediate environment.

planning study trips

The one great difference between a study trip and just going somewhere is that a study trip has educational objectives. Key points for a teacher to keep in mind are presented in checklist 3–4.

92

Checklist 3–4
Guide for the Planning of Study Trips

FIRST CONSIDERATIONS

_____ Have adequate backgrounds, ideas, and objectives been developed?

_____ Are related materials—films, books, pictures—available?

_____ Are there profitable follow-up activities?

_____ Other: _____

PRELIMINARY ARRANGEMENTS

_____ Has administrative approval been given?

_____ Has the approval of parents been secured?

_____ Are eating and toilet arrangements satisfactory?

_____ Has the time schedule been prepared?

_____ Has the guide been advised on problems, needs, and maturity of the group?

_____ Have travel arrangements and expenses been arranged?

_____ Are assistants needed to help supervise the group?

_____ Has a list been made of the names, telephone numbers, and addresses of those children who are going?

_____ Other: _____

GROUP PLANNING

_____ Are questions prepared and understood?

_____ Are recording procedures and assignments clear?

_____ Have behavior standards been developed?

_____ Have safety precautions been considered?

_____ Have the time schedule, travel arrangements, and expenses been clarified?

_____ Has attention been given to appropriateness of dress?

_____ Are monitorial assignments clear?

_____ Other: _____

FOLLOW-UP PLANS

_____ Do experiences that follow contribute to objectives?

_____ What summaries and records should be made?

_____ Is attention given to the development of charts, maps, diagrams, displays, murals, models, scrapbooks, construction, dramatic activities, and floor layouts?

_____ Are procedures in mind to discover and clarify misconceptions?

_____ Are letters of appreciation to be sent?

_____ How is learning to be evaluated?

_____ Other: _____

Sacramento and Colma, California

What can we learn from recordings? What can we learn from old timers? In what other ways can oral history be used to gather data?

It is sound procedure to summarize specific plans on charts, on the chaklboard or on duplicated sheets of paper so that each student clearly understands important points. Charts 3–12 and 3–13 show the planning done by a first-grade group that took a short walk to the food section of a supermarket. After their walk to the store, the children engaged in dramatic play and decided they needed the materials shown in chart 3–14, thus putting to use the information gained from the study trip.

An advanced type of planning for a study trip to an airport is illustrated in chart 3–15, which was developed by a sixth-grade group. The class was divided into four committees, each responsible for five related questions.

Our Walk to the Store	Let's Find Out	We Need for Our Supermarket	
1. Stay together.	1. Where are vegetables kept?	Cash register	Shopping bags
2. Watch where you walk.	2. How is meat kept fresh?	Counters	Tables
3. Ask questions in turn.	3. What is in the storeroom?	Delivery trucks	Vegetable stand
4. Listen to the answers.	4. Who keeps the shelves full?	Refrigerator	

Chart 3–12   Chart 3–13   Chart 3–14

Questions We Want to Answer

COMMITTEE 1

1. How many passengers does a 747 carry? An SST?
2. What airlines use the airport?
3. How many planes come in each day?
4. Where do they come from? Where do they go?
5. At what altitude does a westbound plane fly? Eastbound? Northbound? Southbound?

COMMITTEE 2

6. How many runways are there?
7. What are runways made of? How long are they?
8. How many people work in the control tower?
9. What do they do?
10. Where does the ground crew put the fuel?

COMMITTEE 3

11. What do members of the flight crew do?
12. How long does it take a pilot to get a license?
13. What must one study to become a pilot?
14. How does one become a flight attendant?
15. What do the terminal workers do?

COMMITTEE 4

16. What is a flight log? Who keeps it?
17. How many instruments are on the control board? What do they tell the pilot?
18. What kinds of cargo are carried?
19. Where is the baggage stored? How cold does it get?
20. How many pounds of luggage is one passenger allowed? Why?

Chart 3-15

RESOURCE VISITORS

Community studies are enriched when firefighters, police, journalists, and other workers meet with the class to discuss problems and questions that have arisen. In units about foreign countries such as South America or Japan, individuals who are natives or who have visited the country can share their experiences with the class. Questions that arise in units on industrial America, aviation, transportation, lumbering, and marketing may be answered by individuals who are well acquainted with them. The showing of realia, pictures, and slides along with the discussion enhances the contributions of resource visitors.

A sound procedure is to organize a file of resource persons who can make valuable contributions to the social studies program. A simple card system can be used by noting the following information on index cards:

Contribution _____

Name _____Telephone _____

Hours available _____

Will come to school? _____

Children may visit at home or office? _____

Comments _____

_____

The kinds of people who are available depends on the particular community. One group of teachers in a social studies workshop compiled the following list of possible resource visitors:

Airport employees	Forest rangers	Old-time residents
Authors	Gardeners	Police
Business people	House builders	School administrators
City officials	Industrial workers	Ship workers
Consuls of foreign nations	Lawyers	Social workers
Dairy workers	Librarians	Soil conservationists
Dentists and doctors	Merchants	Store clerks
Farmers	Ministers	Traffic safety specialists
Fellow teachers	Musicians	Travelers
Firefighters	Newspaper workers	Urban planners
Foreign students	News reporters	Utilities workers

interviewing
resource
persons

When a resource person cannot come to school, when essential materials must be kept on the job, or when seeing the person in a working situation is more beneficial, a student or a small group can interview the person at work. Interviews require the same kind of planning as is needed for resource visitors. In addition, attention must be given to good interviewing techniques. Charts 3–16 through 3–18 list sample questions and topics to include in interviews during study trips or with resource persons (see the end-of-chapter reference by Wurman for other examples). The points in chart 3–19 illustrate the standards that can be set up through group planning.

Criteria for Selecting Materials

Teachers are constantly selecting materials for use in their classrooms from those available in the school system and from sources of free and inexpensive materials. Less frequent but of equal importance is their role in evaluating new materials being considered for adoption.

SELECTING MATERIALS FROM AVAILABLE RESOURCES

The following criteria are used to select from among the materials available in the instructional media center, the community, and the school:

1. *Appropriateness* to instructional objectives and maturity and background of students
2. *Content* free of bias, stereotypes, and other distortions; unbiased treatment of women, ethnic minority groups, and differing cultures
3. *Variety* to achieve objectives, promote interest, meet individual needs, and stimulate thinking
4. *Time, effort,* and *expense* reasonable for both students and the teacher
5. *Quality* of format, print, sound, photography, and clarity of presentation
6. *Manuals* available to clarify objectives and instructional uses

The Courtroom

What is the role of each of these?
- Defendant
- Defense attorney
- Judge
- Jury
- Prosecutor
- Recorder clerk

What rules are followed
- To show the judge respect?
- To make an objection?
- To cross-examine witnesses?
- To refuse to answer questions?
- To be found in contempt?
- To declare a mistrial?

Chart 3–16

The Library

What is the role of these workers?
- Accountants
- Administrators
- Bindery repair artists
- Catalogers
- Clerks

What machines are used?
- Binders
- Computers
- Conveyors
- Microfilm
- Photographic book charging
- Pneumatic tubes

What special services are there for the blind?

Chart 3–17

The Newspaper

What is the role of these workers?
- Accountant
- Artist
- Editor
- Photographer
- Reporter
- Secretary
- Writer

What equipment is used?
- Linotype
- Photographic delivery
- Presses
- Recycling
- Teletype

Why is the morgue needed?
What is the editorial policy?

Chart 3–18

How To Interview

Introduce yourself.
State questions clearly.
Listen attentively.
Let the other person talk.
Ask questions on special points.
Take notes on hard points.
Do not waste time.
Express thanks when finished.

Chart 3–19

FREE OR INEXPENSIVE MATERIALS

Special care must be exercised in the selection of free or inexpensive materials—for example, maps, charts, diagrams, pamphlets, leaflets, booklets, and pictures. Many school districts have policies governing the selection and use of materials distributed by companies, consular offices, travel agencies, state and local groups, national organizations, and government agencies. In general, reputable agencies and groups set high standards for the free or inexpensive materials they distribute. Indiscriminate use of such resources without strict adherence to established policies is unprofessional and contrary to the best interest of children, however. Criteria such as the following should be applied:

1. Is the material produced by a reputable group?
2. If controversial issues are included, are they presented fairly and on a level that is meaingful to children?
3. Are concepts, style of presentation, symbols, and language appropriate to the capabilities of the children who will use them?
4. Is the content related to units of instruction?
5. Are sources of information given?
6. Is the material free of bias and prejudice?
7. Is the material up to date and available from standard sources?
8. Are type size, spacing format, and other technical qualities satisfactory?
9. Is material free of objectionable or obtrusive advertising?
10. Will the school be obligated if it uses the material?

APPRAISING NEW MATERIALS

Teachers normally assist in the selection of new materials being considered for adoption by the school district. New materials should be evaluated in terms of criteria such as those in checklist 3-5.

Checklist 3–5
Criteria for Appraising Materials

_____ Directly related to social studies goals and instructional objectives

_____ Satisfactory in terms of program requirements and the following:

_____ Accurate portrayal of men and women in all types of roles

_____ Accurate portrayal of roles and contributions of members of ethnic minority groups

_____ Accurate portrayal of business and labor

_____ No adverse reflection on persons because of race, color, creed, national origin, sex, or occupation

_____ Suited to needs and comprehension level of students who will use them

_____ Accurate reflection of cultural pluralism in our society and in our global society

_____ Appropriate use of various forms of presentation, such as case studies, stories, maps, graphs, exposition, transparencies, and games

_____ Inclusion of material giving varying points of view on issues

_____ Use of metric measures where appropriate

_____ Suggestions for handling controversial issues, providing for differing learning styles, and promoting independent study

evaluating books   When appraising books (and other materials) on foreign cultures, teachers should consider these points:

> Is the author qualified?
>
> Has the author visited or lived there?
>
> Are facts presented accurately?
>
> Has a native reviewed the work favorably?
>
> How are values of the people treated?
>
> How are hopes and aspirations portrayed?
>
> Are stereotypes avoided?
>
> Are costumes, art, dances, and special customs portrayed in perspective along with current ways of living?

A common practice is to include criteria in rating forms so that points can be assigned to each criterion, as shown in checklist 3–6.

Checklist 3–6
Evaluating Textbooks

Directions: Rate each book on the specific points as follows:
5, superior; 4, good; 3, fair; 2, poor; 1, unsatisfactory.

CRITERIA FOR RATING EACH TEXTBOOK

TEXTBOOK
A   B   C   D   E   F

As an instructional resource:

Is it related to the content of the program?

Is it accurate and up to date?

Can the children who will use it grasp the concepts and understandings?

Is the level of reading difficulty—vocabulary, style of presentation, sentence structure—appropriate for children who will use it?

Will it contribute to problem-solving skills?

Do illustrative materials—maps, pictures, drawings—contribute to the meaningfulness of the content?

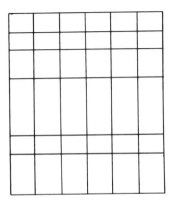

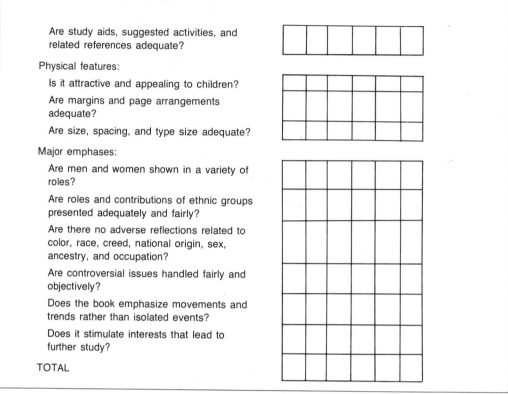

Are study aids, suggested activities, and related references adequate?

Physical features:

Is it attractive and appealing to children?

Are margins and page arrangements adequate?

Are size, spacing, and type size adequate?

Major emphases:

Are men and women shown in a variety of roles?

Are roles and contributions of ethnic groups presented adequately and fairly?

Are there no adverse reflections related to color, race, creed, national origin, sex, ancestry, and occupation?

Are controversial issues handled fairly and objectively?

Does the book emphasize movements and trends rather than isolated events?

Does it stimulate interests that lead to further study?

TOTAL

Other examples of rating forms may be found in school district offices and in the references at the end of this chapter.

At times, data on the actual use of materials with students should be considered in making adoptions. Information obtained by actually using materials under classroom conditions is most valid. Tryouts are needed when serious questions arise about how well materials meet students' capabilities or other factors. In most instances, however, use of criteria such as those listed in checklist 3–6 will prove adequate for making a decision.

estimating readability level
A simple procedure for estimating readability level of books is presented in this section (see Fry's book for other procedures).

Expanded Directions for Working Readability Graph

1. Randomly select three sample passages and count out exactly 100 words beginning with the beginning of a sentence. Do count proper nouns, initializations, and numerals.
2. Count the number of sentences in the hundred words estimating length of the fraction of the last sentence to the nearest one-tenth.
3. Count the total number of syllables in the 100-word passage. If you do not have a hand counter available, an easy way is to simply put a mark above every syllable

Graph for Estimating Readability—Extended
*by Edward Fry, Rutgers University Reading Center,
New Brunswick, New Jersey*

Average number of syllables per 100 words

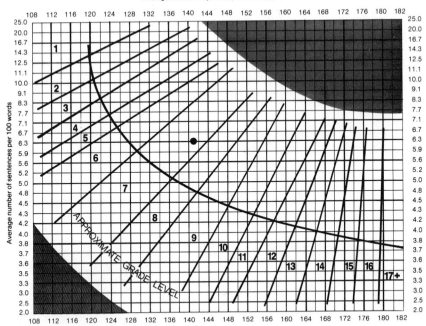

Directions: Randomly select three 100-word passages from a book or an article. Plot average number of syllables and average number of sentences per 100 words on graph to determine the grade level of the material. Choose more passages per book if great variability is observed, and conclude that the book has uneven readability. Few books will fall in gray area, but when they do grade level scores are invalid. Count proper nouns, numerals and initializations as words. Count a syllable for each symbol: *1945* is one word and four syllables and *IRA* is one word and three syllables. For example:

	Syllables	Sentences
First Hundred Words	124	6.6
Second Hundred Words	141	5.5
Third Hundred Words	158	6.8
Average	141	6.3

Readability Seventh Grade (see dot plotted on graph)

over one in each word, then when you get to the end of the passage, count the number of marks and add 100. Small calculators can also be used as counters by pushing numeral *1*, then push the ''+''sign for each word or syllable when counting.

4. Enter graph with *average* sentence length and *average* number of syllables; plot dot where the two lines intersect. Area where dot is plotted will give you the approximate grade level.

5. If a great deal of variability is found in syllable count or sentence count, putting more samples into the average is desirable.

6. A word is defined as a group of symbols with a space on either side; thus, *Joe, IRA, 1945,* and *&* are each one word.

7. A syllable is defined as a phonetic syllable. Generally, there are as many syllables as vowel sounds. For example, *stopped* is one syllable and *wanted* is two syllables. When counting syllables for numerals and initializations, count one syllable for each symbol. For example, *1945* is four syllables and *IRA* is three syllables, and *&* is one syllable.

detecting bias in materials

In all materials the treatment of men and women and ethnic groups should be evaluated, as noted in checklist 3–6. In addition, teachers should guide students to discover bias and unfair treatment in the materials they are using. Charts 3–20 and 3–21 include points that students should check; if the materials being used suggest additional points, add them to the lists.

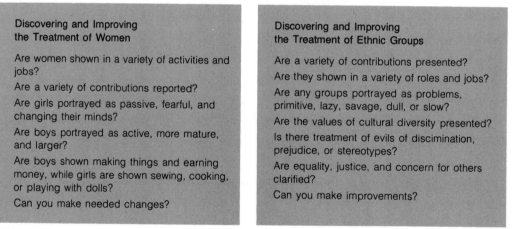

Discovering and Improving
the Treatment of Women

Are women shown in a variety of activities and jobs?
Are a variety of contributions reported?
Are girls portrayed as passive, fearful, and changing their minds?
Are boys portrayed as active, more mature, and larger?
Are boys shown making things and earning money, while girls are shown sewing, cooking, or playing with dolls?
Can you make needed changes?

Chart 3–20

Discovering and Improving
the Treatment of Ethnic Groups

Are a variety of contributions presented?
Are they shown in a variety of roles and jobs?
Are any groups portrayed as problems, primitive, lazy, savage, dull, or slow?
Are the values of cultural diversity presented?
Is there treatment of evils of discimination, prejudice, or stereotypes?
Are equality, justice, and concern for others clarified?
Can you make improvements?

Chart 3–21

the metric system

As noted in the criteria for selecting materials cited earlier, attention is being given to use of the metric system in the social studies program. Use of metric measures must be paced with instruction provided in the mathematics and science programs. Helpful activities include the use of rulers with both metric and English measures, conversion of scales on maps, and conversion of square miles, acres, and other quantities encountered in textbooks and other materials. Children should use metric measures in weighing and measuring themselves, operating the classroom "supermarket," making maps, making and recording weather observations, and other activities. Recently published social studies textbooks include metric measures and tables that show how to convert to and from the metric system. Detailed tables may be found in mathematics books, encyclopedias, and other references. Charts 3–22 through 3–24 are useful for approximate conversion from United States to metric measures.

Conversion to Metric		
Inches	× 25	= millimeters
Feet	× 30	= centimeters
Yards	× .9	= meters
Miles	× 1.6	= kilometers
Ounces	× 28	= grams
Pounds	× .45	= kilograms
Tons	× .9	= tonnes
Pints	× .47	= milliliters
Quarts	× .95	= liters
Gallons	× 3.8	= liters
Bushels	× 2.8	= hectoliters
Sq. inch	× 6.5	= sq. centimeters
Sq. foot	× .09	= sq. meters
Sq. yard	× .83	= sq. meters
Acres	× .4	= hectares
Sq. miles	× 2.6	= sq. kilometers

Chart 3–22

Conversion from Metric		
Millimeters	× .04	= inches
Centimeters	× .4	= inches
Meters	× 1.1	= yards
Kilometers	× .6	= miles
Grams	× .035	= ounces
Kilograms	× 2.2	= pounds
Tonnes	× 1.1	= tons
Liters	× 2.1	= pints
Liters	× 1.06	= quarts
Liters	× .26	= gallons
Hectoliters	× .35	= bushels
Sq. centimeters	× .16	= sq. in.
Sq. meters	× 1.2	= sq. yd.
Sq. kilometers	× .4	= sq. miles
Hectares	× 2.5	= acres

Chart 3–23

Metric Prefixes	
giga	1,000,000,000
mega	1,000,000
kilo	1,000
hecto	100
deka	10
deci	0.1
centi	0.01
milli	0.001
micro	0.000001
nano	0.000000001

Temperature

Celsius = 5/9(F−32)
Fahrenheit = 9/5(C+32)

Chart 3–24

Guidelines for Using Materials

Whatever materials are used in the classroom, they will be more effective if several general guidelines are kept in mind. All materials should be viewed as sources of data to use in studying topics and solving problems, not as entertainment or diversion unrelated to objectives of instruction. Materials on differing levels of abstractness should be included, ranging from objects, models, and pictorial materials to maps, charts, graphs, and reading materials. The classroom should be viewed as a laboratory—a planned learning environment—where materials are arranged and used in learning centers, in individual activities, and in class and small-group activities. A multimedia approach is generally more effective than the traditional textbook approach; it may be facilitated by arranging the materials in a kit in the sequence in which they will most likely be used. Finally, materials should be evaluated not only before use but also during and after use to identify strengths and weaknesses and to plan for future improvements.

Guidelines set forth in checklist 3–7 will help the teacher to plan for the use of materials, to guide their use, to provide for follow-up activities, and to evaluate their contributions to learning:

Checklist 3–7
Using Instructional Media

OBJECTIVES

_____ What objectives are suggested in the manual?

_____ To which core objectives is it related? _____ Knowledge _____Thinking processes _____ Skills _____ Attitudes, values

_____ What questions can be answered by this material?

_____ How does it fit into individual and group inquiry with other media?

READINESS

_____ What suggestions for introducing it are in the manual?

_____ How should objectives be clarified for students?

_____ What terms and concepts need development in advance?

_____ How can it be related to questions in the unit?

_____ What experiences of students should be recalled and related to it?

DURING USE

_____ What suggestions are presented in the manual?

_____ Should students observe? _____ Take notes? _____ Raise questions? _____ Handle or use the material?

_____ What supplementary materials or comments are needed to enrich learning?

_____ Should a break be given for questions and comments?

_____ Should the resource be used a second time to emphasize points, clarify questions, or make explanations?

FOLLOW-UP

_____ What follow-up activities are suggested in the manual?

_____ What points should be stressed in group discussion and evaluation?

_____ How might other resources be used to check any points at issue?

_____ What related activities flow from it? _____ Chart making _____ Construction _____ Map making _____ Reading _____ Research _____ Role playing _____ Other

_____ How might group planning be used to project further inquiry?

_____ What hypotheses or generalizations might be made?

_____ Which objectives were and were not achieved?

TEACHER EVALUATION

_____ Was the resource satisfactory for the group involved?

_____ How can its use be improved?

_____ Should supplementary resources be available before or after its use?

_____ Were there any special difficulties that should be noted for future reference?

_____ Does the manual suggest points for evaluation?

Sources	When special materials that are not available in a school are needed, the
of Information	sources listed below should be checked. Most are available in college
	libraries and in instructional media centers.

1. The catalog of materials in the school system's media center.
2. Catalogs and lists of resources available from the county schools office, the state department of education, state universities, colleges, and other agencies from which your school district obtains materials.
3. The NICEM (National Information Center for Educational Media) indexes of audiovisual media, ecology, black history (Los Angeles: University of Southern California).
4. Detailed analyses of materials: *Curriculum Materials Data Book* (Boulder, Colo.: Social Science Education Consortium); *Educational Product Report* (New York: EPIE Institute).
5. Guides to free or inexpensive materials (also check special sections in the magazines listed in item 7): Ruth A. Aubrey, *Selected Free Materials for Classroom Teachers* (Belmont, Calif.: Fearon Publishers); *Educator's Guide to Free Social Studies Materials, Elementary Teachers' Guide to Free Curriculum Materials,* and *Educator's Guide to Free Films* (Randolph, Wis.: Educator's Progress Service); *Free and Inexpensive Learning Materials* (Nashville, Tenn.: George Peabody College, Division of Field Services); *Vertical File Index* (New York: H. W. Wilson); *Economic Education* (New York: Joint Council on Economic Education); and *Selected United States Government Publications,* Superintendent of Documents, Government Printing Office, Washington, D.C. 20402 (ask to be put on the mailing list).
6. Guides to social studies reading materials: *Basic Book Collection for Elementary Grades, Subject Index to Books for Primary Grades,* and *Subject Index to Books for Intermediate Grades* (Chicago, Ill.: American Library Association), check latest edition; *Best Books for Children and Children's Books in Print* (New York: R. R. Bowker Company), check latest edition; *Bibliography of Books for Children* (Washington, D.C.: Association for Childhood Education), check latest edition; Helen Huus, *Children's Books to Enrich the Social Studies for the Elementary Grades* (Washington, D.C.: National Council for the Social Studies), check latest edition.
7. Periodicals: *Booklist, Bulletin of the Center for Children's Books, Teacher, Instructor, Library Journal, Scholastic Teacher, Social Education, Audiovisual Instruction, Educational Screen, Education Product Report, Preview: News and Reviews of Nonprint Media.*
8. Detailed source lists in professional textbooks on audiovisual materials (see the list of references at the end of this chapter).
9. Information on materials related to ethnic groups: African-American Institute, 866 United Nations Plaza, New York, 10017, publications, and guides to materials; Anti-Defamation League of B'nai B'rith, 315 Lexington Ave., New York, New York 10016; Association for the Study of Negro Life and History, 1538 Ninth Street, N.W., Washington, D.C. 20001; James A. Banks, *Teaching Strategies for Ethnic Studies* (Boston: Allyn & Bacon, 1979); *Materials and Human Resources for Teaching Ethnic Studies* (Boulder, Colo.: Social Science Education Consortium, 1975).

1. Visit an instructional media center or check the center's catalog of materials to identify materials for use in a unit of your choice. Use the checklists in this chapter to guide your search.
2. Examine a textbook and make notes detailing how you might use it in a unit. Which of the objectives noted in the first part of this chapter might you achieve?
3. Make a sketch of a chart you might use in a unit. Indicate what type of chart it is and how you would use it.
4. Select and preview a film or filmstrip. Make a plan for using it in a unit, following the guidelines in checklist 3–7, Using Instructional Media.
5. Examine one or more of the guides to free or inexpensive materials listed at the end of this chapter. Request materials that appear suitable for a unit you plan to teach. Appraise items that you receive in terms of the criteria in checklist 3–5.
6. Select two textbooks for a grade of your choice, and apply the criteria for rating textbooks given in checklist 3–6. Note your reasons for any differences in the ratings.
7. Obtain magazines that contain pictures related to a unit you plan to teach. Cut out and mount useful pictures and organize them in a picture file. Indicate how they may be used to develop interpreting, classifying, and other thinking processes as well as concepts and related vocabulary.
8. Visit a library and examine sets of adult's and children's encyclopedias. For a unit of your choice, list relevant articles for teacher reference and for student reference. Make notes on how you might use the encyclopedias in the unit.

references

Brown, James W., Richard B. Lewis, and Fred F. Harcleroad, *A-V Instruction: Materials and Methods* (5th ed.). New York: McGraw-Hill, 1977. Principles and procedures for using all types of instructional materials and a listing of source materials; criteria for rating materials.

Cianciolo, Patricia, *Adventuring With Books.* Urbana, Ill.: National Council of Teachers of English, 1977. Booklist for prekindergarden through eighth grade.

Foster, Harold M. *The New Literacy: The Language of Film and Television.* Urbana, Ill.: National Council of Teachers of English, 1979. Guidelines for teaching visual literacy.

Fry, Edward, *Elementary Reading Instruction.* New York: McGraw-Hill, 1977. Chapter on experience approach and readability.

Klein, M. Frances, *About Learning Materials.* Washington, D.C.: Association for Supervision and Curriculum Development, 1978. Handbook of sources for identifying and evaluating materials.

Laybourne, Kay, ed., *Doing the Media.* New York: Center for Understanding Media, 1972. Section on making and using storyboards.

MINOR, ED, AND HARVEY R. FRYE, *Techniques for Producing Visual Instructional Media* (3rd ed.). New York: McGraw-Hill, 1978. Techniques for making materials.

"Notable Children's Trade Books in the Field of Social studies," annual review, *Social Education* (April issue).

SPACHE, GEORGE D., *Good Reading for Poor Readers*. Champaign, Ill.: Garrard, 1974. Materials on easy reading levels.

WURMAN, RICHARD, S., ed., *Yellow Pages of Learning Resources*. Cambridge, Mass.: MIT Press, 1972. Questions and study guides for using community resources.

PLANNING AND GUIDING GROUP WORK

focusing questions

What are the values and limitations of group work?
What skills are used at beginning, intermediate, and advanced levels?
What guidelines should be used in conducting discussions?
How can questions be used to improve discussions?
What guidelines should be used to improve learning in small-group activities?
How can study guides be used to improve learning in small groups?

There is no doubt that the quality of children's learning in the social studies is closely related to the skill with which teachers guide group work. The core of instruction is provided in groups, and many independent study activities grow out of group planning, discussion, and evaluation. This chapter presents guidelines and techniques that lead to productive group work.

Values
and Limitations
The class as a whole and small groups set up for special purposes may well be viewed as laboratories for firsthand learning about human interaction and interpersonal relationships. Both individual and small-group study and learning can be motivated and improved by working with others. Objectives can be set, questions can be raised, needed information can be provided on the spot, and concepts can be clarified. Being a part of the group fosters feelings of belonging, security, respect, and mutual trust. Group study taps the best thinking of individuals in the class or in a subgroup. A construc-

Grateful acknowledgement is made to Dr. Ruth Grossman, City University of New York, City College, for suggested revisions in this chapter.

tive and dynamic approach to learning can be nurtured and the excitement of discovering and sharing ideas with others can increase motivation. Democratic attitudes and behavior patterns such as open-mindedness, responsibility, creativity, cooperation, and concern for others can also be developed.

Teachers should also recognize the limitations of group work:

1. Group work should be limited to activities with a purpose group members can share; otherwise individuals in the group will waste time and derive little or no benefit from the activity.
2. Group work should be limited to those activities that use skills that the children already possess or that they can be taught. If children are to benefit from such activities as panel discussion and committee work, for example, they need certain skills, which are noted later.
3. Group work should be limited to activities that call for cooperative action to achieve stated purposes. If an activity can be completed by an individual, or by several individuals working independently, there is no need to organize a working group.
4. Group work should be limited to activities in which effective working relationships can be maintained. If interpersonal conflicts and differences in points of view cannot be reconciled, little will be gained by forcing individuals to work in a group.
5. Group work should be limited to situations that put to use the diverse talents of children. If each child is required to do the same thing in an activity, individual differences will be neglected, and each child's unique contribution will be lost.

Whole-Group Activities

In many learning situations the class works together as a single group. All students may participate in such whole-group activities as

Planning dramatizations, things to make, displays, use of materials, murals, maps, charts, art and crafts projects, stories, simulation games, ways to obtain information, individual and small-group work, and evaluation

Observing demonstrations, films and other audiovisual resources, people and activities on field trips, role playing, committee reports, changes in the neighborhood and community, and resource visitors

Discussing observations, interpretations, generalizations, classifications, inferences, hypotheses, predictions, analyses, syntheses, and evaluations based on data gathered from reading materials, community resources, and audiovisual materials

Evaluating plans, projects, use of materials, displays, dramatic activities, discussion, demonstrations, group behavior, sources of data, role playing, and interviewing and other data-gathering techniques

Small-Group Activities

Small-group activities are needed to carry out work planned by the whole group and to meet special needs and interests of students. Examples are

These groups are gathering data to share with the class. How might
you use small groups to investigate selected topics?

Investigating topics, problems, questions, and hypotheses raised in class discussion through interviews, library research, and use of materials in study centers

Collecting pictures, stories, articles, postcards, objects, and other items related to questions under study

Making maps, charts, graphs, labels, dioramas, murals, clay and papier-mâché figures, instruments, objects needed in dramatizations, booklets, displays, corner arrangements, and plans for reporting and sharing

Small-group activities are usually coordinated so that each group makes a contribution to the work of the class. On field trips, for example, the class may be divided into four or five groups to obtain information on different questions. Several groups may be set up to interview different individuals. The construction of different objects for a supermarket, airport, dramatization, or other activity may be assigned to small working groups. Parts of murals, time lines, bulletin board arrangements, scrapbooks, and other projects may be handled by designated groups.

*Growth
in Group-Work
Skills*

The growth and development of group-work skills from a beginning phase to an advanced phase is shown in chart 4–1. Items in the beginning phases should be emphasized in the early grades with all students and in later grades with students who are inexperienced in group work. Students should be guided to move to the intermediate and advanced phases by providing instruction on the necessary skills. By the time children reach the middle and upper grades they should be able to work at the advanced phase.

Developing Group Work Skills: A Continuum of Skills*

	Beginning Phase	Intermediate Phase	Advanced Phase
Objectives	Brief, specific	→ Longer, yet directed	→ Long, more complex
Planning	Planned primarily by the teacher	→ Planned jointly by the teacher and pupils	→ Planned primarily by pupils
Duration	Short, one or two days	→ Longer, several days	→ Several days to several weeks
Materials and Sources of Data	Use of single source or few sources or materials	→ Varied sources and materials	→ Variety of media and materials
Organization, Interaction	Informal, parallel activities, little interaction	→ Chair selected, tasks varied and assigned, some interaction during work	→ Chair or coordinator, much interaction in all phases
Reports	Parallel reports, or one student reporting with others filling in	→ Each member reports, or pupils share in reporting pooled information	→ Synthesis of information in one report; planned and given by the group
Evaluation	Informal, emphasis on sharing of best ideas	→ Attention to both content and procedures, self-evaluation encouraged	→ Emphasis on self-evaluation of activity in greater depth

Chart 4–1

Space Arrangements for Group Work

Group work of all types is most productive when space arrangements can be made to accommodate groups of varying sizes. Open space schools provide an unlimited number of arrangements. Single classrooms with movable furniture can also provide a high degree of flexibility, as chart 4–2 shows. Notice the spaces provided for learning centers, storage of unit materials, group activities, and related art, reading, and other activities.

*Grateful acknowledgment is made to Dr. Ruth Grossman, City University of New York, City College, for this chart.

Space Arrangements

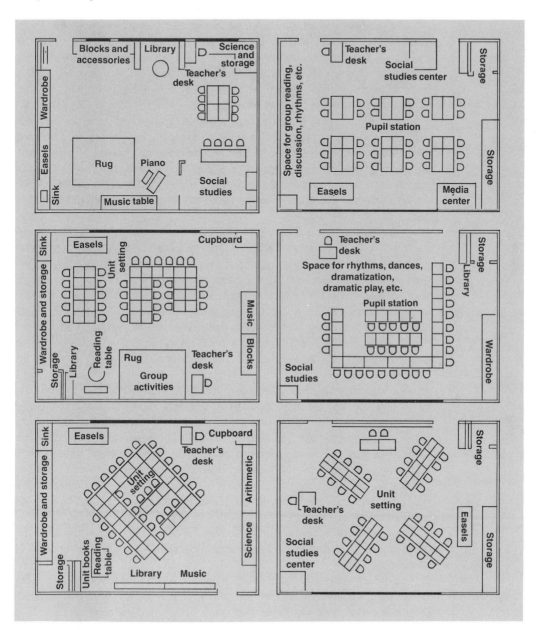

Chart 4–2

One of the most valuable techniques used in group work is discussion. Its use is essential to effective clarification of goals, planning, and evaluation. Discussion provides a practical opportunity to clarify objectives, introduce topics, raise questions, and appraise various experiences in the social studies. Social amenities are practiced, critical thinking is sharpened, and attention is focused on common problems. Ideas are shared, points of view expressed, leaders selected, and responsibilities delegated. Students learn to respect the right of others to express themselves. Discussion is truly an essential technique of democratic education.

Group discussion gives teachers opportunities to note children's behavior, attitudes, and abilities to express ideas. Teachers can observe originality of contributions, sharing of ideas, respect for the opinions of others, consideration of differing points of view, shyness, boldness, and the like and can give special help as individual needs arise. Many teachers find discussion situations to be a most valuable source of information about children's needs, potentialities, and backgrounds.

The teacher has a crucial role in group discussion. He or she must create a supportive atmosphere so that all children will feel that their contributions are valued by the teacher and the group. Shy children should be encouraged, and children who tend to monopolize the discussion should be guided in learning to share discussion time with others. The teacher should clarify the major problem to be discussed and keep it before the group throughout. The teacher should also call for questions, illustrations, and comments as particular items need clarification and allow adequate time for thinking about the points made and questions raised. To be avoided are such pitfalls as not sticking to the point, failing to clarify the problem, wasting time on side issues or repetitious comments, embarrassing participants by rejecting their contributions, omitting key ideas, and allowing a few individuals to dominate the discussion.

The teacher's (or discussion leader's) role is to secure maximum participation of members of the group. This point must be emphasized because sometimes discussion is limited to interaction between the teacher and individuals in the group. For example, the teacher raises a question and a student responds; the teacher comments or raises another question and calls on another student who answers; and this question-and-answer recitation pattern continues. Although this pattern is sometimes useful—as in discussing particular concepts, eliciting information needed for an activity, reviewing key ideas, or achieving other objectives that require close teacher direction—it should not be used all of the time.

In sharp contrast is discussion characterized by interaction among group members. Here the teacher or discussion leader raises a question or makes a comment and several participants respond before the leader intervenes. This pattern brings out a variety of ideas and stimulates questions. It encourages the group to propose hypotheses to guide study; it elicits various points of view and predictions. Stated briefly, this type of discussion is needed to achieve objectives that call for the sparking of thinking through interaction of members of the group.

Charts 4–3 and 4–4 illustrate the difference between these two types of discussion. The rectangle represents the teacher or leader, and the circles represent the participants. The lines indicate the flow of discussion from one individual to another. Chart 4–3 illustrates teacher or leader domination, and chart 4–4 illustrates group interaction.

Teacher-dominated Discussion

Group-interaction Discussion

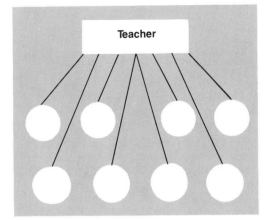

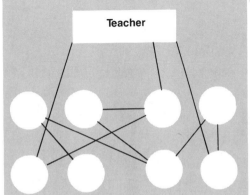

Chart 4-3

Chart 4-4

Sometimes children should lead the discussion, particularly in intermediate and upper grades. Before this is done, guidelines for leading the discussion should be developed. Chart 4–5 shows guidelines developed by a group in the fifth grade to meet problems that had arisen.

Discussion may be improved by introducing special reports and small-group techniques. Group sharing of experiences and objects, group reports on special topics, and panel presentations are used in many units in the social studies. Small discussion groups, sometimes called "buzz sessions," may also be used at times to generate ideas on specific questions or topics. Charts 4–6 through 4–8 illustrate standards and guidelines that have been used successfully with children.

Both the teacher and the group should evaluate discussion, giving specific attention to points and problems that have arisen. The teacher should keep in

Discussion Leaders

Call the group to order.

State the question or topic to be discussed.

Get ideas from the group.

Call on different children.

Keep the group on the topic.

Get answers from the group to any questions that are raised.

Make a brief summary of the discussion.

Chart 4–5

Discussion Groups

Each group has a topic or question to discuss.

Each group includes four to six students.

Seats are arranged so that students can see each other.

The leader opens the discussion.

Each member of the group participates.

The recorder keeps notes and reports to the class.

Chart 4–6

Panel Discussion

Panel members sit in a half circle facing the class.

The panel leader presents the topic for discussion.

Panel members present their part of the discussion.

Members of the class note questions to raise.

The leader asks for questions from the class.

Panel members answer the questions.

The leader makes a summary.

Chart 4–7

Group Reports

The topic is broken into questions or subtopics.

Each member of the group works on a question or subtopic.

Notes are reviewed to avoid repetition.

Length of time for each report is set.

Questions that could be raised are discussed.

Pictures and other items are selected to illustrate reports.

Reports are given and questions are discussed.

Chart 4–8

mind both the essential elements of effective discussion and the maturity of the children. The discussion itself can be appraised in terms of the items listed in charts 4–9 through 4–11 and in checklist 4–1.

The maturity of the group must be considered in guiding and evaluating group discussion. The charts, checklists, and group evaluation criteria should reflect the students' levels of growth. Charts 4–9 through 4–11 show what can be expected of groups at various stages of development.

In addition to evaluation carried on by the group, the teacher must consider how each child participates in discussion so that effective planning and guidance can be carried out. Checklist 4–1 suggests several points to keep in mind as each child's growth in discussion ability is considered. Others may be added or some may be deleted, depending on the instruction provided and the specific needs of the children.

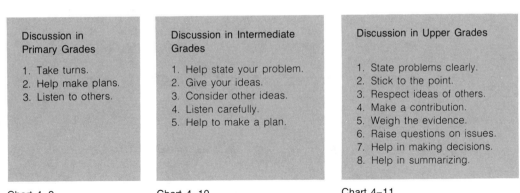

Discussion in Primary Grades	Discussion in Intermediate Grades	Discussion in Upper Grades
1. Take turns.	1. Help state your problem.	1. State problems clearly.
2. Help make plans.	2. Give your ideas.	2. Stick to the point.
3. Listen to others.	3. Consider other ideas.	3. Respect ideas of others.
	4. Listen carefully.	4. Make a contribution.
	5. Help to make a plan.	5. Weigh the evidence.
		6. Raise questions on issues.
		7. Help in making decisions.
		8. Help in summarizing.
Chart 4–9	Chart 4–10	Chart 4–11

Checklist 4–1
Growth in Discussion

Note: Check each child two or three times during the term to see if growth is taking place.

BEHAVIORS TO BE CHECKED	NAMES OF CHILDREN			
Understands the problem				
Listens while others speak				
Is an interested and willing listener				
Interjects ideas at appropriate points				
Considers ideas contrary to his or her own				
Sticks to the topic				
Does not repeat ideas given by others				
Gets to the point without delay				
Speaks clearly and distinctly				
Uses appropriate language				
Uses concepts accurately				
Is interested in comments of others				

ANALYSIS OF DISCUSSION

Analysis of discussion patterns can improve the teacher's role and identify the participation patterns of students. Informal analysis may be made by checking the patterns shown in charts 4–10 through 4–12 and by keeping a list of students who do and do not participate. With such information, the emphasis can be shifted from teacher domination or close direction to group interaction, or vice versa, depending on the needs of students and instructional objectives.

A systematic procedure for checking interaction between teacher and students has been proposed by Flanders.* The teacher may record the discussion and check it later, considering the following:

Teacher Talk

1. Indirect influence with much student freedom and interaction
   a. Teacher accepts feelings expressed by students.
   b. Teacher praises and encourages students.
   c. Teacher accepts or uses ideas of students.
   d. Teacher asks questions of students.
2. Direct influence with less student freedom and interaction
   a. Teacher lectures to students.
   b. Teacher gives directions.
   c. Teacher criticizes or justifies authority to improve student behavior.

Student Talk

1. Student responds to the teacher.
2. Student initiates the talk.

LISTENING SKILLS

Listening skills should be put to use in discussion and in other activities in which students get ideas from others. Effective listening is essential if students are to note points that are made, identify points to question, get a feeling for the mood or tone of expression of others, and make meaningful contributions. In the early grades children listen at a level that enables them to get ideas from others and respond to them. As listening skills develop, they are able to note explanations in detail, then move on to making critical evaluations of opinions and judgments.

Recording a discussion and playing back portions can show students the need for careful listening. As students listen to the tape they should note points of agreement and disagreement, comments that get off the topic, failure to pick up on questions, and lack of courtesy while others are speaking. Directed listening activities may be made a part of follow-up discussions to focus attention on the need to stay on the topic, to get facts and opinions right the first time, and to listen courteously to others. Charts 4–12 through 4–14 list points to emphasize.

*Ned Flanders, *Interaction Analysis in the Classroom: A Manual for Observers* (Minneapolis: University of Minnesota, College of Education, 1960). Procedures for studying teacher-pupil interaction. For a variety of other systems, see Anita Simon and E. Gil Boyer, *Mirrors For Behavior III: An Anthology of Observation Instruments* (Philadelphia, Pa.: Research for Better Schools, 1974).

Listening in Discussions	Listening for Information	Listening to Evaluate
Get the topic clearly in mind.	Have a question or purpose in mind.	What is to be appraised?
Raise your hand if you cannot hear.	Get ideas in order.	What standards are to be used?
Note points made by others.	Relate details to main ideas.	What is the evidence?
Make your points when they fit in.	Ask questions about parts that are not clear.	Which statements are facts? Which are opinions?
Listen to others as you want them to listen to you.	Summarize the main ideas.	What conclusion or judgment can be made? Which standards are met?

| Chart 4–12 | Chart 4–13 | Chart 4–14 |

USING QUESTIONS TO IMPROVE DISCUSSION

The types of questions raised during discussions determine the outcomes that can be expected. Questions raised relate to three basic aspects of discussion: (1) content, (2) responses to students' comments, and (3) structure or format of the discussion.* By planning questioning strategies in advance, the teacher can guide discussion in the desired direction (refer to chapters 9 and 13, which contain strategies for developing thinking and valuing processes).

questions related to content of discussion

The following types of question are directly related to the content of discussion.

Open-ended questions are frequently used to initiate discussion, elicit a variety of responses, and invite students to participate.

What did you see on the field trip?
What should we do to improve bicycle safety?
What do you remember about the Gold Rush?
How many different ways can you think of to solve this problem?

Specifying questions are injected to focus on details and data that are essential to understanding.

What steps in processing almonds did you see on the field trip?
How can we improve bicycle safety around the school?

*Adapted from Helen McGinnis, Director, *Retrieval: A Social Sciences Handbook for Teachers*, Social Science Project, Area III Superintendents (Sacramento, Calif.: County Office of Education, 1972).

119

How were claims established during the Gold Rush?

What can we do right now to help solve this problem?

Clarifying questions are used to establish the meaning of terms, phrases, and statements.

Can you give some examples to show what you mean?

Can that be stated in another way?

Are you saying that they wasted their resources?

What do you mean by civil liberties?

Probing questions call for additions, explanations, alternatives, and further analaysis.

What other causes might there be?

What other reasons can you think of?

In what other ways might the problem be handled?

What are other reasonable explanations?

questions related to students' comments

A classroom climate that is marked by accepting, supporting, and encouraging behavior on the part of the teacher and students encourages meaningful discussions. How should the teacher handle comments off the point, interjection of unrelated ideas, and the erroneous statements that are inevitably made by students? Some students hold back during discussion. How can they be encouraged to participate? The following comments and questions illustrate accepting, supporting, and encouraging behavior on the part of the teacher, behavior that should be emulated by students.

Accepting questions and comments are used when a student gets off the point, repeats an idea, interjects irrelevant comments, or responds to a question raised earlier.

That's interesting, Betty. Can we come back to it later?

I see that you agree with what Paul said.

Have we already listed that? Let's check.

Discussion can also be facilitated by teaching students to precede remarks that may be unrelated to the immediate topic with explanatory comments.

I just thought of something related to an earlier question. . . .

Getting back to what Jane said. . . .

This isn't on the question, but may I say. . . .

An idea that may be useful later is. . . .

Supporting questions and comments are helpful when a child makes an error or needs help in making a point or when an unpopular or shy child comments.

Can we look that up later?
Who can help Alice make her point?
Let's give Robert a chance to have his say.

Encouraging questions and comments bring students into the discussion.

Has anyone else something to say?
Are there any items that should be changed?
Does anyone want to raise a question about any points made so far?

questions
to structure
the discussion

When the emphasis in discussion is on classifying for concept formation, interpreting data, generalizing, and other processes, planned questions are needed to structure or guide the discussion. The questions are used to guide the discussion from one step to the next and on to higher levels at a pace the students can handle.

Focusing questions direct thinking in a step-by-step manner and shift discussion from one phase of a teaching strategy to the next. The following questions were designed to develop concepts through classifying; notice how each question focuses students' attention.

What did you find? See? Hear? Note [focus on data]?
Which ones can be grouped together [focus on grouping]?
Why can they be grouped together? How are they alike [focus on reasons]?
What is a good name for this group [focus on labeling]?

Refocusing questions bring students back to the point under discussion; they may be a repetition or rewording of focusing questions.

What is shown in this chart, not the one on air pollution?
Can we wait on that and get more examples of waste pollution?
Which activities in the home, not in parks, add to waste pollution?

Lifting questions move thinking to higher levels. They are a special type of focusing question in that they move discussion from recalling of information to processing of information; they lift thinking beyond what is given in the information. Give particular attention to the last three questions.

What can you recall about ways to prevent air pollution?
How can we group the different ways [lift to grouping]?
What would happen if everyone helped to prevent air pollution [lift to predicting]?
Why do you think that would happen [lift to analyzing reasons for prediction]?

As stressed in the previous example and in many places throughout this text, efforts should be made to move students from first levels of thinking, such as recalling and observing, to higher levels, such as analyzing and evaluating. When planning discussion questions to lift thinking, consider the three broad levels of thinking, then plan questions and use questioning strategies, such as those in chapters 6 and 9, that fit within each level.

level 1: consideration of data
Questions at this level are frequently used after students complete a reading, see a film, or use another source of information. The objective is to discuss the meaning obtained and to use what has been learned to get at questions and problems under study. Questions such as the following may be used:

What does this map (film, reading, picture, and so on) show?
Which ideas can we use to answer questions we have listed?
In what other ways can we use the information?

level 2: processing of data
Questions at this level ask students to classify, compare and contrast, and generalize, using the information considered at the first level. Students have the meaning clearly in mind and are ready to process or use the data in various ways. For example, questions such as the following focus attention on comparing and contrasting:

Look at our chart on consumers and producers.
What is the main thing consumers do?
What is the main thing producers do?
What is the main difference between them?

level 3: moving beyond what is given
Questions at this level invite students to go beyond the information they have considered at the first two levels. The focus may be on drawing inferences, stating hypotheses, making predictions, analyzing reasons or causes, synthesizing parts in a new way, or evaluating what happened. The following questions were designed to get students to infer the feelings aroused by a current event, film, or other item and to move thinking beyond what is given.

What happened? What is the problem? What did they do?
How do you think they (she, he) felt? Why might they feel that way?
Has something like that ever happened to you? How did you feel? How would you feel if you were in that situation? Why would you feel like that?

Guidelines for Small-Group Activities

Small groups may be used a variety of ways in the social studies. Teams of two or three students may work on specified tasks. A special group may be set up to interview experts in the community on a particular topic. Committees may be formed to investigate different topics and report back to the class. Groups may be organized for almost any need that arises. In this section attention is given to guidelines for using small-group activities to achieve optimum learning.

INITIATING SMALL-GROUP WORK

Guidelines for organizing and starting committees and forming other small working groups are as follows:

1. Make two analyses before starting group work. First, identify individuals who can work well together so that the first attempt at group work will be successful and serve as a model for other groups. Second, identify specific needs for productive small-group work directly related to the unit under study.
2. Make plans to begin with one group. Give attention to the task to be completed, directions to guide work, and arrangement of needed materials and working space.
3. After the rest of the class is busy at work, take the small group to the work area, clarify what is to be done, and see that they are off to a good start. Provide supervision as needed during the work period.
4. After the task is completed, guide the sharing of the group's efforts with the class. Discuss procedures used as well as outcomes, giving attention to any problems that arose and suggesting ways to prevent them in the future. Summarize standards that similar groups can use.
5. Make plans for other working groups in a similar fashion. Move from one group to two or more as needs for group work become clear and children assume the necessary responsibilities. Have worthwhile independent activities ready for children who become overstimulated in small-group work and are not ready to assume a role in group activities.
6. Move from group to group as needed to supervise and direct. Note ideas that provide more effective ways of working together for the follow-up evaluation.
7. As the class members develop group-work skills, provide them with more freedom to work on their own. Arrange groups so that children who are advanced in group-work skills can assume leadership in helping others and in keeping the group moving in profitable directions. Give close supervision to any children who continue to have difficulty working with others.

SELECTING AND ORGANIZING SMALL GROUPS

To organize effective groups the teacher must consider not only the job to be done but also needs of individual students to develop leadership and followership, their readiness for the activity, and the compatibility among students. Children can be allowed to select groups in which they would like to work when choice is a basic consideration and when students are ready and able to participate in the various group activities. When special topics are to be researched in textbooks or library resources it is wise to use reading groups and to provide materials at a reading level that the group can handle.

Teams of two or three students to work on specified tasks should be set up so that each students benefits from team learning (see end-of-chapter reference by Chase and John). The team should be made up of students who can work together and help each other. For example, a team could be composed of a student who excels in reading and can help others with vocabulary and other reading skills, a student who can make diagrams or other graphic materials, and one who is skillful in recording information. A team can also be organized around a special interest—transportation, communication, or other topic in a unit.

Some teachers use sociometric data along with information gained by observing children to form working groups. If such information is used, *great care should be taken* so that students are not embarrassed and made the victims of self-fulfilling prophesies related to their status in the group. Students may be asked to (1) name students with whom they would like to work on a committee or other activity, or (2) assign their classmates to such categories as good discussion leader, good group member, good committee chairperson, and so forth. Choices or assignments may then be used to make a sociogram as illustrated in chart 4–15, in which circles represent girls, squares represent boys, students are identified by number, and arrows show choices. In the group diagramed, boys 1 and 3 chose boy 7, as did girl 1; boys 2 and 4 and girls 3 and 4 chose each other; girl 8 was chosen by four students, and boy 7 by three; and some students were not chosen by anyone. Notice that leaders are placed in the center, isolates on the edge, and others in between.

Because the making of sociograms is so time consuming, some teachers substitute social status scores. To determine social status scores, students are asked to choose classmates for different roles and to list their first, second, and third choices, so that a reasonable range of scores are obtained. In addition to making first through third choices for those they would like to work with, students are asked to make choices for discussion leaders, members of a panel, and the like. A student's social status score is the number of choices he or she receives.

Sociometric data can be used constructively to group and regroup students so as to extend patterns of friendship, improve interpersonal relationships, and help isolates gain group acceptance. In some cases individual interviews and counseling may help students work with others more effectively and improve group work skills. Students that no one or only one other student chooses may be placed with students who have demonstrated concern for others. Groups can also be formed to help students learn to work with members of the opposite sex, to extend friendship patterns beyond cliques, to spread leadership roles, and to help students who consistently choose each other to learn that they can work effectively with many different students.

In forming groups the guiding principle is to organize groups that will achieve stated objectives and at the same time help students improve their skills in interpersonal relationships. In no instance should the classroom become a

Sociogram

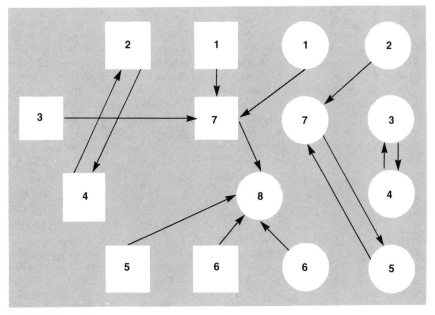

Chart 4-15

place where negative attitudes toward certain children are exhibited. Children should know that the standing rule is to work together so that everyone learns as much as possible.

PLANNING

As problems arise the group must plan and replan its work. Initial planning is carried out in group discussion, and special attention is given to questions, problems, and responsibilities. Replanning is necessary as new needs arise and as special problems surface. Both initial planning and replanning should involve more than a search for sources of information. Attention may well be given to such items as formulating problems, devising ways to secure data, setting up work standards, deciding on things to construct, considering ways to secure and use materials, overcoming obstacles, helping others, extending interests, investigating proposals, submitting suggestions, asking for help, and learning the opinions and ideas of others. Planning is also essential in getting ready for research activities, construction, dramatic play, processing of materials, field trips, and creative expression through art, music, literature, and rhythms.

In guiding group planning, teachers should keep the following principles in mind:

1. All should be encouraged to participate in planning, so that the best ideas of each member are brought to bear upon the problem.
2. Problems and questions expressed by the children should receive major attention. Problems neglected by the children can be pointed out by the teacher.
3. Constructive suggestions should be secured from the group; negative comments should be redirected into positive suggestions.
4. The teacher should guide planning and help when encouragement is needed, impasses are reached, or difficult problems arise.
5. Standards for planning should be developed and used as needs arise.
6. Records should be kept as needed to further group action; examples are charts, directions, reading guides, work sheets, notes, and minutes.
7. Group decisions growing out of planning should lead to specific plans of action.
8. At the end of planning discussions, check to see that each child understands what to do, where to do it, how to proceed, materials to use, work standards to follow, and how to get help if needed.

GUIDING ACTIVITIES

As children engage in group activities, the teacher should gather information to use in group evaluation, observing such behavior as acceptance of responsibilities, cooperation, courtesy, and self-control. During group work the teacher has many opportunities to move about and to give help as needed. One child may have difficulty in locating material in a given reference; another may have difficulty using tools and materials. By giving judicious assistance, the teacher can make sure that effective learning takes place.

Attention should also be given to the various materials being used, techniques that need to be improved, and misconceptions or erroneous ideas that arise. For example, in a unit on pioneer life, the teacher noticed during a research period that several youngsters were having difficulty using the table of contents; others were not sure of the topics to locate in the index. Notes were made for use in a later discussion that centered on skills involved in the location of materials.

The teacher should also note how children use the work standards that they have helped to set. He or she should commend those children who carry out group-made standards and who help others to do so. Occasionally the teacher will have to ask a child to stop an activity for a few minutes and consider if his or her behavior conforms to the group standard. In a few instances some children must be excluded from the group until they realize that they must accept all of the responsibilities involved in the activity. Following the work period, time should be given to a careful reconsideration of the group standards and how well each member of the group helped maintain them.

Particular attention must be given to those few youngsters who appear unsure of what they should do in an activity. If the planning period has been

Special needs can be met through small-group instruction. How might you group students to develop concepts or meet other needs?

carefully organized, very few children will lack a clear sense of purpose. During the work period—whether it is research, dramatic play, or construction—children who do not have clear purposes in mind may need further guidance. Classmates frequently volunteer to help others who are not sure of what they should do to complete an activity. This is a good indication of cooperative behavior and should be encouraged. More important, however, is careful planning at the beginning of the work period to assure that all members of the group participate.

The ways members of the group use materials should also be noted. Courtesy, sharing, taking turns, proper use of tools, proper selection of material, and the ways children help others use materials are of particular importance. Toward the end of the work period, materials should be returned to their places so that others can use them.

EVALUATION

Group evaluation is an essential element in all phases of group action—from initial definition of problems to appraisal of the effectiveness of group work. During evaluation, the group answers such questions as these: Is each individual doing his or her part? Are the plans effective? Are leadership responsibilities being carried out? Are our objectives being achieved? Are additional resources needed? What steps should be taken next? In making appraisals, the group may use discussions and charts or checklists, refer to a log or diary of activities, get assistance from the teacher, examine work materials, or use other evaluative devices. Emphasis should be given to self-evaluation and to suggesting specific ways in which group activities can be improved.

COMMITTEES

Committees should be congenial working groups interested in the job to be done and balanced in terms of needed abilities and talents. The leader may be selected by the group or the teacher after due consideration of needed qualifications. The committee should make clear plans, which the teacher should check before committee work begins. Needed materials and adequate working space should be available; sufficient time to make an effective beginning or to complete the job should be allowed. The committee should develop work standards beforehand and use them as responsibilities are carried out.

Each committee member should know what he or she is expected to do so that confusion and excessive noise can be avoided. Some teachers demonstrate committee work to provide guidelines for students to follow, either by selecting a group to demonstrate for the class or by using the class as a committee with the teacher as leader. As members of the class begin to sense a need for standards, they should be encouraged to develop standards and list them on the chalkboard or on charts. See charts 4-16 through 4-18 for examples of group-developed standards.

Committee Members	Committee Reports	Committee Leaders
1. Know what to do.	1. Stick to the questions.	1. Keep the main job in mind.
2. Divide the work.	2. Use pictures, objects, and maps.	2. Get ideas from all members.
3. Do each job well.	3. Be ready to answer questions.	3. See that each member has a job.
4. Discuss problems quietly.		4. Be fair and do not talk all the time.
5. Plan the report carefully.		5. Urge everyone to do his or her best.
		6. Say *our* committee, not *my* committee.

Chart 4–16   Chart 4–17   Chart 4–18

As established committees proceed with their work, the teacher moves from committee to committee providing guidance as needed and noting points for use in evaluation. The teacher may offer suggestions for improving reports by using pictures, charts, maps, and the like, and should note and commend the interest and seriousness of each child who is being a good committee worker. Through careful observation and direct guidance as committees work, the teacher can bring about rapid growth in group work skills.

Study Guides for Productive Group Work

Study guides allow a team of two or three students or a committee of four or five to learn in small groups. Several types of study guides can be used, ranging from those that contain questions on a single source of information to those created by students themselves.

GUIDE FOR A SINGLE SOURCE
OF INFORMATION

The following example illustrates an easy-to-prepare study guide based on a story that is part of a unit on rights and responsibilities. The same format may also be used for a film, filmstrip, or other data source. Notice that the questions are arranged in a sequence that begins by asking students to recall and interpret basic information, then moves to higher levels, stimulating students to consider inferences, analyze reasons, and make a prediction.

Study Guide for the Telescreen Story

1. Answer the questions listed below as you read the story entitled "The Telescreen" on pages 61 to 66 in *Rights and Responsibilities*.
   a. What different ways were used to watch people [recalling, interpreting]?
   b. What individual rights that we have discussed so far in our unit were disregarded [recalling]?
   c. Does the group agree on the answers to the two questions above [comparing]? If so, proceed to the next questions. If not, reread the story and find out who is right.
2. Discuss these questions in your group and write answers that members of the group agree are the best answers. If agreement cannot be reached, report the different answers.
   a. How do you suppose the people felt when they were watched all of the time [inferring]?
   b. If you were to be watched all of the time, what would happen to your freedom to speak [inferring]?

c. What other freedoms would you lose if you were watched all of the time [inferring]?

d. Look back over your answers to questions a, b, and c. What reasons can you give for your answers [analyzing]?

e. Do you think that anything like what happened in the story will ever happen in our country? Why or why not [predicting]?

GUIDES BASED ON RETRIEVAL CHARTS

Another type of study guide is based on a retrieval chart. The chart is discussed with the class before teams go to work, and each team is assigned responsibility for one section of the retrieval chart. For example, chart 4–19 was designed for use in a unit on Latin America. In using such charts, teams of three to five students are set up to gather information on each country. Work

Retrieval Chart on Latin American Countries

Topics	Argentina	Brazil	Chile	Columbia	Ecuador	Uruguay
Population						
Area						
Main Regions						
Agriculture						
Manufacturing						
Mining						
Trade						
Transportation						
Education						
Art						
Music						
Form of Government						
Capital						

Chart 4–19

may be divided in several ways; some students might gather data on the first three topics, others on agriculture and other economic activities, and so on. Or a team of two or three may find information on economic activities in one country, another team may collect data on education, art, and music, and so on. As the teams report their findings, the information is pooled and displayed on large wall charts.

STUDY GUIDES COMBINING INDEPENDENT AND SMALL-GROUP STUDY

A more detailed type of study guide can be used to combine aspects of independent study and small-group study, as illustrated in the sample study guide for life style that follows. Each member of a team or group receives a copy of the guide, uses it to collect information, compares information and answers with other members, makes revisions after small-group discussion, and submits a final report to the teacher. Such a study guide combines the benefits of interacting with others and getting ideas from them with the benefits of independent study. Several small-group sessions may be needed. The groups that used the following study guide held four sessions: one to compare notes on the materials to read, one to discuss and revise responses to the questions, one to compare notes and discuss the follow-up activity, and one to sharpen ideas on evaluation.

Study Guide for Life Style

OBJECTIVES

To state the meaing of life style

To describe the effects of one's life style on the environment

To state changes that may be made in one's life style to improve the environment

MATERIALS

Read one or more of the following books: *At Home around the World, People Use the Earth, Population, Production, Pollution,* and *The Social Sciences.* Use the index to find the pages on which life style is discussed. Take notes on the filmstrip *Using Our Forest Wisely* when it is shown to the class.

QUESTIONS AND ACTIVITIES

1. What do you think *life style* means?
2. Find and write the meaning of life style in one of the readings. How is the meaning like and different from yours?

3. Describe your own life style by completing the following:
   Foods I eat are _____.
   Clothes I wear are _____.
   Things I do to have fun are _____.
   The way I treat other people is _____.
   Other aspects of my life style are _____.
   Things I do that cause waste pollution are _____.
   Things I do that cause noise pollution are _____.
   Other things I do that hurt the environment are _____.
   Things I do that do not hurt the environment are _____.
4. How is your life style like the life style of people described in the reading material? How is it different?
5. Which changes in life style noted in the reading materials do you think are most important to help the environment? Why?
6. Which changes in life style do you think are most important in the filmstrip on forests? Why?
7. What changes in your life style should be made to help the environment? Why? Do you think that you will make them? Why or why not?

FOLLOW-UP ACTIVITY

During the next three days keep a record of your activities following the form below. (Examples are given in the first box.)

Activities	Energy or resources used	Helps the environment	Hurts the environment	Type of Pollution
Example: Family picnic	Car and food	No	If we litter	Waste
1.				
2.				
3.				

EVALUATION

1. Life style means _____.
2. One's life style may affect the environment in these ways:
   a. _____
   b. _____
   c. _____
3. Three changes in life style of people in our country that should help to improve the environment are
   a. _____

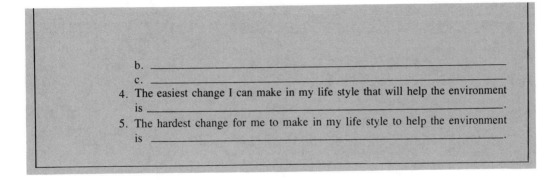

b. _____

c. _____

4. The easiest change I can make in my life style that will help the environment
   is _____.

5. The hardest change for me to make in my life style to help the environment
   is _____.

USING MODELS AS STUDY GUIDES

Models of decision making, problem solving, case-study analysis, and other sets of processes may be used by committees set up to consider proposals, solve a problem, analyze a case, or tackle a particular issue. The use of models in groups is most effective after students have considered them in class discussions directed by the teacher. Examples of decision making and case analysis models follow. They outline the procedure for a group to follow, focus discussion on key points, and serve as guides for preparing oral and written reports. They may be applied to a variety of issues, proposals, problems, and dilemmas that arise in social studies units.

Decision-Making Model

1. Discuss the issue or proposal so that each member has it clearly in mind.
2. Discuss and list the values (justice, freedom, and so on) that are most important in this situation. Note any disagreements that cannot be settled.
3. Discuss and list alternative decisions that might be made. Note reasons for each possible decision.
4. Discuss and list the consequences of each decision that the group agrees is worth considering. If there is disagreement, consider making a minority report.
5. Select the best decision in terms of consequences and values. If there is disagreement, prepare a minority report.
6. Prepare a statement of reasons for the decision that the group accepts. If there is a minority report, state reasons for the decision that it supports.

Case-Analysis Model

1. Determine the facts (evidence in the case).
2. Discuss the issue that must be resolved.

3. List the facts pro and con (for and against).
4. Make a decision or judgment after discussing the pros and cons.
5. List reasons for the decision—how justice will be served.

STUDENT-PREPARED GUIDES

A most valuable learning activity is to have students develop their own study guides. Before students begin, the general plan should be discussed with the class; then teams go to work to develop their own detailed plan. Each team answers the questions listed below, then presents the resulting study plan to the teacher or the class for review and improvement. Think of the skills that students must use and the extra learning they may achieve as a result of sharing ideas and creating their own guide!

Planning a Study Guide

BEGINNING

1. What is the topic of study?
2. What questions should be answered?

IDENTIFYING SOURCES OF INFORMATION

1. What reading materials in the classroom may be used?
2. What library materials may be used?
3. What people may be interviewed?
4. What other sources may be used?

COLLECTING AND ORGANIZING INFORMATION

1. How may note taking and outlining be used?
2. What information should be put on charts?
3. What information should be put on maps?
4. What other ways of organizing information may be used?

SHARING AND REPORTING FINDINGS

1. What are the main parts? Can the report be organized around questions stated at the beginning?
2. In what order should the parts be placed?
3. What ideas should be put on cards for an oral report?
4. How can pictures, maps, or other items be used to improve the report?

Questions, Activities, Evaluation

1. Which of the values and limitations of group work skills do you believe to be most significant? Why? What do you think are some dangers in overemphasizing them at the expense of independent study skills?
2. Note four or five whole-group activities you might use in a unit of your choice. Do the same for small-group or committee activities.
3. Visit a classroom and use the following questions to observe and analyze the teacher's role in guiding discussion. Was the initiating question clear? How did it give a focus to discussion? Note how each of the following types of questions was used:
   a. Open-ended, specifying, clarifying, and probing questions related to content of the discussion
   b. Accepting, supporting, and encouraging questions related to students' comments
   c. Focusing, refocusing, and lifting questions related to the structure and flow of discussion

      On what level(s) was the discussion held? How did students respond to any shifts that were made to raise the level?
4. Select one small-group activity and make a plan for using it in a unit of your choice. Specify how you would select students, initiate the activity, guide it, and evaluate it.
5. Make a plan for a study guide that you might use to improve learning in small-group work, relating it to a unit of work.

references

ASSOCIATION OF TEACHERS OF SOCIAL STUDIES IN THE CITY OF NEW YORK, *Handbook for Teaching of Social Studies*. Boston, Mass.: Allyn & Bacon, 1977. Chapter on questioning.

BANKS, JAMES A., WITH AMBROSE A. CLEGG, JR., *Teaching Strategies for the Social Studies*. Reading, Mass.: Addison-Wesley Publishing Co., 1977. Chapter on questioning.

CHASE, W. LINWOOD, AND MARTHA T. JOHN, *A Guide for the Elementary Social Studies Teacher* (3rd ed.). Boston, Mass.: Allyn & Bacon, 1978. Sections on grouping procedures, team use of study guides, and preparing study guides (chapter 2).

HANNAH, LARRY S., AND JOHN U. MICHAELIS, *A Comprehensive Framework of Educational Objectives*. Reading, Mass.: Addison-Wesley Publishing Co., 1977. Examples of questions for classifying, generalizing, analyzing, and other processes.

HUNT, MAURICE P., AND LAWRENCE E. METCALF, *Teaching High School Social Studies*. New York: Harper & Row Publishers, 1968. Chapter on discussion as a tool of reflective thinking.

JAROLIMEK, JOHN, *Social Studies In Elementary Education* (5th ed.). New York: Macmillan, 1977. Chapter on skills for group interaction.

JOYCE, BRUCE, AND MARSHA WEIL, *Models of Teaching* (2nd ed.), Englewood Cliffs, N.J.: Prentice-Hall, 1980. Chapters on group investigation and social inquiry.

Kurfman, Dana G., ed., *Developing Decision-Making Skills* (47th yearbook). Washington, D.C.: National Council for the Social Studies, 1977. Chapter by Nelson and Singleton on small-group decision making, and chapter by Capron on decision making in elementary schools, including a section on pupil-team learning.

PLANNING AND PROVIDING FOR INDIVIDUAL DIFFERENCES

What strategies and techniques can be used to identify individual differences and to make plans to meet them?

How can learning contracts, activity cards, and the preparing of reports be used to individualize instruction?

How can reading be individualized in the social studies?

What procedures may be used to teach children to individualize for themselves?

How can special needs of the economically disadvantaged, less able, and gifted be met?

What adjustments can be made to meet the needs of physically impaired students who are mainstreamed into a teacher's classroom?

This chapter presents guidelines and procedures for individualizing classroom instruction in the social studies.* No phase of social studies instruction is more difficult or more important. To be successful, teachers must view individual differences among children as a positive value, and they must gain a working knowledge of strategies for planning and managing instruction to benefit each child.

Point of View   Teachers who truly value differences and recognize the unique characteristics of each child are the ones who plan most effectively for individualized instruction. They care deeply about all children and can see the unique characteristics of each child, whether average, physically impaired, disadvantaged, less able, or gifted. Their deep concern for each child provides the necessary drive to complete the hard work of individualizing instruction.

Teachers who effectively individualize instruction are also flexible, open

*For a review of commercially available individualized programs see Gagne, Robert M., and Leslie J. Briggs, *Principles of Instructional Design* (New York: Holt, Rinehart & Winston, 1974).

to new ideas, and willing to put each child's educational welfare above arbitrary grade standards. They believe that each child's maximum growth is more important than minimum standards for the group, that some children can go far beyond grade standards, whereas others can make substantial progress only if instruction is geared to their needs. Such teachers are approachable, they welcome questions and other indications of a need for help, and they accept each child for what he or she is and can do. Instead of blaming other teachers, parents, or home and neighborhood conditions, they try to provide effective instruction for each child. Instead of being defensive when instructional problems arise, they try to find solutions to them.

The value of planning instruction to meet individual differences has been highlighted in the concept of mastery learning (see end-of-chapter reference by Bloom). In essence, this concept states that most students can master basic elements in a subject if diagnostic procedures are used, defined levels of performance are specified, instruction is individualized, each child is allowed the time he or she needs, and students are judged according to their ability rather than a normal curve. Individualization of instruction demands that every possible avenue be explored to equalize learning outcomes as well as learning opportunities. This is possible, it is argued, if each child is given the specific instruction and encouragement he or she needs and is not treated the same as all other children.

Mainstreaming   The mainstreaming of students in need of special educational services has further highlighted the value of planning to meet individual differences. When children with special needs are placed in regular classes, the learning of all students is enriched. Schools that mainstream students foster democratic attitudes and positive self-concepts and discourage negative labeling of others, problems that often arise when children with special needs are isolated in separate classes. Those who are mainstreamed benefit from acceptance and from the variety of role models they are exposed to. They also benefit from more positive expectancies on the part of teachers, parents, and other students. The social studies provide special opportunities because of the variety of activities and materials available for meeting individual differences.

Individual education plans (IEP) are prepared for students mainstreamed into classrooms in schools receiving funds through PL 49–142. The IEP for each student should include objectives, activities, materials, and evaluation procedures that are selected and adapted to meet individual needs. Techniques presented in this chapter may be incorporated into an IEP.

The mainstreaming of students with special needs does not require all teachers to become specialists in the education of exceptional children. Rather, it means that teachers must bring into play the strategies and techniques used to individualize instruction for all children. They should also adjust their instruction to meet the needs of the economically disadvantaged, the less able, and others, as discussed in later sections of this chapter. They should take maximum advantage of the assistance of specialists and the special services provided by the school district.

Planning
Guidelines

Various approaches to individualized instruction commonly follow guidelines that include management and instructional planning—two components of effective teaching. These two components are intertwined as teachers work with a given group of students. In many schools planning begins with needs assessment to identify objectives to be emphasized in various classes. Individual students within a class are diagnosed to pinpoint capabilities, reading level, and other characteristics. The instructional objectives grow out of needs assessment and diagnosis of individual students, setting the stage for decisions on management procedures and teaching plans. Detailed attention must be given to planning a multimedia approach to instruction, arranging the classroom environment, and including a variety of learning activities. The organization of groups, individual study, tutoring, variations and adjustments in teacher guidance, and varying allotted time to fit individual needs also require attention. Finally, standards and procedures of evaluation are modified to match the teacher's objectives to meet the needs and capabilities of students. Checklist 5–1 summarizes these guidelines and suggests focusing questions and points to check as plans are made.

Checklist 5–1
Planning to Meet Individual Differences

NEEDS ASSESSMENT

What special needs have been identified in terms of social studies objectives?

_____ Knowledge   _____ Thinking   _____ Skills   _____ Attitudes,
                           processes   values
_____ Other: _____

DIAGNOSIS OF INDIVIDUALS

What are individual needs, strengths, weaknesses, and achievements?

_____ Interests   _____ Capabilities   _____ Reading level
_____ Problems   _____ Talents   _____ Language skills
_____ Other: _____

INSTRUCTIONAL OBJECTIVES

What objectives should be stated to guide planning and evaluation?

_____ For individual students   _____ For handicapped students
_____ For less able students   _____ For gifted students
_____ Other: _____

USE OF MULTIMEDIA

What instructional materials are available and should be used to meet individual differences?

____ Reading materials on different levels	____ Audiovisual materials	____ Community resources
____ Learning kits or packages	____ Performance-based modules	____ Individual contracts
____ Rewritten material	____ Task cards	____ Taped material
____ Library materials	____ Practice materials	____ Study guides
____ Other: _____		

CLASSROOM ENVIRONMENT

How should the classroom environment be organized?

____ Learning centers	____ Classroom library	____ Viewing station
____ Listening post	____ Group work area	____ Interest centers
____ Other: _____		

USE OF A VARIETY OF LEARNING ACTIVITIES

What intake, organizing, applicative, and creative activities should be used?

____ Reading	____ Painting	____ Constructing
____ Writing	____ Listening	____ Making charts
____ Dramatizing	____ Classifying	____ Collecting
____ Composing	____ Reporting	____ Mapping
____ Observing	____ Role taking	____ Modeling
____ Outlining	____ Interviewing	____ Making murals
____ Drawing	____ Note taking	
____ Other: _____		

ORGANIZATION OF GROUPS

What groups should be organized to achieve various objectives?

____ Reading groups	____ Groups needing special instruction
____ Interest groups	____ Groups to make maps, murals, and other items
____ Committees	____ Groups of two or three for team learning
____ Learning centers	____ Groups for finding materials and for other activities
____ Other: _____	

PROVISION FOR INDIVIDUAL STUDY

What variations and adjustments can be made in individual study activities?

____ Topics to investigate	____ Depth of study	____ Type of report
____ Sources of data	____ People to interview	____ Use of library
____ Individual contracts	____ Use of free time	____ Activity cards
____ Other: _____		

PROVISION FOR INDIVIDUAL TUTORIAL

How can selected students be provided with individual tutoring?

____ By the teacher	____ By a teacher aide	____ By programmed material
____ By a parent	____ By another pupil	____ By computer
____ Other: _____		

TEACHER GUIDANCE AND SUPERVISION

What variations and adjustments should be made in the role of the teacher?

____	Questions	____	Individual assistance	____	Evaluation of learning
____	Directions	____	Assistance to groups	____	Involvement of parents
____	Explanations	____	Class discussion	____	Home visitation
____	Other: _____				

ALLOCATION OF TIME

What variations in time should be made for individuals and groups?

____	Introducing topics	____	Developing readiness	____	Completing activities
____	Assimilating ideas	____	Accommodating new ideas	____	Expressing ideas
____	Making maps or other items	____	Preparing oral and written reports	____	Making murals or other items
____	Other: _____				

STANDARDS AND EVALUATION

What variations and adjustments should be made in standards and procedures of evaluation of each student?

____	Vocabulary	____	Concepts	____	Main ideas
____	Thinking processes	____	Skills	____	Values
____	Self-evaluation	____	Testing	____	Informal evaluation
____	Gifted	____	Handicapped	____	Less able
____	Other: _____				

Key Aspects of Individualizing

IDENTIFYING INDIVIDUAL NEEDS

The teacher must know each child—background, achievements, interests, level of mental maturity, language power, and related abilities—to make adequate provisions for individual differences. In addition to checking cumulative records and available test data, the teacher should also informally diagnose needs during actual classroom activities. For example, as children engage in group planning, discussion, and evaluation, the teacher can identify interests, difficulties, language skills, and levels of understanding about selected topics. As children observe and interpret pictures, maps, graphs, and other resources, the teacher can identify those who need special help and those who have attained adequate levels of development. As students prepare reports, make murals, dramatize activities, and engage in other expressive experiences, the teacher can detect interests, needs for further study, and misconceptions.

Data obtained from tests should always be interpreted with caution. It is well known that intelligence tests do not give an accurate assessment of the ability of students from disadvantaged homes and neighborhoods, that they are culturally biased. Because tests and inventories designed to measure personality, attitudes, and social adjustment are even less reliable than achievement and intelligence tests, their data should be interpreted in the light of continuing direct study of childen as they work in the classroom.

Teachers should be careful not to set up situations that lead to self-fulfilling prophecies. Consider, for example, a child who is classified as less able, disadvantaged, or otherwise handicapped. Thereafter he or she is presumed to have all the characteristics of that classification, and as a consequence, instruction is shaped to fit the classification rather than the individual. Expectations may be set too low, with no challenge to move to higher levels of development or attainment. In one school district, a minority child from a disadvantaged neighborhood was placed in a fourth-grade classroom after the school psychologist and the teacher had used intelligence and achievement test data to establish what seemed to them to be reasonable expectations. But because of the ways he responded to questions, selected materials in the library corner, and participated in group discussion, the teacher realized that the child could reach higher levels in reading and other activities. Had the teacher not been alert, the student could have continued indefinitely at a low level of learning.

TEACHER GUIDANCE AND SUPERVISION

Probably no strategy for meeting individual differences can be modified and adapted on the spot more readily than that of varying the amount and kind of instructional assistance given by the teacher. For example, one child may need help in settling down to work, another may need help in completing an outline, and a group working on a map may be puzzled about the location of particular items. By moving about the room and observing children at work, a teacher can give guidance when it is needed. Because each child is a unique person, the teacher should tailor his or her approach to fit emotional as well as intellectual needs. A smile, an encouraging comment, or an understanding nod may be just right for one child, whereas another may need a thought-provoking question, a specific suggestion, or direct assistance on a problem.

At times a child may need and should receive a direct answer to a question—how to find a booklet, how to complete an outline, or where to locate particular items on a map. At other times the best answer is another question—Have you checked the study guide? Will the outline form on the chart be useful? Do you think the atlas will be a good source? If a student needs to move ahead, then direct assistance may be given, but if the objective is to improve inquiry skills and to help students become more self-directive, then a question or comment may actually be more helpful.

DIFFERING LEVELS OF CONCEPTUALIZATION

There are great differences in the levels at which children state main ideas, make interpretations of pictures and reading selections, draw inferences, and state generalizations. A less able student may interpret a picture of a harbor

How can independent study meet individual differences in investigating one's root culture?

scene by describing the main activities, whereas a more able student may go beyond description to point out the primary function of a harbor. The teacher should aim to progressively lift each student's thinking to higher levels. Examine the questions in charts 5–1 and 5–2. They begin at basic observing or recalling levels and move to interpreting, classifying, or other higher-level processes.

One individualizing technique is to provide questions on different levels and to accept levels of achievement that fit the capabilities of individual students. For example, some students might need to begin with the first question in chart 5–1, and then answer every succeeding question, in this way building their understanding to the levels represented by the last two questions. More able students might begin with the last two questions. In chart 5–2, less able students might work with the first two questions and present findings to the class; then all students might consider the findings as they discuss the next four questions. More able students might work on the last question and present their findings to the class for further discussion and analysis. Still another adaptation that could be made for able students would be to extend chart 5–1 to include a question such as How is location of the three most populous cities related to terrain and transportation facilities? Chart 5–2 could be adapted for less able students by reducing the number of industries to be studied to one or two.

Interpreting the Map of Mexico	Stating Main Ideas about Mexican Industries
What does each symbol in the key stand for?	What data did you find on each industry?
Where is the capital? What is its name?	Which facts seem to go together?
Where are other large cities located?	What is common or general about them?
Where are the main roads?	Have the common facts and ideas been grouped together?
What relationships can you find between the location of cities and roads?	What can we say in general about each industry?
How are the locations of cities, roads, and mountains interrelated?	Do our general statements fit the facts? Are changes needed?
	What is the order of importance of the industries? Why?

Chart 5–1   Chart 5–2

The same principle can be applied in adjusting expectations related to using concepts and making generalizations. Varied responses should be expected and accepted from students as they bring facts together and state main ideas. For example, compare the following generalizations, which vary in complexity and generality: (1) People in the home have different jobs. (2) Work is divided in the home and neighborhood. (3) Division of labor helps to get more work done. By accepting generalizations that fit the facts the student has collected, the teacher is recognizing and making an important adjustment to each child's ability.

PROVIDING DIFFERENT LEARNING ACTIVITIES

As noted in the chapter on unit planning, a variety of learning experiences should be provided to meet individual differences as well as to develop skills in using different types of materials. In providing for individual differences, two basic approaches should be followed. First, give students opportunities to engage in activities that they can handle with success. Encourage them to draw out ideas related to questions under study so that they can contribute to group planning, discussion, and evaluation. Using students' ideas in group activities extends learning, provides for interaction, stimulates interest in further learning, and gives all students a feeling that they are contributing to group goals. Second, plan and guide instruction so that every student engages in a variety of learning activities. All too frequently some students do a single activity over and over because they are good at it. For example, if students who are talented in art spend too much time painting and drawing, they may miss important learnings.

145

Chart 5–3

Chart 5–4

Chart 5–5

Chart 5–6

LEARNING CENTERS AND STATIONS

Setting up learning centers and stations helps to individualize instruction and also provides study and work centers for general use. A learning center that includes a variety of materials may be arranged and the materials changed for a particular unit of study. Learning stations may be set up to listen to tapes and records, to view slides and filmstrips, to make maps, to construct objects or process materials, to engage in games and simulation, to research and prepare reports on selected topics, or to provide other activities. Reading materials on different levels, task cards, individual activity cards, study guides, and other items designed to meet individual needs of students should be included. Students should be introduced to the materials in each center or station and given procedures for using them and rules to follow. Illustrative guidelines are presented in charts 5–3 through 5–6.

PROVIDING DIFFERENT AMOUNTS OF TIME

Probably no two people ever need or take the same amount of time to complete a given activity. Certainly this is true of students as they read, get ideas from maps, prepare reports, and engage in other activities. Varying

146

amounts of time are also needed in building readiness for the use of reading and other materials; for assimilating new concepts, and for fitting new ideas into one's existing framework of knowledge. If attempts at individualization are to succeed, the teacher must plan for variations in the time that may be needed to introduce a topic, collect and organize data, and express ideas in oral or written form.

DEVELOPING LEARNING CONTRACTS

One practical means of varying time, providing for choices, and using the other guidelines noted above to meet individual needs is to develop learning contracts. A learning contract is an agreement between a student and teacher stating what the student will do and when it is to be completed. A contract may be a brief statement of two or three items or a listing of several, as shown in these examples.

My Learning Contract

I _____ agree to do the following by _____ :

1. To find information on shipbuilding in Japan in *Japan,* by Cuban and Greenblatt; *Japan,* by Pitts; and *The World Almanac.*
2. To prepare a report on shipbuilding in Japan
3. To present the report to the class

Student's signature _____

Teacher's signature _____

Learning Contract on Water Pollution

Listed below are items we discussed in planning this learning contract. Read it and discuss with me any questions you have. We should discuss any changes before you begin.

OBJECTIVE

To state the causes and describe the effects of water pollution

MATERIALS

Use these reading materials to find definitions and information. Refer to the index of each book to find pages on which topics are discussed: *Air and Water Pollu-*

tion, Planet Earth, Voices of Earth, and *Water: Riches or Ruin.* Take notes on the following as they are shown to the class: *Water Pollution* (film) and *Water Pollution* (filmstrip).

QUESTIONS

1. What definitions are given for the terms *water pollution, sewage, run off,* and *industrial waste* in the glossary of *Planet Earth* or *Voices of Earth*?
2. What do you think are the main causes of water pollution?
3. What four main causes of water pollution are given in the reading materials? In the film and filmstrip?
4. Which causes of pollution did you list when you answered the second question?
5. What effects of water pollution are presented in the reading materials? In the film and filmstrip?
6. In what areas of the United States is water pollution most serious? Mark these areas on a desk outline map.
7. What steps are recommended to reduce water pollution?
8. What can you and members of your family do to reduce water pollution?
9. Do you believe government should make stricter laws to reduce water pollution? Why?
10. What would you recommend to be included in stricter laws? Why?

ACTIVITY

During the next week find examples of water pollution in our community. Look for news articles as well as activities of people. Suggest what might be done to stop pollution for each example that you find.

SIGNATURES

I, _____ agree to accept the responsibility for completing the above by
_____.

Teacher's signature: _____.

Learning contracts may be prepared cooperatively by a student and teacher, prepared by the teacher to meet a particular need, or prepared by a student to pursue a special interest. Whichever procedure is used, the student should fully understand what is expected and the teacher should be sure that the activities of the contract have value for the student and are not simply busy work. The following planning guide may be used to involve students in the planning of contracts.

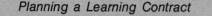

Planning a Learning Contract

1. My objectives are (state specific things you plan to accomplish):

2. I will use these materials (list textbooks, references, and other sources):

3. I will find answers to these questions (list questions you plan to answer):

4. I will complete these activities (list mapping, chart making, interviewing, and so on):

5. I will complete the contract by _____

Signature: _____

PROVIDING INDIVIDUAL ACTIVITY CARDS

The preceding guidelines can also be applied by preparing a set of individual activity cards or sheets, also referred to as task cards. The central idea is to provide activities or tasks that children can handle on their own. Each card or sheet should include a task, which can be stated as an objective, question, or project, along with a list of materials to use and questions and activities to complete. Here are three examples.

To Interpret Pie Graphs

Directions: Write your answers on a sheet of paper. Do not write on this activity card.

1. Find the pie graphs at the top of page 215 in *Towns and Cities*.
2. What color shows people who work on farms?
3. What color shows people who do not work on farms?

4. Do more people work on farms in Bolivia or in Brazil?
5. Which country has the fewest people working on farms?
6. List the countries in order by people working on farms. Begin with the country with the most people working on farms.
7. Why do you think so many more people work on farms in some countries than in others?

To Interpret Historical Maps

Directions: Write answers to the questions below on a sheet of paper, not on this activity card.

1. What is the title of the map on page 101 in *America: In Space and Time?*
2. What symbol is used to show the travels of Cartier?
3. What symbol is used to show the travels of LaSalle?
4. What symbols are used to show the travels of the other two explorers?
5. Which explorer traveled through Lake Ontario, Lake Huron, and Lake Michigan?
6. Which explorers traveled on the Mississippi River?
7. Which of the explorers do you think traveled the most important area in terms of development of our country? Why do you think so?

Stereotypes

OBJECTIVES

To explain the meaning of stereotypes and to state how to limit their influence on your thinking

MATERIALS

Read one or more of the following, using the index to find the pages on which stereotypes are discussed: *The Social Sciences, Concepts and Values; Still More Tell Me Why;* and the encyclopedia. Note ideas from the following as they are shown to the class: *People Are Different and Alike* (film) and *Recognizing Individual Differences* (filmstrip).

QUESTIONS

Answer these questions on a separate sheet of paper.

1. What definition of stereotype is given in the reading you selected?
2. What examples of stereotypes were noted?

150

3. What other examples can you think of?
4. What individual differences exist among members of your family? Are they all the same on any trait?
5. What individual differences exist among members of our class? Are they all the same on any trait?
6. What individual differences exist among whites, blacks, or Chinese?
7. Why is it unfair to judge you or a member of your family by a stereotype of your group?
8. Why is it unfair to judge each individual in a group by a stereotype of that group?
9. What can you do to avoid the judging of an individual in a group by a stereotype?
10. What can you do in a discussion when someone judges an individual by a stereotype?

ACTIVITY

Keep a list of stereotypes that you hear or read about or see on television during the next week. After each one note what you and others can do to limit its influence on your thinking and to be aware of individual differences among members of all groups.

Planning for Differences in Reading Ability

The wide range of reading ability that exists in every class calls for the same care in planning for reading in the social studies as in the developmental reading program. Teachers should collect information on each child, locate appropriate materials, group students for instruction, and develop students' ability to use self-directed reading strategies.

COLLECTING DATA ON EACH CHILD

Information may be obtained from standardized tests, from teacher-made tests, from tests and exercises in workbooks, and from observations of children as they read. This last source of information—observation—is especially helpful in getting clues to a child's ability to read social studies materials. Tests and exercises in workbooks that accompany social studies textbooks are helpful in getting specific information on strengths or weaknesses in such abilities as finding main ideas, noting details, using maps, and reading charts, graphs, and tables. Analysis of reading and study-skills tests provides clues to children's specific needs and problems.

After information is gathered, it should be summarized on a class sheet or on an individual card for each child and should include the items shown below.

Child's name _____ Age ____ Grade ____ Mental age ____
Reading group ____ Scores on reading tests ____ Scores on study skills
test ____ Reading level for individual reading ____ Reading level for group
instruction ____

Ability to use contents ____ indexes ____ glossaries ____

Ability to read maps ____ graphs ____ tables ____ charts ____ diagrams ____

Ability to use encyclopedias ____ atlases ____ dictionaries ____ card
catalogs ____

Comments (special notes on reading difficulties, interests, and the like)*

_____

_____

_____

_____

_____

LOCATING NEEDED MATERIALS

One of the best sources of information is the list of materials in resource
units for each grade. This usually includes materials that are available in the
local school system. In some school systems, kits of materials on varying readability levels have been assembled for different units and may be requisitioned
by the teacher. In other systems, materials may be requisitioned from the instructional materials center. Another good source is the list of additional reading materials included in basic social studies textbooks and accompanying
teacher's manuals, which may include poems, stories, biographies, and other
related materials.

The room library, school library, and neighborhood or community library
are excellent sources of reading material. Cooperation among teachers in sharing books contained in room libraries is helpful. For example, when such units
as our community, our state, or life in early America or other lands are being
studied, one should be sure that reading materials on various grade levels may
be found in different classrooms.

Guides to children's books and free or inexpensive materials should be
used to build up a basic collection of reading materials related to different units
of instruction (see references at the end of chapter 3, "Identifying and Using
Instructional Media").

*Right of privacy of students should be respected. Teachers should check school regulations to be
sure that they are followed.

How can a display such as this stimulate use of reading materials at each child's level of ability?

GROUPING FOR INSTRUCTION

Small-group instruction is most effective for developing vocabulary and comprehension skills, providing practice, and meeting needs that several children have in common. Groups may be organized on the basis of

1. *Achievement level,* in which those who read on approximately the same level are grouped together and materials on the appropriate level are provided for them
2. *Special needs,* in which students are given instruction in using the index, interpreting material, or other basic skills
3. *Assigned topics,* in which students are given a topic or problem to investigate in depth
4. *Common interest,* in which those who have chosen a topic or problem read materials related to it
5. *Partner* or *group-leader study,* in which one child assists a partner, or two or three children, in reading selected materials

The self-directed reading strategies that follow are designed to aid students in upper grades in reading on their own. A widely used one is SQ3R adapted from Robinson (see end-of-chapter references).

SQ3R

S (Survey). Get an overview; check the organization; read headings.

Q (Questions). Have questions to answer based on heading or topic sentences.

R (Read). Find answers to questions.

R (Recite). State or write answers to questions.

R (Reread). Clinch key ideas, check answers, reread key parts.

A helpful and creative activity is to guide students to create their own self-directed reading strategy as illustrated by the following example:

PROVE

P *(Purpose).* Set a purpose or questions to guide reading.

R *(Read).* Achieve your purpose or answer your questions.

O *(Organize).* Place details under main ideas.

V *(Vocabulary).* Note new concepts and words you mastered.

E *(Evaluate).* Did you achieve your purpose?

PREPARING REPORTS

Oral and written reports are an effective means of individualizing instruction. Each child may work on topics of special interest at a pace and level consistent with his or her capabilities. The variety of topics a child may choose is vast indeed, as the following sampling from a few social studies units shows.

Home and Family: How Work is Divided, Care of Pets, Workers Who Come to the Home, How Our Family Saves Energy, How Our Family Has Fun, How Families Have Fun in Other Cultures

Our Community: How Our Community Got Its Name, The First Buildings, The First School, Our Water Supply, Parks with Playgrounds for Children, The City Center Renewal Project, Ethnic Groups in Our Community

Our State: Where Native Americans Lived, The First European Settlers, The First Town, Early Travel Routes, Main Transportation Routes Today, How the Capital Was Chosen, Our State's Nickname, The Story of our State Flag, Products We Send to Other States, Our State's Largest City, Our State Parks, Environmental and Pollution Problems, Future Plans to Meet Problems

Living in Early America: The Plymouth Colony, Town Meetings, What Early Schools Were Like, Games Children Played, Help from Native Americans, How Clothing Was Made, Candle Making, The Saugus Ironworks, Being a Slave on a Plantation, Some of Ben Franklin's Inventions

Living in Other Cultures: Family Life, Foods They Eat, Family Recreation, A Day in the Village of _____ , Places to Visit, Special Customs and Holidays, Ways That We and the People of _____ Are Alike, Their Schools, Art and Music, Main Problems They Are Facing, Future Plans

Ideally, students will have no difficulty finding a topic that interests them. Specific suggestions for both oral and written reports are presented in social studies textbooks. Possible subjects for reports can be explored through group discussion. The teacher should suggest possible subjects to those children who do not choose one on their own so that they will have an opportunity to develop reporting skills and make contributions to class activities.

Guidelines for choosing a subject for a report and for preparing reports are presented in charts 5–7 through 5–10.

Students should be given opportunities to prepare both oral and written reports. Encourage them to supplement the reports with appropriate visual

---

Choosing a Subject

Why is the subject important? How is it related to our unit?

Why do you find it interesting? Why will others be interested?

Where can you find information on it? What sources of information do we have in our room?

Can you finish the report in our time limits?

Chart 5–7

Selecting Ideas for Reports

Think of questions that your report should answer.

List the main topics that you think should be included.

Find information related to each question or topic.

Look for new questions or topics that you may have overlooked.

Chart 5–8

Preparing Reports

State what the subject is in a good title and again in the introduction.

Put the main ideas in the order you think is best to relate them and hold interest.

Put the special points that are needed under each main idea.

Use or make pictures, dioramas, maps, charts, tables, graphs, or time lines to help show ideas or information.

State a short conclusion or summary.

List the sources of your information.

Chart 5–9

Proofreading Reports

Are capital letters used where needed?

Are words used correctly to give the meaning you want to give?

Are sentences complete?

Is the punctuation correct?

Are words spelled correctly?

Have you used the dictionary to check the spelling of new terms?

Has correct form been used for the title, margins, spacing, and sources of information?

Chart 5–10

materials. Informal oral reports by individuals and committees contribute much to class knowledge and discussion. Formal reports on books that have been read, special topics related to a unit, and individual and committee projects may be a part of concluding activities in a unit. In the early grades written reports may be dictated by children and recorded by the teacher. In later grades students can prepare individual papers, scrapbooks, notebooks, booklets, logs, or journals. As a useful team project for a class, start a class newspaper that includes reports on current topics and presents historical events in a "you were there" style.

INDEPENDENT STUDY HABITS

Good study habits are essential to the completion of learning contracts, activity cards, reports, and other individual activities. Because of the variety of opportunities for individual study, the social studies program is particularly well suited to developing effective study habits. Encourage students to apply the habits and attitudes learned in social studies at home and in the library. The foundations for good study habits should be established in the early grades, and refined as students advance. Proper attitudes and procedures are listed in charts 5–11 and 5–12.

Good Study Habits

Know your purpose and keep it clearly in mind:

Stop. Stop other activities so that you get clear directions.

Look. Watch the teacher so that you understand each point.

Listen. Remember the details on what to do.

Ask. Raise questions if you do not understand any part.

Proceed to do it:

Organize. Arrange materials and plan the steps to take.

Concentrate. Stick to your job and ignore distractions.

Finish. Complete the job before starting other activities.

Check. Review your work to be sure it is complete and well done.

Chart 5–11

Improving Home Study

Know exactly what you are to do.

Be sure to take the necessary materials home.

Plan your study time so that you will not have to stay up late.

Study in a place where you can work without interruption.

Arrange the study materials so that you can use them effectively.

Finish the job once you have started it.

Do your own work. (You may get advice on hard parts.)

Review your work and make any changes that will improve it.

Be ready to ask questions the next day on any parts that you do not understand or need help on.

Chart 5–12

In this new approach to learning, teachers provide instruction that enables children themselves to individualize. When the teacher also takes steps to individualize, each child's chances of getting tailored instruction are greatly improved. The guiding principle is to teach students specific ways in which they can vary materials, activities, time, individual work, group work, and standards to fit their own needs. In short, children should discover what has heretofore been kept secret by some teachers. If the goal of learning how to learn is to be achieved, children themselves must be able to identify and apply guidelines and techniques of individualization appropriate to their level of development. Charts 5–13 through 5–18 illustrate ways in which this can be done.

Planning for Special Students

Meeting the special needs of such groups of students as the economically disadvantaged, the less able, and the gifted takes careful planning. One of the many dangers of viewing and labeling students in such ways is that limited instruction will be provided. For example, if a teacher categorized

---

Because We Are Different

We vary the time on some activities.

We work as a class on some projects and in small groups on others.

We have projects each of us can do alone.

We find materials we can use.

We give help on some things and get help on others.

Chart 5–13

Can You Find

Reading materials that give you ideas on questions under study?

Maps, charts, diagrams, and other aids in books and references?

Pictures and clippings in newspapers and magazines that you can use in sharing and reporting?

Other sources of ideas?

Chart 5–14

What Ideas Can You Find

On questions and problems we are studying?

For use in group planning?

For use in discussion?

For use in committees?

For use in oral or written reports?

For other uses?

Chart 5–15

Use Free Time

To work on individual projects

To listen to tapes and records related to our unit

To view slides and filmstrips related to our unit

To find ideas in the picture file

To find materials in the reading center

Chart 5–16

---

a group of students as less able, he or she is apt to overemphasize drill and remedial work to the neglect of critical and creative thinking. A teacher may suggest creative activities for gifted students, forgetting that they also need basic instruction in the development of skills, concepts, and values. The following sections and the checklists within each of them call attention to special needs and guidelines that should be considered. They should not be viewed narrowly as applying only to a particular group, however. View each child as an individual and review all of the checklists when planning instruction for individual students. Many of the items on the checklist for gifted students, for example, are appropriate for students who are not labeled ''gifted.''

PLANNING FOR ECONOMICALLY
DISADVANTAGED STUDENTS

Children from economically disadvantaged homes and neighborhoods must in no way be viewed as culturally deficient, nor should they or the home be blamed for any disadvantages they have experienced. Rather, they should be provided every opportunity to develop their potentialities to the fullest. All children have a rich cultural heritage; they learn the language, customs, and other traits that are needed to function in their homes and neighborhoods. In addition, all children need to develop the ability to function in other settings in our society.

Never assume that students from economically disadvantaged homes will be less able learners. Some will be and some will not be less able; a wide range of ability exists in all social groups. What may appear to be low ability may in fact be a consequence of lack of instruction. Nor should you view economically disadvantaged students as a single group; instead see them as individuals who have not had access to the advantages of our economic system. Specific guidelines to consider are given in checklist 5–2.

158

_____ Encourage participation in question raising, planning, discussion, role playing, and other activities.

_____ Use language that clarifies objectives and directions for learning activities, giving attention to students' language patterns as appropriate.

_____ Develop language power, using bicultural-bilingual materials as needed.

_____ Develop positive self-concepts through growth of personal competence and appreciation of one's own heritage.

_____ Provide opportunities for constructive and rewarding interaction with students of differing backgrounds, stressing respect for each individual.

_____ Utilize special talents and backgrounds of students to develop self-esteem and enrich the learning of all students.

_____ Provide special units and learning activities that meet identified needs, including appropriate multicultural-multiethnic, law-focused, and career education as presented in chapter 7.

PLANNING FOR LESS ABLE STUDENTS

Less able or slower learning children have several characteristics that should be kept in mind as instruction is planned. In general, they have shorter attention spans and less ability to concentrate and to transfer learning than do average students. They need extra stimulation and encouragement to motivate learning; they need praise, commendation, and immediate rewards when they complete activities. Because of the difficulties they have in working with abstractions, they should be given a variety of concrete, firsthand experiences before they are asked to infer, generalize, or synthesize.

Less able students may need extra attention and more time to understand directions for activities. They will need careful explanations of concepts and themes encountered in instructional materials. They should be given additional opportunities for recalling and reviewing basic concepts and concept clusters in order to develop an understanding of the main ideas in a given unit. At times it may be necessary to take a small group aside to give special help in interpreting a map, identifying special features presented in a flow chart, or discussing ideas presented in a film or filmstrip. Guidelines for planning are given in checklist 5–3.

Checklist 5–3
Less Able Students

_____ Provide reading, and audiovisual materials that challenge them but are not beyond their capabilities.

_____ Prepare explanations to clarify objectives, questions, and directions for activities.

_____ Emphasize concrete and specific presentations and discussions.

_____ Provide review and extra practice to ensure learning.

_____ Extend time to complete map work, reports, and other activities.

_____ Prepare simplified study guides based on pictures, diagrams, and charts.

_____ Adjust number of concepts and level of development to challenge but not frustrate each student.

_____ Provide creative activities in art, music, role playing, and making things so that the thrill of self-expression is experienced.

_____ Utilize talents in dramatizing, drawing, and doing other activities in individual and group projects.

_____ Identify special contributions less able students can make in discussion and other activities such as reporting findings gleaned from pictures, maps, charts, diagrams, and easy-level reading materials.

_____ Identify students with whom they can work effectively in team learning, committee work, making murals, arranging displays, preparing group reports, planning contributions to discussion, and other group activities.

_____ Make summaries of achievement at frequent intervals to provide knowledge of progress and encouragement.

_____ Pay attention to regular feedback on progress, make commendations for effort, and give constructive assistance in self-evaluation in order to provide motivation.

_____ Provide for home study with guided home cooperation in finding and using reading materials, pictures, clippings, current events, and other items related to topics under study.

PLANNING FOR GIFTED CHILDREN

Academically talented and gifted students come from all ethnic groups and socioeconomic backgrounds. Some may have academic or intellectual potential far beyond those of their peers. Others may have special talents in artistic, literary, or other forms of expression. Still others may have a combination of intellectual, physical, and social potential that are exceptionally high. If these children are to attain optimum growth in all the objectives established for the social studies program, they need a balanced program. To overemphasize knowledge outcomes at the expense of inquiry processes or group work skills is not recommended. Nor should a student with special talent in art be allowed to spend too much time "making murals for the group" at a cost of neglecting other vital learnings. Like all children, gifted children need learning activities that develop all of their potentialities. Planning should include attention to the items in checklist 5–4.

_____ Provide a variety of challenging reading materials, maps, and other sources to optimize development of inquiry skills.

_____ Provide a balanced program of activities to promote well-rounded development of intellectual, social, physical, and emotional growth.

_____ Extend learning by means of additional opportunities to formulate hypotheses, draw inferences, state generalizations, synthesize main ideas, and contrast points of view.

_____ Provide many opportunities for independent inquiry, use of library and community resources, and synthesis of data from several sources.

_____ Emphasize self-direction, self-evaluation, and individual growth and achievement through practice activities and group work that meet individual needs.

_____ Encourage individual initiative and planning, leadership, concern for others, sharing, teamwork, and appreciation for different types of contributions.

_____ Provide direct instruction and guidance to develop basic skills, concepts, inquiry processes, and emotional stability and to avoid gaps or deficiences in essential learning.

_____ Extend learning through wide reading of materials that take students far beyond basic and supplementary texts.

_____ Emphasize positive traits and attitudes, such as individualism without being overbearing, self-criticism without being overly critical of others, and respect for intellectual attainment without lack of regard for other accomplishments.

_____ Provide opportunities for creative expression in individual and group work, oral and written reports, map making, construction, and other activities.

_____ Avoid activities that may be needed by other students but are boring or irrelevant to the needs and pace of learning of students, such as reteaching of selected material, reviews of concepts taught earlier in the week, drill on terms that may be useful for less able students, and other items already mastered by students.

_____ Provide home study with planned home cooperation to extend and enrich reading, construct models and other objects, use library resources, visit places, and interview experts to gather data on topics under study.

PLANNING FOR PHYSICALLY IMPAIRED CHILDREN

There are several guidelines for working with children who are hard of hearing, partially sighted, crippled, or have other disabilities or impairments. Taking a realistic approach helps each child face up to a given disability and to take positive steps to cope with it. Both teachers and other students should avoid oversentimentality and pampering on the one hand and completely overlooking a child's disability on the other. Avoid labeling children and making negative comparisons. Do not let a disability become an excuse for not attempting to teach a child, and do not let the child use a disability to avoid learning. Give special attention to finding learning opportunities. Each child's independence should be developed to a maximum. Make every attempt to discover and develop whatever special talents these children possess and to emphasize the contributions that they can make to both class and small-group activities.

Services available through the special education department should be used and cooperation with special teachers is essential to carry through procedures and activities that are most helpful. The involvement and cooperation of parents should be secured so that there is an integrated approach in which teachers, parents, and specialists work as a team. Examples of adjustments and variations that teachers can make are listed in checklist 5–5.

Checklist 5–5
Planning for Physically Impaired Children

HEARING IMPAIRED CHILDREN

_____ Speak in a normal voice, without shouting, to facilitate speech reading.

_____ Face students so that they can watch your lips, keep hands away from the face, and do not move about while speaking.

_____ Use a natural tone of voice with emphasis on clear enunciation.

_____ Get attention by touching a student or using an inconspicuous gesture.

_____ Introduce new vocabulary both orally and in writing.

_____ Provide written instructions for assignments and detailed directions.

_____ Use visual materials to clarify concepts, values, and main ideas.

_____ Avoid writing and speaking simultaneously while at the chalkboard.

_____ Have a classmate provide assistance when a situation arises in which a child cannot hear a speaker or recording.

_____ Encourage and supervise the proper use of hearing aids.

VISUALLY IMPAIRED CHILDREN

_____ Provide the best possible lighting and eliminate glare and shadows.

_____ Arrange seating for ease of seeing and hearing the teacher and members of discussion groups.

_____ Avoid exacting visual tasks over long or successive periods of time, blurred or hard to read worksheets, detailed and minute outline maps and graphic materials, and intricate art or craft activities.

_____ Provide appropriate materials such as widely spaced and heavily lined paper, pencils with very black lead, worksheets prepared on typewriters with large type, books with large type, raised relief and uncluttered maps, nonglossy paper, and projection magnifiers that enlarge material.

_____ Provide rest periods to reduce eye strain and tension.

BLIND CHILDREN

_____ Orient the child to the layout of the classroom, seating arrangements, work centers, teacher's desk, own work station, and other features.

_____ Provide "talking books" and material in Braille obtained from the library and special teacher.

_____ Have an aide serve as interpreter to transmit messages to a child manually by signing or finger spelling or through lipreading, and by communicating the child's questions or responses to the teacher (or others).

_____ Provide models, objects, and other realia that blind children can feel, touch, and manipulate.

_____ Use raised relief maps and globes to locate mountain ranges and other surface features by feeling them.

CHILDREN WITH SPEECH DIFFICULTIES

_____ Use activities suggested by the speech therapist and encourage children to apply newly developed skills in social studies activities.

_____ Encourage students to choose activities in which they feel secure, such as giving a chalk talk, using puppets, or participating in choral speaking.

_____ Call on those children who volunteer to contribute to discussion and give them time to respond without pressure or interruption.

_____ Avoid situations that create tensions, lower self-confidence, or create feelings of insecurity.

CRIPPLED CHILDREN

_____ Arrange seating for ease of entrance, exit, and participation in classroom activities.

_____ Emphasize independence in using crutches, braces, wheelchairs, or other devices.

_____ Provide assistance as needed to use scissors, references, equipment, or other resources.

_____ Make necessary modifications so that children can participate in group activities.

_____ Provide substitute activities in situations that demand physical capabilities children do not possess.

 Questions, Activities, Evaluation

1. Visit an elementary classroom and note the following:
   a. Differences among children in the use of language, work habits, involvement in activities, and the like
   b. Techniques and activities used by the teacher to meet individual differences
   c. Learning centers in the classroom and materials that might be used to meet individual differences
2. How might the basic strategies and techniques for meeting individual differences be put to use in a unit you are planning? Which are easiest to use? Which are hardest?

3. Prepare the following for use in a unit of your choice:
   a. A learning contract or individual activity card
   b. A plan for teaching a self-directed reading strategy to students
   c. A plan for teaching students to individualize for themselves
   d. Adaptations you might make in a unit for disadvantaged, less able, or other exceptional students discussed in this chapter

references

BLOOM, BENJAMIN S., *Human Characteristics and School Learning.* New York: McGraw-Hill, 1976. Mastery learning through individualized instruction.

BECHTOL, WILLIAM M., AND ANTHONY E. CONTE, *Individually Guided Social Studies.* Reading, Mass.: Addison-Wesley Publishing Co., 1976. Procedures for a systematic approach to individualized instruction.

HALLAHAN, DANIEL P., AND JAMES M. KAUFFMAN, *Exceptional Children: Introduction to Special Education.* Englewood Cliffs, N.J.: Prentice-Hall, 1978. Suggested adjustments for children with learning disabilities, speech disorders, and other special needs.

LARKIN, JAMES M., AND JANE J. WHITE, "The Learning Center in the Social Studies Classroom," in *Social Studies and the Elementary Teacher: Promises and Practices,* (bulletin 53), ed. William W. Joyce and Frank L. Ryan. Washington, D.C.: National Council for the Social Studies, 1977. Procedures for setting up centers.

ROBINSON, FRANCIS P., *Effective Study.* New York: Harper & Row, Publishers, 1970. Procedures for improving study habits.

SMITH, ROBERT M., AND JOHN T. NEISWORTH, *The Exceptional Child.* New York: McGraw-Hill, 1975. Chapter on fundamental instructional practices.

INCORPORATING CONCEPTUAL AND PROCESS COMPONENTS FROM THE SOCIAL SCIENCES

What concepts, concept clusters, themes, and generalizations can be drawn from the social sciences?
How are concepts used to prepare focusing questions?
What values, models, modes, and methods of inquiry may be put to use in the social studies program?

In every area of the curriculum, instruction is rooted in material drawn from the basic disciplines. The disciplines are sources of both conceptual and process knowledge. *Conceptual,* or substantive, knowledge includes data, concepts, themes, and generalizations; it may be referred to as "know that" content. *Process* knowledge is knowledge about values, models, and methods of study and inquiry; it may be referred to as "know how" content.

In the social studies program, content is drawn from the social sciences and other disciplines. This chapter presents examples of conceptual and process components drawn from a selection of these disciplines. First the core disciplines are examined; then widely used concepts, themes, and generalizations are noted; and finally focusing questions are presented to illustrate how concepts are used as tools to guide study and inquiry. As you study the chapter, try to formulate additional questions that can be used in a particular unit of instruction. The final section of this chapter examines the values, models, and methods of inquiry for promoting study and learning in the social studies.

Core Disciplines

The social studies program draws content from geography, history, economics, political science, anthropology, sociology, psychology, and philosophy. Aspects of law are receiving increased attention, and material from art, music, and literature continues to be important in culture studies.

A few points about the general nature of the disciplines of primary importance in planning should be noted. Geography, history, and anthropology are highly integrative disciplines. Geography is rooted in both the physical and social sciences, and in the schools it is used to give a well-rounded view of areas under study. History may bring together material from the social sciences and such humanities as art, literature, and philosophy to give an integrated view of human events in various periods of time. Cultural anthropology includes comparative studies of the values, beliefs, social structure, economic activities, political organization, aesthetic and spiritual expression, technology, and artifacts of selected cultures. These three disciplines are used extensively to synthesize content: geography in a spatial context, history in a time context, and anthropology in a cultural context.

Political science and economics, the policy sciences, are more specialized and focus on decision-making activities. Material from these two disciplines may be brought into units based primarily on history, geography, or anthropology, or it may be presented in separate units.

Sociology and social psychology, behavioral sciences (as is anthropology), are sources of concepts (such as roles, groups, institutions, processes of interaction, and social control) used extensively throughout the social sciences and in social studies. These fields contribute much to the study of contemporary societies, social problems, and social change. They also provide, along with anthropology, economics, and political science, many concepts used in cultural geography and history.

Philosophy provides concepts and methods of analysis and reasoning invaluable in social studies and used throughout the social sciences. Inferring, using criteria to make judgments, finding fallacies in statements, and studying the grounds for beliefs all call for logical analysis and reasoning. In fact, much of what is done in the social studies in the name of critical thinking can be related to philosophic modes of study.

Chart 6–1 shows several features of the disciplines from which the bulk of social studies content is drawn. It includes examples of concepts that are used to organize and process information. Notice that under history a time gap is shown by means of a broken line; this highlights the fact that past events are not observable and so must be studied nonempirically by referring to whatever records or other remains are available to the historian. Notice also that historical data may be structured around themes within periods, by areas (such as countries), and around topics (such as the Constitution). The section on geography shows how four central concepts may be used to structure the myriad of detailed information on the location of various phenomena. In other sections selected concepts are connected to show interrelationships. For example, decisions made in the economic system are central in determining production, income, consumption, and so on. The study of political behavior calls for the use of several concepts, such as those grouped around the political system. The study of culture calls for study of social, economic, political, and expressive patterns of behavior, as noted in the section on anthropology. The section on

The Core Disciplines

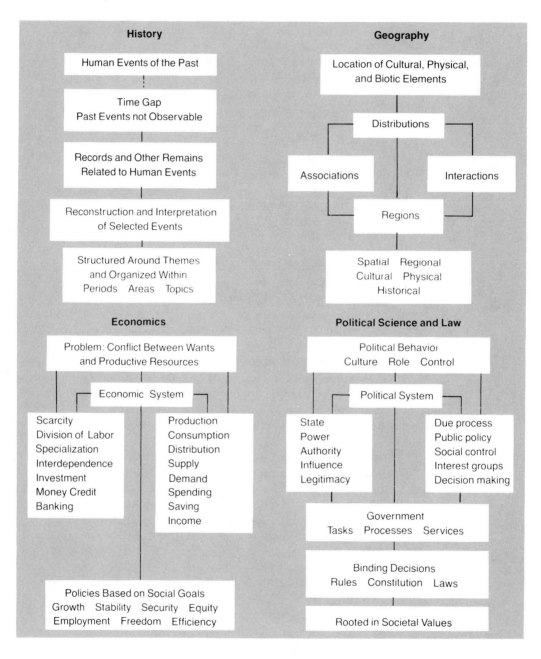

History

Human Events of the Past

Time Gap
Past Events not Observable

Records and Other Remains
Related to Human Events

Reconstruction and Interpretation
of Selected Events

Structured Around Themes
and Organized Within
Periods   Areas   Topics

Geography

Location of Cultural, Physical,
and Biotic Elements

Distributions

Associations   Interactions

Regions

Spatial   Regional
Cultural   Physical
Historical

Economics

Problem: Conflict Between Wants
and Productive Resources

Economic System

Scarcity
Division of Labor
Specialization
Interdependence
Investment
Money Credit
Banking

Production
Consumption
Distribution
Supply
Demand
Spending
Saving
Income

Policies Based on Social Goals
Growth   Stability   Security   Equity
Employment   Freedom   Efficiency

Political Science and Law

Political Behavior
Culture   Role   Control

Political System

State
Power
Authority
Influence
Legitimacy

Due process
Public policy
Social control
Interest groups
Decision making

Government
Tasks   Processes   Services

Binding Decisions
Rules   Constitution   Laws

Rooted in Societal Values

Chart 6–1

The Core Disciplines *(continued)*

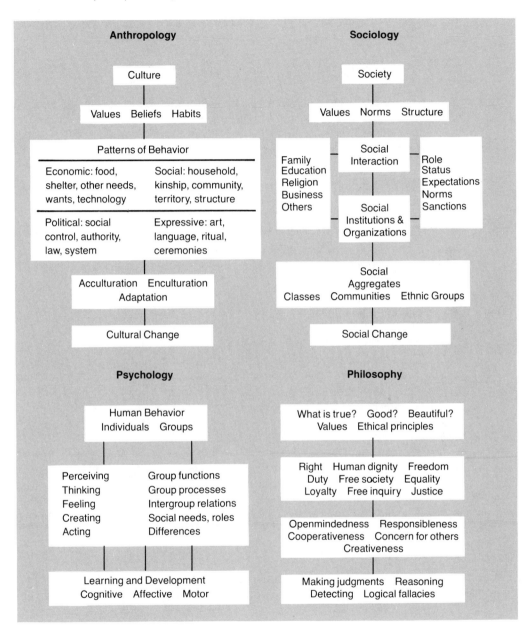

Anthropology

Culture

Values   Beliefs   Habits

Patterns of Behavior

Economic: food, shelter, other needs, wants, technology	Social: household, kinship, community, territory, structure

Political: social control, authority, law, system   Expressive: art, language, ritual, ceremonies

Acculturation   Enculturation
Adaptation

Cultural Change

Sociology

Society

Values   Norms   Structure

Family
Education
Religion
Business
Others

Social
Interaction

Social
Institutions &
Organizations

Role
Status
Expectations
Norms
Sanctions

Social
Aggregates
Classes   Communities   Ethnic Groups

Social Change

Psychology

Human Behavior
Individuals   Groups

Perceiving
Thinking
Feeling
Creating
Acting

Group functions
Group processes
Intergroup relations
Social needs, roles
Differences

Learning and Development
Cognitive   Affective   Motor

Philosophy

What is true?   Good?   Beautiful?
Values   Ethical principles

Right   Human dignity   Freedom
Duty   Free society   Equality
Loyalty   Free inquiry   Justice

Openmindedness   Responsibleness
Cooperativeness   Concern for others
Creativeness

Making judgments   Reasoning
Detecting   Logical fallacies

Chart 6–1 *(continued)*

sociology illustrates the breadth of study involved in analyzing society. The section on psychology deals with key concepts related to the study of the behavior of individuals and groups. Central concepts from philosophy are illustrative of key values, processes, and behaviors central to making judgments.

IDENTIFYING STRUCTURAL COMPONENTS

One step in good planning is to have a concise statement of the structural components of core disciplines. There is no agreement on a single structure for any given discipline, nor is a consensus likely in the near future. Many helpful statements have been prepared, however, as noted in the references at the end of this chapter. In these statements, both conceptual and process or inquiry components may be identified. The conceptual components are

> *Concepts,* such as culture, region, values, division of labor, and role
>
> *Concept clusters,* such as factors of production (land, labor, capital, know-how)
>
> *Themes,* such as the growth of industry and the westward movement
>
> *Generalizations,* such as "culture is a primary determiner of how people use the environment"

The process components are

> *Values of inquiry,* such as objectivity, open-mindedness, and search for truth
>
> *Models of inquiry,* including such phases as defining the problem, stating questions or hypotheses to guide study, classifying and interpreting data, and drawing conclusions
>
> *Methods and materials of inquiry,* such as content analysis of source materials, interviews of individuals, and examination of objects

Most programs include all of these in one form or another. Concepts and concept clusters may be identified in all materials that are based on the social sciences. Generalizations and themes are widely used in organizing content and learning experiences within units of instruction. Values, models, and methods of inquiry are used in varying degrees, depending on the extent to which inquiry is emphasized in the program.

Conceptual Components

Teachers need concise summaries of the conceptual components included in materials to use as a checklist for instructional planning. Each of the summaries presented in the following pages is based on a review of the references cited at the end of this chapter and on materials available to students. Key concepts have been identified for each discipline. Examples of widely used concept clusters have been included to emphasize the point that many key concepts are multidimensional—that is, they include other concepts that must be given specific attention. The examples of generalizations are similar to those found in instructional media. Examples of focusing questions are given to show how concepts and thinking processes can be linked together to guide study and move thinking to higher levels.*

Teachers should add other items to the lists as particular units are planned, including concepts and other elements that are in the materials students will use. The concepts in students' materials are the ones that they will be using, but the teacher may introduce others to improve study and learning.

GEOGRAPHY

Most units of instruction draw extensively on geography to clarify the characteristics of areas under study and the interaction of people with their cultural and natural environments. Five approaches to geographic study are given varying degrees of emphasis throughout the program. *Earth science*, or *physical geography,* is the study of landforms, water bodies, climate, and other physical features. *Area,* or *regional, geography* brings together the physical and cultural features that give the particular place its distinctive characteristics. *Cultural geography* focuses on ways of living and on human use of resources and ecology, with attention to relationships between culture and the environment and between resource use and adaptations to and modifications of the environment. *Locational,* or *spatial,* approaches focus on location of places, relations between places, and the distribution or arrangement of cities, populations, and other features. *Historical geography* deals with changes over time and brings together selected aspects of physical, regional, cultural, and spatial approaches.

Such special fields of study within geography as urban, economic, and political geography are also drawn upon to enrich learning. Concepts from urban geography—zones of a city, specialized cities, settlement patterns, and central places—are valuable. They are used to analyze inner, middle, and outer zones of students' own and other cities. They help students to identify and classify specialized cities as manufacturing, transport, government, or commercial cities. They are used to identify settlement patterns within a given region on a continuum that ranges from isolated settlement, village and town, to suburb, city, metropolitan area, and megalopolis (for example, the area stretching from north of Boston through New York to south of Washington, D.C.).

Major cities such as New York, Chicago, London, and Tokyo, which serve large areas from a central core, are studied separately as are towns and cities that serve relatively smaller areas. Special attention is given to the goods and services central cities provide, their accessibility, and their importance in the social, economic, and political activities of the people they serve. Urban sprawl may be investigated in comparative studies of cities that have mush-

*See chapter 9 for strategies to develop conceptual components.

Social Studies Workshop, University of California, Berkeley

What landforms are clearly evident? What patterns do they make?
Where are the great plains?

roomed outward in a series of concentric circles, strips, and other patterns. The sphere of influence of a city may be studied in terms of the impact of its activities on its satellite cities and towns. The internal structure of a city may be studied, starting with streets in the neighborhood and extending to how the land is used in inner, middle, and outer zones for business, industrial, residential, recreational and other purposes. The study could include transportation networks, the location of the central business district, and relationships to the suburbs. Social variation as reflected in ethnic enclaves and ghettos and in residential areas that reflect differing income levels could also be included.

Concepts from economic and political geography are used to study relationships between communities, states, and nations, changing boundaries, the struggle for resources, and trade between areas. The importance of wise use and conservation of resources is accentuated in studies of resource use, beginning with the local community and extending to studies centered in areas round the world. The importance of resources along with capital, labor, and know-how, a key concept cluster in economics and economic geography, is helpful in analyzing and comparing selected countries and regions. Of paramount importance is the steady growth of the concept of interdependence that begins to emerge in a local context and is extended and deepened throughout the program to lead to the concept of global interdependence.

One of the most pervasive impacts of geography is in instruction on map and globe concepts and skills and map making. Because of their importance, chapter 12 is devoted to them. The examples given here focus on the concepts, concept clusters, illustrative generalizations, and inquiry-conceptual questions that may be drawn from other aspects of geography.

Concepts

The environment; earth-sun relationships; location, spatial distribution, areal association, spatial interaction; region and regionalizing; cultural, physical, and biotic elements; resources; population, urbanization; culture regions; change

Concept Clusters

The environment: spheres (hydrosphere, lithosphere, atmosphere, biosphere or life layer), human elements (people and their works), physical elements (land, water bodies, climate), biotic elements (plants, animals)

Earth-sun relationships: source of energy, rotation, revolution, inclination and parallelism of axis, circulation of atmosphere, seasons, night and day

Location: position (absolute—latitude and longitude; relative—near a known place); site (natural location such as island, continental, or maritime location); situation, such as relative location (strategic, central, or adjacent)

Major landforms: plains, hills, plateaus, mountains

Water bodies: rivers, lakes, bays, straits, seas, oceans

Natural resources: water, soil, animal life, plant life, minerals, climate

Factors in climate: sunlight, temperature, precipitation, humidity, winds, altitude, latitude, major water bodies, mountain systems, ocean currents

Population: size, distribution, centers, density, composition, growth rate, movement, prediction, control, problems, productive potential

Settlement patterns: isolated, village, town, suburb, city, metropolis, megalopolis

Urbanization: growth of urban centers, central cities, location, functions, internal structure (residence, business, industry), interaction with other places, accessibility, changing occupancy patterns, migration, invasion, segregation, desegregation, redevelopment, urban sprawl, urban planning

Specialized cities: manufacturing, commercial, transport, port, government, other

City structure: inner, middle, outer zones; central business district; residential, industrial, suburban areas

Culture regions: Western, non-Western: European, Soviet, Middle Eastern, North African, Southwest Asian, South Asian, Southeast Asian, East Asian, Africa, Anglo-American, Latin American, Australian–New Zealand, Pacific

Generalizations

The location and productive activities of a community are key factors in its interaction with other places.

People everywhere identify and use resources in ways that are shaped by their culture.

Regions defined in terms of one or more common features may vary depending upon the time period and objective of inquiry.

Urbanization has necessitated the redevelopment of cities and better planning for the use of space.

Change takes place constantly on the earth's surface.

Focusing Questions

What natural resources are shown in this map [interpreting]?

What do you think Japan can produce with such limited natural resources [hypothesizing]?

What are the advantages and disadvantages of urbanization [analyzing]?

What kind of map should we make to bring together and show how transportation routes and cities are interrelated [synthesizing]?

Four spatial concepts merit special comment because they may be used to structure geographic data within regions of varying size. These four concepts are helpful in any unit that deals with the spatial arrangement of surface features: they can be used at all levels of instruction if they are couched in appropriate language. Definitions and examples of the four concepts are presented below, along with questions that illustrate how they may be used to guide the study of topics at various levels.

spatial distribution *Spatial distribution* is the pattern or arrangement of phenomena on the earth's surface. Examples are homes around the school, residence, and business sections of a community, highways, wheat-growing areas, population distribution, mineral deposits, climate patterns, mountain systems, and drainage systems in selected areas. Illustrative questions are

> How are homes arranged around our school [observing]?
> What is the population distribution along the East Coast [interpreting]?
> How can we show the distribution of population on our map [synthesizing]?

areal association *Areal association* refers to how distributions are related, how they tend to be found together. Examples are homes and schools, homes and shopping centers, plains and farming, cattle and corn production, and harbors and shipping. Illustrative questions are

> Why are homes and schools usually found near each other [generalizing]?
> What do you think we will discover about how cattle and corn production are related [hypothesizing]?
> How can we explain the relation between elevation and kind of vegetation [interpreting]?

spatial interaction *Spatial interaction* is the flow, movement, or circulation of phenomena. Examples are the movement of children to and from school, people to and from stores, ideas via newspapers and other mass media, and goods and people via transportation networks. Illustrative questions are

> How do we get from home to school and back [recalling]?
> How can we show what is brought from other cities into our city [synthesizing]?
> How do goods, people, and ideas circulate throughout our state [analyzing]?

region A *region* is a defined area that is relatively homogeneous in one or more characteristics. Examples are neighborhoods in a community, defined areas around the community, regions of a state or the United States, regions within other countries, and culture regions of the world. Illustrative questions are

> What is the area around our schools [recalling]?
> How might our state be divided into regions [analyzing]?

What regions can we find in our books [observing]?
Why were they grouped that way [inferring]?

The last question is designed to develop an understanding of regionalizing as the process of using criteria to define regions. Experiences in all grades should contribute to competence in handling the concept of regionalizing as students define regions for various purposes and discover the reasons why others have defined regions in similar and different ways.

Notice in chart 6–2 how basic concepts are used to study areas or regions that vary in size from local areas to states, regions, countries, or groups of countries. The key concepts of distribution, association, interaction, and region guide students as they analyze and synthesize data on the physical setting and on the people and their activities. Notice also how concepts from several disciplines are used, particularly in the study of people and their activities. The order of study may vary, studying either people or setting first, or shuttling back and forth between the setting and people. Typically, a unit first clarifies the setting, then considers how people have used and changed the environment.

some cautions   Several points should be made regarding problems that often arise as geography is studied in the social studies program. Because so many facts are avail-

---

Model for Study of an Area

FOCUSING QUESTIONS

What is the location of the items below? What patterns of distribution can we find?
Which of the items tend to go together? What patterns of association can we find?
What relationships are there between and among items? What patterns of interaction can we find?
How can the area be defined as a region? What characteristics or criteria should we use?

THE PHYSICAL SETTING

Space: area, shape, natural and political boundaries, relation to other areas
Landforms: plains, hills, plateaus, mountains, patterns made by them
Water: underground, rivers, lakes, bays, straits, coastlines, other
Climate: temperature (range, average); growing season; precipitation (average, seasonal amounts, causes)
Resources: soil, water supply, vegetation, animal life, minerals

THE PEOPLE—HUMAN ACTIVITIES

Population: number, growth rate, shifts, settlement patterns, central cities
Economics: agriculture, industry, trade, transportation, communication, relations to other areas
Political system: ideology, government, administrative units, relation to other areas
Culture: links to others, values, social classes, institutions, art, music, literature, changes, history
Problems and plans: economic, political, health, education, urban, ecological, other

Chart 6–2

able on various cultures, cities, and regions, it is easy to fall into the trap of teaching a mass of facts about a variety of topics. It is far better to study selected areas in depth and to view facts as data to be used in solving problems, answering inquiry-conceptual questions, and testing hypotheses. Data should be organized around concepts, concept clusters, and generalizations; students should investigate the use of resources, adaptations to the environment, why cities have developed in some places and not in others, values and levels of technology, and the like. A related pitfall is to emphasize superficial and romanticized studies of bizarre and exotic features of various lands and peoples. The inevitable outcomes are stereotypes and misconceptions.

In the middle and upper grades a curricular issue is the value of a depth study of selected cultures in an area versus an overall study of cultures in the area. The issue has been resolved in some schools by giving an overview of a large region or area followed by an intensive study of one or more representative cultures or countries within the area. Care must be taken so that pupils do not generalize about all countries within the area on the basis of the single country studied in depth. Although certain common geographic, economic, political, and cultural characteristics are to be found among countries in the Middle East, in Africa, or in Latin America, specific differences exist that can be grasped only by studying each country in detail. When representative countries are studied, pupils should understand that the purpose is to get a view of certain characteristics that are generally typical of the area, but that may be manifested differently in other countries. For example, many countries in Africa aspire to improve standards of living, better educational and health services, increased industrial output, and stable government, but the specific ways and means employed to attain them vary greatly from country to country.

The outmoded concept of environmental determinism has been rooted out of most new materials and should be rooted out of instruction. Geographers take the position that although environmental conditions are key factors to consider as ways of living are studied, they are not *the* factors that *cause* ways of living. If this were so, all people in desert areas, for example, would live the same way. Students can quickly discover differences in ways of living in similar environments and interpret them in terms of differences in culture. And they can discover how interaction with the environment changes as changes occur in a people's culture by studying their own community, state, and nation as well as other lands.

When referring to places relative to the equator, the terms *middle latitudes, high latitudes,* and *low latitudes* should be used. The terms *temperate, frigid*, and *torrid zones* are climatic rather than locational terms, and they are not accurate descriptions of climatic conditions in the particular zones they are used to designate. Since some writers still use the terms, however, children should become acquainted with them and understand the inaccuracies and limitations that exist in their usage. An example of how one group of children in the sixth grade handled this problem is shown in chart 6–3.

1. Low latitudes are between 23½ degrees north and south of the equator; this area is sometimes called the torrid zone.
2. Middle latitudes are between 23½ and 66½ degrees north, and between the same degrees south; these areas are sometimes called temperate zones.
3. High latitudes are between 66½ degrees north and the North Pole, and the same degrees south ·and the South Pole; these areas are sometimes called frigid zones.

Chart 6–3

HISTORY

The social studies program contains much material from history. Changes in family life from colonial times to the present, growth of the community and state, United States history, and selected historical developments in other countries have traditionally been included. A promising new addition is oral history. Students interview firsthand observers of events and old-timers in the community, record their accounts, play them back, and interpret and analyze them. They may also listen to oral accounts taped on cassettes, such as *Geronimo: His Own Story, Hard Times,* and *The Immigrant.* Information gathered from oral accounts is synthesized with information from other sources.

Many of the conceptual elements used to interpret and synthesize historical information are drawn from other disciplines. For example, role, division of labor, and cultural borrowing may be used to explain changes in family life, communities, and nations in different periods of time. Time, process, and organizing concepts are also widely used in historical materials, and special emphasis is given to events and themes, as the following summary shows.

Concepts

Time concepts: time, day, week, month, season, year, decade, generation, century, millennium, B.C., A.D., period, epoch, age, era, prehistoric, ancient, medieval, Middle Ages, modern

Process concepts: criticism, analysis, and synthesis of primary and secondary sources; reconstruction of events; interpretation; periodization

Organizing concepts: event, theme, period, place

Events and Themes

Events and themes in local history: first settlers, homes, school, and church; beginning as a town; growth of population, transportation, communication, business, education, public services, the arts; contributions of individuals and groups; problems of growth

Events and themes in United States history: discovery and exploration, living in the colonies, gaining independence, establishing a government, living on the frontier, the westward movement, the growth of sectionalism, the Civil War, the period of reconstruction, growth of agriculture and industry, becoming a world power, the growth of cities, contributions of ethnic groups

Interpretations and Generalizations

Changes in communities have been the result of the actions of many individuals and groups.

Interdependence has increased rapidly in recent times.

Social problems and institutions of today have roots in events of the past.

Ideas about self-government were strengthened on the frontier.

Multiple causes and consequences must be considered in studying events.

Time and space form a framework within which events can be placed.

Focusing Questions

What periods can we use to group events in the growth of our community [classifying]?

How can we show (or report on) the growth of industries in our state [synthesizing]?

What were the most serious acts of discrimination against native Americans during the settling of the West [evaluating]?

ECONOMICS

There have probably been more advances in economics education in recent years than in any other segment of the social studies. Newer instruction materials include a clearly defined set of concepts and main ideas drawn from economics. Concepts such as division of labor are introduced in the beginning

179

How can data gathered at historical sites be used to reconstruct events? What sites in or near your community can be used by students in a unit you are planning?

grades as children compare the production of cookies or other items on an "assembly line" with individual production. The differences between producers and consumers and between goods and services are discovered as children investigate roles of family members, community workers, and people in other places to find out who produces and consumes various goods and services. The opportunity-cost principle is put to use as students consider such questions as "What does Billy give up if he spends his allowance for candy?"

180

"What does a family give up when they take a trip instead of spending the money for other things?" "What does a country sacrifice when it decides to produce some things and not others?" Basic conceptual elements follow.

Concepts

Conflict between wants and resources, scarcity, division of labor, specialization, interdependence, comparative advantage, goods, services, consumers, producers, factors of production, production, consumption, exchange, distribution, market, supply, demand, prices, money, banking, credit, saving, spending, investing, trade, economic systems, economic values, opportunity-cost principle, trade-offs

Concept Clusters

Basic economic problem: conflict between wants and resources, need to make choices, need for an economic system to allocate resources to alternative uses

Specialization: division of labor by occupations, technological applications, and geographic situation; resulting interdependence

Productive resources: human (workers, managers, know-how), capital (tools, machines, factories), natural (soil, water, climate, minerals, forests)

The market: means of allocating resources; interaction of supply and demand; use of money, transportation, and communication; modification by policies related to economic goals

Economic systems: market-directed or private enterprise, centrally directed or command, tradition-directed, mixed

Economic goals: equity, growth, stability, security, freedom, employment, efficiency

Generalizations

Members of families, people in communities, and societies meet the basic economic problem by finding answers to these questions: What shall we produce? How shall we produce? How much shall we produce? How shall we distribute what is produced?

Division of labor increases production and leads to interdependence among individuals, communities, states, and nations.

People in a market system have more freedom of choice than people in a command system.

Firms produce goods and services in a modified market system under policies set by government to protect consumers and producers.

In our system the government provides certain goods and services such as highways, schools, protection, and welfare services.

Focusing Questions

What goods and services are produced at home [recalling]?

How is their use of resources similar to ours? How is it different [comparing]?

What changes in agricultural production in our state are shown on this graph [interpreting]?

What do you think are our most valuable resources? Why [evaluating]?

POLITICAL SCIENCE AND LAW

Material from political science has traditionally been included in social studies under the title of civics. Now we are moving beyond civics to include dynamic aspects of the uses of power and authority in the home, school, and other institutions as well as in government. There is also a trend to include material from law, such as legal rights and responsibilities of individuals and groups. Because elements drawn from political science and law are interrelated, they are treated together in this section. (Additional examples are included in the section on law-focused education in chapter 7).

In the early grades instruction calls attention to rule making, rule applying, and the settling of disputes in situations familiar to children. Later these concepts are extended to legislative (rule making), executive (rule applying), and judicial (rule adjudicating) processes of local, state, and national government. Attention is given in community studies to the mayor, city council, teachers, police, and other public employees; to public services such as education, protection, and recreation; to city planning and redevelopment; and to metropolitan planning to solve transportation and other cross-community problems. State and national studies include such concepts as authority, separation of powers, due process and equal protection of law, and processes of government. Historical studies include material on contributions of the Greeks and Romans to government, the Magna Carta, changes in laws in England, law and government in early America, case studies of struggles for justice, and great documents such as the Declaration of Independence and the Constitution.

Studies of our own and other lands include material on uses of power and authority by leaders, type of government, roles of officials, and relations with other countries. These and other topics may be structured around the following conceptual elements.

Concepts

State, power, authority, political system, government, constitution, rules, laws, legal system, legal processes, civil liberties, due process, equal protection, justice, freedom, responsibility, diversity, privacy

Concept Clusters

Tasks of government: external security, internal order, justice, public services, freedom (under democracy)

Processes: rule making (legislative), rule applying (executive), rule adjudicating (judicial)

Public services: police, fire, postal, education, health, welfare, sanitation, conservation, recreation, labor, business

Due process of law: protection against arrest without probable cause, unreasonable search and seizure, forced confession, self-incrimination, and double jeopardy; right to public trial, counsel, fair judge and jury, habeas corpus, knowledge of accusation; right to confront and cross-examine witnesses, to have witnesses for one's defense, to the assumption of innocence until proven guilty

Sources of law: the Constitution, statutes, common law, administrative rulings, decrees

Generalizations

Rules and laws provide for social stability and control, equality, and individual freedom; they limit behavior that endangers life, liberty, and property.

All societies have individuals and groups with the authority to make, carry out, and evaluate decisions related to individual and group welfare.

Due process of law is needed to provide equal opportunity, protection, and justice for all individuals and groups.

Civil liberties—freedom of thought, speech, press, worship, association, and petition—are essential to human freedom.

Conflicts arise when individuals and groups have competing goals, apply different standards of conduct, and interpret laws differently.

Laws are nonviolent means of handling conflicts.

Focusing Questions

Why do we need rules in school to limit what we do [analyzing]? Why do we need laws in the community to limit what people do [analyzing]?

How are public services like and different from private services [comparing]?

How is equal protection defined in this reading selection [interpreting]?

Which ideas for providing equal protection of all groups in our community do you think are best? Why [evaluating]?

What processes of government are common at the local, state, and national levels [generalizing]?

How can we use the Bill of Rights to decide what is just or unjust in this case [interpreting, evaluating]?

ANTHROPOLOGY

Many concepts and key ideas from anthropology are now included in programs of instruction as the contributions this discipline can make are recognized. Anthropology is especially valuable in developing attitudes, understandings, methods of inquiry, and skills related to the comparative study of cul-

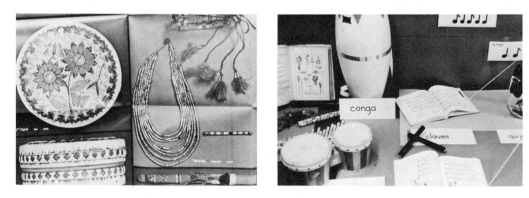

Berkeley, California

How can artifacts such as these be used to develop concepts and appreciation of aesthetic expression in cultures under study?

tures. The inclusive ''culture'' concept, in which values, beliefs, and patterns of learned behavior are brought together in a unified view of ways of living, is the basis for many units of instruction—for comparative studies of families, villages, and communities as well as for studies of selected areas, prehistoric peoples, and early civilizations. Specific units on Eskimos, native Americans, village life in Africa, and other peoples include anthropological material on food, shelter, clothing, utensils, social organization, arts, crafts, rituals, ceremonies, and other aspects of culture. Illustrative conceptual elements follow.

Concepts

Culture, society, values, beliefs, tradition, customs, change, social organization, role, technology, community, civilization

Concept Clusters

Culture: learned patterns of behavior; ways of living; arts, crafts, technology, religion, economic activities, language, other learned behaviors

Processes of cultural change: invention, discovery, diffusion, adaptation

Food-getting activities: gathering, hunting, fishing, herding, gardening, agriculture

Societies: folk or preliterate, preindustrial, transitional, industrial

Families: nuclear, extended; functions (biological, affectional, economic, social)

Community: territory, common culture, collective action; folk, peasant, urban

Characteristics of civilization: writing, accumulation of food and other goods for managed use, division of labor, government, arts, sciences, urbanization, trade

Generalizations

Culture is socially transmitted in all societies, differs from society to society, and is a prime determiner of behavior.

Families around the world have common needs, but they meet those needs in different ways.

Major differences among people are cultural, not biological.

Food-getting activities are closely related to level of technology.

Focusing Questions

What do these art objects and crafts tell us about their culture [inferring]?

What do you think we will find to be the main causes for the change from hunting and fishing to herding [hypothesizing]?

How can we group these societies [classifying]? Folk? Preindustrial? Transitional? Industrial?

In general, what conditions were necessary for the rise of civilization [generalizing]?

SOCIOLOGY

Concepts and key ideas from sociology are included in many units of study. The family and school, two basic social institutions, are usually studied early in the program. The positions and roles of members of the family, the teacher, and other school personnel are included. Values and expectations of children, parents, teachers, and community workers are considered in the context of children's relationships to each other and to adults. Norms and sanctions and their relation to social control are discovered through the children's own experiences and in units that include material on customs, regulations, rewards, punishments, and laws in communities and other places near at hand and far away. In the same manner, understanding of processes of social interaction, such as cooperation, competition, and conflict, are also developed. Historical and geographic studies centered on the community, state, nation, and other places typically include such sociological concepts as role, groups, institutions, values, and social change.

Structural elements drawn from sociology are closely related to those drawn from anthropology and psychology, as shown in the following examples.

Concepts

Society, values, norms, role, status, expectations, social institutions, social processes, groups, social control

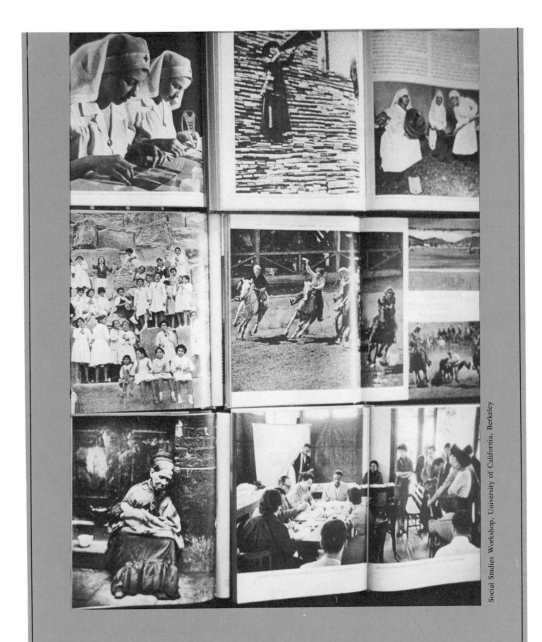

Social Studies Workshop, University of California, Berkeley

How is the role of women changing in our country and in other countries? Why is it changing faster in some areas than in others?

PSYCHOLOGY

Concepts and key ideas from psychology are embedded in units of study at all levels of instruction. For example, the concept of individual differences is important in studies of families, schools, community workers, and people in other places. How the senses—seeing, hearing, touching, and others—help one to observe and to learn may be included early in the program. The importance of attitudes, motives, and interests as key factors in human behavior is brought home in both contemporary and historical studies of people near at hand and far away. How to control feelings and what happens when feelings are not controlled are considered in the context of children's own experiences and in studies of others. Students are taught effective ways of learning; they are taught how to remember and use what is learned and how to improve critical thinking and problem solving. Illustrative conceptual elements follow.

Concepts

Senses, learning, remembering, group processes, attitudes, perceptions of others, personal-social needs, individual differences, intergroup relations, social roles

Concept Clusters

Using our senses to learn: seeing, hearing, smelling, touching, tasting, balancing

Learning and remembering: clear purposes, meaning, practice, use, review, application, grouping around main ideas, contrast, comparison, concentration, knowledge of results, ideas in own words

Perception of others: previous experience, needs, motives, attitudes, expectation, current condition of perceiver, self-concept

Group processes: goal setting, planning, doing, evaluating, decision making

Personal-social needs: acceptance, belonging, security, achievement, self-expression, interaction with others, learning, self-actualization

Individual differences: appearance, personality, role, attitudes, beliefs, family, customs, learning, abilities, habits

Social roles: leadership, followership, aggression, submission

Generalizations

Individual differences exist among members of families, children in schools, and people in communities.

Perceptions of others vary from individual to individual and are conditioned by a variety of factors.

Both individual and group needs may be met through group action.

Learning and remembering can be improved by concentrated effort.

An individual takes different roles in different groups and situations.

How do we use our senses to learn [generalizing]?

What does this picture show about individual differences [observing, interpreting]?

What does that kind of behavior show about their values [inferring]?

What do you think will happen if the leadership is changed [predicting]?

PHILOSOPHY

Better classified as a humanity than as a social science, philosophy is included as a core discipline because concepts related to values and various aspects of inquiry are emphasized in social studies. Wide agreement exists that knowledge about such values as freedom, equality, responsibility, loyalty, and patriotism should be emphasized along with the positive attitudes and feelings needed to make them enduring qualities. Students should also understand the nature of logical fallacies, the meaning of the spirit of philosophical inquiry, and the processes involved in making judgments. The following value-related elements are found in most social studies materials.

Concepts

Values, moral and ethical principles, rights, duty, freedom, equality, justice, truth, human dignity, patriotism, loyalty, free society, free inquiry, common good, individual interest, responsibility, cooperation, creativity, open-mindedness, concern for others

Concept Clusters

The spirit of inquiry: longing to know and understand, questioning of all things; search for data and their meaning; demand for verification; respect for logic; consideration of premises, causes, and consequences

Logical fallacies: appeal to force, argument from ignorance, appeal to pity, emphasis on false cause, snob appeal, neglect of all causes, false premises

Making judgments: clarifying what is to be judged, defining related criteria, analyzing in terms of criteria, making the judgment, checking the judgment with others

Generalizations

The basic value of human dignity underlies our way of life. Free societies keep open the path of free inquiry for their own well-being.

Criteria should be defined in terms of values and used to decide what is good or ought to be.

Ideas and proposals must be subjected to critical examination if their value is to be determined.

Focusing Questions

What values should we use to judge the treatment of minority groups [recalling]?

How does enlightened loyalty differ from blind patriotism [comparing]?

Who can explain the statement that human dignity underlies our way of life [interpreting]?

How can equality of opportunity be improved for this group [analyzing]?

Process Components

Values, models, and methods and materials of inquiry are dynamic aspects of the core disciplines used to investigate topics, questions, and problems. Values of inquiry indicate the attitudes held by those who truly search for the best new ideas and test old ideas about human relationships. Models of inquiry are helpful guides in the study of problems; they are also helpful in planning a balanced program. Specific methods of inquiry can be put to use in units of instruction at all levels.

VALUES OF INQUIRY

Free and open inquiry is clearly valued by anyone who wants to find the best possible explanations for cultural and natural phenomena. Individual opinion, tradition, pronouncements of authorities, and other ideas not based on critical study must be opened to review and investigation.

Several values of inquiry are stressed in current materials and in teaching guides and units of instruction. Especially important are

Curiosity about the causes and consequences of human behavior and ways of studying human relationships

Definition of terms in precise language so that the meaning is clear

Awareness of the effects of one's own background, views, feelings, position, and values on the way problems are viewed, how they are studied, and how findings are interpreted

Objectivity so that findings will be reliable and can be readily checked by others

Skepticism marked by thoughtful questioning and critical review of methods of study, findings, interpretations, and conclusions

Search for evidence to test hypotheses, answer questions, support conclusions, and weigh alternatives

Respect for differing views based on evidence gathered through systematic study and critical analysis of causes and consequences

Regard for logical thinking in defining problems, framing questions and hypotheses, making plans for study, classifying and interpreting data, and drawing conclusions

Rigorous analysis of assumptions, premises, biases, possible errors, special meanings, ideas behind interpretations, and other subjective aspects of inquiry

Corroboration, or double-checking of findings, by repeating studies and making comparisons with the findings of others

Although few individuals hold and practice these values fully, they can serve as ideals toward which to guide the study of human relationships. A beginning can be made early in the social studies program, for curiosity is characteristic of all children and can be kept alive by exploring a variety of problems. Such values as clear definition of terms, demand for evidence, and analysis of ideas can be developed as problems and topics are studied in different units of instruction. Objectivity, control of feelings, thoughtful skepticism, and respect for differing views can be nurtured by considering such questions as

Will we get the same result if we do it again?

Are we consistent in the way we do it?

Did we control our feelings about it?

Is this a good idea because we like it or because it works?

Is this a fair statement?

What questions do we have about it?

Where might mistakes have been made?

What is good about that idea?

How can we use that idea?

Is that a sound argument?

Models must be used flexibly and must be adapted to problems under study. Rigidly following predetermined steps irrespective of new insights gained as one studies a topic is the antithesis of sound thinking. Creative thinking is a key ingredient in inquiry and should be employed to the fullest to adapt models to differing situations.

Models of inquiry used in different disciplines have been adapted from the references at the end of this chapter and are presented in chart 6–4. Notice that the general pattern or sequence begins with identification of problems and ends with conclusions or interpretations and suggestions for further studies. The importance of helping children grow in the ability to identify problems cannot be overemphasized. Also, the need to be on the lookout for what to study next should not be neglected. These two elements of inquiry are directly related to the goal of developing competence in learning how to learn. Notice that the section in the center of the chart lists common phases of inquiry. Note the similarities between these points and those listed under individual disciplines.

Careful analysis of the models in chart 6–4 reveals that for most purposes in the social studies one can use a generalized model that incorporates basic features common to all. In fact, the general model for guiding group inquiry presented in chapter 9 includes the common aspects of inquiry noted in this chart. Sometimes, however, study can be sharpened by relying mainly on two other models. The example given for anthropology is especially useful when planning or conducting field trips (detailed information for field trips is presented in chapter 3). The models for political and economic analysis have much in common and are useful in analyzing and managing value conflicts and in decision-making studies.

METHODS AND MATERIALS OF INQUIRY

In drawing methods and materials from the social sciences the underlying principle is to use only those that are most helpful for obtaining the data needed to attain stated objectives. In historical studies, techniques involved in analyzing and synthesizing data from records and other remnants of the human past are used extensively. In studies of contemporary problems, a variety of techniques and data sources may be needed to obtain up-to-date information.

The various methods of inquiry outlined below are adapted from reports on various disciplines and from recent social studies materials. They should be referred to and used as guides when planning units of study. Students need opportunities to develop skill in using many different methods of gathering data. By embedding them in units of instruction, it is possible to make them an integral part of the problem-solving process.

Models of Inquiry

GEOGRAPHY

Identify and define the topic or problem to be studied.

Consider all factors that may be related.

State questions or hypotheses related to each factor.

Gather data related to each hypothesis or question.

Evaluate and organize data to test hypotheses or answer questions.

Interpret findings and draw conclusions.

Suggest other needed studies.

ANTHROPOLOGY

Define objectives or questions for the field study.

Make a plan for gathering and recording data for each objective or question.

Make necessary arrangements.

Gather data by direct observation, interview, and participation (if feasible).

Organize and interpret data in light of objectives.

Summarize findings and draw conclusions.

Compare findings and conclusions with those of others.

HISTORY

Define the question or problem to be studied.

State hypotheses or questions to guide study.

Collect and evaluate sources of information.

Analyze and synthesize data in the sources.

Organize findings to answer questions and test hypotheses.

Interpret findings in relation to social, economic, and political developments.

COMMON PHASES OF INQUIRY

Define the problem and clarify objectives.

State questions or hypotheses to guide study.

Make and use a plan to gather data.

Appraise, organize, and interpret data.

Make and check conclusions.

Consider further needs for study.

SOCIOLOGY

Define the problem and relate it to existing knowledge.

State hypotheses to guide study.

Select an adequate sample.

Use appropriate techniques to gather data.

Organize and analyze the data to test each hypothesis.

Interpret findings and draw conclusions.

Suggest other studies.

POLITICAL ANALYSIS

Define the problem and clarify related values.

Consider different choices or solutions.

Evaluate each choice or solution in terms of values, facts, and historical background.

Identify possible consequences of each choice or solution.

Evaluate the consequences in light of values.

Make judgments as to which choice or solution is best in terms of values.

ECONOMIC ANALYSIS

Define the problem. Where are we and where do we want to go?

Identify goals and rank them in order of priority.

Consider alternative ways to attain goals with usable resources.

Use concepts to explore the problem and effects of alternative proposals.

Complete an analysis of each alternative in terms of goals.

Choose the best alternative to achieve goals.

Chart 6–4

Collecting Data

SOURCES

Written materials: textbooks, references, letters, diaries, minutes, newspapers, magazines, government reports and documents, business records, biographical materials, case studies

Art objects: paintings, murals, tapestries, vases, plaques, medals, jewelry, wall paintings, portraits, ornaments, sculpture

Orally transmitted materials: folklore, legends, sagas, ballads, anecdotes, stories, eyewitness accounts

Recorded materials: photographs, slides, films, tapes, records, maps, diagrams, graphs, charts

Inscriptions: monuments, plaques, buildings, coins, clay tablets, walls, grave markers, bridges, art objects

Physical remains: buildings, monuments, implements, tools, utensils, weapons, pottery, baskets, clothing, textiles, costumes, furnishings, musical instruments

TECHNIQUES

Content analysis of printed materials, films, and other instructional media to gather data on meanings of terms, changes and trends, uses of resources, sex bias, treatment of minority groups, use of words to stir the emotions, underlying assumptions, and the frequency of occurrence of other items under study

Field trips to collect data on farming, business activities, conservation, transportation, communication, artifacts in exhibits, and other topics under study

Observation of activities of family members, construction workers, and other community workers; of the roles of police, firefighters, and other public officials; of changes in the weather and seasons; of meetings of the city council, school board, and other groups

Interviews, polls, and questionnaires to gather data from fellow students, parents, community officials, business people, health workers, experts on conservation, and other experts on issues and questions under study

Role playing and simulation of activities and decision making in families, markets, banks, and other situations in which identification with others and involvement in decision-making processes are important

Experiments to determine what happens when different procedures or treatments are used, such as selecting and testing hypotheses about division of labor or presenting objects of varying sizes or colors to find out how one's perception of them changes

Recording, Organizing, and Presenting Data

Make notes on or record data obtained through interviews and on field trip.

Construct maps to show the distribution of homes, businesses, population, resources, and other phenomena; how such distributions as transportation networks and cities are related; and the flow of people, goods, and services between places.

Construct models, diagrams, graphs, tables, and charts of objects and processes under study to demonstrate and explain how they work and how they are used.

Prepare sketches, drawings, displays, and exhibits to illustrate processes, show the uses of objects, and highlight relationships between objects and human activities.

Prepare reports, oral or written, to share findings and conclusions with others.

Evaluating Inquiry and Materials

Keep logs, diaries, or other records for use in evaluating both individual and group activities.

Construct and use rating scales, charts, and checklists to appraise reports, maps, films, other sources of information, and individual and group activities.

Participate in discussions to appraise and improve the effectiveness of both individual and group inquiry.

Questions, Activities, Evaluation

1. Examine two or three social studies textbooks and note examples of the following:
   a. Concepts, concept clusters, generalizations, and inquiry-conceptual questions
   b. Models and methods of inquiry suggested in the related teacher's manual
   c. Relative attention to material from core disciplines
2. Examine a course of study and do the same.
3. Examine a unit of instruction and do the same.
4. Which of the models of inquiry presented in this chapter do you prefer? Discuss your choice with others and defend your position.
5. Which of the methods of inquiry do you think will be most useful in a unit you plan to teach? Note examples of how they might be used.

6. Prepare six to eight inquiry-conceptual questions, using concepts presented in this chapter.

references

BANKS, JAMES A., AND AMBROSE A. CLEGG, JR., *Teaching Strategies for the Social Studies,* (2nd ed.). Reading, Mass.: Addison-Wesley Publishing Co., 1977. Social inquiry, separate chapters on disciplines, value inquiry model.

MACHART, NORMAN C., "Doing Oral History In the Elementary Grades," *Social Education,* 43 (October 1979), 479–480. Practical examples and suggestions.

MICHAELIS, JOHN U., AND A. MONTGOMERY JOHNSTON, eds., *The Social Sciences: Foundations of the Social Studies.* Boston, Mass.: Allyn & Bacon, 1965. Chapters on eight core disciplines; major generalizations from the social sciences in appendix.

MORRISSETT, IRVING, AND W. WILLIAMS STEVENS, JR., eds., *Social Science in the Schools: A Search for Rationale.* New York: Holt, Rinehart & Winston, 1971. Sections on the disciplines.

MUESSIG, RAYMOND H., AND VINCENT R. ROGERS, *Social Science Seminar Series.* Columbus, Ohio: Charles E. Merrill Publishing Company, 1965. Volumes on history, geography, economics, political science, anthropology, and sociology.

PRESTON, RALPH C., AND WAYNE L. HERMAN, JR., *Teaching Social Studies in the Elementary School.* New York: Holt, Rinehart & Winston, 1974. Chapters on social sciences.

WESLEY, EDGAR B., AND STANLEY P. WRONSKI, *Teaching Secondary Social Studies in a World Society.* Lexington, Mass.: D.C. Heath & Company, 1973. Chapters on history and social sciences.

INCORPORATING MULTICULTURAL, GLOBAL, LAW-FOCUSED, ENVIRONMENTAL, AND CAREER EDUCATION

focusing questions

What guidelines may be used to incorporate instruction recommended by
various groups?
How are goals and objectives of various programs related to goals and
objectives of the social studies?
What conceptual components are emphasized in different programs?
How may focusing questions be generated to guide study?
What types of learning activities should be provided?

Over the years many different educational programs have been advocated by
the federal government, private groups, and various agencies and organizations.
During the past decade high priority has been given to multicultural, multiethnic, ethnic heritage, law-focused, global, career, environmental, energy,
and values education. The improvement of reading ability has been stressed as
a responsibility of all teachers in all subjects in which reading is used. Teachers
face the challenge of incorporating these programs into the social studies and
other subjects while still maintaining a strong program of developmental instruction.

This chapter discusses multicultural (including multiethnic and ethnic heritage) education, global education, law-focused education, environmental and
energy education, and career education. Chapter 13 presents values education,
and chapter 11 presents procedures for improving reading. The resource unit in
the appendix includes additional material on environmental education.

Grateful acknowledgement is made to Nina Gabelko, University of California, Berkeley, for
suggestions included in this chapter.

There are several guidelines for incorporating recommended programs in the social studies. The following apply to unit planning and to lesson planning as well as to overall program planning.

GOALS

The goals of each program should be clarified to identify their relationships to goals of the social studies and other subjects. For example, although multicultural education is strongly related to the social studies, aspects that deal with aesthetic expression can be included in art, music, and literature. Career education should be a part of all subjects that offer opportunities to develop career awareness. Environmental education is a vital aspect of science education. After goals are clear, the teacher can decide whether to develop interdisciplinary units or to treat materials as a part of a single subject. This is far better than attempting "to do it all" in the social studies.

Goals must also be translated into instructional objectives, as noted in chapter 1. Examples are given in the sections that examine the particular programs.

CONCEPTUAL COMPONENTS

To plan instruction on solid conceptual foundations, key concepts, concept clusters, themes, and descriptive and prescriptive generalizations should be identified.* These conceptual components serve as tools of study, provide a structure for organizing information, and help to generate focusing questions. They also help in preparing plans for developing main ideas, concepts, vocabulary, and the reading-language skills essential to effective learning.

FOCUSING QUESTIONS

Special attention should be given to the generation of focusing questions to guide study. Key concepts and thinking processes should be linked together to focus instruction on central ideas and to lift thinking from the recall level to the generalizing, analyzing, and higher levels.

LEARNING ACTIVITIES

A variety of learning activities should be identified to add zest to learning and to meet individual differences. The full range of activities—initiating, data gathering, organizing, applicative, and expressive activities—should be included, as suggested in the chapter on unit planning. Consider including opportunities for action projects, such as involving students in improving human

*See chapter 9 for strategies to develop conceptual components.

relations in school or improving the environment and curbing pollution in the community.

TEACHER REFERENCES

Volumes that deal specifically with recommended programs should be consulted. Those that teachers have found to be especially helpful are listed in the references at the end of the chapter.

PITFALLS TO BE AVOIDED

When a special program is introduced there is a very real danger of getting so involved in "our new program for the year" that the developmental social studies program is neglected. As one teacher put it, "This year we are doing career education. I'll get back to social studies next year, I hope."

Another pitfall is "drumming in the facts" about our ethnic group, environmental problems, or other topics. This approach is contrary to the recommendations of educators from various ethnic groups and experts on environmental education. Both of these dangers can be avoided if concepts, concept clusters, themes, and generalizations are used to organize information.

The use of exhortation, polemics, and scare tactics when dealing with environmental, ethnic, global, or other problems should also be avoided. Such techniques are self-defeating and must be replaced by an emphasis on critical thinking and decision making.

Another problem is overemphasizing one aspect within a program, such as focusing on pollution problems and neglecting conservation and other aspects of environmental education or dwelling on a single ethnic group to the exclusion of others.

Finally, there is the temptation to present ideas and concerns of interest to the teacher and other adults, but far beyond the comprehension of elementary students. Fascinating as they may be to the teacher, theories of race relations in ethnic studies, technical aspects of nuclear waste disposal in environmental studies, and diplomatic relations in global education are beyond the grasp of children. Such topics are better postponed until students have the background and maturity to understand them.

Multicultural Education

In this section the term *multicultural education* is used in its broadest sense to include multiethnic, bicultural, and ethnic heritage studies in a comparative culture context. The trend today is to study the ethnic minority experience within the totality of human experience. High priority is given to developing an appreciation of one's own and other cultures and to eradicating racism, classism, sexism, ethnocentrism, prejudice, and discrimination. Value systems, life styles, cultural heritages, and current conditions are studied along with the cultural contributions of various ethnic groups. Knowledge of one's own and other groups is brought together to answer these questions: Who am I? Who are we? Who are they? What is special about each individual? Opportunities are provided for students to learn about their root culture, the derived culture of their ethnic group, and the common culture all of us share.

The reality of cultural and ethnic pluralism should be recognized and viewed as a source of cultural enrichment rather than as a divisive factor. All ethnic groups should have opportunities to participate fully in societal institutions and still maintain their ethnic identity if they so desire. They should be able to say "I am an American" in addition to "I am an Afro-America," or "I am an Italian-American," or whatever. No longer can the equality of opportunity and justice that are guaranteed by the Constitution be denied because of prejudice and discrimination. Ethnic identification should be encouraged for those who desire it, with full respect accorded those who seek it and those who do not.

Guidelines have been recommended for curriculum design and instructional planning for multicultural education (see end-of-chapter references by Banks and Grant). The school environment and the hidden as well as the visible curriculum should be attuned to ethnic pluralism, learning styles and cultures of children from various groups, local conditions and resources, and ethnic group languages. Multicultural education should be provided for all students, not just children from minority groups. Attention should be given to the disparities between ideals and realities, ways of narrowing the gap, and the decision-making and participatory skills for making needed changes. Studies of the history, culture, and current conditions of several ethnic groups should be provided. Cross-cultural comparative studies are needed, and events should be interpreted from different ethnic perspectives. Consideration should be given to the influence of African, Mexican, and other cultures on our multicultural society and to ways we can still learn from them.

GOALS AND ILLUSTRATIVE OBJECTIVES

The following goals show the breadth of multicultural, multiethnic, and ethnic heritage studies. Each goal is followed by an example of a related instructional objective that illustrates a specific student attainment.

1. To develop understanding of cultural diversity in our society, of diversity within and among ethnic groups, of ethnic heritage as a factor in life style, and of the history, culture, and achievements of ethnic groups

    Describe gaps between the professed ideals of our society and current realities for native Americans.

2. To apply thinking and decision-making processes to ethnic issues through such activities as differentiating facts from interpretations and inferences, interpreting events from various ethnic perspectives, making cross-cultural analyses and

syntheses of data, proposing action programs, and evaluating proposals and actions

> Evaluate proposals for eliminating racism, prejudice, and discrimination by ranking them in order according to your judgment of their effectiveness.

3. To develop skills needed for participating in different ethnic groups, for communicating with both majority and minority groups, for resolving conflicts, and for taking action to improve current conditions

> Describe steps of procedure that may be used to clarify an issue and to make a plan to resolve it.

4. To develop attitudes, values, and behavior supportive of cultural diversity and ethnic differences, a willingness to combat racism and prejudice, each student's self-concept, respect for individual differences, a sense of political efficacy, and appreciation of diversity as a factor in cultural enrichment

> State reasons why everyone in our society must be accorded justice, equal protection, and due process of law.

CONCEPTUAL COMPONENTS

The following examples illustrate conceptual elements drawn from various disciplines (for a detailed list see end-of-chapter reference by Banks [1979]):

CONCEPTS

Culture	Ethnicity	Racism	Pluralism
Heritage	Race	Ethnocentrism	Assimilation
Lifestyle	Minority	Stereotype	Power
Status	Discrimination	Prejudice	Social protest

How can new interpretations of history contribute to a clearer understanding of the roles and achievements of members of ethnic groups?

Richmond, California

CONCEPT CLUSTERS

Social Interaction: cooperation, competition, conflict, assimilation, accommodation

Democratic values: justice, equality, liberty, concern for others, use of intelligence to solve problems, respect for human dignity

Americans: Afro-, Anglo-, Cuban, Chinese, Japanese, Jewish, Puerto Rican, Italian, German, Greek, and so on

THEMES

Cultural and ethnic pluralism   Unity and diversity in our society
Social protest and action   Discrimination against minority groups

DESCRIPTIVE GENERALIZATIONS

Conflicts tend to develop between the major group and minority groups in a community.

Cultural diversity exists within ethnic groups as well as among ethnic groups.

American culture has been enriched by the achievements of members of many different ethnic groups and cultures.

PRESCRIPTIVE GENERALIZATIONS

The gap between democratic values and social realities must be eliminated.

All groups have a responsibility to take action that will eliminate racism, prejudice, and discrimination.

Civil rights guaranteed by the Constitution must be extended to all groups in our society.

FOCUSING QUESTIONS

The following examples of questions illustrate how concepts and thinking processes may be brought together and sequenced to lift students' thinking:

What different *races* are shown in the pictures at the beginning of this reading [observing, interpreting]?

How does the author define the terms *ethnic group, minority group,* and *race* [interpreting]?

Which of the groups discussed in the reading are *ethnic* groups? Which are *minority* groups [classifying]?

In what ways have the responses of *minority* groups to *discrimination* been similar? In what ways have they been different [comparing]?

In general, which *ethnic* groups have been *assimilated* in our society? Which have not [generalizing]?

Why do you suppose certain ethnic groups resisted *assimilation* [inferring]?

Why do you think some groups formed *ethnic enclaves* in cities? How can your idea be checked [hypothesizing]?

What principles of organization have some *ethnic* groups used to increase their *political power* [analyzing]?

How can we organize and present our findings on the goals, actions, and achievements of *social protest* groups [synthesizing]?

What do you think *social protest* groups will do during the next decade? Why do you think so [predicting]?

Which *actions* have been most effective in achieving goals? Why? Which have been least effective? Why [evaluating]?

ILLUSTRATIVE LEARNING ACTIVITIES

The learning activities presented below are illustrative of those included in multicultural, ethnic heritage, and multiethnic resource units.

Activities for Multicultural Education

In early grades, identify and value unique characteristics and individual differences among members of one's class and members of other groups:

1. Make and share "me books" in which each child includes pictures and drawings that show "what is special (unique) about me," including age, height, weight, and skin color; liked and disliked foods; favorite toys, games, television programs, and other items; things that make me happy and sad; size and composition of my family.
2. Make and share books that show unique characteristics, customs, and behavior of a child in a different ethnic group or culture, similar in format to the "me books" noted above.
3. Make comparative picture charts that show what is unique or special about my family and a family from a different ethnic group.
4. Complete statements such as these:
   A family can be made up of _____.
   Special things about my family are _____.
   Special things about other families are _____.
   Foods my family likes are _____.
   Foods other families like are _____.
5. Make picture charts or booklets of various ethnic groups here and in other lands to show how basic common needs for food, shelter, clothing, and security are met in a variety of different ways.
6. Make comparative charts that show what other ethnic groups like, with emphasis on why they like them just as we like certain things:

	Group A Likes	Group B Likes
Food		
Games		
Toys		
Etc.		

Make a chart of our ethnic heritage background (ethnic identification should be left optional, respecting the wishes of children and their parents):

Afro-American	Mexican-American	Puerto Rican–American	German-American	Italian-American	Jewish-American etc.
___	___	___	___	___	___
___	___	___	___	___	___
___	___	___	___	___	___

Trace one's ethnic roots and build a background on one's ethnic heritage (optional in terms of students' wishes):

1. Interview parents, grandparents, and relatives.
2. Examine photographs and albums made by parents and grandparents.
3. Trace the origin of one's name, referring to such books as *4000 Names for Your Baby* (Dell Publishing Company).
4. Make a family tree or genealogy chart.
5. Write an autobiography or a report on special events in one's own life and in the lives of members of the family.
6. Read and listen to stories and see audiovisual materials on one's ethnic group.
7. Trace one's ancestors, following suggestions in *Genealogy* (Boy Scout Manual), Doane's *Searching for Your Ancestors,* or Wright's *Building an American Pedigree.*
8. Collect family tales, anecdotes, and stories for a booklet on ''My Family's Folklore.''

Make charts that show how many Americans are mixtures of different ethnic groups:

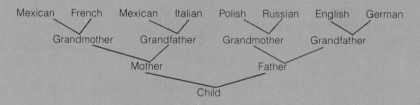

Do a survey of ethnic resources that may be used in ethnic heritage and other studies, with attention to the following:

Ethnic groups in school and in the community

Learning materials in school, libraries, museums, and other places

People to interview or to invite to school

Holidays, festivals, and other events to observe

Make scrapbooks or files of articles and pictures from newspapers and magazines that are related to groups under study.

Make a card file or directory of the variety of ethnic institutions, organizations, businesses, and other organizations in the community, including stores, newspapers, restaurants, radio programs, churches, television stations, organizations, and consular offices.

Make a dictionary card file of such terms as

acculturation	ethnic minority group
assimilation	melting pot theory
discrimination	prejudice
ethnic group	racism
ethnicity	stereotype

Make data bank cards and fact sheets for questions and topics under study, for example:

Data Card on Jewish Americans

Countries they left: _____

Why they left: _____

Problems on arrival: _____

Ways of adapting: _____

Work they did: _____

Examples of Achievements: _____

See a film such as *Geronimo Jones* to develop sensitivity to the conflicts that arise when a Papago boy is torn between two cultures.

See a filmstrip on immigrants, such as *Immigrants: The Dream and the Reality:* follow by discussing such questions as these:

What dream did they have?

What problems did they have?

How did they solve the problems?

To what extend did their dream come true?

What still needs to be done to make their dream come true?

Analyze stereotypes and the faulty thinking that results from using them, forgetting that individual differences may be found in all groups:

1. What images, mental pictures, or thoughts come to mind when you hear these words?

   Africans   Arabs   Artists   Athletes   Bankers   Blacks   Germans
   Irish   Jews   Lawyers   Russians   Scots   Teachers

2. Where did the images or mental pictures come from? Television? Stories? News items? Friends? Other sources?

3. Do you think your mental pictures are true of everyone in each group? Why or why not?
4. What about individual differences? How is each of us different from others in our group? How must others be different from each other in various groups?
5. How might our images of others make us act toward them? How must they feel when they are different from our image? How would we feel if they had incorrect mental pictures of us and acted accordingly?

Analyze sex-role stereotypes and sexist language:

1. Note and change sexist language in materials and discussions.
2. Correct steroetyped views of roles, distortions, and omissions.
3. Develop awareness of the need for equal career opportunities.
4. Identify exemplary role models of equality for both sexes.
5. Share pictures and reports that show both sexes in similar roles, occupations, and activities.

Pantomime or role-play feelings that show in attitudes, facial expressions, and other behavior:

When we are afraid of someone or something

When we feel that others are inferior

When we are embarrassed by someone

When someone does something that makes us happy

When we welcome a new student to our class

Play a "What Do You Think Will Happen If . . . ?" game by drawing slips of paper with examples of behavior on them and asking members of the class to state what they think will happen next to see if they have the same idea in mind as the student who drew the slip. Use statements such as these:

A boy from a minority ethnic group is called hurtful names.

A girl from an ethnic minority group is not given her turn.

A student from a minority group who eats different foods is teased.

Help is given to a minority student who is looking for lost money.

A student from a different ethnic group is asked to play in a game.

Students make friends with a newcomer from a different ethnic group.

Engage in role-taking activities to move students from superficial awareness of conflicts to sensitivity to the feelings of those caught in conflicts:

1. Role-play incidents that involve interpersonal conflicts.
2. Participate in simulation games, such as *Equality*, which deals with slavery and racial prejudice.
3. Take the position of others in discussion, debates, and panels.

4. Create and present a program or playlet that highlights values and customs of other groups.
5. Plan and enact plays and pageants that depict the efforts of ethnic groups to obtain equality, justice, employment, housing, education, and other rights in American society.

Engage in creative writing by completing statements or chain stories that focus on topics under study:

When someone is name calling I _____.
When I am caught name calling I _____.
When someone prejudges others I _____.
When I am told I have prejudged others I _____.
When someone applies a stereotype to me _____.
When I apply a stereotype to others _____.
All people need _____ because _____.
Each person is special in _____ because _____.
Things that make others happy are _____, and things that make them unhappy are _____.

Engage in creative writing about a special event in the lives of members of various ethnic groups with an emphasis on "How They Must Feel":

A person who has just become an American citizen
A person who has been discriminated against in getting a job
A Cuban who fled to the United States on a small boat
A Chinese who was ridiculed because of cultural differences

Write to pen pals who belong to different ethnic groups.

Write newspaper articles, editorials, letters to the editor, and reports that deal with topics, issues, and problems under study.

Make and display scrapbooks, drawings, murals, reports, movie box rolls, and other items related to topics in ethnic heritage and multiethnic units.

Have a multicultural or ethnic heritage fair at which items such as those listed above are displayed and students give descriptions and explanations of them to those who come to the fair.

Exchange scrapbooks, reports, and other materials on ethnic heritage with students from different backgrounds.

Global Education

The current emphasis on global education is part of the long-standing tradition in the social studies to include attention to the development of world-mindedness and international understanding. In the early grades learning begins with children studying families, schools, and communities around the world. Deeper understandings are developed in the intermediate grades through studies of other lands and peoples, relationships between our country and other countries, cultural interaction and sharing, the tightening interdependence among people in places throughout the world, and how we are all part of a global system of human interaction.

Instruction in elementary schools focuses on concrete examples of interdependence. Students learn about relationships between communities and nations, transnational communication, and cultural exchange. Specific attention is given to ways in which family and community life have been enriched by cultural sharing and the networks of communication that link communities and countries together. Children study the effects of pollution on people here and in other places, the impact of the energy crunch, and common environmental and urban problems. Opportunities are provided to identify common human needs and explain the reasons for diverse ways of meeting them. Students discover how our life styles affect others and how their life styles affect us; then they move on to consider the consequences of various courses of action for us and for the next generation. Activities and events in the lives of children and adults here and in other places are used to make instruction realistic and meaningful.

Emphasis is given to *why* cultural differences, problems, and conflicts exist. By responding to *why* questions as well as to what, when, where, who, and how questions, students begin to understand reasons for and causes of differences in ways of living in families, schools, communities, and countries that are all part of our global system of human interaction. Children should be helped to view ways of living around the world with an open mind and to understand beliefs and customs from the point of view of the people under study. This approach avoids the negative outcomes of ethnocentrism. Of fundamental importance is development of understanding and appreciation of cultural and ethnic differences here and now as a background for considering differences in other times and places.

GOALS AND ILLUSTRATIVE OBJECTIVES

Centered on developing an awareness of our involvement in a global system, competence in making decisions and judgments, and exercising influence, the goals of global education are summarized below along with an illustrative objective for each goal (see end-of-chapter reference by King, Branson, and Condon for a detailed outline of goals and objectives).

1. To develop understanding and appreciation of our involvement in a world system marked by cultural diversity, interdependence, conflict, change, and networks of communication

Describe common human needs, problems, and concerns in one's own culture and in other cultures and explain why ways of meeting needs differ.

2. To apply thinking and decision-making processes to our own activities, exploring the impact that personal decisions about the use of resources, life style, and other matters may have on other people

Describe how decisions about life style, use of resources, or use of energy may affect others in our community and in other places.

3. To apply and strengthen reading, study, and other skills by gathering, organizing, and reporting information related to interdependence and other global concepts

Locate and describe examples of how people depend on each other, as shown in the reading on the flow of goods, services, and ideas in and out of communities.

4. To develop attitudes and behavior that reflect respect for cultural diversity, appreciation of differences, understanding of why differences exist, and interest in exerting influence through one's life style, work, and social and political action and through setting examples for others

Make a list of things one might do to help curb pollution and to influence others to do the same.

CONCEPTUAL COMPONENTS

The following examples are core components in the vast array of conceptual elements that may be used in global education.

CONCEPTS

Culture	Change	Interdependence	Developed nations
Cross-cultural	Conflict	Interaction	Developing nations
Transnational	Cooperation	Environment	World view
Global system	Communication	Urbanization	World community

CONCEPT CLUSTERS

Interdependence: among families, communities, states, nations; in trade, use of resources, use of energy, improving the environment, worldwide transportation and communication, search for peace

Change: scientific, technological, social, economic, political, historical

Conflict in goals and values: among social, economic, political, and military goals and values; among interpersonal, intergroup, and international goals and values

Communication, verbal and nonverbal: through language, the arts, music, mathematics; via television, radio, telephone, telegraph, print media

THEMES

Cultural similarities and differences	Resolution of conflicts
Increasing interdependence of people	Interaction of cultures

DESCRIPTIVE GENERALIZATIONS

Conflicts arise because of differences in goals, values, and claims to the use of resources.

How are people in the countries of North America and South America interdependent? How are they part of a global system along with people in other countries around the world?

International networks of transportation and communication link communities and countries around the world.

All people are part of a global system in which change in one part may affect other parts.

PRESCRIPTIVE GENERALIZATIONS

Because of their interdependence all countries have a responsibility to cooperate in solving environmental, energy, economic, political, and other problems and to maintain peace.

High priority should be given to equality, justice, and human dignity here and in other lands.

All human life is to be respected equally.

FOCUSING QUESTIONS

By formulating questions such as those listed below to guide study, concepts will be used as tools of inquiry and students will move from the recalling and observing levels of thinking to generalizing, analyzing, and higher levels of thinking.

How are people in our community *dependent* on people in other communities [observing, interpreting]?

How are intergroup *conflicts* in our community alike and different from conflicts in other communities [comparing]?

Consider our findings about the ways that people around the world are *interdependent*. Which findings can we group under the headings trade, transportation, communication, pollution, and resources use [classifying]?

What general statements can we make about the relationship between *population growth* and *food* supply [generalizing]?

What are the main reasons for the differences between their *culture* and ours [analyzing]?

How can we bring together and share our findings on *communication systems* that link communities around the world [synthesizing]?

Why do you suppose people who share that *culture* place such high *value* on living in harmony with nature [inferring]?

What hunch [*hypothesis*] do you have about the main causes of the growth of cities [*urbanization*]? How can it be checked [hypothesizing]?

What do you think the main worldwide *pollution* problems will be in the year 2000? What are your reasons [predicting]?

Which of the proposals for improving the *food supply* in *developing countries* do you think is best? Why [evaluating]?

ILLUSTRATIVE LEARNING ACTIVITIES

The following activities illustrate the types of learning activities that can be included in global studies. Many of the activities from the section on multicultural education may be adapted and used to develop global perspectives.

Activities for Global Studies

Examine displays of pictures and objects and clippings from magazines and newspapers, textbooks, references, and other materials to find information on family life, activities of children and adults, current problems, and community life in different cultures around the world.

Find out about ways of living and learning of children in other lands, guided by such questions as these:

What foods do they eat? What clothes do they wear? How are their homes like ours? How are they different? Why?

What games do they play? What songs, poems, stories, and dances do they enjoy?

Listen to and read stories about people in other cultures to discover that they also have hopes and fears, joys and sorrows, happiness and sadness, positive and negative feelings and attitudes, and stability and change in their lives.

Collect information from officials in consulates, exchange students, foreign visitors, recent immigrants, and local persons who have recently visited places under study.

Interview the people mentioned above, or invite them to share slides, pictures, ideas, and objects such as clothing, jewelry, pottery, and dolls and to answer questions.

Observe festivals, pageants, and commemorations of local groups that highlight customs, traditions, and values from other lands.

Interpret and make maps, charts, diagrams, graphs, and time lines—for example, maps of networks of air and sea transportation; charts of food, clothing, shelter, and modes of travel; diagrams of the flow of people, products, and ideas between countries; graphs of population change and trade; time lines of events, showing the relationships between our country and other countries.

Investigate as individuals or in small groups such international organizations and agencies as the UN, UNESCO, UNICEF, WHO, CARE, Red Cross, YWCA, and YMCA.

Trace the origins of foods common to many countries, using encyclopedias and such references as Evans's *People Are Important*, Morris's *Dictionary of Word Phrases and Origins*, Sullivan's *How Do They Make It?* and Limburg's *What's in the Name of Fruits*. Then make a chart (or world map) that shows where those foods we think of as American actually originated:

Asia: wheat, rice, chickens, noodles, apples, apricots, other fruits

Central South America: chocolate, gum (chicle), vanilla, potato, sweet potato, peanuts, tomatoes, pineapple

Europe: ice cream, sausage, soda pop, gelatin, pretzels, beets, spinach

Middle East: milk, butter, candy, olives, sherbet, melons
Native American: cranberry, beans, corn, maple syrup, squash, pumpkins

Investigate where various objects were invented or first used, using encyclopedias and such references as Gekierc's *Who Gave Us . . .* and *Waller's American Inventions.* Then make a chart (or world map) that includes such items as these:

China: clock, ink, paper, printing, compass, gunpowder, porcelain dishes, kites (or Greece)
England: soccer, train, baby carriage
France: canned food, parachute
Italy (Rome): calendar, circus
Babylon (Iraq): bricks, roses
Egypt: cat, plow, glass
America: rocking chair, safety pin, zipper, elevator, frozen food
Greece: Olympic games, school system, kites (or China)
South American Indians: hammock, rubber balls

Listen to excerpts from Linton's *The Study of Man* to identify commonly used items that were created in other cultures and to illustrate the impact of other cultures on our own.

The bed originated in the Near East and was modified in Europe.
Cotton was domesticated in India.
Glass was invented in Egypt.
Moccasins were made by native American Indians.

Make a retrieval chart of the ways in which our culture has been enriched by the achievements and contributions of immigrants, including medicine, inventions, politics, art, music, sports, education, and recreation.

Learn folk songs, dances, anthems, poems, myths, legends, folklore, and proverbs of another place; compare them with our own and with those of other peoples.

Make data bank cards, fact sheets, booklets, and scrapbooks on such topics as another country's food, shelter, clothing, transportation, communication, relations with our country, relations with other countries, trade, family life, community life, activities of children and adults, environmental and energy problems, art, music, literature, games, and folk tales.

Make murals, montages, and collages that highlight distinctive aspects of a country's culture, such as family life, modes of travel and communication, arts, crafts, ceremonies, costumes, utensils, and musical instruments.

Make comparative analyses of human activities here and in other places, using pairs of questions:

How do we depend on each other at home? How do they?

How do we depend on each other at school? How do they?

How do we depend on each other in the community? How do they?

Analyze interconnections in transportation, communication, and trade:

How do networks of air and sea transportation link nations?

How do television, radio, telephone, and telegraph link countries?

How does trade of products and resources affect economic interdependence?

Participate in plays, pageants, and role-playing activities that portray ways of living in other cultures.

Exchange scrapbooks, tape recordings, drawings, and other items with classes in sister cities. Write to pen pals in other countries, as suggested by the following groups:

Students Letter Exchange, Waseca, Minnesota 56093

International Friendship League, 40 Mount Vernon Street, Beacon Hill, Massachusetts 02108

Letters Abroad, 209 East 56th Street, New York, New York 10022

People to People, Box 1201, Kansas City, Missouri 64141

Make decisions and judgments and evaluate those made by oneself and by others, including description and analysis of the following:

1. One's life style and how it affects others
2. Others' life styles and how they affect us
3. Changes in life styles that all people can make for the good of all people now and in the future
4. Public and private group decisions related to the environment, use of resources, intergroup relations, and other aspects of our global system
5. Alternative proposals and possible consequences of various ways of improving the management of conflict, change, environmental concerns, and other problems
6. Fairness of treatment accorded children, women, and minority groups
7. Provisions for the health, safety, education, and welfare of children and adults

Exert influence to improve the functioning of our global system through such activities as these:

1. Identifying and making changes in one's own life style that will enhance individual and group welfare

2. Describing changes in school and community activities that will improve the environment
3. Participating in activities of Junior Red Cross, CARE, UNICEF, and other groups
4. Eliciting the cooperation of others at the local, state, and national levels, including elected officials and lay persons
5. Setting examples and modeling one's behavior to demonstrate concern for responsible involvement in our global system

Law-Focused
Instruction

The recognition that legal knowledge is a necessary component of civic competence has lead to a rapid growth in law-focused studies. This growth reflects today's concerns about such problems as juvenile delinquency, justice for all in our society, and the imperfections of our legal system. Its aim is to overcome ignorance of individual rights and obligations under law. Law-focused education takes the position that to be an effective citizen in today's society one must understand the rights and freedoms guaranteed by the Constitution and the laws that protect the individual and promote group welfare. One must be aware of the legal procedures to follow when in need of help, know how to hold authorities accountable, and understand the responsibilities that each must assume to make our legal system work.

Programs of instruction have been developed by bar associations, educators, and civic-minded citizens. Many explain the dynamic and changing nature of our legal system: how it works, how it reflects personal and social values, how it affects all of us, and how it operates to resolve disputes. Some programs also explore the close relationship between social issues and legal issues: how law is both protective and promotive as well as prescriptive and punitive, and ways in which our system of law and justice can be improved to serve all groups fairly in our society.

In early grades, instruction focuses on the rules and decision-making procedures needed to work, play, and live together at home, in school, and in the community. Instruction in later grades is extended to include both contemporary and historical events that highlight such concepts as justice, equal protection, due process, and civil rights. Special emphasis is given to aspects of law that touch the lives of students, such as rights and responsibilities, use of authority, and rules and regulations related to health, safety, recreation, and property.

GOALS AND ILLUSTRATIVE OBJECTIVES

Close relationships exist between the social studies and law-focused studies, as shown in the following statement of goals and examples of instructional objectives.

217

1. To clarify the need for rules and laws in daily life and within a legal system designed to keep a balance between individual freedom and group welfare

   State three rules or laws for bicycle safety and give examples of how they promote individual and group welfare.

2. To develop understanding of concepts related to our legal system, including justice, equal protection, authority responsibility, due process, property, civil liberties, and privacy

   State the meaning of property rights and describe examples of violations of property rights that occur in school.

3. To develop understanding and appreciation of the Constitution as the basis of our legal system, roles and responsibilities of representatives of our legal system, and the need for continuing improvement

   List civil liberties guaranteed by the Constitution and give an example of how each one is important in our daily lives.

4. To develop thinking processes and decision-making ability through activities that call for comparing, classifying, interpreting, analyzing, and evaluating legal issues, topics, and procedures

   Evaluate procedures for settling a dispute by stating whether all parties had a fair hearing, whether wrongs or injuries were corrected, and whether a fair decision was made.

5. To develop skill in finding, organizing, evaluating, and presenting information related to legal issues and topics

   Collect and classify facts for and against an issue in a case study of the right to privacy.

6. To develop respect for the rights of individuals, the general welfare, the legal procedures for settling disputes, the proper use of authority, and diversity

   Describe a situation in which an individual from an ethnic minority group used legal procedures to obtain equal protection of the law.

7. To increase students' feelings of efficacy and reduce feelings of indifference and alienation related to laws and legal processes

   Describe at least three procedures that an individual or group can use to challenge the misuse of authority.

CONCEPTUAL COMPONENTS

Below are illustrative examples of conceptual elements drawn from political science and jurisprudence:

CONCEPTS

Rules	Authority	Equality	Responsibility
Laws	Power	Justice	Participation
Regulations	Rights	Privacy	Equal protection
Due process	Freedoms	Property	Legal system

NEA

What contributions can local officials make to law-focused education?

CONCEPT CLUSTERS

Rights: of minors, women, accused, citizens; to public trial, bail, privacy, property, vote; due process, equal protection, protection from unreasonable search and seizure

Freedoms: religion, speech, press, assembly, petition

Justice: fairness, equity, impartiality; fair distribution of benefits and burdens, fair decision making, correction of wrongs

THEMES

The need for rules and laws	Individual rights and responsibilities
The resolution of conflicts	Extension of civil liberties

DESCRIPTIVE GENERALIZATIONS

Rules and laws provide for individual and group welfare.

The Constitution serves as the basis for our legal system.

Laws are a reflection of basic social values.

PRESCRIPTIVE GENERALIZATIONS

Laws must be changed to meet new conditions and improve the quality of life for all groups.

Individuals must exercise their rights and assume responsibilities to make our legal system work.

Equal protection must not be denied any individual in our society.

FOCUSING QUESTIONS

How is *fairness* (justice) defined in this case study [interpreting]?

In general, how do *laws* help to promote *justice* [generalizing]?

What problems would we have if no one had *authority* in school? In the community [inferring]?

What main reasons for making *laws* are given in this reading [analyzing]?

How can we show on a chart the *freedoms* guaranteed by the *Bill of Rights* [synthesizing]?

What changes will be made in *laws* to improve the quality of *justice* for members of minority groups? Why do you think so [predicting]?

Which of the housing *regulations* suggested in this reading will best serve members of minority groups? Why [evaluating]?

ILLUSTRATIVE LEARNING ACTIVITIES

Programs of instruction in the schools are attuned to questions, issues, and topics of value to students. Instruction in elementary and middle schools is kept close to the experiences of students, to current affairs that are appropriate for study, and to topics in basic units of study. Illustrative learning activities follow:

Activities for Law-Focused Studies

Examine pictures of people in authority, such as parents, teachers, police, and judges, and discuss such questions as these:

What authority does this person have? Why is it needed?

What do we expect this person to do? Why is that important?

What might happen to those who do not comply? Is that fair? Why or why not?

Investigate and discuss the authority of people in particular institutions, such as the school, guided by such questions as these:

What authority do teachers have?

What authority does a principal have?

What authority do monitors, team captains, play leaders, and teacher aides have?

Make a list of rules and regulations represented by signs that students observe in the community, including signs that regulate people, traffic, and behavior in parks, playgrounds, libraries, and other places; discuss such questions as Why are they needed? What happens when people do not follow them?

Investigate and discuss how rules at home, in school, and in the community help people, and how laws related to food, health, safety, housing, and other items close to the lives of students are designed to serve students, their families, and people in the community.

Listen to recordings, reports, resource visitors, and material read by the teacher to get information related to such questions as these:

What does equal protection mean? How does it affect us?
What groups have been denied equal protection? What gains have been made? What steps still need to be taken?

Read (or listen to) stories, case studies, and accounts in textbooks and other materials in which the characters are involved in conflicts or are facing issues related to authority, justice, privacy, or other concepts.

Interview a resource person such as a judge, attorney, or police officer, or invite the person to come to the classroom, to obtain answers to such questions as these:

What is a juvenile court? Who is in charge of it?
How does it operate?
What rights do minors have?
What legal assistance is available to minors?

Take study trips to a small claims court, a police station, a juvenile court, a detention center, or a legal aid society.

Make data bank cards, fact sheets, or retrieval charts on rules and laws related to topics under study, following a format similar to this:

Topic	Rules or Laws	Penalties
Bicycle riding		
Dogs		
Trespassing		
Firearms		
Drugs		
Etc.		

Investigate services available from the local bar association, legal aid society, law enforcement agencies, Better Business Bureau, American Civil Liberties Union, Better Housing League, and law schools in colleges and universities.

Collect and analyze news clippings that deal with legal topics and issues such as vandalism, petty theft, disturbing the peace, accidents involving traffic violations, drug abuse, trespassing, and littering.

Analyze authority (and other concepts) in depth in units on the home, school, community, state, and nation, guided by such questions as these:

> Who has authority? Why? How did they obtain their authority?
>
> What are the limits of authority (of teachers, police, and others)?
>
> What are the penalties for not obeying authority (of teachers and others)?
>
> What can one do if a person does not use authority fairly (police and others)?
>
> Why is authority needed in games? At home? In a community? In a state? In a nation? In the international scene?

Collect and analyze examples of incidents that occur in school and in the community and that are presented in learning materials to illustrate how law

1. Is a reflection of what people value
2. Sets standards of behavior and related penalties
3. Defines procedures for settling disputes
4. Defines and sets limits of authority
5. Provides a means of achieving justice
6. Is changed to meet new conditions

Analyze case studies of events, incidents, and decisions related to sticking to rules and regulations, justice for members of minority groups, equality for women, freedom of expression, the trial of Peter Zenger, the Salem Witch trials, and other historical events, following such procedures as these:

1. Identify the facts in the case.
2. State the issue(s) in the case.
3. Present arguments for and against the issue(s).
4. Make a decision.
5. State reasons for the decision.
6. Compare your decision and reasons with those made by a jury or judge.
7. Discuss possible reasons for any difference between the student's decision and that of the jury or judge.

Analyze a television program that deals with law enforcement, court procedures, roles of judges and attorneys, or other aspects of law, inviting a local attorney or judge to assist in finding accurate and inaccurate information.

Analyze advertisements in terms of truth in advertising, emotional appeals, and consumer protection laws.

Analyze moral dilemmas presented on filmstrips or proposed by the teacher on such issues as telling the truth, stealing, cheating, and respecting the property rights of others:

What Is Their Responsibility?

Jim and Mary were just entering their classroom. They saw Jane take a candy bar from another student's lunch pail. Jane was their friend and lived in the same block. What should Jim and Mary do? Why? What if Jane were not their friend? Should this make a difference in what Jim and Mary do? Why or why not?

Complete statements designed to clarify values related to legal issues and topics:

I learned that _____.
I wonder what would happen if _____.
Three rules (or laws) that are needed are _____.
If we didn't have classroom rules _____.

Evaluate events in terms of justice (or use of authority, responsibility, and other concepts) by applying standards of fairness to the following:

1. The distribution of benefits and burdens at home, in school activities, in the community, and at the state and national levels
2. Penalties given to bicycle riders, car drivers, and others for violations
3. Procedures used to make decisions about who is to blame for a fight, hearing both sides of an argument, how a city council gets ideas from citizens when faced with a decision
4. Correction of such wrongs as not giving others their turn, taking something that belongs to others, and littering in a park

Evaluate the effectiveness of strategies for holding people in positions of authority responsible for their actions, appraising the following alternatives in the context of incidents in which authority has been misused:

1. Appealing to a higher authority (the person's supervisor)
2. Presenting charges in a hearing
3. Calling attention to rules or laws that have been broken
4. Taking court action, suing for damages, seeking removal from office
5. Mounting voting campaigns in behalf of other candidates
6. Demonstrating, striking, boycotting, engaging in civil disobedience
7. Asking pressure and interest groups to act against the offender

Role-play conflicts that arise in the lives of students or are identified in instructional materials, such as disobeying a teacher, team captain or other authority, crossing a street against a red light, and trespassing, followed by a discussion guided by such questions as these:

What rule or authority was not obeyed? Why did this happen?
What may happen to those who break rules? Why do you think so?
What may happen to those who do not comply with authority? Why?
What should be done to get people to comply with rules and authority?

Simulate a small claims court session or conduct a mock trial on cases related to topics under study.

Engage in simulation games, such as *Micro-Community*, in which students make a constitution and laws, or *Truth in Advertising*, in which consumer protection laws are highlighted.

Make a scrapbook of news reports, organizing them in sections on civil rights, equal protection, authority, truth in advertising, or others related to topics under study.

Create and present case studies related to issues of concern to students, using stories, historical events, letters, current events, or information drawn from textbooks or other materials.

Propose ways to improve the quality of justice in a community, giving attention to fair distribution of benefits and burdens, decision-making procedures, and correction of injustice in incidents that occur in school and in the community. Use examples related to children and youth, ethnic minority groups, and problems of special concern to students.

Environmental and Energy Education

In the past eight decades three major waves of concern about various aspects of the environment have occurred. The first, which took place during the 1900s, was led by Gifford Pinchot and supported by President Theodore Roosevelt. It focused on saving and expanding our great public domain. The second, during the 1930s, stressed conservation and management of natural resources. The third, during the 1970s, recognized the need to improve the total environment, reduce pollution, and use energy more efficiently.

GOALS AND ILLUSTRATIVE OBJECTIVES

Broadly conceived to include all of the above concerns, the central goals and objectives of environmental and energy education are to develop:

224

1. Awareness of environmental problems and conditions, causes and consequences of deterioration, corrective measures currently under way and needed in the future, and action that individuals and groups may take

   Describe three environmental problems in our community and the steps that are being taken to solve them.

2. Understanding and appreciation of the impact of energy use on the environment and the economy, of the need for alternative energy sources, and of the consequences of energy shortages

   State two or more effects on family life that may occur when existing oil reserves are exhausted.

3. Thinking and decision-making processes by analyzing problems, taking and defending a position on issues, and evaluating proposals related to energy use, conservation of resources and energy, and improvement of the environment

   Evaluate each suggestion listed on the chart for saving energy; tell how much energy each suggestion will save and determine how many students will follow it.

4. Skills involved in studying environmental problems, such as reading, interviewing, interpreting maps and other materials, and working with others in action projects

   State the main idea and supporting details in this reading about individual responsibility for preventing waste pollution.

5. Attitudes, values, and appreciations related to quality of life, a commitment to improve the human and physical environment, and the need for individual, group, and worldwide cooperative action

   Demonstrate a commitment to energy conservation by making and carrying out a plan to save energy at home and in school.

CONCEPTUAL COMPONENTS

Conceptual elements are drawn from both the social and natural sciences. The following are examples illustrative of those found in current materials.

CONCEPTS

Environment	Interdependence	Energy	Population
Ecology	Adaptation	Conservation	Industrialization
Ecosystem	Food chain	Pollution	Urbanization
Balance of nature	Resources	Pollutants	Quality of life

CONCEPT CLUSTERS

Conservation: human, water, soil, forest, wildlife, grazing lands, minerals, public domain, recreational areas; wise use, restricted use, substitution, recycling, education of producers and consumers

Energy Sources: solar, wind, biomass, wood, sea gradient or sea thermal, ocean currents, waves, hydroelectric, oil, coal, nuclear

Pollution: air, water, thermal, soil, food, wildlife, plant life, solid waste, aesthetic, noise; causes, effects; corrective and preventive measures; needed action; action groups

Quality of Life: personal, social; physical, mental, emotional; rural, suburban, urban, inner city, state, regional, national, global

THEMES

Interaction and interdependence   Variety and pattern
Adaptation and survival   Continuity and change

DESCRIPTIVE GENERALIZATIONS

All living things affect the environment and are affected by conditions, interactions, and changes in the environment.

Population growth, industrialization, and urbanization are causes of environmental problems.

Critical current problems are overpopulation, food supply, energy use, and pollution of the environment by industrialized nations.

PRESCRIPTIVE GENERALIZATIONS

Industrialized nations, in cooperation with others, must devise programs that promote personal, social, economic, and technological change that will restore and maintain the environment.

Decision making related to proposals, action programs, and technological developments must include examination of risks and benefits, consequences of alternatives, and effects of changes on the quality of life.

Immediate and long-range action should be taken by individuals and groups and by both public and private agencies.

FOCUSING QUESTIONS

The examples of focusing questions listed below illustrate ways to link concepts with thinking processes and lift thinking from recalling and observing to higher levels:

resources

How many ways can you think of to conserve energy at home [remembering]?

How many ways of conserving energy are shown in this film [observing]?

What is meant by the statement that improvement of the environment and conservation of energy are mainly a matter of individual choice [interpreting]?

How are environmental and energy problems alike in our country and in Japan? How are they different [comparing]?

Into which of the groups listed below should the natural resources shown on the map on page 81 of our textbook be placed [classifying]?

Energy Resources   Mineral Resources   Water Resources

In general, what does the evidence show about progress in forest conservation in our state [generalizing]?

Why do you think greater progress has been made in forest conservation than in water conservation [inferring]?

What are the risks and benefits of using herbicides in forest conservation [analyzing]?

How shall we present our findings on the causes and effects of water pollution [synthesizing]?

What do you think the main environmental and energy problems will be in the year 2000? Why [predicting]?

Which of the committee's suggestions for improving the environment and saving energy in our community do you think are best? Why [evaluating]?

ILLUSTRATIVE LEARNING ACTIVITIES

The selected activities listed below illustrate those that might be used in environmental and energy education. Others are found in the teaching unit in chapter 2, Planning Units of Instruction, and in the resource unit in the appendix.

Activities for the Study Of Conservation Problems

Introduce the study by discussing a display for pictures, clippings, pamphlets, books, and other materials on conservation.

Investigate conservation problems and practices through such activities as the following:

1. Identifying natural resources available in our country and natural resources that we get from other countries
2. Defining renewable and nonrenewable resources and classifying resources available in our country as either renewable resources or nonrenewable resources
3. Collecting materials from local, state, and national organizations
4. Interviewing local experts on conservation and taking field trips to gather data
5. Interpreting physical and land-use maps of the United States to locate forest areas, mineral areas, and bodies of water and to identify the proportion of the nation's area that each occupies
6. Interpreting maps of other countries and regions of the world and comparing them with areas of the United States, as noted above
7. Making data bank cards on the estimated amount, location, and primary uses of such resources as coal, oil, natural gas, iron ore, and other minerals
8. Making data bank cards and reporting on the contributions of such conservationists as

George P. March	Fairfield Osborn	Paul B. Sears
J. Sterling Morton	Gifford Pinchot	Jay N. Sterling
John Muir	Theodore Roosevelt	Charles R. Van Hise

9. Forming committees of four to five students to prepare and present recommendations for action that can be taken to improve conservation of resources at home, in school, in the community, in the state, and in the nation

Activities for the Study of Forest Conservation

Introduce the study by arranging a display of forest areas and discussing:

How many of you have been in a forest? Where is it located?
What was it like? What did you do? What fun did you have?
Was any timber being cut? Were new trees being planted?
Did you hear a lecture by a forest ranger? What was said about conservation?

Collect materials and gather information related to focusing questions through such activities as these:

1. Collecting pictures, maps, graphs, newspaper and magazine clippings, and other materials to make booklets, reports, scrapbooks, and displays
2. Writing to the National Forest Service to obtain maps, folders, and other materials needed to answer questions, prepare oral and written reports, and make displays
3. Visiting a nearby lumber mill (or watching films or filmstrips) to gather information on how lumber is processed
4. Seeing films and filmstrips and reading materials from lumber and paper producers to identify practices that conserve forests, prevent waste, maintain an adequate supply of lumber, and protect the environment

Organize, summarize, and present information through such activities as these:

1. Mapping major forest areas and national parks in the United States and identifying those that students have visited
2. Summarizing steps that are being taken by the government and by private and commercial organizations to conserve forests
3. Summarizing steps that individuals who visit forest areas and vacation in national and state parks can take to conserve forests
4. Preparing and sharing reports on how forest conservation helps to preserve wildlife, watersheds, soil, wilderness areas, and lumber supply

Express thoughts and feelings creatively by

1. Completing such statements as
   If I were in charge of forest conservation I would _____.
   If I owned a large forest I would _____.

If I were in the lumber business I would _____.

Three things everyone should do when in forests are _____.

2. Writing a haiku poem about some aspect of forests (haiku poems have words with five syllables in line one, seven syllables in line two, and five syllables in line three)

Activities for the Study of Conservation of Energy

Introduce the study by discussing a display of pictures, pamphlets, and other materials on energy use, guided by such questions as:

What forms of energy do we use every day?

What steps can we take to save energy?

How much energy would be saved if people who drive alone in a car would use public transit systems?

Social Studies Workshop. University of California, Berkeley

What energy sources should be considered as alternatives to oil? Why?
What is the future outlook for safe sources of energy?

Compare the costs and the time for going to work by different means of transportation.

1. Look at the following information on costs of going to work:

   CAR: Gasoline $.75   Parking $.60   Other costs $.75   Total $2.10
   BUS: Fare $.75   Parking $.00   Other costs $.00   Total $.75
   TRAIN: Fare $1.00   Parking $.50   Other costs $.25   Total $1.75

2. Which way is least expensive? Which is most expensive? What reasons might someone have for going by car? By bus? By train?
3. Look at the following information on time required to get to work:

   By car: 35 minutes   *By bus:* 45 minutes   *By train:* 25 minutes

4. When might the amount of time be important in deciding how to go to work?
5. In general, when both cost and time are considered, which way of going to work do you think is best? Why?

Form committees to collect, organize, and present information on energy alternatives to oil: coal, nuclear, water, solar, and wind. Include the advantages and disadvantages of each.

Analyze and evaluate alternative sources of energy in terms of economic costs, environmental costs, arguments for and against each alternative, and impact on quality of life.

Analyze and evaluate advertisements, television commercials, and materials from utility and oil companies and producers of cars and appliances, paying particular attention to the following:

Which suggestions in them are aimed at saving energy?

Which suggestions are designed to promote good will?

Which suggestions are made to promote sales?

How are current advertisments different from those used before the energy crisis?

Make a checklist of ways to save energy at home, in school, and in the community.

Project future prospects, and consider responsibility for present conditions and continuing action:

1. What energy sources will we have in 2000? Will our dependence on other nations increase, decrease, stay the same? Why do you think so?
2. How can we adjust to dependence on other nations for oil? How can disrup-

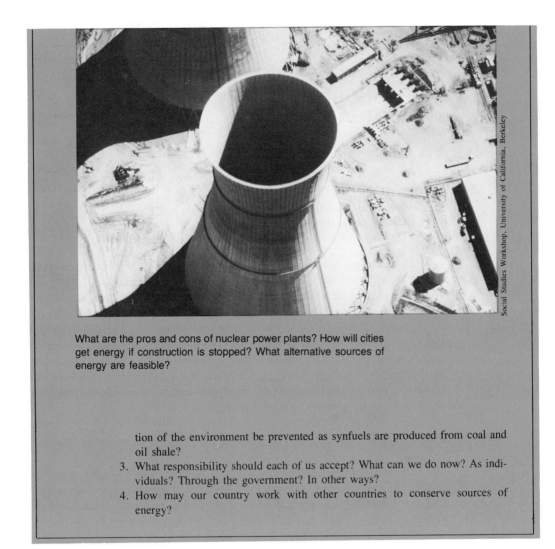

Social Studies Workshop, University of California, Berkeley

What are the pros and cons of nuclear power plants? How will cities get energy if construction is stopped? What alternative sources of energy are feasible?

tion of the environment be prevented as synfuels are produced from coal and oil shale?

3. What responsibility should each of us accept? What can we do now? As individuals? Through the government? In other ways?

4. How may our country work with other countries to conserve sources of energy?

Career
Education

Career education should begin in early childhood education and continue throughout life. Well-designed programs of instruction emphasize individual development, educational awareness, decision making, and contributions of general education to all careers. Such programs view life careers as including the realms of work, leisure, aesthetics, and ethical behavior. The social studies can help students to develop positive attitudes toward the world of work, to appreciate the contributions of selected workers, and to understand and appreciate the role of work in one's life career and in personal and group welfare.

Social Studies Workshop, University of California, Berkeley

What important roles do workers have in medical centers and drug stores? To what career families do they belong?

The focus of instruction in the elementary schools is career awareness, not vocational education. In the early grades children investigate the roles of workers in their community. In the middle grades career awareness is extended to units that go beyond the student's immediate environment to include a variety of career clusters in the public and private sectors of our society. In the upper grades, middle schools, and junior high schools, attention is given to career orientation and exploration. Career preparation takes place at secondary and higher levels of education. At all levels the elimination of sex-role and ethnic-role stereotyping and recognition of the need to give equal opportunities to everyone in our society is emphasized.

GOALS AND ILLUSTRATIVE OBJECTIVES

Career education, in its broadest sense, seeks the well-rounded development of the individual for a productive life career. Central goals of career education are presented below; each is followed by an example of a related instructional objective.

1. To develop a positive self concept, self-evaluation skills, and an awareness of one's interests, aptitudes, and values

   List some personal interests and state how they are similar to those of workers in an occupation of your choice.

2. To develop understanding of the social and economic structure of our society and an awareness of the variety of occupations that are essential to individual and group welfare

   State three ways in which community workers depend on each other for goods and services.

3. To develop concepts and main ideas about the world of work that enrich one's general education and extend career awareness

State the meaning of these words: *work, leisure, life style, occupation,* and *career.*

4. To develop an understanding of the place of work in one's life style that includes the realms of work, leisure, aesthetics, and reflection

    Describe the life style of a community worker of special interest to you.

5. To develop appreciation of the importance of education, special skills, attitudes and values, and standards of workmanship in a life career

    State a generalization about the relationships between education and an occupation in which you are interested.

6. To develop positive attitudes toward different types of work and the dignity of workers in different occupations

    List three personal satisfactions that health workers derive from their careers.

CONCEPTUAL COMPONENTS

The following are illustrative of conceptual elements drawn from various disciplines:

CONCEPTS

Career	Work	Occupation	Aptitudes
Career awareness	Leisure	Specialization	Interests
Career families	Goods	Interdependence	Values
Career clusters	Services	Life style	Achievements

CONCEPT CLUSTERS

Individual differences: interests, aptitudes, capabilities, values
Occupations: carpenter, nurse, doctor, sales clerk, teacher, and so on
Career clusters: agriculture, communications, transportation, and so on

What important roles do workers have in department and hardware stores? To what career families do they belong?

Social Studies Workshop, University of California, Berkeley

THEMES

Producers of goods and services   Interdependence of workers
Significance of all types of work   Work and life styles

DESCRIPTIVE GENERALIZATIONS

People can learn to work in a variety of occupations.

An individual's interests, values, capabilities, and education are key factors in choosing an occupation.

Wise use of leisure time contributes to health and happiness in one's career.

PRESCRIPTIVE GENERALIZATIONS

Discrimination must be eliminated so that women and members of minority groups have full access to the world of work.

Workers in all occupations should be respected.

Awareness of a variety of career opportunities should precede decision making about careers to explore in depth.

FOCUSING QUESTIONS

The following focusing questions illustrate ways in which thinking processes and concepts may be linked together to guide the study of particular topics and issues, and to lift students' thinking from observing and remembering to higher levels, such as analyzing and evaluating:

What *construction* workers are shown in this filmstrip [observing]?

Which *construction* workers have you seen on the job [remembering]?

What new ideas about the *role of workers* did you get [interpreting]?

How is the work of *carpenters* like the work of *roofers*? How is it different [comparing]?

In what *career family* should we place carpenters, roofers, plumbers, and plasterers [classifying]?

In general, what is a common *goal* of these *workers* [generalizing]?

What do you suppose is most satisfying about *construction work* [inferring]?

How has *specialization* increased *interdependence* among construction workers [analyzing]?

What should be included in a scrapbook on *construction* workers [synthesizing]?

What do you think *construction* workers like the most about their work? How can we find out [hypothesizing]?

What changes may occur in the *role* of *construction* workers in the next decade? Why do you think so [predicting]?

What kind of *construction* work would you like most to do? Why [evaluating]?

ILLUSTRATIVE LEARNING ACTIVITIES

The illustrative activities that follow have been arranged in three categories:

1. Introductory activities to use to initiate a unit
2. Developmental activities to provide for the intake, organization, application and demonstration, and expression of information
3. Concluding activities to wrap up the unit through sharing and evaluation

---

Activities for Career Education

INTRODUCTORY ACTIVITIES

Arrange a display of pictures of selected workers headed by the question, What is the role of each of these workers?

Invite a worker to give an overview of main activities of and qualifications for a career group to be studied, and ask the worker to answer questions raised by students.

Show a film or filmstrip that gives an overview of a career family.

Read a story that portrays a challenging and interesting aspect of the occupation to be investigated.

Link the unit to a preceding one by making comments or posing questions such as the following: This group of workers belongs to the same career cluster, but they do different things. In what ways do you think the work of members of this group is similar to and different from the work of those we just studied?

Preassess students' background of understanding through discussion of such questions as these:

Do you know anyone who does this type of work?

What do you think is the main thing these workers do?

What education is needed to work in this occupation?

DEVELOPMENTAL ACTIVITIES

List and discuss the jobs of members of students' families, telling why each job is important.

Identify different occupations of special interest to students; investigate, singly or in groups, the roles, contributions, and job requirements of these occupations.

See a filmstrip such as *Work? Play?* Then define *work* and *play*, describing how work for one person may be play for another and describing how play for one person may be work for another.

Watch a filmstrip such as *The Lollipop Factory* to find out why many workers, each doing a special job, are needed in factories.

See films and read or listen to stories about different types of workers. Then discuss such questions as

Why is that type of work important?

What skills are needed? What education is needed? What tools and equipment are needed?

What aspects are most interesting? Least interesting?

Examine tools, equipment, and materials used by workers in a particular occupation.

Collect news articles and read such materials as Baggell and Ackerman's *All In A Day's Work* to find new roles for men and women, such as male nurses, secretaries, and day care teachers, and female truckers, plumbers, and telephone installers.

Take study trips to observe workers in action, and conduct interviews to get answers to questions about the roles of workers, working conditions, likes and dislikes, and related aspects of an occupation.

Find examples in current events or classroom materials of how sex, age, race, ethnicity, and amount of education may aid or hinder one's opportunities; then discuss steps that would further equality of opportunity for everyone.

Interview a worker in an occupation of special interest, asking such questions as these:

Why did you choose this kind of work?

What special skills are needed? What tools and materials are used?

What interests and attitudes are important?

What education is needed?

What is the outlook for workers in your field?

Complete data bank cards or fact sheets on different workers, including such information as the following:

Name of occupation	Career cluster	Main activity
Required education	Essential skills	Working conditions
Effect on life style	Income	Other aspects

Make retrieval charts such as the following that can be used to clarify concepts and to develop generalizations about the roles of selected workers.

Construction Workers	Activities	Tools	Materials
Carpenters			
Plumbers			
Electricians			

Classify a list of jobs into career clusters, such as communication, transportation, business, construction, recreation, manufacturing, health services, public services, personal services, and environment.

State and check hypotheses about how changes in the seasons affect the work of those in such occupations as the following:

Product Occupations	Service Occupations
Automobile producers	Postal workers
Cannery workers	Ski instructors
Dairy workers	Store clerks
Toy makers	Teachers
Wheat farmers	Truckers

Role-play work done by members of the family, community workers, and workers studied in units on transportation, communication, and other topics.

Demonstrate the importance of each worker's role in an activity by describing what may happen or by role-playing an activity (such as mail service) with one worker's role omitted (mail sorter or mail carrier).

Play a simulation game such as *Complete a City* to increase understanding and appreciation of community needs, the importance of working together to solve problems, and education needed for social service occupations.

Make picture collections, booklets, and murals of different types of work by members of families, community workers, and workers in other settings.

Compare individual production with assembly line production by having one group of students make complete items while another group makes the same items on an assembly line (making paper hats, party favors, bookmarks, vocabulary cards). Then discuss such questions as these:

Why is production faster on the assembly line?
How does each worker on the line depend on others?

Which items are more uniform in appearance?

Which is more boring? Why?

What are the advantages and disadvantages of each type of production?

CONCLUDING ACTIVITIES

Share individual and committee projects with the group, emphasizing the roles and contributions of the workers under study.

Ask students to state the main idea in their own words, drawing upon charts, reports, or other materials to state such main ideas as these:

The work people do influences their life style.

More service workers will be needed in the years ahead.

Educational preparation varies with the type of work.

Complete and share movie box rolls, scrapbooks, and murals that highlight activities and contributions of the workers under study.

Evaluate students' understanding through discussion, test, or checklists.

 Questions, Activities, Evaluation

1. Select any one of the programs discussed in this chapter and do the following:
   a. Note examples of ways that you might include instruction in a regular teaching unit of your choice, such as community workers, our state, or our country.
   b. Plan two or three lessons or a short teaching unit that includes instructional objectives and related learning activities.
2. Examine a local course of study or unit of instruction, and note the following:
   a. Goals stated for multicultural, environmental, or other programs
   b. Conceptual components that are identified
   c. Types of questions that are suggested to guide study
   d. Examples of learning activities different from those presented in this chapter or in the appendix
3. Visit a classroom in a local school to observe instruction on one or more of these special programs. Note ideas that you can use.

references

Multicultural Education

American Association for Colleges of Teacher Education, Clearinghouse for Evaluation of Multicultural Materials. Bibliographies and reports.

Anti-Defamation League of B'nai B'rith. Catalog of instructional materials on ethnic groups, prejudice, and other topics.

BANKS, JAMES A., *Curriculum Guidelines for Multiethnic Education*, NCSS Task Force on Ethnic Studies Curriculum Guidelines. Washington, D.C.: National Council for the Social Studies, 1976. Rationale and guidelines for multiethnic education.

BANKS, JAMES A., *Teaching Strategies for Ethnic Studies* (2nd ed.). Boston: Allyn & Bacon, 1979. Guidelines, activities, and resources.

Bulletin of the Council on Interracial Books for Children, 1841 Broadway, New York, New York 10023. Stories, materials, and suggestions for multiethnic instruction.

GRANT, CARL A., (ed.), *Multicultural Education: Commitments, Issues, and Applications*, ASCD Multicultural Education Commission. Washington, D.C.: Association for Supervision and Curriculum Development, 1977. Guidelines and examples of classroom activities.

ROSE, PETER I., *They and We: Racial and Ethnic Relations in the United States*. New York: Random House, 1976. Background information.

Global Education

Center for Global Perspectives, 218 East 18th Street, New York 10003. Teaching guides with a variety of activities related to interdependence, conflict, communication, and change.

JELINEK, JAMES J., *Improving the Human Condition: A Curricular Response to Critical Realities*. Washington, D.C.: Association for Supervision and Curriculum Development, 1978. Chapters on environment, science and technology, and global and international perspectives.

KING, DAVID C., MARGARET S. BRANSON, AND LARRY E. CONDON, *Education for a World in Change*. New York: Center for Global Perspectives, 1976. Goals, objectives, concepts, and sample lessons.

OVERLY, NORMAN V., AND RICHARD D. KIMPSTON, eds., *Global Studies: Problems and Promises for Elementary Teachers*. Washington, D.C.: Association for Supervision and Curriculum Development, 1976. Rationale, content, and list of materials.

Social Education, 41 (January 1977), 13–54. Issue on global education; objectives, activities, and list of materials.

Law-Focused Instruction

American Bar Association, Special Committee on Youth for Citizenship, 1155 East 60th Street, Chicago, Illinois 60637.
Directory of Law-Related Activities (by states and of national interest).
Bibliography of Law-Related Curriculum Materials: Annotated.
Media: An Annotated Catalogue of Law-Related Audiovisual Materials.
Gaming: An Annotated Catalogue of Law-Related Games and Simulations.
Update (three issues yearly; articles, reviews of new materials).

GALLAGHER, ARLENE F., ed., *The Methods Book*. Chicago, Ill.: Law in American Society Foundation, 1977. Strategies for law-focused units, including case studies, values analysis, role playing, simulations, and mock trials.

GERLACH, RONALD A., AND LYNNE W. LAMPRECHT, *Teaching About Law*. Cincinnati, Ohio W. H. Anderson Co., 1975. Classroom activities, model lessons, materials, community resources, and evaluation techniques.

Law in American Society, journal of the National Center for law-focused education. Teaching strategies, reviews of materials, and games.

QUIGLEY, CHARLES N., *Law in a Free Society*. 5115 Douglas Fir Avenue, Calabasas, Calif. 91302. Activities for elementary and secondary students; units on authority, diversity, freedom, justice, participation, property, and responsibility.

TURNER, MARY JANE, ed., *Handbook of Legal Education Resources*. Boulder, Colo.: Social Science Education Consortium, 1977. Reviews instructional materials for use in elementary and secondary schools.

Environmental and Energy Education

BLAUSTEIN, ELLIOT H., AND ROSE, BLAUSTEIN, *Investigating Ecology*. New York: Arco Publishing Co., 1978. Projects and activities.

CARSON, RACHEL L., *Silent Spring*. Boston, Mass.: Houghton Mifflin Company, 1962. The volume that stirred many to action.

Energy and Education. Bimonthly Newsletter of the National Science Teachers Association, 1742 Connecticut Avenue, Washington, D.C. 20009. Reports on new developments and materials; ask to be placed on mailing list.

ERIC/SMEAC Information Reference Center. Columbus: Ohio State University, College of Education. Materials and blbliographies on environmental education.

KRALL, FLORENCE, MARGO I. SORGMAN, AND DONALD M. UHLENBERB, "Hooking the Geographer in Children with Field-Based Studies," *Journal of Geography*, 77 (May 1978), 108–110. Activities for studies of the community, solid wastes, and energy conservation.

MILES, BETTY, *Save the Earth*. New York: Alfred A. Knopf, 1974. Handbook of activities and community projects.

1979 Conservation Directory. Washington, D.C.: National Wildlife Association, 1979. Organizations concerned with conservation/environmental problems.

POSTHUMA, FREDERICK E., ed., *Energy and Education: Teaching Alternatives*. Washington, D.C.: National Education Association, 1978. Miniunits, sample lessons, and list of materials.

ROSCOE, GEORGE B., *200 Ways to Save Energy in the Home*. New York: Acropolis Books Ltd., 1978. Practical handbook.

SALE, LARRY L., GARDNER WEBB, AND ERNEST W. LEE, *Environmental Education in the Elementary School*. New York: Holt, Rinehart & Winston, 1972. Objectives, activities, organizations, and sources of information.

U.S. Department of Energy, Technical Information Office, P.O. Box 62, Oak Ridge, Tennessee 37830. Sample instructional materials for different grades.

Career Education

FULLER, JACK W., AND TERRY O. WHEATON, *Career Education: A Lifelong Process*. Chicago: Nelson-Hall Publishers, 1979. Guidelines, procedures, materials.

HEDSTROM, JUDITH E., AND MARY J. TURNER, *Career Education Sourcebook*. Boulder, Colo.: Social Science Education Consortium, 1977. Review of career education materials, annotated bibliography of items in ERIC, games and simulations, and references for teachers.

HOYT, KENNETH B., AND OTHERS, *Career Education: What It Is and How To Do It.* Salt Lake City, Utah: Olympus Publishing Company, 1974. Goals, concepts, and procedures.

MARLAND, SYDNEY P., JR., *Career Education: A Proposal for Reform.* McGraw-Hill, 1974. Rationale for a broad program, examples of programs, and pros and cons of career education.

TAYLOR, BOB L., AND OTHERS, *Tips for Infusing Career Education in the Curriculum.* Boulder, Colo.: Social Science Education Consortium, 1977. Guidelines and illustrative activities.

INCORPORATING CURRENT AFFAIRS AND SPECIAL EVENTS

How does the study of current affairs and special events contribute to social studies objectives?

What criteria should be used to select current affairs?

What approaches to the study of current affairs are used?

What guidelines and techniques should be used to handle controversial issues?

What guidelines should be used to provide instruction on holidays and special events?

Current affairs and such special events as holidays and commemorations are included in the social studies at all levels of instruction. This chapter presents guidelines for making these two recurring topics a dynamic and integral part of teaching and learning. It shows how such events can contribute to social studies objectives and gives criteria for selection, approaches to instruction, and teaching strategies.

Contributions to Social Studies Objectives

The study of current affairs and special events adds relevance, reality, and immediacy to the social studies program. Meaningful bridges can be built between life in and out of school and between the past and present.

Students' interests can be extended and deepened as they investigate events, issues, and holidays related to their own concerns, to long-term social trends, and to actions of individuals and groups. Units of study and material in textbooks, films, and other instructional media can be brought up to date. A beginning can be made in developing a continuing interest in the analysis of current affairs, the ability to evaluate the information that flows from the mass media, and an appreciation of the significance of holidays and other special events.

Current affairs and special events directly contribute to the attainment of social studies objectives. Concepts and generalizations are extended and enriched as students identify and describe the roles of individuals, situations that involve due process and other concepts, and special events that highlight valued aspects of our culture and other cultures. Students learn to apply thinking processes as they interpret, analyze, and evaluate events. They sharpen their reading, study, map, and other skills as they gather, organize, and report data on events. They consider attitudes and values and learn valuing processes as they analyze and evaluate actions and decisions in current affairs.

Current affairs instruction makes students aware of changes in their community, state, and nation and in the other places they study. It provides an opportunity to focus on topics of great social concern, such as equality for women and minority groups, environmental and energy problems and proposals, and the impact of mass media and other technological developments. The present can be linked to the past and related to the future as students consider current events in the context of trends in human affairs. And as students progress they can learn how to keep abreast of changes on their own by critically selecting, interpreting, analyzing, and evaluating the outpourings of mass media.

*Selecting
Current Affairs
for Study*

The multiplicity of current events, issues, and problems makes the selection of those to be studied no simple task. Although help can be obtained by relying on children's weekly newspapers, problems still exist in selecting local and state events, adding events not included in such periodicals and screening out some that have been included. As with the selection of content for the overall social studies program, teachers should apply the following criteria:

1. *Educational value:* Will children learn something significant? What contributions can be made to conceptual, process, skill, and affective objectives?
2. *Appropriateness:* Is the topic appropriate in terms of the maturity, understanding, and competence of pupils? Is it appropriate in terms of community conditions, values, and feelings?
3. *Relatedness:* Is it related to past and future learning? Can it be related to basic units of study?
4. *Available information:* If needed, can background information be obtained? Are suitable teaching materials available?
5. *Available time:* Is sufficient time available to obtain adequate depth of understanding?
6. *Reliability:* Is accurate information available? Can facts be differentiated from opinions? Can any bias in it be detected and analyzed by students?
7. *Timeliness:* Is it current? Is up-to-date information available? Is it related to basic trends? Are significant consequences discernible?

Every effort should be made to select events that are *significant for the particular class in which they are to be used.* Children should be guided so that

Sharing the News	Finding Current Events
About parents' work	Is it important?
About our own work	Do I understand it?
About trips we take	Can I report it well?
About community activities	Will it be interesting to others?
About changes in seasons	Is it related to other topics?

Chart 8–1   Chart 8–2

they will avoid sensational, lurid, and trivial events. In addition, specific attention must be given to the teaching of criteria, and direction must be provided in the selection of current events to be shared in class.

An effective procedure is to direct the students' search for current events related to a topic or unit they are studying. Problems and topics in such units as home and family, community workers, environmental problems, transportation, living in our state, regions of the United States, living in Canada, and living in Mexico make excellent focal points around which student-selected current events can be organized. When this is done, skills in critical and evaluative reading are enhanced, and the events are placed in a setting that gives them meaning.

Teachers can apply the same idea to current events bulletin boards, panel discussions, and other activities by setting a major theme or concept to guide the selection of events. Some teachers also use such basic concepts as cooperation, interdependence, creative contributions, and people's use of resources. When current events are gathered and discussed in terms of these basic concepts, growth in depth and breadth of understanding invariably takes place.

Scrapbooks or notebooks prepared individually, by small groups, or by the class can also be organized around specific concepts and themes, such as community changes, the environment, interdependence, or justice. Or several related concepts, such as environmental problems, air pollution, waste pollution, water pollution, and conservation of resources, may be used, placing the clippings about each concept in a separate section.

Whatever approach is used, the purpose is to help children relate the selection of current affairs to main objectives and to the activities used to achieve them. Continuing guidance of selection is essential and can be improved by utilizing standards that children themselves have helped to formulate, as shown in charts 8–1 and 8–2.

Approaches to the Study of Current Affairs

The several approaches to the study of current affairs described below have strengths and weaknesses. Many teachers use a combination of approaches, depending on the objectives to be achieved, the significance of the events involved, the units under study, and the materials available.

245

In general, the teacher should relate current affairs to basic units of instruction; then the problem of obtaining background material and giving perspective to current affairs becomes less difficult. As regional units such as areas of our state, midwestern United States, and regions of South America are studied, current events can be selected to highlight recent developments. As historical units such as early times in our state and colonial life are studied, current events can be selected to contrast then and now. Charts 8–3 through 8–6 show how topics in selected units can be used as guides for finding related current affairs.

The greatest problem in relating current affairs to units of instruction is one of timing. As one teacher put it, "So many significant events occur either

**We Need News Items
on Our Changing Community**

Activities of people
Conservation problems
Health and safety problems
Highways and traffic
Housing developments
New schools and libraries
Recreation facilities
Relations with other communities
Water supply

Chart 8–3

**We Need News Items
on Our State**

Agriculture	Industries
Cities	People
Communication	Population
Conservation	Recreation
Education	Relations with
Exports to	other states
foreign places	Rural areas
Government	Safety
Health	Transportation

Chart 8–4

**Find Items on These Regions
for Further Use**

Far Western states
New England states
North Central states
Rocky Mountain states
South Central states
Southeastern states
Southwestern states

Chart 8–5

**Look for News Items
on Canada Related to**

Cities	Relations
Communication	with the
Conservation	United States
Education	St. Lawrence
Government	Seaway
Mining	Trade and
Oil pipelines	industry
Provinces	Transportation
Relations with	Value of the
other countries	dollar

Chart 8–6

before or after I teach a unit.'' Many teachers meet this problem by using current events to launch units and, when possible, by timing the introduction of certain units to coincide with holidays, sessions of the state legislature and Congress, and other scheduled events. They relate current events to past units and continue certain strands, such as transportation, communication, and conservation, from unit to unit. They assure their classes of a good supply of current materials by collecting clippings and having students collect clippings for the units to come and by filing copies of children's periodicals that pertain to units they plan to develop.

WEEKLY STUDY OF PERIODICALS

Many teachers allot one period each week to the study of children's periodicals. It is convenient and relatively easy to assign the reading of articles, carry on discussion, and have students complete the activities and tests included in each weekly issue. But there are dangers in this approach. Too often it can lead to routine reading and answering of questions, superficial learning caused by an attempt to cover too many topics, and failure to relate current events to basic topics and units. The suggestions presented later in this chapter in the section on weekly periodicals for children should help teachers to avoid these dangers and to get maximum benefit from the weekly study of current affairs. In addition, a sound procedure is to direct the study of weekly periodicals by stressing points noted in chart 8–7.

MISCELLANEOUS REPORTING

Reporting on news items may be done on a daily or weekly basis or at irregular intervals. Teachers in primary grades and in some middle grades frequently use daily sharing. Some teachers prefer to have reporting on a weekly

Studying Weekly Newspapers

Skim it first to get a general idea of the contents.
Study pictures, maps, charts, tables, and graphs.
Note articles related to topics we are studying.
Note articles on which background material is given.
Note articles on which background material is needed.
Look up the meaning of any words you do not understand.
Look for facts, opinions, and differing points of view.
Be ready to raise questions and make comments during discussion.
Check your understanding by completing the tests.

Chart 8–7

basis or at assigned times. Children select items from newspapers, radio and television newscasts, and children's periodicals. Five to ten minutes may be set aside for daily sharing; a full period may be scheduled if a weekly plan is followed.

The weaknesses in this approach include the reporting of trivial events, superficial learning because of a lack of depth of study, isolation of events from past experiences and basic units of study, and the tendency for discussion to wander. These weaknesses can be overcome in part by directing the selection of current affairs, suggesting better sources of news items, systematically relating current affairs to basic topics and units, holding to discussion standards, and providing for deeper study of more important current affairs. What at first may appear to be isolated events can sometimes be related to significant topics. For example, a bicycle accident may lead to a discussion of safety rules with emphasis on showing concern for others; a news item on minority groups may lead to a discussion of rights and responsibilities, fair play, and other democratic values in community living.

Because of television and discussions with adults at home, children may raise questions that are beyond their level of maturity. Such questions should be dealt with on levels of experience and understanding appropriate for the group. After adequate comment or discussion, the teacher should direct the group's attention to other, more appropriate questions, reports, or topics. At times, particularly in the primary grades, children may report personal family events that are not proper topics for group discussion. When this happens, the teacher should be prepared to make a tactful and unobtrusive shift to other topics. Sometimes a wise course is to suggest that a particular topic is one that the child may want to discuss later with the teacher.

SHORT CURRENT AFFAIRS UNITS

Current affairs of special significance cannot always be dealt with in the daily or weekly period, nor can they always be incorporated in units of work. An important community or state event or problem, a major election, activities related to commemorations, the coming of a nation to the forefront in international affairs, the study of an individual of current national and international importance—any of these may require an intensive short unit using current materials and related background material. Sometimes special units featured in children's weekly periodicals need a more extended period of study. By noting related materials and suggestions contained in the teacher's edition of the weekly newspaper and by collecting pamphlets, books, films, and other resources, a teacher can plan to achieve important objectives by introducing special units.

Whichever approach or combination of approaches is used, every effort should be made to have students attain the highest possible levels of thinking and understanding. Three levels may be quickly identified as one visits

The Boeing Company

Travel agencies and transportation companies have pictures related to new developments. How might such materials be related to the study of current events?

classrooms. The *first level* is the routine reporting of events. Each child has seen, read, or heard about an event and shares it with the group with little or no discussion and without analyzing its relationship to other experiences. At the *second level* the reporting of an issue or event is followed by discussion of the most interesting points. This level requires more thinking by the class, may prove to be entertaining for those who participate in discussion, and may stimulate the interest of others. Usually it does not penetrate far beneath the surface to uncover basic concepts, trends, and relationships; it does not encourage any critical analysis of related issues and problems. At the *third level* students use problem-solving and critical thinking skills to explore the significance of the event or issue. They review supporting facts, consider differing points of view, and collect any additional data that is needed. To be sure, this third level cannot and should not be applied to all current affairs. When truly significant events are selected for study, however, children can usually be guided from the first to the third level, thus increasing the value of the experience.

Activities and Sources of Information

Many activities and sources are needed to develop a dynamic and interesting current affairs program. In selecting them, teachers should consider those that can be used by individuals and small groups as well as by the entire class. Here are some examples.

Illustrative Learning Activities

Set up a news bulletin board; assign a group of four or five students to add current news items each week, and encourage other students to bring items on a voluntary basis.

View telecasts or listen to broadcasts of ceremonies, inaugurations, festivals, holidays, commemorations, and other special events at home or in school; then report and analyze highlights.

Encourage individual students to volunteer to report on a current development in community activities, environmental or energy problems, or another topic that they have followed.

Conduct mock television and radio newscasts with students taking such roles as anchorperson, on-the-spot reporter, editorial commentator, weather reporter, and sports reporter.

Conduct round-table and panel discussions in which four to six students plan and present the topic (after critically reviewing news articles) and respond to questions from the class.

Make maps, charts, and graphs based on news reports related to such items as changes in population, proposals for the building of dams and electric power plants, journeys of public officials, events in countries under study, and trade between countries.

Make scrapbooks or notebooks that include events on a topic over a period of time to show how one event is related to others, how individuals and groups interact, how consequences flow from the decisions people make, and how changes are made in response to various conditions and demands.

Interpret maps, charts, diagrams, graphs, and tables that appear in students' periodicals and, as students gain experience and can handle the material, in newspapers and news magazines for adults.

Use students' periodicals, or daily newspapers with advanced students, to develop special skills such as scanning headlines to locate items on a topic; using the index to find the editorial page, travel section, or other section; and finding the pros and cons on particular issues.

Complete practice exercises designed to develop skills:

Find the index and write the letter of the section and the number of the page for the following subjects:

Business: section _____ page _____ Classified: section _____ page _____
Editorial: section _____ page _____ Sports: section _____ page _____
Television
and radio: section _____ page _____ Travel: section _____ page _____

Find examples of "doublespeak" in the article in the handout. List examples in the space below.

Playing up their own good	Playing up the bad of others
Playing down their own bad	Playing down the good of others

Analyze and evaluate news reports, editorials, and letters to the editor to identify point of view, positions on issues, bias, stereotypes, and prejudice.

Write editorials and letters to the editor on issues and topics of special concern to students.

Plan and publish (ditto) a newspaper for which students collect, write, edit, and proofread items related to (1) the unit under study, (2) other significant events, and (3) events of concern to students.

Students as well as the teacher should help select activities, and they should be involved in finding and using a variety of sources of information. Charts 8–8 through 8–14 include activities and sources that may well be considered as the teacher and students play ways to improve the study of current affairs. Notice the skills stressed in the last four charts.

Which of These Should We Use?

Individual reports	School intercom	Pictures	News maps
Committee reports	Bulletin board	Charts	Globe
Panel or debate	Quiz games	Murals	Models
Classroom newscasts	News files	Scrapbooks	Exhibits
Tape recorder	Picture file	Cartoons	Dramatizations

Chart 8–8

Finding Current Events

Bulletin board
Interviews of experts
News file
Newspapers and magazines
Radio and television newscasts
School and neighborhood library
Weekly newspaper

Chart 8–9

Periodicals in the Library

Current Events	The Times
Evening Star	Time
Junior Scholastic	U.S. News & World
News Explorer	Report
Newstime	Weekly Reader
Newsweek	Young Citizen

Chart 8–10

Preparing News Reports

Note the main ideas.
Select the most important facts.
Have pictures or other items to show.
Be ready to locate it on a map.
Be ready to answer questions.
If possible, relate it to a topic under study.

Chart 8–11

Checking Reports

Is it accurate?
Is it up to date?
Who reported it?
How can facts be checked?
Are there opinions in it?
What do others say?

Chart 8–12

Reporting Current Events

Is it important to the group?
Do I know it well?
Can I give illustrations?
Can I give it in my share of the time?
Do I have the main ideas?
Can I relate it to other topics or events?

Chart 8–13

Listening to News Reports

Do I understand it?
Do I have questions to ask?
Is it related to my report?
Is it related to topics we are studying?
What other information is needed?
Is it controversial? If so, are all sides given?

Chart 8–14

WEEKLY PERIODICALS FOR CHILDREN

Fortunately, well-prepared classroom periodicals are available for elementary school students. These newspapers and magazines are prepared by highly qualified writers, editors, and illustrators and contain a variety of current affairs that meet the criteria discussed earlier. Properly used in the classroom, they are an excellent resource. The following are used in many schools throughout the country:

My Weekly Reader (grades K–6) and *Current Events* (grades 7–8)—Xerox Education Publications, Education Center, Columbus, Ohio 43216

Let's Find Out, News Pilot, News Ranger, News Trails, News Explorer, News Citizen, and *Newstime* (grades K–6), and *Junior Scholastic* (grades 6–8)—Scholastic Magazines, 902 Sylvan Avenue, Englewood Cliffs, New Jersey 07632

Junior Review—Civic Education Service, 1733 K Street, Washington, D.C. 20006

These publications include significant current affairs, problems and concerns, information on holidays, and special events. A critical selection is made of topics appropriate for study in different grades. Points of view are presented on issues, related background information is frequently given, and tests and practice exercises are included. Suggestions for guiding study in the accompanying teacher's issue are to the point and consistent with sound teaching principles.

To get maximum value from children's newspapers and to avoid misusing them, the following guidelines should be observed:

1. Individual needs can be met by selecting editions that are appropriate to the reading levels in a class. Thus, editions on three or four reading levels may be needed in the same class.
2. Teaching techniques should include attention to developing readiness and understanding purposes for reading, building vocabulary, anticipating difficulties, interpreting maps and graphs, and discussing and summarizing key ideas. As with textbooks, films, and other resources, children's periodicals do not take the place of good teaching.
3. An effort should be made to use each issue of the periodical at a time when it will be most effective. Although one period each week may be set aside for intensive study, many teachers set aside a particular issue until related topics are being studied.
4. The whole-class approach to the study of selected sections of the weekly newspaper may be appropriate at times, but it should be supplemented by individual and small-group study to meet individual needs.
5. Whenever possible, relationships between the current affairs presented in the newspaper and basic units of instruction should be pointed out. Isolated items and incidents are soon forgotten, but events and issues related to basic studies become a part of the child's growing background of concepts and knowledge.
6. Learning resulting from the use of current periodicals should be both formally and informally evaluated. Tests provided in the periodicals, discussion, sharing, reporting, follow-up activities, and observation can be used to appraise basic outcomes.
7. A teacher should not expect a weekly periodical to provide the entire program of current affairs study. He or she must still include a careful selection of significant

local and state news items as well as important national and international items that may not have been mentioned in a particular issue.

8. By maintaining files of back issues, a teacher can provide reference material on topics and units in the basic program.

9. Maps, tables, charts, and other graphic materials should be used to improve competence in interpreting and making them.

CONTROVERSIAL ISSUES

The statement is sometimes heard that "elementary school children have inadequate backgrounds to study controversial issues." Ordinarily the speaker means that children are unable to study critical issues currently being debated by adults and achieve adult levels of understanding. Certainly, many current issues are beyond a child's understanding; but controversial issues do come up in social studies, and experienced teachers wisely select to study some of them. Such study assumes that some issues will be approached as unanswered questions toward which there are differing points of view that should be studied in a thoughtful manner. Some may be handled briefly, others may simply be introduced as continuing problems that will be reviewed in the future, and still others may be studied in detail because of their importance.

In the primary grades, attention is generally given to issues and problems close to the lives of children—issues and problems that come up in school, in the neighborhood, and in the community. Examples of these are differences of opinion on ways of carrying out classroom activities, how to conserve resources, ways of using parks and playgrounds, fair play in the treatment of others, the contributions of others, and conflicts between individuals and groups. At times, the teacher may include issues raised by children—perhaps a labor dispute, a demonstration, housing problems, or ways of preventing discrimination against others. Problems growing out of community living should not be ignored, nor should they be handled in a way that is beyond the ability of children to understand. A simple answer, an explanation of the problem, a clarification of the issue, or a brief discussion may suffice. The important thing is to keep the way open for such questions, to discuss them on an appropriate level, and to begin to lay a foundation for ongoing study of issues.

In the middle and upper grades, more involved issues and problems are encountered as children undertake such units as our state, the United States, Mexico, Canada, countries of Latin America, the Middle East, or Africa; and growth of democracy. Current events periodicals raise issues that may be related to basic units of study. Children may be exposed to other issues through television and radio programs, newspapers, and discussion at home.

The board of education often sets policy governing the study of selected current issues and problems. The following statement is typical of the policies established in many school systems:

1. Only significant issues and problems understandable to children, and on which children should begin to have an opinion, should be selected for study in the elementary school.
2. Instructional materials must present differing points of view, discussion should include all points of view, and respect for the views of others should be shown.
3. Teachers must guide learning so as to promote critical thinking and open-mindedness, and they must refrain from taking sides or propagandizing one point of view.
4. Special attention must be given to a consideration of background factors, possible consequences of various proposals, the need for additional information, and the detection of fallacies of thinking, logic, and argumentation.
5. The importance of keeping an open mind—that is, the willingness to change one's mind in the light of new information—should be stressed.

The criteria listed in the first part of this chapter must be applied rigorously in the selection of current issues and problems for study in the elementary school. Of special importance are those criteria related to educational value, significance, and appropriateness in terms of children's background of experience and community conditions. Generally, issues are not selected if they are offensive to individuals and groups in the community or will place the school in the center of a heated debate. Checking with other teachers and with the principal is a good idea when there is any doubt about the appropriateness of a particular issue.

Serious problems arise when a teacher becomes a crusader for a cause and pressures students to adopt the same point of view. Such behavior violates professional ethics and is a misapplication of the concept of freedom in teaching. Teachers at all levels of education are expected to guide the study of controversial issues in an impartial, unemotional, and unprejudiced manner. The teacher's prestige and position in the classroom must not be used to promote a partisan point of view. When the teacher is asked to express an opinion, it should be given and noted as an opinion, and not as the final answer.

The behavior of teachers should be a model for students. Charts 8–15 through 8–22 contain points that teachers may demonstrate through their own behavior and emphasize in instruction for students.

Special Events

Special events—holidays, special weeks, and commemorations—are a vital part of every cultural heritage. They have been set aside as a time for celebration and the expression of treasured values, ideals, and beliefs. Special days and weeks call attention to significant events, institutions, documents, great men and women, and customs that have been valued through the years. The manner in which special days and weeks are presented, the depth and quality of understandings and appreciations that are achieved, the historical perspective that is developed, and the attitudes that result determine in large measure their meaning and significance in the lives of children.

Defining Issues and Problems

How shall we state it?

Do we understand each term?

What are the subproblems?

What parts are most important?

Do we have ideas about any part?

Which parts need most study?

Chart 8–15

Checking Materials

What is the author's background?

What group sponsors or publishes it?

What is the group's purpose?

What are other points of view?

What materials present other points of view?

Chart 8–16

Discussing an Issue

Define it clearly so that all sides are known.

Consider each position.

Find facts related to all sides.

Verify and organize facts.

Make and change conclusions on the basis of facts.

Chart 8–17

Checking Points of View

What facts do I have?

How do I feel about it?

What do others believe?

How do they feel about it?

What would I believe and feel if I were in their place?

Chart 8–18

Working on Problems

Recall ideas related to it.

Think of possible ways to solve it.

Find information related to each possible solution.

Check and summarize information.

Try out the best solutions. Select the one that works best.

Chart 8–19

Forming Conclusions

Wait until facts are checked and organized.

Be sure facts are separated from opinions.

Consider outcomes and consequences.

Test tentative conclusions.

Make final conclusions.

Chart 8–20

CONTRIBUTIONS TO BASIC OBJECTIVES

The study of special days and weeks can contribute to the development of wholesome attitudes and deeper appreciations. Children learn about the contributions of great men and women (see chart 8–23), discover the deeper meaning of Thanksgiving, find out how Christmas and New Year's Day are celebrated in different countries, express friendship and affection for others on Valentine's Day, and discover how they can show appreciation on Mother's Day and Father's Day. The responsibilities of citizenship take on deeper meaning through the observance of Bill of Rights Day, Constitution Day, General Election Day, Veteran's Day, Washington's Birthday, Memorial Day, Flag Day,

Watch Out For

Name-calling and not giving the facts

Making general statements that sound nice but are vague

Using popular words so that the idea will be accepted

Saying that so-and-so believes it, therefore we should believe it

Saying that plain folks believe it, therefore we should

Giving only those facts that support one side

Stating that many people are accepting the ideas, so we should too

Chart 8-21

Watch Out For

Name-calling and not giving the facts

Making general statements that sound nice but are vague

Using popular words so that the idea will be accepted

Saying that so-and-so believes it, therefore we should believe it

Saying that plain folks believe it, therefore we should

Giving only those facts that support one side

Stating that many people are accepting the ideas, so we should too

Chart 8-21

Feelings and Issues

Control your feelings and help others control theirs.

Try to put yourself in the other person's place.

Try to understand other points of view.

Give facts when stating your own position.

Search for deeper causes of the difficulties.

Try to find reasonable proposals and next steps.

Make tentative conclusions and be ready to change them when feelings calm down.

Chart 8-22

What Contributions Did These Women Make?

Jane Addams	Paulina Wright Davis	Mary Church Terrell
Susan B. Anthony	Lucretia C. Mott	Sojourner Truth
Marian Anderson	Florence R. Sabin	Harriet Tubman
Ida Wells-Barnett	Sacajewea	Mary E. Walker
Mary McCleod Bethune	Elizabeth Cady Stanton	Emma H. Willard
Marie S. Curie	Henrietta Szold	Frances E. C. Willard

What others can we find?

_____   _____   _____
_____   _____   _____
_____   _____   _____

Chart 8-23

and Independence Day. Concepts such as interdependence, cross-cultural sharing, and cultural diversity are deepened and broadened as children discover similarities and differences in modes of celebrating holidays at home and in other lands. Intergroup understanding may be increased as children observe Brotherhood Week and join with others in observing Hanuka as well as Christmas, a practice increasingly common in recent years. International understanding may be increased as Pan-American Day and United Nations Day are observed. Reading, study, discussion, and other skills are sharpened as children find and share information related to special days and weeks.

GRADE PLACEMENT

Two policies are widely followed in determining the grade level at which special days and weeks will be included. First, certain holidays are studied in all grades, beginning in kindergarten and first grade. In succeeding grades opportunities are provided for more advanced learning through background studies, short units, relationships to basic social studies units, and varied activities. Second, certain special days and weeks are assigned to particular grades, when appropriate to the background and experience of children and the basic units in the program. An examination of grade placement charts usually reveals a pattern similar to this one:

Kindergarten and grade 1: Halloween, Thanksgiving, Christmas, New Year's, Washington's Birthday, Lincoln's Birthday, Valentine's Day, Easter, Hanuka, Mother's Day, Father's Day, and Flag Day are studied.

Grades 2 and 3: The above are continued on higher levels and Columbus Day, American Indian Day, Fire Prevention Day, Veteran's Day, Book Week, American Education Week, Arbor and Conservation Day, Memorial Day, Independence Day, and the day our community was founded are added.

Grades 4 through 6: The above are continued on higher levels and the following are added: Labor Day, United Nations Day, Constitution Week, Admission Day, Bill of Rights Day, Franklin's Birthday, Susan B. Anthony's Birthday, Brotherhood Week, Black History Week, Pan-American Day, Women's Equality Day, International Goodwill Day, Armed Forces Day, other special days and weeks of significance in the community or state, and special days of importance in other countries that are studied.

A CALENDAR OF SELECTED DAYS AND WEEKS

In some school systems a calendar or listing of special days, weeks, and ethnic holidays is provided so that teachers may select and plan ahead for those their class will study. Because practices vary greatly among school systems and among states, the calendar must be developed to fit local and state policies. The calendar in chart 8–24 was prepared by a group of teachers in a social studies workshop.

Teachers should be alert to special days and events not shown in chart 8–24 that are of importance to various ethnic groups. These could include German Day, Polish Bazaar, Mexican Independence Day, Cabrillo Day, and the Chinese Moon Festival in September; Madonna Del Lume (Italian), Irish Festival Week, Dia de la Raza, and Ohi Day (Greek) in October; Finnish Independence Day, Our Lady of Guadalupe, and Santa Lucia Day (Swedish) in December; Republic Day (India) and Chinese New Year in January; Our Lady of San Juan de Los Lagos (Mexican), St. Patrick's Day, and Greek Independence Day in March; Russian Easter, Cinco de Mayo (Mexican), Polish Constitution Day, and Norwegian Constitution Day in May.

Calendar of Selected Days and Weeks

September

Labor Day	first Monday
Citizenship Day	17
Constitution Week	includes 17
American Indian Day	fourth Monday

October

Junior Red Cross Enrollment	date announced
Fire Prevention Day	9
Columbus Day	second Monday
United Nations Day	24
Veteran's Day	fourth Monday
Halloween	31

November

Veteran's Day	11
Book Week	date announced
American Education Week	date announced
General Election Day	first Tuesday after first Monday
Thanksgiving	fourth Thursday

December

United Nations Human Rights Day	10
Bill of Rights Day	15
Christmas	25
Hanuka	date announced

January

New Year's Day	1
Martin Luther King, Jr.'s Birthday	15
Franklin's Birthday	17
Inauguration Day	20
Franklin D. Roosevelt's Birthday, March of Dimes	30

February

Lincoln's Birthday	12
Brotherhood Week, Black History Week	includes 12
Valentine's Day	14
Susan B. Anthony's Birthday	15
Washington's Birthday (observed third Monday)	22

March

Luther Burbank's Birthday	7
Conservation Week	includes 7
Arbor Day	various dates
Easter Week	in March or April
Passover	date announced

April

Pan-American Day	14
Kindness to Animals Week	date announced
National Youth Week	date announced
Earth Day	date announced

May

May Day, Loyalty Day, Law Day, Child Health Day	1
International Goodwill Day	18
Mother's Day	second Sunday
Armed Forces Day	third Saturday
Memorial Day	last Monday

June

Flag Day	14
Father's Day	third Sunday

July

Independence Day	4

August

National Aviation Day	19
Women's Equality Day	26

Chart 8–24

Richmond, California

Plan ahead to maximize learning during Black History and other special weeks.

Differentiating Experiences from Grade to Grade

Because many special days and weeks are given attention in each grade, overall planning is needed to make sure that children develop deeper appreciations and understandings as they progress through the grades. The following example on Arbor and Conservation Day includes activities that may be provided beginning in kindergarten and through sixth grade. Notice how many of them can be made a part of such units as the family, our community, living in our state, and conservation.

Activities for Arbor and Conservation Day

KINDERGARTEN THROUGH GRADE 2

Take a nature walk in the neighborhood.
Make collections of leaves.
Observe birds and listen to bird calls.
Observe the growth of certain trees and shrubs.
Care for plants and pets.

Learn about the many uses of wood.

Read and hear stories and poems about trees.

Write original poems and stories.

Make a display of leaves.

See films on forest animals.

Draw pictures of trees, flowers, and animals.

Take a study trip to see a house under construction.

Learn about synthetic fibers, paper, and other things made from wood.

Make picture books and scrapbooks.

Participate in a tree-planting ceremony.

GRADES 3 THROUGH 4

Observe and identify trees in the community.

Learn about commercial, recreational, and decorative values of trees.

Learn about logging and other aspects of the lumber industry.

Visit a sawmill.

Make a collection of different kinds of wood.

Learn about the importance of trees in the conservation of water, soil, and animal life.

Learn about our state's watersheds and water supply.

Learn about new uses of wood in construction, industry, and hobbies.

Plan a program and share it with parents or another class.

See films on logging, lumbering, reforestation, and water resources.

Make charts, a mural, or a movie roll box to summarize basic concepts.

GRADES 5 THROUGH 6

Establish a nature trail and make signs to mark trees, plants, and other objects.

Establish feeding and watering stations for birds.

Arrange an exhibit of flowers and leaves of common trees and shrubs.

Invite conservation experts to discuss questions and problems raised by the class and to report on newer practices.

Learn about the consequences of poor conservation practices in ancient civilizations in China and the Middle East.

Learn about present-day problems in the United States.

Learn how resources are interrelated.

Discuss the balance in nature and how people must work in harmony with nature.

Find out the steps that are being taken to improve conditions.

Read and report on contributions to the conservation movement of men such as Theodore Roosevelt and Gifford Pinchot.

Study and make maps of forest areas and state and national parks.

Make rules of camping.

Create poems, pageants, and programs that highlight conservation needs, problems, and forward-looking practices.

See documentary films or television pograms.

Plan and carry out a tree-planting ceremony to which other classes will be invited.

Make scrapbooks containing pictures, clippings, and notes on conservation.

PRACTICES IN PRIMARY GRADES

In the primary grades, major emphasis is given to introducing customs, traditions, ceremonies, rituals, the special meaning of terms, and the significance of selected special days and weeks. Activities and materials are matched to the children's maturity and their background of experience. Beginning with storytelling, simple art activities, and participation in classroom and school activities, the program moves to reading stories, reporting and sharing ideas, and more advanced activites.

Units of instruction in the social studies provide many opportunities for deeper study of special days and weeks. The home and family unit gives background to Mother's Day and Father's Day. The contributions of many different workers, a key learning related to Labor Day, takes on greater meaning as school and community workers are studied. Thanksgiving activities may be made a part of units on Indians or Pilgrims. Many teachers use Valentine's Day in the study of the post office. As communities in other lands are studied, attention may be given to ways in which New Year's, Christmas, and other holidays are celebrated. Arbor Day activities may be related to the study of conservation, a basic strand in many units from grade to grade.

Classroom parties may be held to celebrate such special days as Halloween, Thanksgiving, Christmas, Hanuka, Valentine's Day, and Easter. Children plan and make room decorations, greeting cards, party favors, hats, masks, and other items and enjoy appropriate songs, games, rhythms, poems, and stories. Bulletin-board displays, flower arrangements, centers of interest, and exhibits may be arranged, and murals, movie box rolls, and programs may be planned and shared with others.

Gifts and greeting cards may be made in connection with such special days and weeks as Junior Red Cross Week, Veteran's Day, Christmas, Valentine's Day, Easter, Mother's Day, and Father's Day. Often children stage special ceremonies, assemblies, parades, and pageants. Films, television and other audiovisual resources, reading materials, interviewing individuals in the community, creative activities, and study trips to places in the community are also utilized.

MORE ADVANCED LEARNING IN LATER GRADES

Instruction in middle and upper grades should be planned to increase children's depth and breadth of understanding. Both the teacher and the class should search for new stories, poems, pictures, articles, and activities related to special days and weeks. After discussing what children have learned in earlier grades about a given day or week, some teachers use leading questions to guide the search for new ideas and materials: How did this special day originate? How was it celebrated in early times? What early customs have we kept for our own? How is it celebrated in other lands? What individuals worked to make it a holiday in our country? What are some famous stories and poems about this holiday?

Questions such as these can be applied to a large number of special days and weeks. Other, more specific questions relate to particular holidays. These ask the meanings of special terms, refer to specific individuals, and show whether the holiday has civic, religious, or personal-social significance. The examples that follow illustrate questions that can be used to guide children's study of background material related to different types of special days.

> *Veteran's Day:* When was Armistice Day first proclaimed? Why was Armistice Day changed to Veteran's Day? Why is the unknown solider honored each year at the National Cemetery in Arlington? What is meant by "preservation of fundamental principles of freedom?" What obligations should each individual assume for the peace, welfare, and security of our country?
>
> *Thanksgiving:* What were harvest festivals like in ancient times? Why did people have them? According to various authorities, what was the first Thanksgiving like in our country? How was it different from earlier harvest festivals? Who was Sarah Joseph Hale, and what did she do to make Thanksgiving a national holiday? Which president issued the proclamation that made Thanksgiving a national holiday? How has the celebration of Thanksgiving changed?
>
> *Washington's Birthday:* Where did Washington live as a boy? What was his home like? How was he educated? What are the main periods of his service to our country? What traits of leadership caused his countrymen to call on him to be the first president? Why is he honored as "the father of our country"? What is meant by "First in war and first in peace"?

Certain special days and weeks are explored in detail at a time when the class is studying a particular unit; this may be in addition to a short observance held as a part of classroom or school activities. For example, Constitution Day, Bill of Rights Day, United Nations Day, and the contibutions of Franklin, Lincoln, Washington, and other historic leaders are included in units on the United States and the growth of democracy. Pan-American Day and International Goodwill Day take on deeper significance when tied in with such units as South

America and other lands. Great men and women and special days of importance in the child's state should be included in the unit on our state.

Short units are needed to give background on a certain special day or week. Examples are fire prevention, Red Cross activities, and the Parent-Teachers Association. Short units on topics such as these give children the background they need to understand the purposes and activities of organizations and agencies that render services of benefit to both children and adults. Other short units may be developed on great men and women, special weeks, or days of special importance in the community or state. Individual study and preparation of reports on related background information are used to develop greater depth of understanding. The following are examples of reports written by children in the fifth grade.

Harvest Festivals before the Pilgrims Had Their First Thanksgiving

Long ago, before the Pilgrims landed, people had celebrations at harvest time. They were happy to have a good harvest. Some would make offerings to the spirits and gods that they thought made seeds fertile and made the crops grow.

The oldest known harvest festival, Succoth, was in Israel. Thanks were given for finding a place to live and for the harvest.

In ancient Greece there was a celebration that lasted nine days. It was in honor of the goddess of the harvest called Demeter. Demeter was also the goddess of corn.

The festival of the harvest moon was held in old China long ago. The Chinese would bake moon cakes. They also thought that a rabbit lived in the moon.

Some of our early settlers had learned about harvest festivals in England. The English would have feasts and share what had been raised. People in the villages would get together and each family would buy something.

The peasants in Old Russia had feasts and dancing. One custom was to place a wreath of grain by the house. A new one was put there each year. They thought it would help make a good harvest.

The Iroquois Indians had feasts at different times. One was in the spring at maple syrup time. Another was at planting time. Still another was at harvest time. They also had a bean and a corn festival. All together they had about seven festivals a year.

Some teachers take time before the school year ends to consider special days that occur during summer vacation. For example, Independence Day and the events leading up to it can be studied as a part of units on the United States. Children can be asked to watch for special reports and activities as celebrations take place during the summer. National Aviation Day, August 19, should not be overlooked as an opportunity for children to collect clippings and other materials for use in transportation and aviation units when school starts in the fall. Similarly, Labor Day celebrations and activities in early September are sources of experience and information that can be put to use at the beginning of the school year.

A variety of activities and materials for special days and weeks should be used to improve learning. Some examples follow.

Learning Activities for Special Events

Investigate origins of holidays, contributions of men and women, holidays in other lands, and customs brought from places around the world.

Interview workers at special agencies and organizations; experts on conservation, fire prevention and other topics; and writers and scholars who have studied special events and famous people.

Visit special exhibits, historic places, homes of famous people, and special agencies and organizations.

View films, filmstrips, slides, photographs, television programs, picture files, and exhibits that show special events.

Listen to stories, tapes, records, guest speakers, panel discussions, and individual and group reports.

Read stories, articles, poems, essays, biographies, autobiographies, diaries, local documents, reference materials, and clippings.

Arrange bulletin boards, flowers for special occasions, room decorations, centers of interest, and exhibits of book jackets and other items.

Design and make room decorations, greeting cards, costumes, hats, masks, puppets, gifts, gift wrappers, party favors, booklets, scrapbooks, shadow boxes, peep boxes, movie box rolls, dioramas, time lines, murals, and charts.

Create and share songs, poems, plays, skits, quiz games, and stories.

Participate in or witness role playing, pageants, festivals, ceremonies, parades, plays, and games.

Sources of Information

Children's weekly newspapers and monthly magazines include stories and articles on great men and women, holidays, and special weeks. At times they feature new stories and activities that may be used to provide fresh learning experiences. The teacher's guides that accompany weekly periodicals occasionally list related films, filmstrips, television programs, books, pamphlets, and other materials.

Children's encyclopedias are excellent sources of information. The background materials, stories, pictures, time lines, reading lists, dates of holidays, and other information they contain can be used for individual study and reference. *The World Almanac* lists the dates set for holidays each year and includes information on holidays observed in different states and public days in Canada.

Teacher and *Instructor,* both magazines for teachers, include stories, articles, units, bulletin-board suggestions, construction activities, reading lists, bibliographies, and other material. Excellent sources for teachers, they are also useful to more able children who are pursuing individual studies or who wish to find directions for making things related to a particular holiday.

Television and radio program listings should be checked in newspapers, weekly program guides, and program bulletins issued by broadcasting companies and school systems. Newspapers and magazines for adults feature special reports and articles that can be read and shared by many children. Specific suggestions on special days and weeks are included in courses of study, units of instruction, and bulletins on special days available in local school systems.

Questions, Activities, Evaluation

1. Select a current event from a local newspaper, using the criteria suggested in this chapter. Note objectives that might be achieved and make a plan for using the event, including a selection of learning activities from this chapter.
2. Select a holiday or other special event and make a plan for teaching it, including objectives and learning activities.
3. Review several periodicals for childen and identify articles, maps, charts, test items, and other material that you might use in a unit of instruction.
4. Make a calendar of special days and weeks that are celebrated in your community. Indicate the grades in which certain days and weeks might be emphasized.
5. Which of the charts presented in this chapter might you use in your teaching? What adaptations would you make to meet the needs of children in different grades?

references

For specific suggestions on holiday observances, see current issues of *Instructor, Teacher, School Activities,* and *School Arts.*

FRANKSON, CARL E., AND KENNETH R. BENSON, *Crafts Activities Featuring 65 Holiday Ideas.* West Nyack, N.Y.: Parker Publishing Co., 1970. Practical activities for special days.

JAROLIMEK, JOHN, *Social Studies in Elementary Education.* New York: Macmillan, 1977. Chapter on current affairs.

MUESSIG, RAYMOND H., ed., *Controversial Issues in the Social Studies: A Contemporary Perspective* (45th yearbook). Washington, D.C.: National Council for the Social Studies, 1975. Models for teaching followed by discussion of selected issues.

MYERS, ROBERT J., *Celebrations: The Complete Book of American Holidays.* New York: Doubleday & Co., 1972. Helpful to middle- and upper-grade students as well as to teachers.

PRICE, CHRISTINE, *Happy Days.* New York: E. P. Dutton & Co., 1969. A UNICEF book of special days in different countries.

DEVELOPING CONCEPTS, GENERALIZATIONS, AND THINKING PROCESSES

What teaching strategies are used to develop concepts and generalizations?
What guidelines can be used to develop critical and creative thinking?
What strategies can be used to develop intellectual processes that are basic to effective thinking?
How can problem-solving procedures be used to unify and sequence intellectual processes?

Development of concepts, generalizations, and thinking ability is given high priority in the social studies. This chapter presents the teaching strategies found most useful in classroom instruction. First it gives an overview of basic aspects of thinking; then it discusses procedures for developing concepts and generalizations. Detailed attention is given to strategies for developing intellectual processes that are central to thinking ability. Model questions presented for each process can serve as guidelines for planning units, lessons, and discussions. The final section of the chapter discusses how group problem solving may be used to bring together various aspects of thinking in daily classroom instruction. Chapter 10 focuses on the development of creative thinking through expressive activities.

Basic Aspects of Thinking

Chart 9–1 shows aspects of thinking that are important in instructional planning. Notice that thinking involves the use of symbols that stand for objects and events. In the social studies word symbols, map symbols, and number symbols in tables, graphs, and other media are used.

269

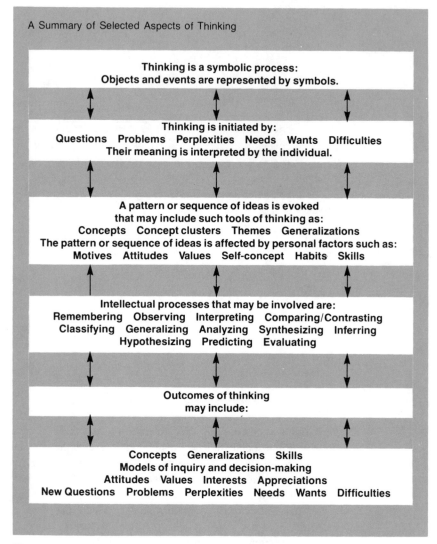

A Summary of Selected Aspects of Thinking

Thinking is a symbolic process:
Objects and events are represented by symbols.

Thinking is initiated by:
Questions Problems Perplexities Needs Wants Difficulties
Their meaning is interpreted by the individual.

A pattern or sequence of ideas is evoked
that may include such tools of thinking as:
Concepts Concept clusters Themes Generalizations
The pattern or sequence of ideas is affected by personal factors such as:
Motives Attitudes Values Self-concept Habits Skills

Intellectual processes that may be involved are:
Remembering Observing Interpreting Comparing/Contrasting
Classifying Generalizing Analyzing Synthesizing Inferring
Hypothesizing Predicting Evaluating

Outcomes of thinking
may include:

Concepts Generalizations Skills
Models of inquiry and decision-making
Attitudes Values Interests Appreciations
New Questions Problems Perplexities Needs Wants Difficulties

Chart 9–1

Thinking is initiated by problems, questions, perplexities, needs, wants, or difficulties. To think in really profitable directions, the student must be able to identify, recognize, and clarify the questions and problems to be studied in units of instruction.

The tools of thinking—what a student uses to think—include the concepts, concept clusters, themes, and generalizations gleaned from past experience and current activities. What students remember and observe, therefore, are key processes in determining the quality and level of their thinking. Of critical importance are the concepts, generalizations, and other tools of thinking developed in the social studies.

Also important are the intellectual processes that are linked with concepts and used to process information. Remembering, observing, interpreting, classifying, and generalizing are central in concept development, the deriving of generalizations, and the use of higher level processes. Inferring, hypothesizing, and predicting extend thinking beyond given information. Analyzing breaks a whole into parts, and synthesizing integrates parts into a whole. Evaluating involves critical thinking in which standards are used to make judgments of worth.

The outcomes of thinking in social studies are as broad as the objectives—conceptual, inquiry, skill, and affective learning. Also important as outcomes are new questions and problems that can be used to begin new rounds of thinking in an ongoing sequence.

Critical and Creative Thinking

Of special importance in all phases of the social studies program are critical and creative thinking. Ways they may be used and developed should be kept in mind as instruction is planned and as learning experiences are developed in the classroom.

CRITICAL THINKING

In critical thinking, making an evaluation in terms of standards or criteria is emphasized. To make a sound appraisal, students must understand concepts involved in the standards or criteria, clearly perceive what is being appraised, suspend judgment until the evidence is weighed, and control feelings.

The social studies often call for critical examinations of ideas, proposals, issues, points of view, discussion procedures, committee work, statements in reading materials, and ideas presented in audiovisual materials. For example, in evaluating discussion, the direction of thinking is set by standards embedded in questions such as these: Did we stick to the topic? Did each individual participate? Were different points made?

Critical thinking is also used to evaluate ideas presented in instructional materials—statements in textbooks and current materials, arguments presented on current issues, descriptions of cause-effect relationships, terms and phrases that stimulate emotions, treatment of women and ethnic groups, propaganda techniques, and exaggerated and incongruous points. Facts are differentiated from opinions, relevant and irrelevant information noted, the evidence for various statements examined, and conclusions checked against the facts presented to support them (see charts 9–2 and 9–3).

As children gain experience, critical thinking is put to use to examine beliefs and values that are meaningful to them. Taking turns, fair play, equal opportunity, and rights of others may be considered in terms of why we value them, how they improve working relations, and how we can extend them to new situations. Beliefs or values that are just "taken on" because of association with others will not be firmly grounded in understanding. A person who takes on beliefs uncritically is trained, not educated. If learners reflect, reconstruct, and test beliefs, they will be more likely to base their beliefs on evidence, not just emotion. This enhances both the meaning and the significance of treasured values and beliefs. Additional examples and a teaching strategy are presented in the section on evaluating. Chapter 13, "Developing Attitudes, Values, and Valuing Processes," illustrates vital applications of critical thinking.

CREATIVE THINKING

The term *creative* implies new or original. For a child it may be a new interpretation, a grasp of new relationships, an original synthesis and expression of ideas, a new proposal or hypothesis, or a new way of doing something. Signs of creative thinking are originality rather than conformity, divergent thinking that calls forth multiple responses rather than convergent thinking that gives unifying responses, and production of new ideas rather than reproduction of old ideas. Basic to creativity are such traits as sensitivity to problems, fluency of ideas and words, expressional fluency, semantic flexibility and elaboration, originality, perception of objects and activities in new ways, and redefinition of symbols.

In social studies, creative thinking is stimulated whenever children are encouraged to suggest new ideas or ways of doing things, express thoughts and feelings in original ways, and propose solutions to problems. Creative thinking may be developed by planning and arranging work centers and displays, framing hypotheses, organizing and summarizing information in new ways on maps and charts, constructing objects, dramatizing, expressing thoughts and feelings through art and music, expressing ideas through oral and written language activities, and planning activities to culminate a unit of instruction. But creative thinking is not limited to special activities; rather it is approaching problems or viewing them in a way that opens new horizons. As different pictures, films, and other materials are used in units of instructions, questions such as the following will stimulate creative thinking:

> What do you see in this picture that is new? In what other ways could it have been shown? How could we express it?
> What do you think about that statement? Which words have special meaning? How could it be improved?
> How is this film related to an experience you have had? How is it different?
> How did this part make you feel? How would you tell it or write it to express your feelings?

Creative thinking is also applied to reading. Creative reading takes the reader beyond literal interpretation to implied meanings, appreciative reactions, and evaluation. The reader visualizes what is read, identifies with characters, recalls experiences and compares them with experiences presented in the text, anticipates what is coming, notes biases, searches for new relationships, and tries to bring together ideas from several sources. Charts 9–4 and 9–5 illustrate specific points related to creative reading.

To promote creative thinking it is first necessary to build a rich background of experience. During this phase, the teacher works to help children perceive relationships and develop concepts. The children's background is enriched through the use of expressive terms and phrases, use of pictures and other materials that stimulate imagery, and reading of materials that help to build word pictures. Students discuss reactions and consider the most significant aspects of the topic under study. A closely related phase of creativity is the organizing, reorganizing, and consolidating of new learnings.

Some preliminary attempts at creative expression may be seen in the discussion, sharing, planning, and evaluation that take place as children clarify meanings, express reactions, and begin to explore possibilities. Fluency of thinking and flexibility in handling ideas develop along with increasing depth of understanding and the ability to reorganize ideas into new patterns. Then new insights and relationships, and possible ways of expressing them, are discovered. Some writers refer to this as the stage of illumination, or discovery; the individual says, "I've got it!" For children it is the discovery of a fresh and original way to express the thoughts and feelings that have been building up within them. (See chart 9–6.)

In the next phase, students proceed to try out, or express, the creative idea they have discovered. In the process of creating something—whether it be a mural, model, dramatic portrayal, picture, or hypothesis—a child may

Creative Readers	Getting a Feeling for Others as You Read	Creative Thinkers
Find special meanings of words and phrases.	Try to picture how they live.	Build up a background of ideas.
Grasp the main ideas and supporting details.	Look for words and phrases that stir your feelings.	See objects and activities in new ways.
Relate ideas to their own experiences.	Look for humor, exaggeration, and comparisons.	Organize ideas in new ways.
Discover hidden or implied meanings.	Try to put yourself in their place.	Search for original ways to express ideas.
Think of ways ideas and meanings can be related.	Try to figure out why they do things their way.	Select the best from the old and new.
Search for ways to apply ideas.	Try to guess how they do things, and then check to see if you are right.	Are willing to try new ideas.
		Put ideas to use in other activities.

Chart 9–4   Chart 9–5   Chart 9–6

change it, redo it, alter a part of it, or start anew after evaluating the adequacy of expression of the original idea. Vital elements in this phase are the original conception of the idea, the perception of progress in expressing it, and the integration of various elements into a harmonious whole. The child's self-evaluation is important in determining how to proceed and what form the final product will take. Additional suggestions are presented later in the section on synthesizing and in the following chapter.

Concept Development

Concepts are basic tools of thinking and inquiry in social studies. Continuing attention must be given to their development, and both direct and vicarious kinds of experiences should be provided. For example, study trips, constructing and processing materials, and dramatic representation along with films, pictures, and models can provide the kinds of direct or sensory experiences that make concepts meaningful. But learning should not stop at this point. Vicarious experiences are needed to take students far beyond objects and events they can experience directly. Through reading, use of maps, discussion, individual research, and other vicarious experiences, thinking and learning can be extended as old concepts are enriched and new ones developed. The following examples are illustrative (additional examples are presented in chapter 10, "Developing and Applying Reading Skills," under building concepts and vocabulary).

In a unit on the farm, a group of lower-grade children developed and used concepts represented by such words as *silo, corral, feeding, milking, crush, bottle, calf, seeds, garden, barn, chute, hay,* and *fodder* through the following activities:

Visiting a dairy farm to see farm buildings and the feeding and milking of cows

Engaging in and discussing dramatic play related to chores on the farm

Constructing and using corrals and barns in dramatic play

Collecting seeds, planting them, and caring for a garden

Finding out how plants grow with different types of soil and varying amounts of sunshine and water

Reading and listening to stories related to life on the farm

Expressing group and individual experiences through art, rhythms, discussion, group chart making, and songs

Seeing a film on farm life

Teachers can develop various shades of meaning by using literature, art, and music. A reading of tales about Daniel Boone extends the meanings of scout, defending the fort, and adventures of early explorers. Recordings of songs sung by the pioneers as they went west and carefully selected pictures that depict the joys, sorrows, hopes, and aspirations of the pioneers as they

How might you use activities such as these to develop concepts?

San Diego, California

established homes and towns give overtones of feeling to terms, such as *husking, bees, clearing, attack, homemaking, hardship, courageous,* and *fearless,* that can be attained in no other way. Similarly, folk dances help children see how the pioneers enjoyed themselves. Such qualitative aspects of concept building must not be overlooked.

Group sharing of experiences through discussion, reporting, and storytelling aids in concept building; pictures, models, and objects should also be used to clarify special meanings. Children and resource persons who have taken trips to places being studied can tell about the places and show pictures and photographs to the class. Materials brought by children that relate to concepts in the unit can be discussed, demonstrated, and used to increase understanding. During a study of Mexico, for example, one child brought in pottery, clothing, and jewelry. In a study of China two children brought in and demonstrated the use of ehru, temple bells, and a gong. Another child brought pictures of Chinese boats and pointed out the differences between junks, sampans, and other Chinese boats.

Clarification of problems, evaluation, and reflection on relationships to past experience and future action, activities have little value without discussion of objectives. One child illustrated this point very well during an activity involving construction designed to develop concepts of a Mexican bazaar. When asked what he was making, he said, "I'm just nailing boards to this box." He had not been in on the planning, discussion, and evaluation of the bazaar for use in the study of Mexico. In terms of his learning experiences, he was truly just nailing boards.

Both the number and the difficulty of the concepts must be considered; introducing too many concepts at one time may lead to misconceptions, confusion, boredom, word-calling without meaning, and little or no comprehension. A long, tedious list of ideas to check on a study trip, during a film, or in a dictionary may result in superficial learning. In each unit, children need opportunities not only to develop new concepts but also to enrich and extend concepts they already have. For example, in a well-planned study of colonial and pioneer life, concepts such as these will be learned: town meeting, dame schools, church services, candlemaking, ways of travel, utensils, and weapons.

TYPES OF CONCEPTS

A concept may be viewed as a cognitive category into which items with common attributes or characteristics may be placed. Different types of concepts should be recognized so that instruction may be adjusted to the special features of each.

Two types of concepts may be identified by level of abstraction.* *Concrete* concepts such as round, red, lake, island, and furniture may be developed

---

*Robert M. Gagne and Leslie J. Briggs, *Principles of Instructional Design* (New York: Holt, Rinehart & Winston, 1974).

by observing firsthand or by seeing pictures to identify attributes or properties; they are the easiest to teach. *Defined* concepts are more abstract and have meanings that go beyond directly observable properties. Examples are family, justice, and freedom. Note that each requires careful definition, examples, and identification of relationships—for instance, relationships among members of a family.

Three types of concepts may be identified as calling for a combination of attributes.* *Conjunctive* concepts, such as legislator, conservation, and truck, are based on observed characteristics that are additive. For example, the meaning of legislator includes residence plus age plus election. Students must bring together all essential characteristics that are part of a conjunctive concept. *Disjunctive* concepts have either/or characteristics that must be identified—for example, citizenship by birth, by passing examinations, or because one's parents were born here. Students must identify the alternative characteristics or attributes. *Relational* concepts, such as population density, per capita income, area, and speed, are defined in terms of how one element varies in relation to another. Instruction should be focused on the relationships and operational definitions that indicate the procedures or operations that are involved—for example, population density is determined by dividing the number of people in an area by the square miles or kilometers in the area (population density = population ÷ area).

A distinction is also made between concepts that are value-neutral and those that are value-loaded. *Descriptive* concepts, such as resources, production, and role, are usually value-neutral. *Valuative* concepts, such as equality, democracy, loyalty, and prejudice, have preferential elements and stir feelings. Consideration must be given to emotional dimensions of valuative concepts, to positive and negative uses of them, and to the context in which they are used. Teachers should recognize that feelings associated with valuative concepts are among "the facts to be considered."

Of special importance is instruction designed to help students recognize the *specificity* and *generality* of concepts used in social studies. Land, resources, family, community, and nation are generally applicable across cultures, time periods, and geographic areas. Concepts such as muckrakers, caste system (in India), the Loop (in Chicago), and New England colonies are specifically applicable only in designated cultures, places, or time period. Generally applicable concepts are used to formulate generalizations that cut across topics or settings under study. Specifically applicable concepts are used to highlight features of particular cultures, places, and time periods. Students should recognize the culture-bound, place-bound, and time-bound characteristics of specifically applicable concepts and not, for example, confuse the caste system in India with the social class system in other places or life in the New England colonies with life in the southern colonies.

*Jerome S. Bruner, Jacqueline J. Goodnow, and George A. Austin, *A Study of Thinking* (New York: John Wiley & Sons, 1956).

CONCEPT DEVELOPMENT STRATEGIES

Four strategies are used to develop concepts: defining, distinguishing examples from nonexamples, listing-grouping-labeling, and problem solving. All give attention to the class or category to which the concept belongs and the characteristics or rule for placing it in the category. For example, the concept *taxes* is a class of payments (different from fines and tariffs) and is levied according to law and paid to the government.

defining Textbooks and other materials provide definitions and teachers state them so that students can put them to immediate use. Students find and share definitions, using glossaries, dictionaries and other sources to get definitions that fit the context in which they are used. Several types of definition should be used, as illustrated in the following examles:

> *Demonstrating:* Watch while I show what candle dipping means.
> *Showing:* This picture shows what a tugboat is.
> *Using analogies:* A governor is like a president except he runs a state.
> *Using synonyms or antonyms:* Rapid means fast. Rapid is the opposite of slow.
> *Using glossaries or dictionaries:* The glossary says that a vaquero is a cowboy.
> *Stating behavior (behavioral definitions):* A legislator campaigns for office, writes bills, serves on committees, things like that.
> *Stating operations (operational definitions):* You figure population density by dividing the population of an area by the square miles in the area.

These model questions and charts 9–7 and 9–8 may be used to focus attention on different types of definition.

> What do you mean by _____ (producer, goods, urban function)? What does _____ mean?
> What is a good way to clear up the meaning of this term? Using a picture or model? Demonstrating the meaning? Other?
> Who can define _____ (carpenter, judge, scout) by telling what he or she does?
> Who can define _____ (average income per family, population density) by stating how it is figured?
> Which meaning(s) of _____ (bank, pollution, democracy) should we use? Which one best fits the context?

distinguishing examples from nonexamples This strategy is used to develop specific concepts students need in learning activities; it is frequently used in conjunction with the defining activities noted above. Major steps are as follows:

1. State the concept to be learned or pose a question.

> Today we are to learn about peninsulas.
> What is a peninsula?

Questions to Guide Defining	How Do Feelings Affect the Meaning of These Terms?	
What is to be defined (word, phrase, map symbol, behavior, operation, feelings)? How is it like and different from others we know? What is included? Not included? What kind of definition (example, analogy, picture, demonstration, behavioral, operational) will be most useful?	Communism Demands Democracy Dictator Environment Fair play Freedom Ghetto Justice	Lobbyist Majority Minority Police Politician Pollution Poverty President Rights

Chart 9–7   Chart 9–8

2. Identify defining characteristics (critical attributes).

> Look at this example on the wall map. Which parts are surrounded by water?

3. Present other examples of the concept.

> Look at the map on page 22. See the peninsula at the bottom. Find the one on the next page.

4. Present nonexamples.

> Look at the island on page 22. Why is that *not* a peninsula? Find others that are *not* peninsulas.

5. Have students state or write a definition.

> A piece of land nearly surrounded by water and connected with the mainland

listing-grouping-labeling

This is an inductive strategy developed in the Taba project as one of three cognitive tasks (see end-of-chapter reference by Taba and others). The classifying process and discovery by students are involved to help students group items encountered in materials and activities:

1. Have students identify and help list items to be grouped.

> What did you see (hear, note)?
> What items are shown in this picture?

2. Identify items that can be grouped together.

> Which items seem to belong together?

3. State characteristics of items that belong together.

> Why do they belong together? How are they alike?

4. Label the group.

> What is a good name or label for the group?
> Why is that a good name (label)?

279

Concept development, extension, and enrichment may be fostered through problem solving, particularly when the concepts being considered are ones like justice, equality, democracy, prejudice, and others that grow in meaning as they are encountered in differing contexts. Through problem solving the meaning of concepts is clarified in ongoing activities, put to immediate use, and used to pose questions, gather and process data, and state conclusions, as the following example from a unit on prejudice illustrates (a detailed discussion of problem solving is presented at the end of this chapter).

1. Define the problem

   What is prejudice and how does it affect us?

2. Pose questions (or hypotheses) to guide study.

   What is prejudice? What causes it? What are different types of prejudice? What are the effects on oneself and on others? How can prejudice be reduced?

3. Collect and process relevant information.

   What information do we have on each question? How shall we organize it? Can we use the headings *causes, types, effects,* and *ways to reduce?*

4. State a conclusion.

   What can we conclude about causes, types, effects, and ways to reduce?

5. Suggest needs for further study.

   What new questions do you have? How can we find answers to them?

The previously noted strategies above may be used to develop concept clusters and themes. Each concept in a cluster or in a theme must be given special attention, however. For example, the cluster of concepts included in *landforms*—plains, hills, plateaus, mountains—may be developed by identifying examples and nonexamples of plains, then hills, and so on. In addition, differences between plains and hills and between plateaus and mountains should be identified. Focusing attention on clusters of concepts allows meaningful comparisons to be made between pairs of concepts; moreover, meaningful examples and nonexamples are contained within the clusters. For instance, after identifying examples of plains, students may identify hills and plateaus as nonexamples. Another advantage is that relationships among the concepts in a cluster make for meaningful learning that promotes the ability to recall, recognize, and apply concepts. This may be illustrated by the comment of a student who stated, ''As you go across the plains you come to hills and then on to plateaus and finally to mountains—the Rocky Mountains.''

Themes, such as ways of living on the frontier, the westward movement, equality for ethnic minority groups, and extending civil rights to all groups, call for concept development plus extended learning activities within a unit of instruction. For example, the theme of ''extending civil rights to all groups''

280

calls for initial instruction on civil rights, followed by a series of learning activities on the struggles of various groups to achieve them. Similarly, the meaning of "ways of living on the frontier" is deepened and extended as students participate in a series of learning activities and process information obtained from readings, films, filmstrips, and other media.

Development of
Generalizations

Generalizations are summarizing and concluding statements based on information and indicating the relationship among concepts. They have many uses in the social studies—they can generate questions or hypotheses to guide study, to explain human behavior and relationships, or to build a model or theory. For instance, students who comprehend the generalization that

How can photos such as this one be used to illustrate *adaptation to the environment?*

International Society for the Study of Education, Tokyo

"people use resources to meet basic needs" may then ask "How do people in another land use resources to meet their needs for food, shelter, and clothing?"

Generalizations range from limited statements that apply to a particular culture, time, or place to statements that have universal applicability. For example, a generalization about the causes of the Civil War is bound by time and place, but the law of supply and demand has universal application. Some generalizations are conditional and take an if-then form: "If the supply of an item increases, the price will decrease (other things being equal)." A cause-effect relationship is implied in if-then generalizations.

Students should learn to distinguish between descriptive generalizations that are value-neutral and prescriptive generalizations that are valuative, just as they are expected to distinguish between statements of fact and opinion. Most generalizations in the social studies are descriptive, as they are in the social sciences. They take such form as "Population growth, industrialization, and urbanization are among the causes of environmental problems." Fewer in number but of equal importance are prescriptive, or valuative, generalizations. They include a preference, demand, value, or value principle, such as "Population growth, industrialization, and urbanization must be controlled if the environment is to be improved." Notice that in descriptive generalizations the emphasis is on *what is;* in prescriptive generalizations the emphasis is on *what ought to be.* The implication for instruction is to clarify the basis or standards and related evidence for the prescription or recommendation. Although descriptive generalizations can be developed through consideration of adequate samples of data, prescriptive generalizations call for the additional step of evaluating proposals for change.

Teachers may focus on the development of different types and levels of generalization by providing for three types of study. The descriptive and widely applicable (or universal) generalizations may be developed through studies that draw samples of data from selected times, places, or cultures. Students analyze the data to identify common elements that form a basis for generalizations. Descriptive and limited generalizations may be developed in units that focus on particular times, places, and cultures. Students bring together the particular features characteristic of such places as our community, Israel, or China, and they formulate appropriate time-, place-, and culture-bound generalizations. Prescriptive generalizations call for use of decision-making processes. Students consider alternatives and consequences and make a decision or judgment regarding the best alternative in light of goals.

TEACHING STRATEGIES

Four teaching strategies for developing generalizations are summarized in charts 9–9 through 9–12. In all of them attention must be given to the meaning of the concepts that are included, the information on which the generalization is based, and the relationship that is expressed. The information is analyzed to identify what is common or general. The concepts need to be understood in

Inductive: From Data to a Generalization	Deductive: From Generalization to Supporting Data
Collect, organize, and examine data. Identify common elements, or what is generally true. State a generalization based on common or general elements. Check against the data to see if the generalization holds up.	Present the generalization to the group. Present supporting data, cases, or evidence. Refer students to sources of additional supporting data. Ask students to find supporting data in the sources.

Chart 9–9

Chart 9–10

Inquiry to Develop a Generalization	Decision-Making to Develop a Prescriptive Generalization
Define the problem to be investigated. State a hypothesis or question to guide study. Collect, appraise, and organize related data. Test the hypothesis or answer the guiding question. State a generalization (conclusion) based on the data.	Define the issue or problem. Clarify the values or standards most important in the situation. Consider alternatives for dealing with the problem. Consider the consequences of each alternative. Select the best alternative in terms of the values or standards. State a prescriptive generalization based on the above.

Chart 9–11

Chart 9–12

terms of attributes and examples. The relationships expressed may be cause-effect, part-whole, quantitative, sequential, or analogous. For example, consider this generalization: "People identify and use resources in ways that are shaped by their culture." The concepts of resources and culture must be clear, information on several groups of people in different cultures must be analyzed, and the cause-effect relationship between culture and human behavior must be considered.

The *inductive* strategy, moving from data to a generalization, is widely used in the social studies. For example, students may be guided to collect, organize, and examine data on various rules and laws, analyze the data, find that a common function of rules and laws is to provide for individual and group welfare, and state this generalization: "Rules and laws are made to provide for individual and group welfare."

The *deductive* strategy, moving from a generalization to supporting data, is often used to demonstrate or verify a generalization. For example, the teacher may present the above generalization about rules and laws, give supporting information, and indicate where additional data or examples can be found; students then find other examples in the sources.

The *inquiry* strategy develops generalizations in the context of ongoing study. A question is posed, such as "Why do we have rules and laws?" Hypotheses are considered, information is collected to test the most promising hypothesis, and a conclusion or generalization is stated.

The *decision-making* strategy takes students beyond the other strategies and requires them to make a judgment or decision for a prescriptive generalization. Consider this generalization: "Every person in a community has responsibility for improving the environment." Students must clarify values, assess alternatives and the consequences of each alternative, select the best alternative in terms of the values, and state a prescriptive generalization.

Each of the four strategies may be adapted to a teacher-directed or a discovery mode. Sufficient teacher direction should always be provided to assure effective learning. As students gain experience in using the different strategies, the teacher gives less direction and lets students make more discoveries on their own.

GROWTH OF CONCEPTS AND GENERALIZATIONS

The meaning of concepts and generalizations should grow deeper and broader as students move from level to level and encounter them in new settings. For example, the concept of community may begin with one's own community, be expanded to include other communities, and eventually embrace the idea of national and world community. A generalization about using resources to meet human needs may begin with local uses and move to state, national, and worldwide uses of resources. Such spiral development of concepts and generalizations is illustrated in chart 9–13, which shows how the four concepts in the cluster "cultural change" and related generalizations may be brought to higher levels of development in units at various levels.

Essential to the development of critical and creative thinking and to the development of concepts and generalizations are intellectual or cognitive processes. They are discussed next.

Strategies for Developing Intellectual Processes

An effective way to improve children's thinking ability is to provide instruction on basic intellectual or thinking processes that can be put to use in the instructional program. But what processes should be emphasized? One answer to this question lies in identifying the processes used in new instructional materials. This section is based on a content analysis conducted to identify basic processes and related teaching strategies.*

*John U. Michaelis, *Inquiry Processes in the Social Sciences* (Berkeley, Calif.: School of Education, University of California, 1973); Larry S. Hannah and John U. Michaelis, *A Comprehensive Framework for Instructional Objectives: A Guide to Systematic Planning and Evaluation* (Reading, Mass.: Addison-Wesley Publishing Co., 1977).

Spiral Development of a Concept Cluster
and Related Generalizations

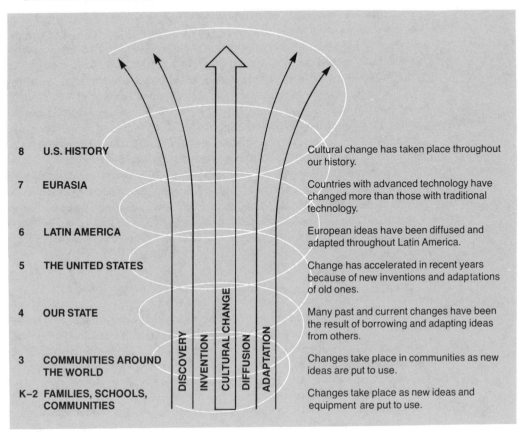

8	U.S. HISTORY	Cultural change has taken place throughout our history.
7	EURASIA	Countries with advanced technology have changed more than those with traditional technology.
6	LATIN AMERICA	European ideas have been diffused and adapted throughout Latin America.
5	THE UNITED STATES	Change has accelerated in recent years because of new inventions and adaptations of old ones.
4	OUR STATE	Many past and current changes have been the result of borrowing and adapting ideas from others.
3	COMMUNITIES AROUND THE WORLD	Changes take place in communities as new ideas are put to use.
K-2	FAMILIES, SCHOOLS, COMMUNITIES	Changes take place as new ideas and equipment are put to use.

Chart 9–13

Attention is given first to the simpler intellectual processes: recalling and observing to generate data; defining and interpreting to clarify meaning; comparing/contrasting, classifying/ordering, and generalizing to organize data. The more complex processes are then considered: analyzing and synthesizing to reorganize data: inferring, hypothesizing, and predicting to apply and extend data; and evaluating to clarify values and use related standards to make judgments of worth.

Before discussing the individual processes, several points need emphasis. First, the processes include those in Bloom's taxonomy of the cognitive domain discussed in chapter 1 plus others that are essential to effective thinking and inquiry. Second, the set of processes may be used to formulate questions in units and lessons as suggested by Hannah and Michaelis's *A Comprehensive*

Framework for Instructional Objectives, which includes the basic cognitive operations used in thinking. Third, no rigid order of the use of the processes is implied, although the order in which they are presented is frequently followed in instructional materials. Inferring, however, may follow interpreting as students "read between the lines," and hypothesizing may be done early to guide data collection. Fourth, some processes included in other lists are subsumed under those in this section. For example, translation is part of interpreting. Communicating is a broad and inclusive activity that may be used to express observations, generalizations, and other thoughts and feelings gained by using processes. Application of data, concepts, and principles is involved in such processes as inferring, hypothesizing, and predicting; in fact, application may be involved in all processes in an inquiry-conceptual program because concepts are used as tools to guide observing, interpreting, and other processes.

In the pages that follow, each process is defined and key questions for initiating use of the process are noted. Teaching strategies are presented for several processes, including the three proposed by Taba. The strategies and the sample questions and illustrations may be readily adapted for use in any unit of instruction. The accompanying charts contain ideas that may be used directly with students.

REMEMBERING AND OBSERVING

These two processes are basic to all others because they provide the data for inquiry. Students draw on their own backgrounds of experience and make observations to gather data as various topics and problems are studied. They need to use the knowledge they have plus new data obtained from observation to make comparisons and interpretations or to use other processes.

remembering   To *remember* as a part of inquiry is to retrieve *selectively,* to recognize, or to recall items related to the topic under study. Both cognitive and affective elements may be recalled. A key outcome for the teacher is identification of a student's knowledge about a topic, degree of interest, and misconceptions or biases—all of which can be used to improve learning. Open-ended questions are used to guide recall during initiating and opening activities, and to initiate classifying, interpreting, and other processes The examples that follow and the items in charts 9–14 and 9–15 provide guidelines for instruction.

What do you know about _____? What can you recall about _____?
What have you learned before about _____? What does _____ make you think of?
Who remembers what _____ means? What feelings do you have about _____?
Who can recall activities that may be useful in studying _____? Can you think of materials that may be helpful?

observing   To *observe* is to perceive, examine, or focus attention on an object or activity with a purpose in mind. Observation is an intake process used to collect data; it

Improving the Ability to Recall

Have a clear purpose for study.

Take notes, make an outline, put ideas in your own words and use them in discussion and other activities.

Try to get ideas the first time, but review as needed to clarify them.

Organize facts around key terms (concepts) and main ideas.

Think of how ideas may be used on other problems and how they may be applied to other situations.

Chart 9–14

Clues to Aid Recalling

Key dates, persons, places, events

Retrieval charts in which facts are grouped under people, problems, causes, effects, resources, or other items

Organizers such as production, goods, role, customs, region, equality, and other concepts

Activities and materials used before on similar problems

Difficulties met on similar problems and how they were solved

Chart 9–15

may be direct or indirect. Direct observation is firsthand perception of objects and activities by looking, listening, touching, smelling, or tasting. Indirect observation includes reading and listening to secondary sources and examining pictures, maps, and other data. The following model questions may be adapted for use in a variety of units to guide observing:

What do we need to find out about _____? What should we look for?

How can we find out? Look? Listen? Ask someone? What other ways might be used?

What can we find in this _____ (picture, map, reading)?

Effective observing requires use of the abilities noted in charts 9–16 and 9–17.

Good Observers

Know what they are looking for and keep a a sharp focus

Use direct observation—look, listen, touch, smell, taste as appropriate

Use indirect observation—read, watch films, and use other data sources

Check findings with others and against other sources

Chart 9–16

Observing

Know what you want to find and keep a focus.

Use a question, concept or hypothesis as a guide.

Identify major and minor items.

Make records as needed for future use.

Double-check findings to be sure they are accurate.

Chart 9–17

287

INTERPRETING, COMPARING/CONTRASTING,
CLASSIFYING, AND GENERALIZING

These processes are essential to clarify, organize, and summarize the meaning gleaned from reading materials, audiovisual media, and community resources. They are often used in the above sequence, with a smooth flow from interpreting through generalizing. And they are used to develop concepts and generalizations, as described earlier in this chapter.

interpreting To *interpret* is to explain the meaning, to state the significance, or to translate or illustrate the thoughts and feelings one has obtained from looking at and thinking about a map, graph, picture, or other data source. Interpreting can be broadly defined to include inferring and other processes, but it is not done here because of the importance of accurate interpretation of the intended meaning that should be derived from a given source of data. After interpretations are made and checked for reasonableness and accuracy, students should proceed to generalizing, inferring, or other processes. The following model questions and the items in charts 9–18 through 9–20 may be used to guide the interpretation of data.

What main idea(s) and supporting evidence did you find in this _____ (film, reading, table)?

Can you explain the diagram that shows the main steps in _____ (processing mail, making clothes, passing a bill)?

What relationships did you find on the map between _____ and _____ (location of homes and schools, travel time and terrain)?

Can you explain this _____ (activity, behavior, and the like) in your own words?

How can we _____ (summarize, demonstrate, act out) the main points presented in this material?

What is your interpretation if you use _____ (specialization, interdependence, factors of production) to explain it?

Using Concepts and Main Ideas to Interpret Findings	Interpreting Maps
How can we use division of labor to explain family activities?	Check the title to note content.
How can we use interdependence to interpret trade between them?	Check the key to define symbols, colors, and scale.
How can we use equality of opportunity to explain their position?	Identify directions by finding the north arrow, parallels, and meridians.
How can we use expectation of others to explain his or her role?	Use colors, flow of rivers, contour lines, and hachures to identify changes in elevation.
	Identify relationships between items.

Chart 9–18   Chart 9–19

Procedure	Focusing Questions	Illustrative Application
Study the data source to determine the intended meaning.	→ What does this show? Contain? Tell? Present? How can we use the data?	→ What does this transportation route map show? How do the title and map key help to interpret it?
Identify and discuss basic data and main ideas.	→ What did you see? Find? Note for use? Which ideas are most important?	→ Who can describe the main transportation routes? What major cities are linked by them?
Identify and describe relationships, similarities, and differences.	→ Which items are related? What similarities and differences are important?	→ How are the transportation routes and city locations related? How are the main routes alike? Different?
Summarize, explain, or conclude (be sure to stick to the data.)	→ How can we summarize the key ideas? What can we conclude?	→ What can we conclude about main routes and location of cities? How might we explain the relationship?

Chart 9–20

comparing/
contrasting

To *compare* is to identify similarities in objects and activities; to *contrast* is to identify differences. In everyday usage the term *comparing* is used to include the identification of both similarities and differences. Probably no questions are used more in the social studies than those that focus attention on comparing and contrasting:

How are they alike? How are they different?

How are _____ and _____ (work of mothers and fathers, goods and services, imports and exports) alike? How are they different?

How can _____ (jobs or community workers, these two cities) be compared? Or, on what points can we compare _____?

Who can summarize how they are alike? Who can state how they are different?

Comparing is also used to place items in order or in a sequence. Questions such as the following are used:

How may we arrange these from _____ to _____ (largest to smallest, longest to shortest, most important to least important)?

How can we rank these in order according to _____ (population, area, amount of production, distance from New York)?

In what order should we place _____ (dates on a time line, pictures for a pictorial graph, columns in a bar graph)?

International Society for the Study of Education, Tokyo

Why is a farm like this in Hokkaido? How might the concept of cultural borrowing be used to make an interpretation?

Charts 9–21 and 9–22 illustrate conceptual models that may be used to guide students in systematic comparing and contrasting of selected topics.

A Model for Comparing Communities	
Population	Major zones
Location	Government
History	Urban problems
Industry	Renewal plans
Transportation	Minority groups
Recreation	Special features

Chart 9–21

A Model for Comparing Populations	
Number	Settlement
Growth rate	patterns
Ethnic makeup	Areas of
Distribution	concentration
Migrations	Central cities
Predictions	Other cities

Chart 9–22

Grouping Workers	Why Should We Classify Items?	Ways to Group
Which ones produce goods? Which ones produce services? Which ones work at home? Which ones work in town?	To develop the meaning of a concept To store ideas for later use To compare and contrast items more effectively To identify how items are related To help interpret, analyze, or evaluate	By uses—tools, materials, other items By appearance—color, size, other features By relationships—parts of a whole, causes and effects, and the like
Chart 9–23	Chart 9–24	Chart 9–25

classifying

To *classify* is to group, sort, or place items in categories according to identified characteristics or other criteria. As noted earlier, the grouping of items into categories or classifications is basic to concept development. Classifications may be single-stage—that is, based on one criterion, such as goods made by mothers—or they may be based on two or more criteria—such as goods made by mothers that are worn by members of the family. Three widely used means of grouping in the social studies are by descriptive characteristics, by function or use, and by relationships. These model questions and charts 9–23 through 9–25 provide some guidelines.

How can we group these _____ (fruits, houses, and the like, by descriptive characteristics)?
Which ones are _____ (red, large, nearest, and other descriptive characteristics)?
Which items are used for _____ (food, recreation, other)?
Which ones are _____ (health, postal, and so on, by function or activity) workers?
How can these _____ and _____ (resources and products, events and time periods, and other related items) be grouped?
Which items are part of _____ (a dairy farm, steel production, and so on, to show part-whole relationships)?

The teaching strategy for classifying shown in chart 9–26 begins with clarifying what is to be grouped, moves to identification of common features as a basis for grouping, and ends by labeling the groups and considering other possible groupings. Notice that observing, recalling, comparing, and defining are involved.

generalizing

Generalizing is central to the effective use of higher level processes such as hypothesizing, synthesizing, and evaluating. It is frequently linked with inter-

291

A Strategy for Classifying		
Procedure	*Focusing Questions*	*Illustrative Application*
Observe and identify items to be grouped.	→ What did you see? Hear? Find? Read? Note?	→ What items (goods and services) are shown in these pictures?
Identify common features for use in grouping.	→ Which ones may be grouped together? Or, how might we group them?	→ How are some items alike? How are others alike?
Decide on a basis for grouping.	→ Why can they be grouped this way? Or, how are these alike?	→ Which ones are things someone makes? Which are not things, but are useful work?
Name, label, or define each group.	→ What is a good name for each group?	→ Who has a name for each group? Which can be called goods? Services?
Consider other possible groupings, if appropriate.	→ What other groups might we make? How are they alike?	→ Are there other ways we can group them? How about work of police? Work of firefighters?

Chart 9–26

preting and inferring as students move beyond interpreted data and inferences drawn from data to formulate main ideas. It provides generalizations that serve as a basis for analyzing, synthesizing, predicting, and making other applications of learning.

To *generalize* is to derive a principle or main idea from data. Two or more concepts are included in a generalization—for example, ''Many schools are located in the residential part of the community''; ''All cities provide education, transportation, business, and other services''; ''How people use their environment is influenced by their culture.'' To qualify as generalizations, statements should be (1) based on evidence; (2) shown widespread, prevalent, or usually the case; (3) based on two or more concepts; and (4) applicable to most if not all members of a group. Charts 9–27 and 9–28 contain guidelines and questions that may be used to improve ability to generalize.

The following model questions focus attention on how different types of generalizations are formed:

In general, what can we say about _____ (the uses of lumber, the role of mayors)?

What are the main _____ (causes of air pollution, functions of government, reasons for urban problems)?

According to the evidence, what are the relationships between _____ and _____ (scarcity and prices, supply and demand, travel routes and location of cities)?

What is the main difference between _____ and _____ (producers and consumers, the work of mayors and governors)?

292

What are the main ways that _____ (homes, cities, the New England states) have changed?

What general statement describes _____ (the advantages of dividing the work, the weaknesses in the Articles of Confederation, how specialization and interdependence are related)?

In the teaching strategy outlined in chart 9–29, first the data on which the generalization is to be based is identified; next common elements are identified and a tentative generalization is formulated. The tentative generalization is checked against the data and, if necessary, revised or made subject to conditions or other qualifications. The generalization may be further checked against other data to see if it applies in other situations. This last step is essential in

---

What Can We Say in General

About the main problems cities are facing?

About the work of urban planners?

About the purposes of urban renewal plans?

About the main difficulties in renewal projects?

About action to take?

Chart 9–27

How to Generalize

Get data from pictures, reading materials, and other sources.

Find what is common or general in the data.

State a main idea that describes what is common or general.

Check to find out if the main idea fits data in other situations.

Chart 9–28

A Strategy for Generalizing

Procedure	Focusing Questions	Illustrative Application
Get the data (facts) clearly in mind and interpret them.	→ What did you find? See? Hear? Read? Note?	→ What did you find to be major governmental activities at the local and state levels?
Identify common elements, relationships, or main ideas.	→ What common elements did you find? Which items are related?	→ What common activities (executive, legislative, judicial) did you find?
Make a tentative generalization.	→ What can we say in general?	→ What seems to be a sound conclusion about activities common at both levels?
Test the tentative generalization against other data.	→ Does our generalization hold up as we check other data?	→ What does this report (film, filmstrip, reading) show to be the main governmental activities at both levels? Is our generalization valid?

Chart 9–29

formulating generalizations of broad applicability. Recall that if a prescriptive generalization is to be made, evaluation of alternatives and consequences is necessary, as noted in the evaluation strategy at the end of this section.

ANALYZING AND SYNTHESIZING

These two processes may be viewed as opposite sides of a coin. Analyzing focuses on breaking a whole into parts; synthesizing focuses on bringing parts together in a new way.

analyzing To *analyze* is to take apart, to divide, to identify elements, relationships, and principles. The focus of analysis may be on (1) parts, kinds, types, groups, qualities, objectives, motives, and assumptions; (2) common elements in several events or different elements in a single event; (3) time/space elements and relationships; or (4) causes, reasons, effects, consequences, and organizing principles. The following model questions and charts 9–30 and 9–31 can be used to guide the making of different types of analyses.

> What are the main _____ (parts of this picture, mural, reading selection; regions of this country; time periods in the growth of our state)?
> Why did the _____ (author, artist, speaker) break the problem or topic into these parts?
> How are the steps in _____ (making bread, passing a bill, the leader's rise to power) related?
> How are the parts of this _____ (story, report, mural) related?
> How are _____ (problems, activities, regions, time periods, concepts, themes, values) used to organize this material?

The strategy presented in chart 9–32 begins with clarification of the need to break the topic or problem into parts, then moves to ways in which it might be analyzed—causes, regions, and the like. The meaning of each part selected

Analyzing Stories	Analyzing Pictures
What are the main parts?	What main things are shown?
How does it begin? Move ahead? End?	What is the central idea? How are other items related to it?
In what order are the main events presented?	How can we use the information to answer questions?
How are your feelings about characters related to what they said or did?	How do reactions or feelings aroused by it affect what we see in it?

Chart 9–30

Chart 9–31

A Strategy for Analyzing

Procedure	Focusing Questions	Illustrative Application
Identify useful ways to break the problem into parts.	→ How can we break the problem into parts? What main parts (types, reasons, causes) should be studied?	→ How can we break down our question on urban land use? What are the main types of land use in cities?
Define each part clearly.	→ What is the meaning of each part? What does each part include?	→ How can we define each type? Commercial? Industrial? Residential? Recreational? Other?
Identify and organize data related to each part.	→ What information do we have on each part? How are these parts related?	→ What data can we classify under each type of land use?
State summary, conclusion, or explanation based on the analysis.	→ What does our analysis show? What can we conclude?	→ Who can summarize the types of land use in order from greatest to least? How might we explain the differences?

Chart 9–32

for analysis should be defined so as to guide the identification and organization of related data. After information is classified under each part and explored, a summary or conclusion should be made.

synthesizing To *synthesize* is to bring parts together into a meaningful whole, to integrate, to create a new product. Parts or elements are put together to form a unified structure around a key concept, theme, question, principle, or other organizer, as in chart 9–33. The completed synthesis may take the form of an original oral or written report, exhibit, map, mural, dramatization, or other creative product, as shown in chart 9–34.

Presenting Ideas on Community Life

What to present: early settlement and growth, main zones of the community, transportation networks, or other items?

How to present them: pictures, charts, maps, booklet, reports, exhibit, or other forms of presentation?

Chart 9–33

How Can We Use These to Combine Ideas in New Ways?

Models	Flow charts	Rhythms
Murals	Diagrams	Dances
Maps	Time lines	Games
Reports	Stories	Simulations
Booklets	Poems	Dramatization
Scrapbooks	Exhibits	Role playing

Chart 9–34

295

Because a desired outcome of synthesizing is a new and original product created by the students, special attention should be given to creativity. If originality is not evident, the activity is better classified as generalizing, interpreting, or some other process, depending upon the operations involved. The following questions are illustrative of those that may be used to spark creativity in synthesizing:

How can we show the main features of _____ (living in the neighborhood, the westward movement) in a new way?

Who can think of a good way to use _____ (pictures, reports, stories, objects, other items)?

How can thoughts and feelings of most importance be highlighted (in pictures, stories, a mural)?

What _____ (concept, theme, main idea) will be useful to organize or arrange the parts?

What form of presentation should we use? Scrapbook? Booklet? Mural? Flow chart? Other?

The teaching strategy presented in chart 9–35 begins with a focus on what is to be synthesized. The main parts or items to be combined are typically considered next, followed by organizing ideas and ways of combining the parts. It is essential that students be open to ideas when they are considering themes or other organizing ideas, pondering the use of exhibits, murals, or other forms

A Strategy for Synthesizing

Procedure	Focusing Questions	Illustrative Application
Clarify the purpose, or what is to be produced (synthesized).	→ How can we bring together the main ideas of this topic in a new way?	→ What are some new ways we can show major aspects of frontier life?
Identify basic parts or items to include.	→ What are the most important items (ideas, activities) to include?	→ What should we include? Shelter? Clothing? Recreation? Food? Protection?
Identify organizing idea(s) and form(s) of presentation.	→ How should the parts be organized (arranged, portrayed, shown)?	→ What theme(s) might we use? What form(s) of verbal and pictorial presentation should we use?
Decide on fruitful plan(s) and proceed with the synthesis.	→ What plan(s) do you prefer? Why? What is needed to proceed?	→ What theme(s) do you prefer? Why? What form of presentation? Mural? Scrapbook? Report? Dramatization?

Chart 9–35

of presentation, and the like. After exploring alternatives, students should make plans that will enable them to proceed with the synthesis.

INFERRING, HYPOTHESIZING, AND PREDICTING

These three interrelated processes go beyond the data at hand. An inference is logical, reasonable, sensible, and applicable in a specific situation. A hypothesis is more general and should apply to all similar cases; it should also be testable. A prediction should be reasonable and supported by evidence, but one must usually wait to see if it is accurate—as, for example, a prediction about an election.

inferring To *infer* is to state a logical consequence, draw an implication, read between the lines, or derive other thoughts and feelings that are not explicit in a given data source. The following model questions illustrate those used in instructional materials to focus attention on inferring. Charts 9–36 and 9–37 contain examples, questions, and guidelines that may be used in various units of study.

How do you think they must feel about _____ (moving into a new neighborhood, the new civic center, his election)?

How do you think they must have _____ (felt about it, learned to do that, done so much in such a short time)?

Why do you say that _____ (they felt happy, he did it to help others, the writer of the article is biased)? Or, why do you think that _____?

What might be _____ (the next step, her reason for doing it, the effect of that decision)?

What do you suppose someone would do if _____ (he were in that situation, some individuals violated the rules, she were appointed to the pollution control committee).

What to Infer	Can You Infer
How someone may feel in a given situation	Why the population is greater in some areas than in others?
What someone may think about a problem	What may be produced from the resources they have?
What someone may say or do in a situation	What minority problems they may have from the information on population makeup?
What the motives or purposes of an individual may be	What the climate may be from the data on location and elevation?
What behavior or action may follow from an incident	What their feelings about neighboring countries may be from the treaties they have signed?
What the reasons may be for an event	

Chart 9–36   Chart 9–37

Why do you suppose _____ (the behavior surprised them, they decided to take that action, these areas are more populated than others)? Or, what are the possible reasons that _____?

hypothesizing   To *hypothesize* is to state a tentative explanation, solution, generalization, or proposition that shows how two or more items are related. Hypotheses are useful in guiding the search for data. They may be generated during introductory activities, as study of a unit progresses, and at the end of one topic to lead into the study of another. Hypotheses confirmed by evidence become conclusions or generalizations. Hypotheses can be stated as questions, if-then propositions, or generalizations—for example, "What reasons did people have for moving westward?" "If people moved westward, did they move for different reasons?" "People moved westward for many reasons, not a single one." Hypotheses such as these indicate a condition (moving westward) and what is usually related to it (reasons).

The following model questions may be used to stimulate hypothesizing about different types of relationships, along with the material in charts 9–38 through 9–41.

What are the main causes of _____ (population growth, urban decay, water pollution, inflation, revolutions)?

What is generally believed to be a good location for _____ (schools, forts, cities, wheat farms)?

If people live in _____ (suburbs, inner city areas, deserts), what problems can they expect?

Why do _____ usually _____ (members of a family usually divide the work, community workers usually specialize, cities usually have different zones, political systems usually have three branches of government)?

How are _____ and _____ (price and scarcity of an item, time and mode of transportation, population of a city and pollution problems) related?

How are the roles of _____ and _____ (parents and teachers, mayors and city managers, presidents and prime ministers) alike?

A Good Hypothesis	Hypothesizing
Is a question, statement, or if-then proposition that can be answered or tested.	Should we state it as a question, statement, or if-then idea?
Shows how two or more items are related.	What evidence, principle, or experience can we use as a basis?
Helps to explain the topic or problem under study.	What should be stated as given and what should we look for?
Is a tentative generalization of data or inferences.	What cause-effect or other relationship is involved?
May be drawn from experience, evidence, inferences, and principles.	Does it apply to all or most cases, not just a particular one? Can it be tested?

Chart 9–38   Chart 9–39

How Can the Following Be Completed?	Stating What Usually Happens
If workers specialize, then dependence on others _____.	What usually happens when one part of an ecosystem is damaged?
If the supply of an item is greater than demand, the price _____.	What environmental problems usually arise in densely populated cities?
If a place has a Mediterranean climate, then living conditions usually are _____.	What usually happens when building construction exceeds the rate of forest renewal?
When people migrate, the main reasons usually are	What benefits can be obtained from recycling of wastes?

Chart 9-40   Chart 9-41

A Strategy for Hypothesizing

Procedure	Focusing Questions	Illustrative Application
State preliminary hypotheses that show relationships.	→ What usually happens if _____? What is the effect of _____? How is _____ related to _____?	→ What may happen if we divide the work in making party favors? Will more or fewer favors be produced?
State reasons for preliminary hypotheses.	→ Why do you think that usually happens? Why do you say that?	→ Why do you think more will be produced? What reasons can you give?
Refine the statement so that it can be tested.	→ How can we state our idea so that it can be tested?	→ How can we sharpen the statement "More favors will be produced if the work is divided than if individuals work alone"?
Identify essential conditions and procedures for testing.	→ What is a fair way to test the hypothesis? What procedures and materials are needed?	→ How can we test our idea? What tools and materials do both groups need? What other conditions are essential?
Analyze the data to find if the hypothesis is supported.	→ Do the findings support the hypothesis? Did we get the expected outcome?	→ Which group produced more? Who can summarize and explain the findings?
Decide if more evidence is needed.	→ Do we need more data? If so, how can we gather them?	→ Are we sure of our findings? Do we need to run another test?

Chart 9-42

The strategy in chart 9-42 begins with the stating of propositions that show how two or more items are related. The hypothesis should be more general than an inference, because a good hypothesis covers most or all cases or instances under study. Students can be led to think in more general terms than when they are inferring by asking such questions as "What usually happens if . . . ?" or "How are these items related in most situations?" After students state tentative hypotheses and give reasons for them, they should try to refine their statements for testing. Next comes the testing, followed by discussion of the findings. Finally, a decision should be made as to whether additional evidence is needed. If it is, another test may be devised.

predicting To *predict* is to forecast, prophesy, or anticipate what might happen. A prediction is based on relevant information but goes beyond it to identify what may happen in (1) a different time dimension (what the future population may be), (2) a different sample (what one city may do to curb pollution because of what others have done or plan to do), and (3) a related activity or topic (an increase in steel production because of projected increase in car production). The following model questions and charts 9–43 and 9–44 may be used to guide the making of different types of predictions.

What do you think _____ (a person, group, the character in a story, a committee, legislature) will do next?

What do you think they (he or she) will do if _____ (Billy does not find the lost bicycle, the pollution laws are passed, the treaty is signed, the original boundaries are restored)?

What do you think will happen if _____ (the school bonds are not approved, new housing is located on the outskirts of town, aid to African countries is stopped)?

What do you think will be the main effects of _____ (the urban renewal project on business, their decision to move ahead with low-cost housing, their intervention in the Middle East)?

What do you estimate the _____ (school enrollment, population of our state, production of steel) will be in ten years?

Where do you think they will locate the _____ (new school, shopping center, factory, nuclear power station)?

What Do You Predict?

What new laws on water pollution may the legislature pass?

What may happen to agriculture after the new dam is finished?

What may happen to the environment after it is built?

What critical problems can we expect if the antipollution program is approved? If it is not approved?

Chart 9–43

Checking Predictions

Basis: What change or process is involved?

Conditions: Under what conditions will the change occur?

Probability: What is the likelihood of its occurrence?

Consequence: If it does occur, what might be the effect?

Chart 9–44

A Strategy for Predicting		
Procedure	*Focusing Questions*	*Illustrative Application*
Clarify what is to be predicted.	→ What changes (trends, developments) are shown here? What might we predict from this evidence?	→ What do these data indicate about population growth in our community? What changes can you find?
Analyze the data to find a basis for predicting.	→ What is a good basis for making predictions?	→ How much growth was there during each period?
Make tentative predictions.	→ What predictions can we make? What do you think will happen?	→ What do you think the growth will be during the next period?
Review reasons or bases for predictions.	→ Why do you think that will happen? How can you support your prediction?	→ What was your basis for the prediction? How many think the growth rate will be the same?
Consider related data or conditions that may have been overlooked.	→ What else may be important to consider? Are other facts needed?	→ What about the reports on decreased birth rate and lack of land for houses?
Modify predictions to fit new data or conditions.	→ How should we change our predictions? How can we use new data to improve our predictions?	→ How should we change our predictions because of the data on birth rate and lack of land?

Chart 9–45

The teaching strategy in chart 9–45 begins by defining what is to be predicted, then searches for a basis for making predictions. Various predictions and the reasons for them are considered next, followed by giving attention to any factors that may have been overlooked and final shaping of the predictions to fit the data and relevant conditions.

EVALUATING

To *evaluate* is to make a judgment of merit, worth, or value in terms of defined criteria. Clarification of the standards or criteria to be used is essential, for otherwise students can only give opinions instead of forming considered judgments. Evaluation may be done along with other processes to test the effectiveness with which they are being used, or it may be a final step to appraise objects and events (see charts 9–46 and 9–47).

Focusing questions are needed for two different types of evaluation. In the first type internal evidence or standards are used to assess the reports, documents, reading selections, and other materials. Typical standards are accuracy, consistency in use of terms, flow of ideas, soundness of arguments, and relation of conclusions to evidence. These model questions focus on internal evidence:

How can _____ (our report, map; this graph, plan) be improved? Is it accurate_____ Well organized_____ Meaningful? Useful for our purpose?

How accurate (adequate, useful, consistent, biased) is this _____ (document, diagram, flow chart, report)?

To what extent are the _____ (conclusions, generalizations, inferences) supported by evidence?

In the second type of evaluation external standards related to the objectives to be achieved and the means of achieving them are used. The standards may be the objectives, commonly used criteria, or comparison with a recognized standard of excellence. Examples of each type of standard are (1) using objectives for urban renewal as criteria to assess plans, (2) using defined standards of freedom of speech to judge the conduct of a meeting, and (3) comparing one conservation program with another acknowledged to be outstanding. These model questions focus on external standards:

To what extent will this _____ (plan, program, type of action) lead to the stated goals?

Which of the alternatives is most desirable in terms of _____ (individual benefits, group benefits, objectives)?

To what extent were standards of _____ (justice, freedom, personal security) upheld during this period?

How does this _____ (report, antipollution proposal, airport, political system) compare with the model of an outstanding one?

The strategy presented in chart 9–48 begins by identifying and defining what is to be appraised, then determining the standards or criteria that should be used. In actual practice these phases may be joined together, provided students understand the focus of the evaluation. Next, evidence is gathered and inter-

Procedure	Focusing Questions	Illustrative Application
Identify and define the focus of evaluation.	→ What is to be appraised? Why should _____ be assessed?	→ Why should we evaluate the renewal plans? How can we judge them?
Identify and define standards of appraisal.	→ What standards (values, criteria) should be used?	→ What are the goals for urban renewal? Are they up to standards? What other standards might be used?
Collect data related to each standard.	→ What is the evidence? What data can we find for each standard?	→ What evidence do we have to show how the objectives will be achieved?
Identify possible outcomes (effects, consequences) of each proposal.	→ What are likely outcomes of each proposal? Which one will have the most desirable outcomes?	→ How may each proposal affect traffic, business, beautification, or other objectives?
Make a judgment, including suggestions for improvement.	→ Which one best meets the standards? How might it be improved?	→ In general, which proposal is best? Why? In what ways can it be improved?

Chart 9–48

preted to show the extent to which the defined standards are met. The next step is necessary if alternatives—different plans, materials, or proposals—are being assessed. Possible outcomes or consequences of each alternative are considered and an attempt is made to identify the one that is most desirable in light of the standards. Finally, the quality or merit of the item(s) under appraisal should be judged, and suggestions for improvement made as appropriate.

Problem Solving as a Unifying Procedure

Problem solving can bring together the various aspects of thinking and inquiry. The model that follows is especially useful in group work and also provides a setting for generating individual activities. The different processes are brought in as needed. Like any model, this one should be used flexibly, varying the steps or phases as appropriate to guide the creative study of selected topics and to avoid the pitfalls of a regimented, step-by-step procedure. The major phases are these:

1. Defining questions and problems to guide study
2. Recalling information and hypothesizing
3. Clarifying steps of procedure
4. Finding, interpreting, appraising, and classifying information
5. Generalizing and further processing of information as needed
6. Evaluating procedures and outcomes

Work at Home	Boonesboro	Early Times in Our Community
What jobs are there?	Why was it built?	Who were the first settlers?
What skills are needed?	Who built it?	What were the first buildings like?
What can children do?	Where was it?	Where was the first school?
What do others do?	When was it built?	Where were the first streets?
	How was it built?	When was the railroad begun?
	How did people travel to it?	What changes have taken place?

Chart 9–49   Chart 9–50   Chart 9–51

DEFINING QUESTIONS AND PROBLEMS

As new units are introduced and as different problems arise in a unit that is under way, questions and problems must be clearly defined. The objective is to get pupils to recognize and understand what is to be studied. During the initiation of a unit, materials may be selected to stimulate thinking. Pictures, maps, objects, and other resources can be arranged to highlight significant questions or problems. After the students have examined the materials, they should discuss the questions or problems to be attacked first. As initial problems are defined and clarified, they may be listed on the chalkboard or on charts, as illustrated in charts 9–49 through 9–51.

Throughout the unit of instruction recognition and clarification of problems should be emphasized; each unit should become a series of problem-solving experiences with a smooth transition from one problem to the next. For example, when students move from the work of family members to the ways a family obtains food, new questions and problems must be defined. Similarly, in units on our community, our state, the westward movement, and other lands, a series of specific questions and problems should be defined, with each new series growing out of the preceding ones.

RECALLING INFORMATION AND HYPOTHESIZING

This phase of problem solving should be both systematic and creative. As the teacher asks questions, students may recall both previous information and information introduced during the initiation of the unit: "What can you recall about this topic?" "What have you learned before that we might use?" "How is it like other topics we have studied?" The teacher may next ask questions designed to elicit hypotheses: "What ideas do you have on this topic?" "What do you think we will find?'' ''What answers might we find to the questions we have listed?'' The objectives of these two sets of questions are to retrieve information related to questions posed by the group during definition of the problem, to get students to state hypotheses regarding what they may find, to identify misconceptions they may have, and to motivate the search for data.

Teachers sometimes ask, ''Should tentative answers or hypotheses be proposed for every problem that arises?'' No! When students lack the background for hypothesizing, the teacher should begin by studying the questions noted during definition of the problem. But if a unit flows out of a preceding one, students should be able to state hypotheses and set the stage for effective investigation. Opportunities to hypothesize also arise during a unit as relationships are explored and key concepts developed, but this phase of problem solving is sometimes neglected. The following examples are given to indicate the nature of children's hypotheses:

> In a unit on the post office, the question under discussion was "What happens to letters that are put in mail boxes?" Children's comments were:
>
> "A mail carrier picks them up. Then they are taken to the right place."
> "Wait! They have to be sorted by somebody. I think they are taken downtown. Maybe they are sorted by workers or a machine."
> "There must be a plan or a system. Then a mail carrier can deliver them."
>
> In a unit on the westward movement, the group was considering this problem on travel routes: check the relief map of the United States and plan a route to California from St. Joseph, Missouri; then check to see if your proposed route is the same as one of those used by early settlers. The children made the following hypotheses:
>
> "Go straight across the plains and mountains to San Francisco. If you go this way, you would have to find mountain passes through the Rockies and Sierras."
> "Go along the Missouri to the Platte River and on to the coast across Utah and Nevada. If you would keep close to rivers, you could get water and there would not be many steep grades. I heard that some railroads and highways are built along water level routes."
> "Go along south to Santa Fe and on to Los Angeles across New Mexico and Arizona. This would be a good route in the winter."
> "Why couldn't we start our trip in St. Louis? Then we could use boats all the way to San Francisco."

In all these examples, the teacher was encouraging students to draw on previous learning to suggest tentative solutions or hypotheses. Children applied creative thinking as they tried to relate past experiences to new problems. Divergent thinking appeared as they made multiple suggestions and considered different proposals. Critical thinking was brought into play as they evaluated the proposals and suggested ideas to support them. Suspended judgment was emphasized and the need for additional information was established. The question or problem was further elaborated and clarified, and the stage was set for identifying procedures to follow.

This phase may be directed by the teacher or planned by the group. Ways to gather information, possible sources of information, and assignment of responsibilities are considered. Questions such as the following are raised: How shall we proceed? What are the next steps? How can we obtain needed information? What sources of information should be used? Should any jobs be assigned to individuals or small groups? Does everyone know what he or she has to do? A wide range of sources and procedures may be explored, as noted in charts 9–52 and 9–53. The best possibilities are carefully selected, and children are urged to watch for others.

Sources of Information		Procedures to Use	
Clippings	Newspapers	Collecting	Note taking
Encyclopedias	Pictures	Constructing	Observing
Films	Slides	Demonstrating	Outlining
Filmstrips	Study trips	Drawing	Reading
The library	Textbooks	Experimenting	Writing for
Magazines	Visitors	Interviewing	information
Maps and globes	Find others	Mapping	Find others

Chart 9–52   Chart 9–53

FINDING, INTERPRETING, APPRAISING, AND CLASSIFYING INFORMATION

With plans in mind, students proceed to gather and interpret data needed to answer their questions, solve their problems, or prove their hypotheses. Observation and related study skills are used to collect data. Terms are defined; pictures, maps, and other data sources are interpreted; comparisons and contrasts are made; and information is evaluated for accuracy and relevance. Difference sources of information are used and cross-checked. If differences are noted in interpretations or if there is doubt about the accuracy of data, double-checking may be necessary. At times a film may need to be shown again, a section of a reference reread, or one reference checked against another. An expert may be interviewed to resolve a difference in fact or in interpretation of data.

As information is gathered it may be listed on the chalkboard or placed on retrieval charts for further use. If directions for making something or steps in a sequence of events are involved, they may be noted on a chart or on the chalkboard. An outline, a set of notes, or simply sharing and grouping information may be adequate. The objective is to organize information for generalizing and further processing as needed.

GENERALIZING AND FURTHER PROCESSING
OF INFORMATION

Generalizing frequently follows the phases discussed above, although other processes could also be used at this point. In most units of instruction, students proceed to draw inferences, test hypotheses, formulate generalizations, make predictions, and synthesize findings in new forms. For example, after interpreting data related to population growth in their city, students may draw and check inferences about possible environmental effects, state generalizations about the main causes of growth, make predictions about future growth and future ecological problems, and synthesize findings in graphs or maps to highlight growth during selected periods or in defined zones of the city. The following examples are illustrative:

In a unit on our changing community, one group moved beyond interpretations and made the following generalizations and predictions:

"Changes have been faster in recent years. Some changes were made to take care of population growth. Some changes were occasioned by inventions and new ways of doing things."

"We predict that school enrollment will be 23,000 in ten years. Population will probably be around 112,000."

In a unit on environmental problems, students proceeded to infer, generalize, predict, and synthesize as follows:

"Feelings about flood control and environmental problems seem to be high enough to get some action. Some people seem to be changing their ideas about what is important."

"The proposed legislation on environmental problems will be passed. If it is passed, the dam will probably be constructed at point A on the map, because it is best for preserving wildlife."

Students then made a map to show location of flooded areas, points at which damage occurred to wildlife and to people, and possible sites for a dam.

EVALUATING PROCESSES AND OUTCOMES

Evaluation is a continuing process. It begins with the definition of the problem and moves on to the forming of generalizations and the final appraisal of the effectiveness of individual and group work. During each phase of problem solving, attention is given to evaluation. As problems are defined, the teacher may ask: Is the problem clear? Have main parts of the problem been considered? As procedures are discussed, the teacher may ask: Have good sources of information been noted? Does each individual know what to do? Similarly, the following questions may be asked during the classifying, interpeting, and further processing of information: Are facts related to main ideas? Are relationships shown? Have we selected the best means of summarizing information? By getting clues through observation, the teacher raises questions and makes comments that help students to appraise and to improve the skills, concepts, and processes they are using.

In addition to the ongoing evaluation that is part of daily activities, there is periodic and systematic appraisal of various aspects of thinking and learning. Teachers may use tests to check grasp of vocabulary, concepts, basic information, reading skills, and study skills. Charts, checklists, and other devices may be used to appraise work habits, use of materials, discussion techniques, committee work, outlines, reports, maps, and other activities and products. Charts 9–54 through 9–56 list criteria to use in evaluation. Both self-evaluation and teacher appraisal help students to improve the attitudes, skills, and understandings that are essential to effective thinking. (A detailed discussion of principles and procedures of evaluation is presented in chapter 14.)

Teachers should be able to recognize certain errors and difficulties in thinking as they evaluate and plan work. Among the more common errors in thinking are confusing the real and the fanciful, mixing facts and opinions, generalizing in terms of purely personal experience or from just a single instance, taking an either-or position when clear-cut alternatives do not exist, failing to check information, making errors in observation, organizing ideas to favor a point of view, and failing to consider consequences. The teacher should be alert to such problems and point them out as they arise. After students have identified errors and difficulties in their own thinking and problem-solving activities, they should gain experience in applying what they have learned to new situations. Charts 9–57 and 9–58 illustrate points that may be given direct attention in discussion and used in both self-evaluation and teacher appraisal.

Appraising Sources of Ideas	Judging Facts and Opinions	Appraising Talks and Reports
Is it related to the topic?	Is it related to our questions?	Is the title descriptive of the topic?
Is it recent enough for our purposes?	Is the source reliable?	Does the introduction set the stage?
Is it reliable? Valid?	Is it consistent with related ideas?	Are the ideas in good order?
Is it published by a special interest group?	Is it supported by evidence?	Are main ideas supported by facts?
Does it contain enough information?	Is it too general to be useful?	Are opinions distinguished from facts?
Can it be checked against reliable sources?	Is it advanced for a worthy cause?	Do conclusions tie ideas together?
Chart 9–54	Chart 9–55	Chart 9–56

Chart 9–57

Chart 9–58

Questions, Activities, Evaluation

1. Indicate two or three examples of creative and critical thinking that you might include in a unit.
2. Identify four or five concepts that should be developed in a unit of your choice. Note two or three direct and vicarious experiences that might be used to develop them. Note how one of the concept development strategies might be used.
3. Identify a generalization that should be developed in a unit of your choice. Note how one of the strategies for developing generalizations might be used to develop it.
4. Examine a recently published social studies textbook to identify the types of questions that are included. Using the model questions in this chapter as a guide, classify them according to the process that is the focus of each question. Which processes are used most? Least? Revise several of the questions so that the focus is shifted to analyzing, synthesizing, or other higher-level processes.
5. Make a set of questions that you might use in a unit of your choice. Be sure to include two or three for each process, arranging them in a sequence that you think will be meaningful for students. Base the questions on a reading selection, map, filmstrip, or other resource.

references

FAIR, JEAN, AND FANNIE R. SHAFTEL, eds., *Effective Thinking in the Social Studies* (37th yearbook). Washington, D.C.: National Council for the Social Studies, 1967. Principles and procedures for developing thinking skills.

309

FRASER, DOROTHY MCCLURE, ed., *Social Studies Curriculum Development: Prospects and Problems* (39th yearbook). Washington, D.C.: National Council for the Social Studies, 1969. Article by Tanck on concepts and generalizations.

HANNAH, LARRY S., AND JOHN U. MICHAELIS, *A Comprehensive Framework for Instructional Objectives: A Guide to Systematic Planning and Evaluation.* Reading, Mass.: Addison-Wesley Publishing Co., 1977. Examples of objectives, questions, and evaluation devices for each intellectual process.

HILLS, JAMES L., "Building and Using Inquiry Models in the Teaching of Geography," in *Focus on Geography* (40th yearbook), pp. 305–335. Washington, D.C.: National Council for the Social Studies, 1970. Eleven processes identified and illustrated.

JOYCE, BRUCE, AND MARSHA WEIL, *Models of Teaching* (2nd ed.). Englewood Cliffs, N.J.: Prentice-Hall, 1980. Chapters on information processing.

TABA, HILDA, MARY DURKIN, JACK R. FRANKEL, AND ANTHONY MCNAUGHTON, *Teacher's Handbook for Elementary Social Studies* (2nd ed.). Reading, Mass.: Addison-Wesley Publishing Co., 1971. Strategies for concept development, generalizing, and applying principles (predicting).

DEVELOPING CREATIVE THINKING THROUGH EXPRESSIVE ACTIVITIES

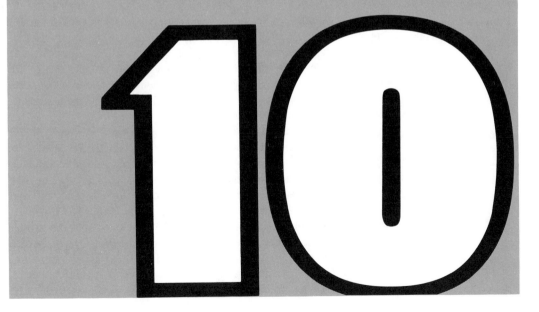

10

What types of expressive activities may be used to develop creative thinking in the social studies?

How can creative writing, role taking through dramatic expression, and simulation games be used in units of instruction?

How can music, arts and crafts, construction of objects, and processing of materials-be used in units?

Creative thinking should permeate all phases of the social studies program. Special opportunities to develop creative thinking abound in the expressive activities that are a dynamic part of each unit of instruction. Six types that add zest and delight to learning and involve children deeply and personally are presented in this chapter: creative writing, simulation games, music, arts and crafts, construction, and processing of materials. Through all of them students can express their thoughts and feelings creatively.

Expressive activities nuture creative thinking in many ways. New shades of meaning may be developed around qualitative and subjective aspects of human relationships as portrayed through music and other modes of aesthetic expression. Cognitive, affective, and skill dimensions of learning may be brought together and expressed in spontaneous and original ways. Thoughts and feelings may be synthesized in creative expression that brings the "doing" phase of thinking into play. New insights may be developed into the hopes, feelings, and aspirations of others as students identify themselves with people and activities under study. And creative thinking is sparked as students plan, carry out, and evaluate expressive activities on their own and in group projects.

Expressive activities enhance creative thinking by individualizing and personalizing learning. All students—able, disadvantaged, or average—can creatively express their very own thoughts and feelings. When students write stories, poems, and songs, when they paint pictures and construct objects, and when they take different roles and play simulation games, they are individualizing their learning by expressing themselves in ways that fit their cognitive and affective learning styles. And through the personal touches that are truly their own they are personalizing their learning by creating and expressing.

Expressive experiences are included in the social studies in two basic ways. First, material is included on the characteristic art, music, industrial arts, dramatic activities, and rhythmic expression of the people under study. For example, in such units as Indians of the Southwest, living in Japan, and South America, the rich storehouse of materials dealing with ''the arts'' should be drawn on and used. Second, children are given opportunities to express and interpret thoughts and feelings gleaned from experiences in each unit. For example, children may create poems, stories, descriptions, pictures, murals, skits, plays, and songs to highlight ideas and feelings for others as they are developed in units. In short, both ''impression'' and ''expression'' are essential to well-rounded learning.

Creative Writing

Children should have opportunities to create and share poems, stories, and descriptions. After backgrounds of understanding have been built up in a unit of instruction, the teacher should encourage the children to express their thoughts and feelings in written form. In the early grades, the group may dictate their ideas to the teacher for recording on the chalkboard and on charts. As children develop independent writing skills in later grades, they can express their thoughts and feelings in written form and share them with the group. When children discover the typical patterns of poetry from other lands—such as haiku, with its pattern of five syllables in the first and last lines and seven syllables in the middle line—they can adapt these forms to express their own feelings and experiences (see chart 10–1).

Related art and music activities may be coordinated with creative writing.

Haiku

When the evening sun
shoots deep red lights in the sky
nighttime is close by.

Golden leaves flutter
as cooler winds start blowing
summer into fall.

Howling winds bending
tall pine trees in the forest
as white clouds pass by.

Chart 10–1

Ideas for Creative Writing	Finding Expressive Terms
1. Stories and poems—topics, events, travel, people, activities 2. Descriptions—persons, places, things, events, and activities 3. Dramatization—sketches and plays 4. Booklets, scrapbooks, leaflets, charts 5. Quiz programs 6. Radio and television programs 7. Movie box rolls	1. Check the vocabulary chart. 2. Use the picture dictionary. 3. Listen as others discuss topics. 4. Look for them in our books. 5. Use the classroom dictionary. 6. Get ideas from pictures. 7. Get ideas from films. 8. Think of feelings as well as facts.

Chart 10–2   Chart 10–3

Over a period of time, collections may be made and kept in individual or class scrapbooks, posted on the bulletin boards, and used in culminating activities in units of instruction. Charts 10–2 and 10–3 list items for children to consider in group planning, discussion, and the evlauation of creative written work.

Role Taking through Dramatic Representation

Role taking enables students to identify with the persons and situations being studied. Role-taking activities range from taking a role in a discussion to playing a role in a value-laden situation. This section focuses on role taking through dramatic representation.

Dramatic representation is an excellent substitute for firsthand experience with people, events, and situations far removed from the classroom. Although children cannot direct activities in a control tower at the airport, a railway classification yard, or a wagon train, they can participate in dramatic representation and thus gain insight into how such activities are directed. They cannot be fire fighters, post office workers, pilots, colonists, pioneers, scouts, or early settlers, but they can identify with such people through dramatic activities. They cannot take study trips to distant lands or go back in history to early times, but they can realistically recreate and interpret distant events, activities, and situations.

Children are familiar with dramatic representation. They have used it before entering school, in make-believe and imaginary play—''being'' a mother, father, teacher, bus driver, fire fighter, or airplane pilot. On entering school children are eager to act out activities they are studying and to portray their impressions of people, events, and situations. The wise teacher will take advantage of their interest and skill in dramatic representation and use it to steer learning in worthwhile directions.

Dramatic representation in school, however, is different from make-believe play at home. At home children engage in dramatic play on their own;

314

in school they are guided and supervised so that their play achieves its purpose. At home children base their dramatic play on ideas and impressions they have gathered in an incidental fashion; in school they gather specific background information and make it the basis for dramatic representation of social studies experiences. At home make-believe play keeps children occupied; in school dramatic representation develops definite concepts, skills, attitudes, and appreciations.

Dramatic representation offers excellent opportunities to evaluate children's learning. As teachers observe children in dramatic activities, they can appraise how children use concepts, grasp main ideas, express attitudes, identify with others, and express themselves creatively. Children spontaneously reveal the ideas, feelings, and impressions they have gained, and the alert teacher can detect and use misconceptions and erroneous ideas to plan and guide subsequent study.

FORMS OF DRAMATIC REPRESENTATION

Dramatic representation takes a variety of forms in the social studies. Among the most valuable are these:

Dramatic play is used frequently in the early grades to portray activities in units on the home, school, neighborhood, and community. Dramatic play allows children to stage an informal and creative portrayal of experiences without a set pattern, refined staging, costumes, or memorization of parts.

Dramatic rhythms involve the interpretation of activities and events by means of rhythmic bodily movement. Dramatic rhythms differ from dramatic play in that rhythmic movement is emphasized. Dramatic rhythms differ from creative dance in that the child is interpreting something learned in the social studies. They are similar to creative dance in that children give their own personal interpretations, not those of others.

Role playing develops insight into human relations, problems of others, a main idea, or the feelings and values of individuals in a critical situation. After the role is portrayed in different ways, such questions as these may be discussed: Which role did you prefer? Why? Which role was least desirable? Why? How did each role make you feel? How might individuals feel in the actual situation? What might be done to improve the situation? (A role playing strategy is presented in chapter 13).

Dramatic skits are more formal than dramatic play; they involve the enactment of a selected event or activity in which assigned roles are taken and lines are learned to portray a significant incident such as the signing of the Mayflower Compact or the landing at Plymouth Rock.

Pageants are used to portray a sequence of incidents or activities related to such unit topics as the history of our community, the development of our state, the growth of America, and living in Mexico. Dramatic skits prepared by small groups within the class are easily arranged as a pageant.

Pantomimes may be used to portray simply and briefly such an activity as a plane landing, the movement of a boat into the harbor, or a scout on the lookout for Indians.

Dramatization may be employed to present a playlet or play in which a script, costumes, and a stage setting are used.

Marionettes and puppets may be used for both creative dramatics and formal dramatization. Children may construct them, plan for their use, use them to present skits and plays, and use them in new situations by preparing new lines, staging, and costumes. Some teachers use them to build confidence in shy children as well as to provide a different form of dramatic expression for typical children.

Mock trials enable students to simulate courtroom activities, including the roles of the judge, plaintiff and defendant and their attorneys, witnesses, and the jury.

Mock meetings may be planned and conducted in the upper grades to simulate New England town meetings, city council meetings, and legislative sessions.

Unfinished stories or *reaction stories* may be used to stimulate the enactment of situations in which children show what they would do if they were involved. After hearing a story about such problems as fair play, helping others, carrying out one's responsibilities, respecting property, or minority group relations, children act out a solution and evaluate the enactment.

In the following sections, major attention is given to creative and informal dramatic activities, primarily because they are more difficult to plan and guide than are formal dramatics in which a script is followed. A teacher who has not observed or guided creative dramatic activities might first experiment with a play written for children. Next the teacher might plan with the class short skits related to topics under study. This may be followed by longer dramatic activities, until finally the group has moved to a creative and informal approach to dramatization.

Sometimes a teacher may decide that a play written for children—for example, a program for a special occasion or a dramatic activity related to the commemoration of a special event—is more appropriate than creative dramatics. If so, an appropriate play should be selected, rehearsed, and presented in a way that develops backgrounds of understanding, involves the students in planning and evaluation, and achieves other educational values.

EXAMPLES OF DRAMATIC ACTIVITIES

The following examples of activities that lend themselves to dramatization have been taken from different types of units of instruction. As you read them, note examples that you might use in a unit you are planning.

The home: cleaning, gardening, washing and ironing; taking care of the baby, taking care of pets; preparing and serving meals, having a tea party; enjoying leisure activities, telephoning friends

The supermarket: being the grocery clerk, butcher, cashier, fruit and vegetable clerk, a customer; stocking shelves, making signs and price tags, weighing items, sweeping

Community workers: being a fire fighter; working in the post office, receiving, sorting, and delivering mail; operating a filling station, cleaning trucks; broadcasting news; running the airport; being other community workers

The farm: pitching hay, feeding and watering animals, herding cows, milking cows; fixing the corral, plowing land, planting seeds, irrigating, harvesting; picking, washing, and bunching vegetables; loading, hauling, and distributing produce in trucks

Our state: early ways of transporting goods and communicating with others; hunting, trading, other life activities; outstanding episodes and personalities in the growth of the state; modern ways of transporting goods, earning a living, and communicating with others

Colonial life: Pilgrims leaving Holland, the trip in the Mayflower, the Mayflower Pact, landing at Plymouth Rock, the first Thanksgiving; starting the first community, meeting Indians, getting food, cutting logs, planning the houses, planting and hunting, spinning and carding wool, making soap and candles; playing games such as leap frog, wood tag, spinning tag; a town meeting, a day in the colonial home, a visit with Indians, a quilting bee; reactions of Indians to the arrival of colonists

China: festivals such as New Year's, Festival of the Lanterns, Festival of the Dragon Boats, and the Mid-Autumn or Moon Festival

DRAMATIC RHYTHMS

Children are quick to respond to the rhythm in life around them. Grain swaying in the field, waves rolling in to shore, birds flying from tree to tree, people at work in the community, trains starting and stopping—all these will stimulate natural and spontaneous rhythmical expression. Similarly, rich experiences in the social studies lead to dramatic rhythms that are meaningful demonstrations of the children's impressions.

"I'll show you how the liner comes in," said a boy demonstrating the slow, even movement of a large ocean liner.

"Out goes the pilot boat," said a girl moving gracefully and speedily as she gave her interpretation of the pilot boat she had seen on a trip to the harbor.

"Here comes a tug to help," said another child moving slowly but powerfully to assist the liner.

"Here comes another tug. Chug! Chug! Chug!" said a boy who had seen a tug work in the harbor nearby. With considerable realism, he moved over to help bring the liner in.

Thus do children spontaneously and eagerly use rhythmic expression through bodily movement to interpret experiences they have had.

Children spontaneously add rhythmic expression to many of the dramatic activities listed in the preceding section. For example, they may "catch the beat" and use rhythmic expression to portray such activities as digging, raking,

Rhythmic expression adds zest to learning.

and working in the garden; loading and unloading trucks; movements of freight trains as they start, gain speed, speed along, slow down, and stop; and activities of farmers as they ride horses, milk cows, and plow a field. When musical accompaniment is added, students bring together dramatic, rhythmic, and musical modes of expression to enrich their interpretations of activities under study in a unit. Suggestions for rhythmic musical activities are presented later in this chapter.

In addition to interpretation through dramatic rhythms, folk games and folk dances have a place in the social studies. Many units would be incomplete if folk dances were omitted. For example, in units on Mexico the Fandango, "La Cucaracha," and "St. Michael's Wheel" and in units on pioneer life "Old Dan Tucker," "Virginia Reel," and "Captain Jenks" are most appropriate. Other examples can be found in references listed at the end of this chapter.

Growth in dramatic rhythms progresses from simple interpretation of single episodes to more complete patterns of expression centered in a unifying theme. At first, children's responses to rhythm are short and simple. A single phase of an activity, such as the train starting, may be interpreted with real satisfaction. Other phases, such as gaining speed, slowing down, or going up a

318

steep hill, may be added later. Still later, several phases are brought together in a pattern of rhythm as the child portrays the complete activity. Finally, several children cooperate in rhythmic bodily expression of related activities, such as the train backing up to couple cars, starting up, traveling along, leaving cars at different places, and arriving at its destination. In this final stage, the group develops a unifying pattern that is a creative synthesis of individual interpretations.

MOCK TRIALS

Mock trials help students develop concepts of justice, learn key aspects of courtroom procedure, analyze issues, interpret facts, and evaluate decisions. To carry out a mock trial students must learn the roles of judges, jurors, attorneys, and witnesses. They also need to know courtroom procedures and rules of evidence. Visits to courts, interviews of judges and attorneys, study of materials for students, television programs, and films are useful sources of information (see end-of-chapter reference by Gallagher).

An inexperienced group should begin with a simple mock trial in which a judge hears the case and makes the decision with no attorneys present, as in small claims court. After students have built up a background of knowledge and experience, a civil court mock trial may be simulated. The main steps in a mock trial are briefing (preparation), conducting the trial (simulation), and debriefing (evaluation). Briefing should be thorough so that participants understand their roles, the issue, and the facts. The simulation should follow the steps as outlined in charts 10–4 and 10–5. Debriefing contributes much to learning as students evaluate the following: How were the roles played? How might they be changed? What was the issue? Which facts were relevant? How effectively were they presented? How sound were the arguments on each side? How might they be improved? Why do you agree or disagree with the decision? Can you think of sound reasons for an appeal?

Small Claims Court

The plaintiff and defendant appear before the judge.

The plaintiff states his or her case.

The defendant states his or her case.

The judge asks questions to clarify facts in the case.

The judge makes and explains the decision.

Chart 10–4

Civil Court

The court is opened, and the jury sworn in.

Attorneys for the plaintiff and defendant make opening statements.

Attorneys examine and cross-examine witnesses.

Attorneys present closing statements.

The jury receives instructions, deliberates, and gives a verdict.

Chart 10–5

An essential first step in guiding dramatic activities is to develop adequate backgrounds of understanding so that children will dramatize events and activities authentically and creatively. This requires much planning, discussion, and study, as shown in the following list of steps taken by a group of ten-year-olds who dramatized the journey of pioneer families into Kentucky.

1. Read and discuss stories about the journey and make a list of important points to incorporate in the play:
   a. Welcoming Daniel Boone home
   b. Talking things over with the settlers
   c. Preparation for the trip
   d. Problems of travel over the trail
   e. Ways of living in Russell Camp
   f. The returning home of many settlers
2. Find out what the settlers took with them.
3. Find out the ways the pioneers traveled. Decide which trail they took and find out about the dangers. Locate the trail and rivers on a map.
4. Read material about early settlers, listen to stories read by the teacher, and write a creative story about them.
5. Find out how to mark trees, cut down obstacles, and stay on the trail.
6. Plan and incorporate these ideas in dramatic activities.
7. Carry out the plan and evaluate the effectiveness of individual and group activities.

Once rich backgrounds of understanding have been developed, group planning may be employed effectively. Attention should be given to such questions as these:

What shall we dramatize?

What space do we need?

What materials do we need?

What characters do we need?

Who should take each part?

By beginning with *what* to do, the children can open up many possibilities without undue concern about *who* will take each part. Decisions on who will take each part may well be left until the last stage of planning, after what is to be included in the dramatic activity is clear.

After plans are made, the group should try out the different suggestions, discuss them, and make changes as needed. During dramatic activity, the teacher should be alert to needs, problems, and suggestions for improvement that may be used during follow-up discussion. It is wise to take notes so that specific guidance can be given during evaluation.

After a group has dramatized an episode, time should be set aside to share and evaluate problems, questions, needs for materials, needs for additional information, and ways to make improvements. The teacher should guide the discussion so that appropriate points noted during the activity are considered. Group standards should be set up when needed to improve the value of the activity. For example, during a unit on the harbor, one group developed the standards in chart 10–6 after a dramatic activity ran into difficulties because of "wrong boat sounds," "boats clogging the harbor," and "fire boats tugging liners in." Following a skit involving life in Boonesboro, another group listed the standards in chart 10–7 because several children had failed to dramatize their roles authentically.

Continuous planning is needed to utilize dramatic activities effectively. Checklist 10–1 presents specific factors that may be used for planning, guiding, and evaluating dramatic activities.

Running the Harbor

1. Share the boats with others.
2. Remember how each boat sounds.
3. Keep the harbor open for liners.
4. Let the tugs pull the liner in.
5. Listen to the captain's signals.

Chart 10–6

Protecting Boonesboro

1. Sentinels should keep a sharp lookout.
2. The gates should be closed on the signal.
3. Gun loaders should load guns and not shoot.
4. Scouts should sneak out through the little gate.
5. Get gunpowder out of the powder horns.

Chart 10–7

Checklist 10–1
Dramatic Activities Checklist

TEACHER PREPLANNING

_____ What needs have arisen for dramatic activities?

_____ Are materials available?

_____ Are space arrangements adequate?

_____ Are new ideas and information needed? How should they be introduced?

_____ Which children probably will wish to participate first? Which should?

_____ What will others do?

GROUP PLANNING

_____ Is attention given first to what to dramatize?

_____ Do the children select important aspects of living to portray?

_____ Are needs for materials considered?

_____ Do individuals suggest roles that are essential?

_____ Are new ideas and materials introduced to enrich the activity?

DURING THE ACTIVITY: CHILDREN

_____ Are the children identifying with the person and objects involved?

_____ Are important aspects of living portrayed?

_____ Are space and materials used effectively?

_____ Are the suggestions made during planning carried out in the activity?

_____ Are concepts being used accurately?

DURING THE ACTIVITY: TEACHER

_____ Are new needs emerging for

_____ a. clarification   _____ c. group standards

_____ b. authentic information   _____ d. language expression

_____ Are concepts being expressed accurately in language and in action?

_____ Are any individuals confused or uncertain as to purpose, use of materials, or role?

_____ Are changes needed in space arrangements or materials?

GROUP EVALUATION

_____ Does the group appraise the activity in terms of the roles discussed during planning?

_____ Are newly discovered needs and problems considered?

_____ Are inaccuracies and misconceptions clarified?

_____ Have leads developed to other group and individual activities that will extend and broaden interests and keep the unit moving forward?

SIMULATION GAMES

Simulation games are scaled-down models of actual situations, problems, or activities. The players assume realistic roles and make decisions according to specified rules. Such games can enlist student involvement, develop and extend concepts, clarify key aspects of life situations, and develop the abilities to weigh alternatives and make decisions. Simulation games are more restricted and patterned than dramatic play and role playing. Roles, rules, and materials are designed to portray realistically the activity to be simulated. Students compete to win the game and must play within its rules and constraints. Games for the social studies have been constructed around urban, economic, political, and social problems and activities. Titles that indicate the nature of games for use in the elementary school are Neighborhood, Dividing the Work, Market, The Barter Game, Making a Profit, Urban Planning, How Competition Works, and Caribou Hunting.

A description of The Barter Game serves to illustrate the main features of simulation games. Key instructional objectives are to demonstrate the nature of bartering and the importance of using workers and resources wisely. The three tribes in the game each have different resources—food, tin, and copper. Each tribe must decide how to use workers, what to produce, and what to trade. The goal is to maintain an adequate food supply and to get as much tin and copper—the raw materials for bronze axes—as possible. The winning tribe is the one that ends up with an adequate food supply and the most bronze axes. Students play the game by choosing leaders, assigning workers to various jobs, and making decisions as to what to trade. Each tribe gets cards indicating units of food, tin, and copper in relation to the number of workers assigned to different jobs. Each tribe decides what to trade and proceeds to barter with the other tribes. (For detailed directions see the pamphlet by Younger and Aceti listed in the end-of-chapter references.)

Simulation games are not without their problems, but many difficulties can be anticipated and avoided. Teachers claim that some games take too much time and are too complex for elementary students or that children overlook key objectives in their eagerness to play the game. Sometimes games become substitutes for important field studies, action projects, or other worthwhile activities. Arguments may arise over rules and roles, or the emphasis on winning may interfere with learning and attaining specific objectives. Such problems can be avoided by selecting games that are not too complex and that fit into available time limits, by planning for a balanced set of activities within each unit, by clarifying rules and roles in group planning, and by setting clear objectives before the game is started. Checklist 10–2 includes specific points to guide the use of simulations and to prevent the foregoing problems from developing.

Checklist 10–2
Simulations Checklist

PREPLANNING

_____ What problem or life situation should be simulated?

_____ How is it related to the unit under study?

_____ What concepts or principles are involved in its use?

_____ How can directions be made clear to students?

_____ What materials and space arrangements are needed?

_____ How many students will be involved, and what will their roles be?

_____ Which students should be assigned to different teams in order to provide for balance in abilities?

GROUP PLANNING

_____ Are objectives clear to the participants?

_____ Do participants understand their roles?

_____ Are rules, use of materials, and time limits clear?

_____ What questions should be answered before beginning?

DURING THE SIMULATION

_____ Are roles being carried out in line with the rules?

_____ How can any confusion about objectives, concepts, and rules be overcome?

_____ What specific suggestions might be made to improve the activity?

_____ What items should be given attention during evaluation?

GROUP EVALUATION AND DEBRIEFING

_____ Which decisions and strategies were most useful? Least useful? Why

_____ Which aspects were true to life? How can distortions be corrected?

_____ How can any problems or difficulties be overcome?

_____ What improvements might be made in directions, rules, and roles?

_____ How might the simulation be modified? Can a better one be created?

Simulations directly related to problems and situations under study are easily constructed. After stating objectives, make a simplified model; specify the roles of each player; set the rules, conditions, and time limits; and prepare necessary cards and other materials. For example, a Gold Rush game could simulate the problems, hardships, and luck that prospectors experienced. Using a board and game procedures similar to Monopoly, players endeavor to avoid such hardships as claim jumping, illness, running out of money, and failing to get a grubstake as they try to obtain mining claims of greatest value. Other simulations might include Deciding on a Vacation, Saving at a Sale, Urban Planning, Curbing Pollution, Lost and Found, Touring a Country, City Council, Getting a Bill Passed, Exports and Imports, and the Stock Market.

The following guidelines aid in constructing simulations:

1. Note the concepts and principles from economics, geography, or other fields to be emphasized.
2. Make a simplified model that shows the elements to be simulated.
3. List the information and materials participants need to carry out the simulation.
4. Specify the groups needed and the roles in each group that individuals should play, noting goals for each participant.
5. Write the directions for starting, carrying out, and concluding the simulation, giving attention to rules, use of materials, time limits, and use of space.
6. Try out the simulation with a small group and make revisions as needed to clarify objectives, roles, and rules.

Music Activities

The world's musical heritage is a rich source of content and activities that help students understand people and their ways of living. People in cultures at home and around the world have expressed their customs, traditions, and values in music. Patriotic music has been written to stir feelings of loyalty, to highlight great events, and for festivals, ceremonies, and religious activities. Poems, stories, legends, and other literary works have been set to music. Folk songs and dances have evolved from everyday activities. Musical instruments have been invented to provide unique modes of expression. And as the music created in one part of the world has reached people in other parts of the world, cultural interdependence has increased.

Six types of music activity are used in social studies units of instruction: singing activities, listening activities, rhythmic activities, instrumental activities, creative expression, and research activities. By directing children's participation in each type of activity, a teacher can guide children to make meaningful cross-cultural comparisons, one of the main reasons for giving attention to music in the social studies.

SINGING ACTIVITIES

Singing is the most extensively used music activity in the social studies. Children's music books contain many songs related to topics in each unit of instruction. Children's identification with others is increased as they sing songs about human experience and activities—working and playing at home, working on the farm, living in a hogan, trekking westward across the plains, and living in other lands. Children develop sensitivity to the effects of natural conditions on human activities as they learn songs about nature and get a feeling for the icy winds of the northern steppes, the hot dry desert, the steaming jungle, the grandeur of high mountains, the vastness of the prairies, and changes in the seasons. Feelings about and appreciation of events in our country's history may be stirred as children sing "The Star-Spangled Banner," "America the Beautiful," "Battle Hymn of the Republic," and "Columbia, the Gem of the Ocean." A feeling of kinship with others may be kindled as children sing the folk songs of different regions of America and of other lands.

In the social studies, special attention is given to the development of backgrounds of understanding of the songs included in each unit. The questions in chart 10–8 may be used to guide children's study and discussion.

**Understand the Songs We Sing
in Our Unit**

What thoughts and values are expressed?

What is the mood, the rhythmic pattern, and the melody?

Is this a song of work, play, worship, adventure, nature, fantasy, or patriotism?

Is this song sung at home, at festivals, or at ceremonies?

Chart 10–8

Through directed listening experiences, children can learn much about the folk songs, dances, instruments, festivals, holidays, patriotic events, composers, and performing artists of greatest importance in each unit. Recordings of different types of music give realism and authenticity to children's learning. Radio and television programs, community concerts and folk festivals, individuals invited to school, and children's own recordings can also contribute to learning. Chart 10–9 lists questions that may be used to guide listening experiences in the social studies.

Listening to Music from Other Lands

How did you feel as you listened?
Who can demonstrate the rhythmic pattern?
Can you tell what instruments were used?
What was unusual about the tonal patterns?
How is their music related to customs and traditions?
What clues did you get about their values?

Chart 10–9

RHYTHMIC ACTIVITIES

Four types of rhythmic activity may be provided in the social studies:

1. *Informal rhythms* allow children to express rhythmic patterns without direction from the teacher.
2. *Formal rhythms* are directed by the teacher, and children move to the rhythm (skip, gallop, and the like) as music is played.
3. *Creative rhythms* encourage children to express their responses in original ways.
4. *Dramatic rhythms* were discussed in the preceding section.

As these activities are used in the social studies, special attention is given to the rhythmic patterns characteristic of the music, folk dances, and activities included in units of instruction (see charts 10–10 through 10–12). Rhythm instruments, recordings, native instruments, the piano, and the autoharp are used to accompany rhythmic activities and to play rhythmic patterns.

INSTRUMENTAL ACTIVITIES

Musical instruments of various types may be used to extend children's learning. Rhythm instruments such as drums, sticks, blocks, bells, triangles,

Rhythms Around Us	Rhythmic Patterns		Finding Rhythms
Bells ringing	Gallop	Skip	Activities of people
Hammers pounding	Gavotte	Slide	Animals moving
Horns tooting	Hop	Swing	Folk dances
Horses trotting	March	Tango	Radio and television
Motors humming	Minuet	Trot	Recordings
People working	Polka	Walk	Songs and poems
Trees swaying	Schottische	Waltz	Trains, planes

Chart 10–10   Chart 10–11   Chart 10–12

cymbals, gongs, rattles, and tambourines may be used to accompany rhythmic and singing activities, produce sound effects, and play rhythmic patterns. Chording instruments such as the autoharp and harmolin may be used to accompany various activities and to demonstrate harmonic and rhythmic patterns. Simple melody instruments such as melody bells, tuned bottles or glasses, song flutes, and recorders may be used to play tunes created by children as well as melodies discovered in the songs and recordings presented in units. Native instruments may be examined and played to give authenticity to music activities. Examples of these are the claves, guiro, maracas, cabaca, bongo, conga, antara or pipes of Pan, quena or flute, and chocalho in units on South America; and the bamboo xylophone, gong, temple block, and finger cymbals in units on oriental countries. (See also chart 10–13.)

How Can We Use These Instruments in Our Unit?

PERCUSSION

Castanets	Jangles	Sticks
Cymbals	Maracas	Tambourines
Drums	Scrapers	Triangles
Gong	Shakers	Woodblocks

MELODY

Bells	Psaltery	Tonette
Harmolette	Recorder	Water glasses
Harmonica	Songflute	Xylophone

HARMONY

Autoharp	Harmolin	Marimba

Chart 10–13

Creative expression through music may be brought to high levels in the social studies as children develop insights and appreciations through activities in units of instruction. Poems and verse created by children may be set to music as children hum tunes or play them on simple melody instruments while the teacher records them on the chalkboard, a chart, or a tape recorder (see chart 10–14).

Children can create accompaniments for songs, rhythmic movement, choral reading, and dramatic activities as they catch the mood and rhythm of thoughts and feelings to be expressed. They can create special sound effects and background music for skits, plays, and pageants. They can make simple instruments from gourds, bamboo, bottles, glasses, and other materials. Creative expression through art, writing, dramatics, and rhythmic movement can be stimulated as children listen to recordings. A range of creative processes can be brought into play as children plan and develop concluding activities that include a script, lyrics and melodies, costumes, staging, musical accompaniments, and their own special effects.

Composing a Song for Our Unit

What moods or feelings shall we try to express?

What words and phrases shall we use?

Shall we hum, whistle, play, or sing to create the melody?

What rhythms shall we use?

Shall we record the lyric and the melody?

Chart 10–14

RESEARCH ACTIVITIES

Individual and group research activities may be undertaken to find background information on the music emphasized in units of instruction. A trip may be taken to a nearby museum to examine instruments and to see costumes used in folk dances. Experts may be interviewed or invited to come to the classroom to give demonstrations. Encyclopedias, library resources, and supplementary music books may be reviewed. Notebooks and scrapbooks may be compiled to summarize information. Illustrative questions to guide children's research activities are listed in chart 10–15.

The diversity of the musical heritage among people in different cultural settings should be explored by the class. For example, in South America, Africa, Europe, Canada, and the United States, many different types of music are

Chart 10–15

found, and as students study them they can discover the influences of diverse cultural backgrounds. Folk music, adaptations of music from other lands, music created by native composers, and famous performing artists may be studied as a part of units. The following examples are drawn from units on countries in South America.

Argentina: Influences of the Italians, Indians, and Spaniards are evident. "El Estilo," a melancholy, nostalgic song of the pampas, shows the Italian influence. The tango shows Spanish influence. The rich folk music shows the Indian influence. The compositions of Alberto Ginastera and Juan José Castro and the folk music recordings and publications of Carlos Vega show the richness of Argentina's musical heritage. Well-known songs that may be found in children's music books are "Sí Señor," "Palapala," "Adiós Te Digo," "Chacerera," "Song of the Pampas," "The Gaucho," "Vidalita," and "Ay, Zamba."

Brazil: Influences of the Indians, Portuguese, and Negroes are evident. Tender and sentimental ballads show the influence of the Portuguese, who sang the "Modinha" to drive away homesickness. The Chôros is a rhythmically rich musical form that includes improvised variations; it originated during the Second Empire. The samba, one of the most sophisticated of the carioca dances, shows the Negro influence. Among the famous Brazilian singers are Bidú Sayão, Elsie Houston, and Olga Coelho. Two renowned composers are Heitor Villa-Lobos and Francisco Mignone. Illustrative of the Brazilian songs included in children's music books are "The Painter of Cannahay," "My Pretty Cabacla," "Tutu Maramba," "Cantilena," "Sambalele," "Bambamulele," "In Bahia Town," "O Gato," and "Come Here, Vitu."

Chile: The gay mood of the folk and popular music of Chile shows a strong Spanish influence. The scarf dances *(danzas de pañuelo)* in which couples dance separately have been brought to a high level of artistic develoment. The *cueca,* or *zamacueca,* is the most popular dance. A new *cueca* may be created to commemorate special events ranging from the winning of a football game to an outstanding historical event. Among the renowned musical figures in Chile are Claudio Arrau (pianist), Domingo Santa Cruz (composer), and Ramon Vinay (tenor). Illustrative songs are "San Severino," "The Lovely Chilean Maid," "Buy a Dozen," "El Marinero," "Pol Perica," "Dance Song," and "Bom Bom Bom."

329

A classroom music center may be arranged and changed as different units of instruction are developed. Song books, instruments, other music materials, and pictures showing musical activities may be placed in the music center. If headphones are available for listening to recordings, children may go to the center at different times for individual listening.

The bulletin board in the music center might display news clippings about musicians in places under study, announcements of related programs on television and radio, a list of recordings for individual listening, and pictures showing native musical activities. The center might also include a listening post (record player with several headphones) for individual and small-group listening, maps showing the locale of songs and musicians, an autoharp and rhythm instruments, and a flannel board for showing rhythmic and tonal patterns.

Arts and Crafts

From ancient times to the present, people have expressed their thoughts and feelings through various art forms. Artists and artisans of each generation have selected ideas and created forms that clarify, simplify, and interpret the ideals, beliefs, and customs of their times. Line, form, color, texture, space, and other elements have been unified in ways that are expressive of the artist's intentions. Touches of beauty have been added to dwellings, clothing, utensils, festivals, ceremonies, and other objects and activities. Folk crafts have been developed to add beauty to everyday objects and have provided opportunities for creative expression in homes and villages throughout the world.

Art activities enrich children's learning. Deeper insights and appreciations are developed as children discover the impact of art on homes, furnishings, cars, trains, airplanes, buildings, bridges, and other objects. They come to ap-

How Are These Portrayed in Arts and Crafts?	
Aspirations	Hopes
Beliefs	Ideals
Customs	Ideas
Events	Nature
Fears	Recreation
Feelings	Religion
Freedom	Superstitions
Heroes	Traditions

Chart 10–16

Which of These Items Do They Make?	
Baskets	Leather
Bead work	work
Blankets	Mosaics
Containers	Pottery
Copperware	Rugs
Featherwork	Shawls
Figurines	Silverware
Instruments	Tiles
Jewelry	

Chart 10–17

Can You Discover Creative Uses of the Following?	
Balance	Perspective
Color	Repetition
Design	Rhythm
Emphasis	Space
Form	Subordination
Integration	Texture
Line	Unity
Movement	Variation

Chart 10–18

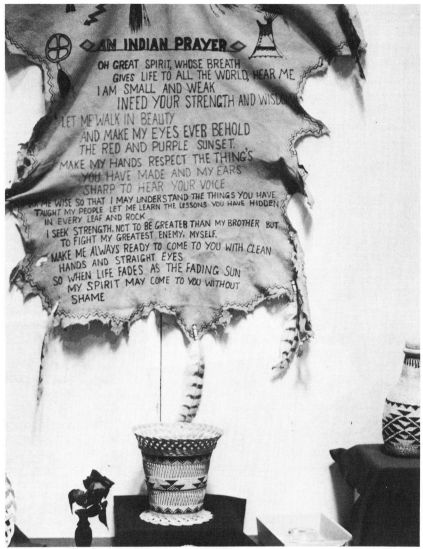

AN INDIAN PRAYER

OH GREAT SPIRIT, WHOSE BREATH GIVES LIFE TO ALL THE WORLD, HEAR ME I AM SMALL AND WEAK I NEED YOUR STRENGTH AND WISDOM LET ME WALK IN BEAUTY AND MAKE MY EYES EVER BEHOLD THE RED AND PURPLE SUNSET. MAKE MY HANDS RESPECT THE THINGS YOU HAVE MADE AND MY EARS SHARP TO HEAR YOUR VOICE MAKE ME WISE SO THAT I MAY UNDERSTAND THE THINGS YOU HAVE TAUGHT MY PEOPLE LET ME LEARN THE LESSONS YOU HAVE HIDDEN IN EVERY LEAF AND ROCK I SEEK STRENGTH, NOT TO BE GREATER THAN MY BROTHER, BUT TO FIGHT MY GREATEST ENEMY, MYSELF. MAKE ME ALWAYS READY TO COME TO YOU WITH CLEAN HANDS AND STRAIGHT EYES SO WHEN LIFE FADES AS THE FADING SUN MY SPIRIT MAY COME TO YOU WITHOUT SHAME

Sacramento, California

How can artistic expression as represented by such artifacts as these be used to enrich multicultural studies?

preciate the beauty in nature as they study their community, the state, the nation, and other lands. Subtle shades of meaning may be brought out as children consider the work of artists who have portrayed great events, heroes, landscapes, poems, songs, everyday activities, ceremonies, festivals, and holidays. Basic concepts may be enriched as children see and discuss pictures that simplify and clarify changes in the seasons, the dense jungles, storms lashing a seacoast, a ship being tossed by the stormy sea, a lagoon by a tropical isle,

**Find Out How People Express
Themselves through Art**

Study pictures in our textbooks.

Look at reproductions of pictures and art objects.

See films, filmstrips, and slides.

Visit a museum or art gallery.

Examine textiles, pottery, jewelry, and other objects.

Interview people who have visited other cultures or studied their art.

Read art books, reference materials, and current periodicals.

Collect pictures from magazines, newspapers, and travel folders.

Chart 10–19

**Which of These Crafts
Are Used in Other Cultures?**

Weaving mats, tapestries, cloth, rugs, and wall hangings

Basket making from reeds and raffia

Creating designs on cloth, bark, woven raffia, parchment, skins, metal, stone, clay, and wood

Embroidering or appliquéing on clothing, costumes, and textiles

Carving in wood, stone, ivory, and bone

Modeling and constructing objects out of clay

Making objects out of metal

Dyeing cloth, leather, bark, and other materials

Making masks, costumes, and objects for use in ceremonies and festivals

Chart 10–20

Which Should We Use?

Drawing, painting, sketching, illustrating

Making items out of paper, cardboard, metal, wire, wood

Weaving, sewing, stitching, embroidering, appliquéing

Modeling, carving, sculpturing, whittling

Making dioramas, panoramas, shadow boxes

Chart 10–21

Making a Mural

What main ideas shall we show?

What related ideas are needed?

How shall the ideas be arranged?

What materials shall we use?

What colors will be most effective?

What contributions can each person make?

Chart 10–22

earth-moving machines cutting a road through mountains, and workers toiling in the fields. A feeling for modes of expression enjoyed by others may be kindled as children discover the concepts of nature in sand paintings of the Navahos, the simple beauty of the Puritan church, the delicate patterns in Japanese paintings, the search for harmony between people and nature in Chinese art, the recurring themes and patterns in Egyptian art, the stateliness of Roman architecture, and the desire for freedom boldly revealed in Rivera's murals. Cultural interdependence may be highlighted as the thunderbird, the cross, geometric forms, and other designs are discovered in the art of peoples in different lands. Charts 10–16 through 10–22 suggest ways to bring art activities into units.

Creative and appreciative experiences may be intertwined as children engage in art activities. For example, the sand paintings of the Navahos may be considered in terms of the concepts of nature, human activities, myths, and ideas that they portray. Paralleling such study may be activities in which children engage in sand painting to portray their impressions of selected activities. In a study of Mexico, pictures of the murals of Diego Rivera may be explored to discover the ideas, hopes, and feelings expressed. This may be paralleled or followed by an activity in which children create a mural to portray their own impressions of life in Mexico. When such parallel activities are provided, be sure that children's expression is truly creative, truly their own, and not a copy of that of others.

As a general guideline, originaltiy should be emphasized in both appreciative and creative activities. As the art of other people is studied, each individual, whether a child or an adult, will respond in unique ways. To be sure, children may have similar understandings of background ideas about the culture in which the art product was created and certain common understandings about the processes involved. But the individual's reaction, response, and feelings are always highly individualized. Similarly, as children engage in art activities, every effort should be made to encourage creative expression in each child. What is desired is individual interpretation and expression of thoughts and feelings.

But what if a child has misconceptions and erroneous ideas about the people or activities portrayed? Misconceptions are corrected through additional study; simply telling or showing a child how to draw something is not a substitute for developing backgrounds of understanding of people and their ways of living. The ideas to be expressed and the media and processes used in an art activity may be enriched through directed study. But when children proceed to express the ideas, they must use their own techniques if the experience is to be called an art activity. Otherwise it is merely copying, illustrating, or reproducing the technique of another person. It is not art.

TYPES OF ART ACTIVITY

Checklist 10–3 includes the main types of art activity used in the social studies. Each major type is followed by examples of items that may be made, designed, or arranged by children.

Checklist 10–3
Art Activities

Drawing and Painting: ____Backgrounds ____Borders ____Cartoons ____Decorations ____Designs ____Friezes ____Greeting cards ____Illustrations ____Landscapes ____Murals ____Pictures ____Posters ____Sketches

Modeling, Sculpturing, and Carving: ____Animals ____Beads ____Bowls
____Candlesticks ____Dishes ____Figurines ____Jars ____Jewelry ____Jugs
____Plaques ____Pots ____Tiles ____Trays ____Utensils ____Vases

Designing: ____Announcements ____Backgrounds for collages ____Booklets
____Borders ____Containers ____Fans ____Greeting cards ____Markers
____Mats ____Mosaics ____Prints ____Programs ____Stage scenery
____Wrappers

Arranging: ____Cornucopias ____Displays ____Driftwood ____Exhibits
____Flowers ____Fruits ____Gourds ____Textiles

Paper and Cardboard Construction: ____Booklets ____Buildings ____Collages
____Containers ____Decorations ____Designs ____Dioramas ____Furniture
____Marionettes ____Masks ____Mats ____Mobiles ____Montages
____Mosaics ____Notebooks ____Ornaments ____Panoramas ____Posters
____Puppets ____Scrapbooks ____Shadow boxes ____Stabiles
____Table covers ____Wall hangings

Weaving, Sewing, and Stitching: ____Bags ____Belts ____Caps ____Costumes
____Curtains ____Headbands ____Mats ____Rugs ____Scarves
____Stuffed animals ____Wall hangings

Using Mixed Media: ____Chalk and paper sculpture ____Chalk, crayon, and paint
____Combinations of discarded materials ____Cut paper and tempera
____Paint and yarn ____Paper, cork, and wire ____Water color

Printing and Stenciling: ____Announcements ____Borders ____Decorations
____Designs ____Greeting cards ____Programs

THE CLASSROOM ART CENTER

A work center for the arrangement of art materials facilitates pupils' work and makes possible more effective utilization of art activities in the social studies.

Materials selected from those listed in checklist 10–4 may be placed in the art center. Materials should be changed as new topics are studied. Related pictures may be displayed on the bulletin board, and selected art objects may be exhibited on nearby shelves, window sills, or tables. Space should be provided to display children's completed art work and to store unfinished work.

Checklist 10–4
Art Materials

Paper: ____Construction ____Drawing ____Newsprint ____Wrapping ____Other

Crayons: ____Large colored ____Large, primary size ____Standard size

Paint: ____Finger ____Poster ____Powdered ____Watercolor ____Other

Brushes: ____Easel ____Paste ____Wash brush ____Watercolor ____Other

Chalk: ____Large, colored ____Standard ____White for sketching

Clay: ____Glaze ____Modeling ____Slip ____Wedged ____Workboard
____Other

Crafts: ____Cardboard ____Looms ____Papier-mâché ____Soap ____Wood
____Other

Printing, Stenciling: ____Block-printing items ____Ink ____Pens ____Other

Other: ____Charcoal ____Knives ____Paste ____Pins ____Rubber cement
____Tape

Industrial or Practical Arts

Two types of industrial or practical arts are useful in the social studies program. The first is construction of objects for use in various social studies activities. The second is the processing or changing of raw materials to usable forms. Both types of activity help children develop realistic and authentic concepts and understandings related to people's use of objects and resources to meet basic needs.

CONSTRUCTION

Construction, as used in the social studies, may be defined as the use of tools and materials to make authentic objects needed to promote growth of social concepts and understanding of social processes. A construction project involves the development of objectives, group planning, selection of materials, appropriate use of tools, manipulative skills, group evaluation, and planning for use in related social studies activities. Examples include making and using model airplanes, trucks, boats, looms, furniture, weapons, and utensils. The value of construction lies in its contribution to inquiry, not in the products that are made. Lasting values can be achieved only if construction achieves significant objectives, involves careful planning, is authentic, and is used to motivate learning in the unit of instruction.

Construction may be closely related to dramatic activities. Dramatic representation of activities in units on the home, the farm, the harbor, the airport, colonial life, Mexico, and other lands creates needs for objects, models, props, and scenery. Children can plan and make essential items and thus relate making objects to stated objectives.

Precision and authenticity in construction grows steadily as children gain in maturity. In the primary grades, children are satisfied with blocks, boxes, boards, and simply made items. A box may be used as a truck to haul things, two boards nailed crosswise can serve as an airplane, blocks may be arranged to serve as a corral, and a can fastened to a board can become a tank car or oil truck. Older children require more detail and precision in materials used in dramatic play: the freight car has sliding doors, the wagon can be pulled and is authentic in detail, the airplane is complete from "prop to tail assembly," and the airport is a realistic representation of one they have visited.

335

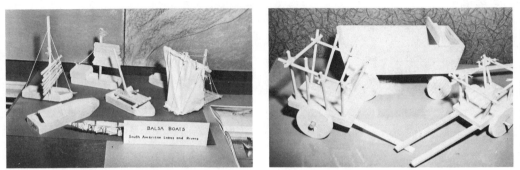

Education Workshop. University of California, Berkeley

How might the construction and use of objects like these be used to further inquiry in a unit you are planning?

criteria If the educational values are to be achieved, criteria such as the following must be used to select activities involving construction.

1. Does this activity help to attain stated objectives?
2. Is it practical in terms of available time, tools, and materials?
3. Is it more effective than other experiences that could be provided?
4. Will it help to develop accurate concepts?
5. Does it bear a direct relationship to other experiences in the unit?
6. Do children have the necessary backgrounds and construction skills?

The following are examples of objects students may construct at home or at school to use in units under study.

The home: playhouse furnishings, including chairs, tables, cupboards, flower boxes, rugs, curtains, wall paper, borders, and dishes

Community life: simply made houses, stores, schools, churches, and other community buildings; various types of trucks, such as oil, lumber, pick-up, milk, mail, and delivery; crates, boxes, bags, fruits and vegetables, hand trucks, and sheds for use in the market

The farm: farmhouse, barn, fences, chicken coops, pens, corrals, silo, trucks; milking and feed barns, nursery for the calves, bottling plant, stanchions, feeding troughs, grain sacks, and milk trucks

Boats: an oil tanker, tug, liner, freighter, lumber boat, fire boat, speedboat, rowboat, fishing boat, and pilot boat; items for a harbor, such as piers, breakwater, buoys, dry dock, and drawbridge

Colonial life: colonial kitchen, fireplace, beds, tables, rag rugs, chairs, benches, cupboards, lamps, candles; spoons, ladles, brooms; horn books, powder horns, bullet pouches, rifles; tape and box looms

Air Transportation: model planes, gliders, wind sock, control tower, hangars, maintenance shops, runways, model airport

Only simple tools are used in construction in the social studies. Saws, C-clamps, hammers, T-squares, brace and bit, mallet, chisels, and a hand drill are adequate for most activities. Proper use of tools, safety measures, and care of tools are taught systematically so that accidents and injuries can be avoided. Portable tool racks permit many groups to use the same tools and also provide a good storage place for tools and materials.

Materials for construction may be obtained in the community. Soft pine wood is especially useful. Crates and boxes can be used for buildings such as houses, barns, stores, hangars, and depots. Boards of varying sizes are used to make boats, trucks, looms, airplanes, and the like. Doweling ranging in size from a quarter inch to one inch can be used to make masts, steering shafts on trucks, derricks, funnels, smokestacks, and any other item that is cylindrical and of appropriate size. Wooden buttons ranging in size from one to three inches in diameter can be used for wheels. An awning pole, two-and-one-half inches in diameter, is excellent for making tank cars, tanks for milk and oil trucks, and locomotive boilers. Tin roofing caps make excellent headlights or hub caps on trucks. Tops of cans, scraps of tin, bottle tops, spools, screws, screw eyes (for hooking railroad cars and trailer trucks), sandpaper, nails, brads, brushes, and paints round out the list of supplies used most frequently. Once materials such as these are assembled, children under the guidance of a creative teacher will think of innumerable objects to construct and will show real ingenuity in using different combinations of materials.

PROCESSING MATERIALS

Processing materials is similar in many ways to construction in that similar values, techniques of planning, instructional procedures, and skills are involved. Processing materials in the social studies may be defined as changing raw or semiprocessed materials (yarn, for example) into finished products. Typical examples are making cottage cheese, processing wool and flax, dyeing fabrics, weaving, drying fruit, and making soap. As children engage in such processes, emphasis should be on the development of concepts and understandings regarding creative ways in which people have met their needs without benefit of technological developments.

In early times, children helped to process materials or saw them processed in their everyday life in the home and community. They helped with planting wheat, harvesting it, grinding it into flour, and making bread; shearing sheep, and washing, carding, spinning, and weaving wool; catching, cleaning, and salting fish; processing meat; felling and sawing trees, and using the lumber for buildings; and cleaning and tanning hides to make shoes and clothing. They collected berries used in dyeing clothes and saved tallow to make candles. They watched the blacksmith as he forged implements from iron and saw flour ground at the mill. Today, children see finished products in the store and have little opportunity to learn about the processes involved in making them.

The social studies program offers many possibilities for processing activities in units at different grade levels:

The home: making popcorn, applesauce, and cornstarch pudding; decorations and clay dishes

The dairy farm: churning butter and making cottage cheese

Mexico: drying corn and peppers; grinding corn with a metate; making candles; carding and spinning wool; making pottery; weaving; preparing and using natural dyes; cooking Mexican foods; making adobe bricks; making sombreros, serapes, and rebosos

China: cooking rice, Chinese cabbage, and bean curd; making tea; raising silkworms, reeling silk from cocoons; making paper, ink, and block prints

Colonial and pioneer life: weaving and quilting; dipping and molding candles; tanning hides; making soap; rippling, retting, curing, breaking, scutching, heckling, and spinning flax; carding and spinning wool; knitting; making a quilt; making dyes; drying apples; making salt; making brooms and brushes; making clothing

Communication: making and using ink, paper, and parchment; clay tablets, papyrus, and simple books.

Steps to take in carrying out selected processing activities are presented in charts 10–23 through 10–28.

The planning and guiding of construction and processing activities are similar in many ways to the planning and guiding of study trips, dramatic activities, and other ''doing'' activities in the social studies. Four basic steps are involved: (1) planning by the teacher, (2) planning with the class, (3) providing guidance during the activity, and (4) evaluating progress after the activity, as shown in the first two checklists in this chapter.

Making Butter

Materials: ½ pint of whipping cream, ¼ teaspoon salt, a pint jar.

Pour cream into jar and seal it.

Shake until butter appears.

Pour off bluish milk.

Place butter in a bowl and add salt.

Add a few ice cubes and water; work with spoon to remove milk.

Pour off water and mold butter into a block.

Chart 10–23

Washing, Carding, and Spinning Wool

Materials: wool sheared from a sheep, soap, pair of cards for carding.

Wash wool in soapy lukewarm water, rinse it, and dry it.

Place a small amount of wool on one card and draw other card over it.

Continue carding until fibers are separated into slivers.

Shape slivers into a fluffy roll by rolling them between back of cards.

Stretch and twist the roll into yarn for weaving.

Chart 10–24

Dipping Candles

Materials: 3 lbs. tallow, candle wick cut into 7-inch lengths, 2 tall cans

Chop tallow into small pieces and fry out grease.

Pour grease into one can and keep it hot.

Pour water into other can.

Dip wicking into grease and then into water.

Repeat dipping until the candle is the desired size.

Chart 10–25

Making Apple Leather

Peel some apples and cook them in water.

After apples are cooked to a mush, spread them on a cloth to dry.

Let them stand for a day or two.

Chart 10–26

Making Pumpkin Rings

Cut a pumpkin crosswise into halves.

Remove seeds and cut rings ½ inch thick.

Place rings on a pole to dry.

Put small ends and pieces on a string to dry.

Chart 10–27

Making Pumpkin Leather

Peel small pieces from the pumpkin.

Cook the pieces in water.

Stir until water is cooked out and mixture is thick.

Spread the cooked peelings on a board to dry.

Chart 10–28

  Questions, Activities, Evaluation

1. What two or three creative writing activities can you include in a unit of your choice?
2. Which forms of role taking through dramatic representation do you believe to be most useful in the social studies? Indicate ways in which you might use them.
3. Review a music book for a grade of your choice and identify songs, rhythms, listening activities, and instrumental activities that you might use in a unit.
4. Make a brief plan to show how you might provide for creative musical expression and for investigating the music of a culture under study.
5. Review the checklist of art activities and indicate specific ways in which you might use each major type in a unit.
6. Select one construction activity and one processing activity and note how you might use each in a unit.

339

references

DIMONDSTEIN, GERALDINE, *Exploring the Arts with Children*. New York: Macmillan, 1974. Teaching procedures for various art forms.

GALLAGHER, ARLENE F., *The Methods Book: Strategies for Law-Focused Education*. Chicago, Ill.: Law in American Society Foundation, 1977. Chapters on role playing, simulations, and mock trials.

KALTSOUNIS, THEODORE, *Teaching Social Studies in the Elementary School: The Basics of Citizenship*. Englewood Cliffs, N.J.: Prentice-Hall, 1979. Chapter on dramatics and games.

PATE, GLENN S., AND HUGH A. PARKER, JR., *Designing Classroom Simulations*. Belmont, Calif.: Fearon Publishers, 1978. Guidelines and examples.

NYE, ROBERT, AND VERNINE NYE, *Essentials of Teaching Elementary School Music*. Englewood Cliffs, N.J.: Prentice-Hall, 1974. Practical guide to development of concepts and skills.

REESE, JOY, *Simulation Games and Learning Activities*. West Nyack, N.Y.: Parker Publishing Company, 1977. Simulation and role playing activities.

SHAFTEL, FANNIE R., AND GEORGE SHAFTEL, *Role-Playing for Social Values*. Englewood Cliffs, N.J.: Prentice-Hall, 1967. Guidelines for expressing values through role playing.

STEWIG, JOHN W., AND SAM L. SEBESTA, eds., *Using Literature in the Elementary Classroom*. Urbana, Ill.: National Council for the Teachers of English, 1978. Section by Simpson on creative drama.

YOUNGER, JOHN C., AND JOHN F. ACETI, *Simulation Games and Activities for Social Studies*. Danville, N.Y.: Instructor Publications, 1969. Pamphlet containing directions for several simulation games.

DEVELOPING AND APPLYING READING SKILLS

focusing questions

How can skills developed in the reading program be applied and further developed in the social studies?
What procedures and activities may be used to identify and develop the vocabulary needed to read social studies materials?
What procedures and activities may be used to apply and refine comprehension skills used in social studies learning?
How can reading-study skills be applied and improved?

No skills are of greater importance in the social studies than reading skills. Through reading students are able to open gateways to a multitude of new ideas and discoveries about life styles in their own and other cultures. They can identify with others, develop new concepts, extend and enrich concepts, derive generalizations, gather information to answer questions and test hypotheses, make critical evaluations, and achieve other objectives. They can also apply and improve skills developed in the reading program as they read new and challenging material in textbooks, references, literary works, and other selections related to social studies units.

Both reading to learn and learning to read are emphasized in well-planned social studies instruction. Some individuals believe that students only read to learn in the social studies, but effective teachers recognize that reading skills can and should be taught, applied, and improved in the social studies and other subjects.

Three basic aspects of reading instruction have been singled out for emphasis in this chapter: vocabulary development, comprehension, and reading-

Grateful acknowledgement is made to Dr. Ruth Grossman, City University of New York; City College, for suggestions regarding the revision of this chapter.

study skills. The guiding principle to keep in mind is that reading instruction in the social studies should be compatible with and build on instruction provided in the developmental reading program. In keeping with this principle this chapter gives concrete examples of strategies and activities drawn from the developmental reading program and shows how they may be applied in the social studies. Planned instruction is needed to assure the transfer and application of skills taught in reading as well as to improve learning in the social studies.

Building Vocabulary

This section presents procedures and activities that may be used to develop concepts and the words used to express them. Attention is given first to the identification of words to clarify. This is followed by a discussion of the many types of meaning-building activities that clarify the meaning of concepts and related words that children do not understand. The remaining sections include procedures and activities for developing vocabulary and using decoding skills such as picture clues, context clues, phonics, and structural analysis.

IDENTIFYING WORDS TO CLARIFY

The following categories of words used in the social studies serve as overall guides to help identify vocabulary to be developed:

Core words such as *role, values, interdependence,* and *adaptation* are used in some textbook series to structure the program. They are found in different contexts, beginning with the home and community and moving to regions of our country and to other lands.

Technical social science words vary in use from unit to unit. Examples are *region, landforms, frontier, goods, market, institution,* and *civilization.* These words are usually defined in the glossary of a textbook.

Unit words are found in particular units. For example, *kayak* and *walrus* occur in readings on Eskimos, and *plantation, antislavery,* and *overseer,* in readings on southern colonies.

Names of particular people, events, times, and places are also found in certain units. Examples are *Roger Williams, Salem witch trials, Middle Ages,* and *Fertile Crescent.*

Quantitative terms are found at all levels, ranging from *near* and *far* and *big* and *little* in materials for the early grades to *area, population, per person income, degrees of latitude and longitude,* and *decade, century,* and *millennium* in materials for later grades.

Similar-looking words that may be confused include *when* and *where, far,* and *bar, house* and *horse, conservation* and *conversation, principal,* and *principle,* and *illegal* and *illegible.*

Figurative terms used in middle- and upper-grade materials include *rush hour, surging crowd, hat in the ring, cold war, bamboo curtain, hot line, closed shop,* and *avalanche of votes.*

Abbreviations and *acronyms* are usually defined in reading materials but should be called to the attention of students. Examples are A.M., P.M., B.C., A.D., U.S., UN, UNESCO, TVA, N.Y., CORE, NAACP, AFL–CIO.

Several specific procedures can help the teacher identify the actual vocabulary that should be introduced before students read a selection. One of the most helpful is to check the teacher's manual that accompanies the textbook. It usually notes new terms and gives suggestions for introducing them.

Teachers should also note the terms for new concepts to be used in a unit of instruction. Key concepts are frequently listed at the beginning of a unit or in different sections where they are used. After noting the concepts, a teacher should check the reading materials and make plans for developing this vocabulary prior to reading.

Teachers should use two other procedures. They should scan a reading selection ahead of time and note words that children find difficult. They should also keep a list of words that children find difficult as they read a selection. Note words that children ask about as they read and encourage children to note any terms they do not know.

Examples of informal assessment devices and directions for building a word card file are presented below. These are designed to focus the attention of students on key words and to develop the ability to identify vocabulary to be learned, a basic skill in independent reading. The devices may be presented on the chalkboard or on duplicated worksheets.

Study of Transportation

Mark a + by each word you know and can read without difficulty. Mark a ? by each word you do not know or have difficulty reading.

_____ subway   _____ underground   _____ elevated   _____ rapid transit
                                                  trains
_____ station   _____ transportation   _____ network   _____ express

---

*Do You Know the Meaning
of These Words?*

Listed below are words we will be reading in our unit on colonial life. Mark each word as follows:

+ if you know what it means
? if you do not know it

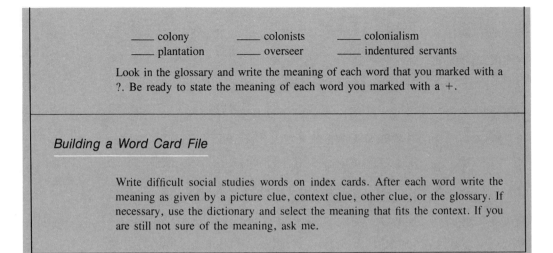

Building a Word Card File

Write difficult social studies words on index cards. After each word write the
meaning as given by a picture clue, context clue, other clue, or the glossary. If
necessary, use the dictionary and select the meaning that fits the context. If you
are still not sure of the meaning, ask me.

DEVELOPING A MEANINGFUL VOCABULARY

Activities that build meaning are a key part of vocabulary development;
they may be used before, during, or after reading a selection. The meaning of
concepts represented by words that are new to students should be developed
prior to reading. Since no teacher can anticipate every concept that is unfamiliar to a child, it may at times be necessary to clarify meaning during or after
reading.

Activities selected to develop meaning should be matched to children's
capabilities, level of achievement, and background of experience. A selection
may be made from the examples that follow and from those suggested in
teacher's manuals that accompany social studies textbooks. In addition to providing specific activities, the teacher should encourage wide reading because of
its value as an independent means of extending and enriching vocabulary.

Both the denotative and connotative meaning of certain concepts and related vocabulary should be given attention. For example, a range of feelings
and shades of meaning are associated with such concepts as friendship, concern
for others, fairness, equality, race, culture, and courage. The connotations of
such concepts should be explored in the context of their use so that students get
a well-rounded grasp of their meaning, including both cognitive and affective
dimensions.

Three groups of meaning-building activities are presented below. The first
group includes firsthand, concrete concept development strategies used to build
meaning prior to reading. The second group includes verbal concept development strategies and defining activities effective in building meaning during the
reading experience. The third group includes interpretive concept development
strategies and expressive activities that enable children to extend, enrich, and
apply meanings in follow-up reading experiences.

Activities that Build Meaning

FIRSTHAND AND VISUAL ACTIVITIES

Take field trips to get a firsthand view of objects and activities in the community, such as a fire station, city council meeting, small claims court, a lake shore or harbor, and museum artifacts (spinning wheel, flintlock rifle, powder horn, and so on).

Watch demonstrations of candle dipping; carding, spinning, and weaving wool; making a relief map; or constructing a loom.

Engage in activities such as operating a loom, dipping candles, singing a song, playing an instrument, or doing a folk dance from the culture under study.

Observe people at work or see films and filmstrips that show the role of carpenters, nurses, firefighters, and other workers.

Examine exhibits, displays, models, and realia to clarify the the meaning of *canoe, kayak, serape, carreta, Conestoga wagon, processing of silk, utensils, textiles, candle molds,* and other objects.

See pictures that show a corral, silo, factory, warehouse, fiord, firebreak, harpoon, canal, rice paddy, sodhouse, jungle, or glacier.

Select from a mixed group of pictures those that show examples of particular meanings of words such as *friendship, transportation, desert* or *services.*

GUIDED DEFINING ACTIVITIES

List, classify, and label pictures or names of items according to uses, characteristics, or other criteria:

> Group *telephone, television, letter,* and *radio* under *communication.* List *river, lake, gulf,* and *ocean* under *water bodies.*

State behavior (what people do) to clarify the meaning of *doctor, carpenter, electrician, public defender,* or other workers:

> An electrician installs, repairs, maintains, or operates devices that run on electricity.

State operations (what to do) to clarify the meaning of *baking, harvesting, mapping,* or how to figure *area, population density, latitude:*

> *Harvesting* means the gathering of corn, wheat, or other crops. Figure *population density* by dividing the number of people in an area by the square miles or kilometers in the area.

Give examples and distinguish them from nonexamples:

Which of the following are examples of natural resources?

animal life	plant life	houses	bricks	minerals
sailing ship	mountains	water	soil	lumber

Describe the special features, uses, or attributes of an object or activity:

A canyon is a deep and narrow valley with steep sides.

Make comparisons or contrasts to indicate the meaning of a new word by relating it to the meaning of a known word:

A governor is like a mayor except he or she is the chief administrator of a state instead of a city.

Use synonyms or antonyms to link the meaning of a new word to the meaning of a known word:

Interdependence means depending on others for some things. It is the opposite of being on one's own.

Listen to explanations and pronunciations of special terms and names of people and places and note how they are written: *metropolitan, Mesabi Range, Cartier, Tokyo, Byzantine, Byzantium.*

Use glossaries to find the meaning of terms as they are used in a textbook:

A *terrace* is level land cut out of the sides of hills or mountains and shaped like stairs.

Use dictionaries to select the meaning of a word that fits the context:

The pilot will *bank* an airplane to make a turn.

Discuss the meaning of words that contain the same word, prefix, suffix, or root: *courthouse, greenhouse, warehouse, statehouse;* and *coworker, coequal, cooperate, coexist.*

Discuss the meaning and note the spelling of homonyms: *air, heir; alter, altar; bail, bale; bazaar, bizarre; cannon, canon; fate, fete; hoard, horde; rain, rein, reign; serial, cereal; straight, strait; step, steppe; stationary, stationery.*

Listen to stories, poems, or songs that give shades of meaning, stir feelings, or create a mood related to such terms as *courage, bravery, hardship, responsibility, cooperation, and concern for others.*

Discuss the meaning of figures of speech and figurative language, such as *cunning as a fox, fighting like a tiger, an avalanche of votes, the bamboo curtain,* and *hat in the ring.*

INTERPRETIVE AND EXPRESSIVE ACTIVITIES

Role-play to deepen meaning and to get a feeling for selected persons and events: playing the role of a mail carrier or other community worker; pantomiming a police officer directing traffic or behavior of other workers; taking the role of a judge, lawyer, or member of a jury in a mock trial; participating in simulation games that involve bartering, making a profit, urban planning, competition, or other simulated activities.

Make objects or models such as furniture for a playhouse; a floor map of the neighborhood that shows a school, library, and other buildings; a model of a tugboat, airport, log cabin, or stockade.

Model bowls, dishes, vases, and other objects out of clay.

Draw or sketch the distinguishing features of an island, peninsula, canoe, kayak, teepee, hogan, longhouse.

Write summaries or creative stories using vocabulary developed in the unit.

Create murals, dioramas, panoramas, and exhibits that highlight events and activities in the lives of people under study.

Arrange displays of utensils, costumes, textiles, and other artifacts related to the culture under study.

BUILDING A SIGHT VOCABULARY

Directly tied to the meaning-building activities noted above is the development of a sight vocabulary that enables one to read without unnecessary pauses to recognize words. Activities should be provided to make sure that the basic words encountered in various reading materials become sight words. The whole-word method of building a sight vocabulary is emphasized in this section. Decoding skills or word recognition techniques presented in the next section should also be viewed as a means of building a sight vocabulary, not as crutches to use over and over on the same terms. As a child put it, "Once I know new words, I can really cruise along."

The following techniques and activities are helpful in a whole-word approach to developing a sight vocabulary that enables students to "cruise along" as they read a selection. They may be used along with or immediately following the previously discussed meaning-building activities.

Place selected terms on a flannel board or bulletin board under pictures that show what the terms mean.

Match words with pictures: *shirt, skirt, raincoat,* or other clothing before reading a selection on clothing for a family; *grassland, farmland,* and *swampland* before a selection on farming; *canal, harbor,* and *pier* before a selection on water transportation.

Recognize labels on objects and pictures in the classroom: *north, south, east,* and *west* on the walls of the classroom; pictures of plains, hills, plateaus, mountains on the bulletin board; pieces of cloth made of wool, silk, cotton, nylon.

Ask what a new word means and how to pronounce it as it is encountered in a reading selection.

Recognize words written on the chalkboard or on flashcards prior to reading: *kitchen, stove, vegetables,* and *cooking* before reading a selection on preparing food for a family; *igloo, dogsled,* and *kayak* before a selection on Eskimos; *urban, suburban,* and *rural* before a selection on city life; *attorney, jury, judge,* and *decision* before a selection on court procedure.

Distinguish similar terms presented on the board or on cards: *bake, cake, lake, take; thought, through; overflow, overthrow, overload, overland; govern, governor, governed, governing.*

Make picture dictionaries, booklets, and scrapbooks of illustrations labeled with words to be used in reading.

Make experience, retrieval, or word charts that contain words to be used in reading materials.

Make a card file of basic words to be used in a unit, for example, *arctic, climate, deciduous, fiord, ice age, region, taiga,* and *weather* for a unit on northern forest lands.

Make word banks consisting of large envelopes or word boxes with such labels as *weather words, food words, clothing words, transportation words, communication words,* and *law words.* (Children write words and definitions on cards or slips of paper and deposit them in the word bank. Words are withdrawn and used at various times in sentences, stories, and other activities.

Match synonyms and antonyms: *hot* and *torrid, cold* and *frigid; equality* and *inequality, justice* and *injustice*.

Complete sentences by selecting a card with the correct term on it or by writing the term:

When it is raining, the coat to wear is a (raincoat).
The line that divides the globe into northern and southern hemispheres is called the (equator).

Play word games, such as Fish, Word Baseball, or others, using social studies terms.

APPLYING DECODING SKILLS

This section discusses techniques taught in developmental reading and shows how these techniques can be applied to words used in the social studies. Double mileage can be obtained by applying them to social studies terms. First, students get useful practice in applying decoding skills. Second, they increase their reading vocabularies, thereby increasing their skill in reading social studies materials.

Four sets of techniques or skills are used in decoding. *Picture clues* are helpful in decoding words in the social studies; the many illustrations in current materials are placed there to clarify basic terms. *Verbal context clues* are also helpful with most new materials providing definitions, examples, and other clues. *Phonics* and *structural analysis* may be applied to many terms. When using phonics special attention should be given to exceptions; students should watch for them as they do in reading instruction. Such exceptions may well be anticipated by teaching them as sight words prior to reading, as noted in the preceding section. The various decoding skills are frequently used in combination. For example, using both context clues and phonics is usually more effective than using either one alone. The desired outcome is to develop the ability to recognize words quickly and to interpret them correctly.

picture clues Picture clues can be used extensively in the social studies. Current textbooks are replete with photographs and drawings directly related to social studies terms. Especially useful are picture dictionaries; picture charts; maps with pictorial representations of such terms as *plateau, gulf, island, peninsula,* and other surface features; illustrations in classroom dictionaries; and pictures in reference materials. Films, filmstrips, slides, and pictures from magazines can also help to clarify terms and improve word recognition skills. Special care must be exercised, however, to clinch recognition of the actual words so that children will read the words and not rely solely on the pictures. Illustrative activities follow.

Picture Clue Activities

See films, filmstrips, or slides that clarify such terms as *broad grassy plains, towering redwoods, hot steamy jungle, glacier,* and *fiord.*

Prior to reading, direct attention to pictures in the selection and present the related terms on cards or on the chalkboard.

After reading, ask students about agreement between a word suggested by a picture and the text: Does the word fit the picture and the meaning in the text? Does the suggested meaning make sense? Does the suggested word match the sound of the one in the text?

Show a picture as a new word, such as *lamp* or *fiord,* is presented on a card or on the chalkboard.

Discuss a picture in a selection, then have children skim the text to find the related word.

---

verbal context clues`

The ability to use verbal context clues is a central skill in reading social studies material. In addition to contributing to the reader's ability to recognize terms and figure out their meanings, skill in using verbal context clues improves the comprehension, interpretation, and application of what is read. Furthermore, use of verbal context clues keeps the child's focus on reading to get the meaning by interpreting the words, phrases, sentences, and paragraphs that are contained in a selection. Readers who use verbal context clues along with other decoding skills can increase their vocabularies at a rapid rate.

Publishers of recent textbooks and supplementary materials have taken special care to provide verbal context clues and to suggest activities for developing skill in using them. Activities for using verbal context clues follow.

Using Verbal Context Clues

Find and discuss the different types of verbal context clues in reading materials:

Definition in a sentence: A *frontier* is the edge of an area where people live.

Definition in apposition: They increased their *exports*—goods sent out of the country—during the past decade.

Definition by examples: A *disaster* is a flood, fire, or earthquake.

Definition by description: A *freeway* is a highway with several lanes where people drive long distances without cross roads.

Comparison or contrast: A *pagoda* is like a temple. A *stream* is much smaller than a river.

Synonyms or antonyms: *Justice* means fairness to everyone. Being *prudent* is the opposite of being rash.

Statement of what a person does (behavior): A *tax assessor* sets the value of property as a basis for taxation.

Statement of what to do (operation): Figure *latitude* by measuring degrees north or south of the equator.

Explanation of word origin: They put the horses in a *corral*. *Corral* comes from the Spanish word *corro*, a ring or a yard.

Solve word riddles, using as few clues as possible:

What is it? It is found on a farm. They store hay in it. They milk cows in it. (*barn*)

What is it? It is found in very cold regions. It is a huge mass of ice. It moves slowly. (*glacier*)

(Note: The above may be combined with phonic clues by stating for the first one "It starts with a *b*," and by stating for the second one "It starts with *gl*.")

Combine parts of sentences to make complete sentences and to note word order:

The horses were   in the milking barn.

The chickens were   in the corral.

The cows were   in the henhouse.

Make sentences by arranging words in proper sequence:

They   building   carpenters   saw   houses

Respond to questions that focus attention on selected sentences, such as "May's friends brought *presents* to her birthday party." What do children usually bring to a friend's birthday party?

State or write a definition after reading a sentence:

The funnel-shaped *tornado* blew cars off the road and lifted roofs from houses. A tornado is (a destructive, whirling wind).

Use clues obtained from information presented in a preceding paragraph or earlier part of a selection:

> The best place for *paddy land* is near large rivers. (Students use description of rice paddy in preceding paragraph to decode *paddy land*.)
>
> The result was the beginning of *service industries*. (Students use description of services and industries in two preceding paragraphs to decode *service industries*.)

State or write the missing term in a cluster of words that are usually used together:

> All people have basic needs for food, shelter, and (clothing).
> Major landforms are plains, hills, plateaus, and (mountains).

Complete sentences taken from reading materials:

> A map (scale) is used to find distance between two places.
> North is toward the north (pole).

State or write the *meaning* of words needed to complete sentences read by the teacher or presented on duplicated worksheets:

> They filled the water bags before crossing the hot, dry (desert).
> The exhaust from cars is a major cause of air (pollution).

Use cloze procedure by filling in sentences from which words have been deleted:

> At night the people moving westward pulled their (wagons) into a circle. During the (evening) they gathered around a fire to talk and sing. Sentries stood watch through the (night) to prevent a surprise (attack).

State or write the meaning of a term with several meanings (for example, *fair* as right, just, equal, good, impartial, or unbiased) in such sentences as:

The judge made a *fair* decision.	(just)
Fair shares will be given to each one.	(equal)
The hearing will be *fair*.	(impartial)
The final report was *fair*.	(unbiased)
Paul did the *fair* thing.	(right)
Tomorrow will bring *fair* weather.	(good)

Double-check to be sure the verbal context clues agree with clues obtained by means of other decoding skills:

> Is there agreement with clues obtained from pictures? From sounding (phonic) clues? From word structure?
>
> Does the word make sense in terms of word order? Does the word have the same meaning in other sentences?

Use context clues to determine the pronunciation of a term:

> The scout will *lead* them through the pass.
> They used *lead* to make bullets.

Use context clues to clarify the meaning of words that sound alike but are spelled differently:

> They decided to *meet* in the supermarket in front of the *meat* counter.
> The *air* was clean and fresh. He was *heir* to the throne.

use of phonics   Decoding by sounding out may be applied to many unfamiliar words in the social studies program as children apply techniques and principles learned in the developmental reading program on a daily basis. As particular decoding skills are taught during reading instruction, they should immediately be applied to words used in the current social studies unit. Unit words may also be included in weekly spelling instruction. Learning activities adapted from the reading program may be used with the social studies vocabulary, as the following examples illustrate.

Phonics Activities

Name and label objects and pictures of things in various units that start with the same consonant or consonant digraph, such as *pot*, *pan*, *picture*, and *paint*, or *plant*, *plumber*, and *playhouse* in a unit on homes and families; and *grow*, *growth*, *growing*, *grass*, *grain*, and *granary* in a unit on farming.

Identify and list examples of consonants with more than one sound such as *c* in *city* and *capital*, *s* in *increase* and *cause*, and *g* in *gold* and *general*.

Make cumulative lists of words as they are encountered, using initial consonant digraphs, such as *ch* in *charter* and *change* (but different in chasm), *sh* in *shelter* and *shed*, *wh* in *wheat* and *wheel*, and *th* with the voiced sound in *thick* and *thin* but voiceless sound in *thaw* and *thatch*.

Keep one chart of unit words having a long vowel sound signaled by a final *e*, such as *lake*, *space*, *time*, *scale*, *trade*, and *zone*, and contrast these with words on a separate chart of exceptions to the "final *e*" rule, such as *store*, *income*, *climate*, and *justice*.

Circle silent letters in such terms as *sack, might, lake, neighbor, know, house, horde,* and *steppe.*

Make a set of word cards for each dipthong, using words from units, readers, and children's oral vocabulary, such as *oi* in *soil, spoil, coil; ou* in *outside, rout, clout, stout, house;* and *oy* in *toy, boy, enjoy, envoy, destroy.*

structural
analysis

Decoding by analyzing the structure of words has many applications in the social studies. The examples that follow include compound words, prefixes, suffixes, roots, word endings, and syllables.

Compound words may be broken into parts as children encounter them: *playground, playhouse, plaything, playback; freeway, expressway, airway, seaway, waterway;* and *overcoat, overcast, overbuild, overflow, overage, overgrowth.*

Prefixes may be used to derive the meaning of a variety of social studies terms: *im, il, ir, dis, in,* and *un* meaning *not* in such words as *impolite, illegal, irresponsible, dishonest, inactive,* and *unable; anti* meaning *against* in *anti-labor, antibusiness, antislavery, antiwar,* and *anti-American; mid* meaning *middle* in *midday, midnight, midway, midstream, midweek, midwestern,* and *midwinter; pro* meaning *in favor of* in *prolabor, pro-Israel, pro-African, pro-ponent; inter* meaning *between* or *among* in *interact, interurban, international; ex* meaning *out* in *exit, expel, export, extract; sub* as *under* or *below* in *subsoil, subway, submarine, substandard;* and *trans* meaning *across* or *over* in *transfer, transmit, transit, transcontinental.*

Suffixes that occur frequently in social studies terms include *less* meaning *without* in *helpless, hopeless, fearless; ern* meaning *direction* in *eastern, western, northern,* and *southern;* and *ward* meaning *course* or *direction* in *forward, backward, toward, homeward, westward.*

Roots that are frequently used include *act* meaning *do* or *move* in *enact, react, activity, activate; civ* meaning *citizen* in *civil, civic, civilian; port* meaning *move* in *transportation, portable, export, import; gram* meaning *letter* or *written* in *telegram, diagram, cablegram; graph* meaning *write* in *autograph, biography, cartography; liber* meaning *free* in *liberty, liberate, liberal;* and *tele* meaning *distant* in *telegraph, telephoto, telephone, televise.*

Word endings may be identified or changed to provide practice in analyzing words and in building words: *farm, farms, farmer, farmers, farming; bake, baker, bakery;* and *legislate, legislator, legislature, legislation.*

Syllables may be identified to aid students in recognizing such words as *classroom, tableware, grandmother, continent, desert, heartland, industrial, interdependent, manufacture, suburban, temperature, vegetation, volcano, un-wise,* and *irresponsible.*

355

Structural Analysis Activities

COMPOUND WORDS

State, point to, draw a line between, or write the words that are combined to make compound words listed on the chalkboard or a chart: *birdhouse, schoolhouse, statehouse, farmhouse;* and *grandmother, grandfather, grandparents, grandson.*

Complete sentences in which one word of a compound word is omitted:

The heavy rains caused a land (slide).

The (state) house is in the capital city.

Match two words that can be put together to make a compound word:

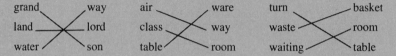

grand	way	air	ware	turn	basket
land	lord	class	way	waste	room
water	son	table	room	waiting	table

Match cards on which a single word has been printed that can be combined with a word on another card to form a compound word: *feed, lot; worth, while; book, store;* and *bath, room.*

Build word lists, make word charts, use word wheels, and play word games that call for making as many compound words as possible when one word is given:

How many words can you make by adding a word to *over?*

Use the word wheel to find words that can be added to *play.*

Who can make the most words by adding words to *land?*

Make as many words as you can by adding a word to *way,* as in *highway.*

PREFIXES, SUFFIXES, AND ROOTS

Recognize prefixes, suffixes, or roots in words selected from reading materials and presented by the teacher in a three-step teaching strategy:

1. The teacher explains the meaning of the prefix: The prefix *anti* means against. It is a part of such words as *antibusiness, antilabor,* and *antislavery.*
2. After discussing the meaning of a term, the teacher uses it in a sentence:
   Both old and young people joined the *antiwar* demonstration.
   The *antislavery* movement was strong in the New England States.
3. Students give or find additional examples and use them in sentences:
   Some women have joined *antifeminist* groups to stop the ERA.
   His stand was both *antilabor* and *antibusiness.*

Circle prefixes, suffixes, and roots in groups of words:

Circle the letters in these words that mean *not: unable, unused, incapable, dislike, unwise.*

Circle the letters in these words that mean *before* or *prior to: predate, preheat, prepay, precondemn, predict.*

Circle the letters in these words that mean *place: locate, location, local, localize, dislocate.*

Make charts that include prefixes, suffixes, or roots, their meaning, and examples of words that contain them:

Prefixes	Meaning	Example
un	not	unknown
il	not	illegal
im	not	improbable
anti	against	antilabor

Compile a list of words with the same root, obtaining definitions of them, and discuss how differences in prefixes and suffixes modify the meaning: *port, porter, import, export, importer, exporter, transport.*

WORD ENDINGS

Build word lists by changing the ending of words: *serve, serves, serving, services, serviceable;* and *govern, governs, governing, governor, government, governmental.*

Complete sentences in which an ending has been omitted:

Every community has producers of goods and serv(ices).

The workers were build(ing) a house.

Select endings from a list and use them to complete a sentence:

Choose the correct endings from the following and complete the sentence below: *s, ing, or, ment,* and *mental.*

A govern(or) is the head of state govern(ment).

SYLLABICATION

Look for words that make up a compound word and use them to break the word into syllables: *landform, landslide,* and *landlord.*

Use prefixes, suffixes, and roots to break words into syllables: *predict, prediction,* and *predictable.*

> Recognize that "looking for little words in big words" does not work in such words as *somewhere, sloping,* and *station.* (Use of *me* and *her* in *somewhere, pin,* in *sloping,* and *at* in *station* leads to errors.)
>
> Find two consonants in the middle of a word and draw a line between them: *problem, support,* and *frontier.*

Developing Comprehension Skills

Comprehension may be viewed as taking place on three levels. The first is the literal or factual level, which can be characterized as "reading the lines." The second is the inferential level—"reading between the lines." The third is the applicative level—"reading beyond the lines." Some add a fourth level, described as the appreciative and creative level—"creating new lines."

All of these levels are used in the social studies. The literal or factual level provides the foundation for movement to higher levels. The inferential level is used to draw inferences and implications, identify possible purposes and motives of an author, and explore assumptions that are not self-evident. The applicative level is used to solve problems, make predictions, evaluate what is read, and put ideas to other uses. The appreciative and creative level is reached as students respond by expressing new feelings, empathy, insights, and appreciations.

DEVELOPMENT OF BASIC COMPREHENSION SKILLS

A practical way to develop the comprehension skills needed to move from the literal to higher levels is to provide learning activities that further the development of skills stressed in the reading program. These skills help students achieve such objectives as interpreting the meaning intended by the author, finding the main idea, selecting important details, drawing inferences, predicting outcomes, and making critical evaluations.

interpreting the meaning

To understand social studies reading materials students must have the ability to interpret the meaning. The reader must be able to grasp the meaning of terms, phrases, sentences, paragraphs, and longer passages. He or she must be able to define terms and figurative language in context and to express the mood or feeling created by a selection. The reader must also be able to interpret the pictures, maps, tables, graphs, posters, and cartoons that supplement the text. Only after the author's intended meaning is grasped can the reader move beyond the literal level of interpretation to inferential, applicative, critical, and creative levels. Examples of activities that develop this ability follow.

358

Provide a place and time for independent reading to improve
learning and to sharpen comprehension skills.

2. Explaining the meaning of words, phrases, figurative terms, and paragraphs
3. Describing the feelings or mood created by a phrase, sentence, paragraph, or longer passage
4. Responding to such questions as

How would you state the meaning of this sentence in your own words?

Who can explain the meaning of this word as it is used in this sentence?

How can this paragraph be summarized in one sentence?

What are the three main points in this section?

What mood or feeling does this reading selection arouse?

Interpret pictures to clarify the meaning of terms used in the text, to visualize land scenes, objects, and activities, and to answer such questions as

What is shown? What meaning does it add to the text?

What word, concept, idea, or feeling does it illustrate?

What scene, objective, or activity is shown? Where is it? What is happening?

Which items stand out? Which are most important? Why?

Interpret maps by noting the title; clarify symbols in the key; identify the location of what is shown; find relationships between places and travel routes, products and resources, and other items; and describe the size and shape of places (see chapter 12 for detailed procedures).

Interpret the meaning of posters, guided by such questions as

What is the purpose? What single idea is emphasized?

How are lines, space, and color used to focus attention on the key idea?

How convincing is it? What feelings does it arouse? Is it effective in stirring one to action? Why or why not?

How is it related to events in the text?

Interpret cartoons, guided by such questions as

What is the title? What event or issue does it highlight?

What is the purpose? To ridicule? To explain something? To reveal an injustice? To present a point of view?

What symbol is used? What is the meaning of it?

What ideas are distorted or exaggerated? What is your reaction to the distortion?

What are other points of view? How can they be used to counter the cartoonist's view?

What meaning does it add to the text?

Interpret tables, guided by such questions as

What is the title? Does it indicate what is presented?

What questions can be answered by using data in the table?

What changes or trends are shown?

What are the largest, average, and smallest amounts that are included?

What conclusion can be drawn?

How is information related to the text?

Interpret graphs, guided by such questions as

What is the title? What changes, trends, amounts, or predictions are shown?

If symbols are used, what do they represent?

If it is a bar or line graph, what is the scale?

What is the source of information?

What conclusion can be drawn?

How is the information related to the text?

Interpret time lines, guided by such questions as

What is the title? What time periods are included?

What type of event is emphasized? Political? Economic? Social? Military? Other? How are events related?

What key or pivotal dates are included? What changes follow them?

What trends are shown in the sequence of events?

What meaning does the time line add to the text?

finding the main idea This skill is used in the social studies to identify the main idea in paragraphs, sections of a chapter, a current event, a story, or other selections. Good readers are able to distinguish the main idea from details, identify topic sentences in paragraphs, use titles and headings as clues, and state the main idea in their own words. Illustrative learning activities to develop this skill follow.

Activities for Finding the Main Idea

Read a paragraph or selection in the textbook, then state or write the main idea in your own words.

Read a paragraph and choose from a list of titles, phrases, or sentences the one that best expresses the main idea.

Express a title for a group experience chart that reflects the main idea of the student's story or account.

Choose from several pictures the one that shows the main idea in a selection.

Answer questions that focus attention on the main idea:

What is the main idea in the first paragraph on page 12?

What is the topic sentence in the second paragraph on page 12? Is this sentence the main idea? If not, state the main idea in your own words.

What is the main idea in the section on pages 13–14?

Which of the pictures on the bulletin board best shows the main idea of the selection we have just read?

Number in order the titles or sentences representing the main ideas of a sequence of three or four related paragraphs.

identifying
important details

Identification of details is used to find information that supports a main idea or hypothesis or information that can be used to answer a question. This skill is also used to gather data needed to derive a generalization or to make a critical evaluation. Good readers distinguish relevant from irrelevant facts or details in light of the objective guiding their reading. They are able to state the details in sequence when reading to follow directions, and they can identify events in the order of their occurrence. They can match details with main ideas, with pictures, with topics in outlines, and with headlines of news reports. They are also able to select details to use in describing people, places, and events.

Activities for Selecting Significant Details

Find and state the details that support a main idea identified in a paragraph or selection.

Make a list of details while reading a selection in the social studies textbook or other material.

Make a chart on which details are placed under such headings as *food, clothing, forms of transportation,* or other topics.

Make an outline of details that fit under headings listed on the board, such as *natural resources, uses of natural resources,* and *ways of conserving natural resources.*

Make a list of details used to describe an object or event in the culture under study.

Write a description of yourself using as many details as possible to see how quickly classmates can identify the writer as they read the description.

summarizing and
organizing

Summarizing and organizing are used to bring together in succinct form key ideas and related details. This skill includes the ability to identify relationships between main ideas and details, to select details needed to give a concise summary, to select details for an outline, to group or classify items with common features, and to organize information in notes.

Summarizing and Organizing Activities

State or write a summary of a selection in your own words.

Select from three summaries presented by the teacher the one that best fits a selection.

Classify items identified in a reading selection under such headings as *food, furniture; resources, products;* and *physical traits, cultural traits.*

Arrange items in order by size, time of occurrence, or other characteristic—for example, main events in the development of the community, the population of cities in a state from largest to smallest, and the area of states in a region according to size.

Make an outline, chart, graph, table, or map that summarizes and organizes information: an outline of steps in baking bread; a flow chart that shows the processing of steel; a graph that shows how much a family spends for food, shelter, clothing, recreation, and other items; a table that shows population growth; and a map that shows the location of major cities in a country.

Answer questions that focus attention on summarizing and organizing:

Who can summarize the key idea in the first paragraph?

Who can summarize in two or three sentences what was presented in today's reading?

Who can summarize the main features of the inner zone of a city?

What headings should we use to outline today's reading?

following
directions
This skill is used to find directions for such activities as constructing an object, making a map, conducting an investigation, evaluating an object or activity, doing an interview, and using a reference. It calls for skills in reading for details, with special attention to the proper sequence. Related study skills are taking notes, outlining, or listing steps of procedure, determining what materials are needed, and finding other essential information.

Activities for Following Directions

Make a set of clear directions for classmates to follow on a treasure hunt in the classroom or schoolyard or on a map used in the unit under study.

Play a classroom game that calls for listening, recalling, and then following three or four oral directions—for example, "Put a yellow pencil on the windowsill, write tomorrow's date on the chalkboard, and tap someone who is wearing blue on the left shoulder."

Read and follow directions presented by the teacher on cards, a chart, or the board.

Follow directions presented in the textbook for making a map, graph, chart, diagram, or other object.

Follow directions for conducting an investigation, interviewing an expert, playing a game, or carrying out another activity.

Answer questions that focus attention on directions:

What directions are given in the story for making cookies?

What are the steps farmer Jones followed to make butter?

What directions for conducting a meeting are given on page 67?

What directions for making a bar graph are given on page 88?

finding
relationships

Of key importance in the social studies is the ability to find and explain cause-effect, part-whole, analogous, quantitative, sequential, and place relationships. Discovering relationships calls for various reading skills, such as finding the main idea, selecting important details, and drawing inferences.

Activities for Finding Relationships

CAUSE-EFFECT RELATIONSHIPS

Find and discuss causes and effects of individual behavior, group action, and historical events. Discover the relationship between family and community problems, weather and climate, and economic and other problems.

Answer questions that focus attention on causes and effects:

What causes were mentioned? What effects were described?

Why did that happen? What reasons were given?

What were the effects of the invention discussed in the story?

Why are there usually several causes and several effects of human events?

PART-WHOLE RELATIONSHIPS

Find and discuss part-whole relationships: contributions of members of the family; the interdependence of neighborhoods, communities, states, and regions; relationships among parts of a transit system; relationships between lower and higher courts and their relationship to the total judicial system.

Answer questions that focus attention on part-whole relationships:

How do members of the family depend on each other? How can each one help to improve cooperation in the family?

What are the relationships between the business and residential areas of our city?

How do people in neighborhoods depend on each other? How do people in one neighborhood depend on people in other neighborhoods? How does everyone depend on city services?

What are the main parts of our city transit system? What happens if one part breaks down?

ANALOGOUS RELATIONSHIPS

Find and discuss similarities and differences in family life in different cultures; in neighborhood and community activities; in the work of mayors, governors, and presidents; in the making of clothing and other items at home and in factories; and in modes of transportation and communication in different times and places.

Answer questions that focus attention on making comparisons and contrasts:

How are they alike? How are they different?

What is common in both activities? What differences are there?

What are common things that mayors and governors do?

QUANTITATIVE RELATIONSHIPS

Find and discuss relative time and distance to various places, area and population of states and nations, duration of time periods in historical events, density of population, income per person, and value of resources, products, and services.

Answer questions that focus attention on quantitative relationships:

How far is it from New York to Tokyo? How much time does it take by air? By sea through the Panama Canal?

How much of the family budget is spent for housing? Food? Clothing? Transportation? Recreation? Health care? Other items?

Which is larger? How do they compare in size?

What is their most valuable natural resource? How much of it do they export?

SEQUENTIAL RELATIONSHIPS

Find and discuss the order in which a series of events occurred or the steps of procedure for an activity—for example, steps in processing iron ore or making steel; main periods in the history of a community, state, or nation; and steps taken to get a bill passed.

Answer questions that focus attention on sequential relationships:

In what order did the events occur? How are they related?

What are the main steps in baking bread? Making silk?

Why was that event called a turning point? What preceded it? What followed it?

PLACE RELATIONSHIPS

Find and discuss relationships between the location of the school and the homes around it, between shopping centers and homes or main streets, between large cities and waterways or other transportation systems, between farms or industries and land, water, or resources, and between elevation or distance from the equator and climate.

Answer questions that focus attention on place relationships:

Why was our school located in a residential section of the city?

Why are so many large cities near waterways?

Why are there so many farms in that location?

Where is Buffalo in relation to New York?

How is the climate of Denver related to its elevation, nearness to the Rockies, and distance north of the equator?

deriving
generalizations
This skill requires an ability to find details and summarize and organize information, then to go a step beyond and derive a generalization. To derive a generalization one must get the details or facts clearly in mind, identify what is common or general among them, and state a conclusion or generalization based on the facts. Students must learn to check the facts, to have sufficient evidence for a conclusion, and not to go beyond the facts or evidence (overgeneralization).

Activities for Deriving Generalizations

State or write in one's own words what can be said in general about a topic discussed in a selection—for example, "All members of a family are consumers of goods and services.

Complete statements after reading a selection:

How people use resources is determined primarily by _____.

Select from a list of generalizations the one that best fits a reading selection the class has just finished.

Distinguish factual statements from general statements:

Mark *F* by each statement that is a fact and *G* by each statement that is a generalization.

_____ Our city has a central business district.

_____ The business district in our city is in a central zone.

_____ Cities have central business districts.

Answer questions that focus attention on forming generalizations:

What general statement can we make about causes of the event described in this selection?

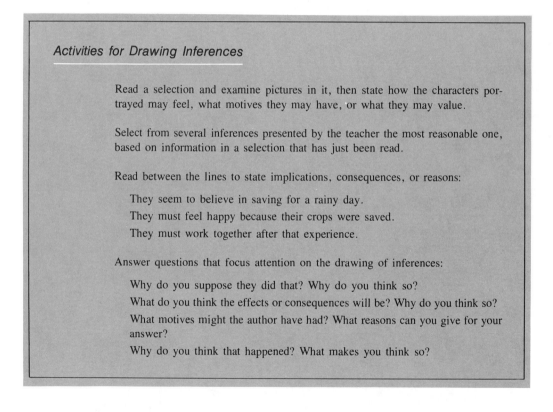

Based on facts presented in this chapter, what can we say in general about the climate of the North Central States?

What conclusion can you draw from the facts in today's reading selection?

drawing
inferences

The ability to draw inferences as one reads takes the reader beyond literal interpretation to identify implications, consequences, motives, feelings, and values. It requires the ability to distinguish an inference from an observation and from a generalization based on given facts and to state reasons for an inference, checking to be sure the inference is reasonable or logical.

Activities for Drawing Inferences

Read a selection and examine pictures in it, then state how the characters portrayed may feel, what motives they may have, or what they may value.

Select from several inferences presented by the teacher the most reasonable one, based on information in a selection that has just been read.

Read between the lines to state implications, consequences, or reasons:

They seem to believe in saving for a rainy day.
They must feel happy because their crops were saved.
They must work together after that experience.

Answer questions that focus attention on the drawing of inferences:

Why do you suppose they did that? Why do you think so?
What do you think the effects or consequences will be? Why do you think so?
What motives might the author have had? What reasons can you give for your answer?
Why do you think that happened? What makes you think so?

stating and
checking
hypotheses

The ability to state and check hypotheses can be put to many uses in reading social studies materials. For example, as children read about the role of members of a family, carpenters, or other people in the community, they can form a hypothesis that similar roles will be found in other settings. To check the hypothesis they proceed to gather information through further reading, thus motivating reading as an activity and adding interest to it. This skill requires the ability to use given information as a basis for the hypothesis, to state a proposition that can be tested, and to collect and analyze information needed to test it.

---

*Activities for Stating
and Checking Hypotheses*

Complete a statement presented by the teacher: If the work is divided, (production is usually increased)

State a hypothesis in your own words after reading a selection:

I think I will find that all North Central States have hot summers and cold winters.

Examine a map that shows water bodies and landforms, then state hypotheses about the location of cities, travel routes, agricultural areas, and manufacturing centers.

Select from several statements presented by the teacher the one that is the best hypothesis, given the information in a selection.

Answer questions that elicit the stating of hypothesis:

Do you think that all fathers have the same role as the one in today's story? Why or why not? How can we find out?

Do you think that all communities depend on other communities for many things, as described in our reading? Why or why not? How can you find out?

What does the author of today's story say usually happens when the work is divided?

According to what we just read, how does the price of an item change when the item becomes scarce?

---

predicting
outcomes   This skill is used to anticipate what may happen next as one reads and to make predictions about the future based on ideas gleaned from reading. It requires the ability to identify conditions, cause-effect relationships, and trends and developments that indicate what is likely to happen. Illustrations, graphs, and tables in reading materials should be used along with the text to gather the information that predictions will be based on.

making critical evaluations — This skill is used to evaluate the content, clarity of presentation, relevance, authority, underlying assumptions, and other aspects of what one reads. Key abilities include defining and applying standards or criteria, identifying an author's purpose, distinguishing facts from opinions, identifying persuasion techniques, checking the accuracy and completeness of information, collecting evidence related to the standards being used, and stating why the judgment was made.

Identify words that signal opinions or judgments, such as "People in _____ generally prefer . . . , or "The greatest achievement of the _____ was . . ."; and identify words with emotional shades of meaning, such as *patriotic, industrious,* and *disloyal.*

Examine and discuss pictures, maps, graphs, and selected passages to appraise them in terms of such criteria as clarity of presentation, provision of meaning clues, usefulness or relevance, and treatment of the sexes and ethnic groups.

Check the qualifications of the author, the currency of material, the accuracy of the sources of information, and the completeness of information.

Discuss the use of such persuasion or propaganda techniques as name calling, glittering generalities, getting on the bandwagon, common folks, testimonials, playing up the good of one group and the bad of other groups, down playing the bad of one group and the good of other groups.

Answer questions that focus attention on critical evaluation:

Which family in today's story would you most like to visit? Why?

Which pictures in this chapter are fair representations of activities of minority groups? Which are not? Why do you think so?

What use has been made of qualifying terms such as *some, sometimes, usually,* and *often* to avoid overgeneralizing?

What references can we use to check the accuracy of the information in this chapter?

Is this generalization based on adequate information? If not, what additional information is needed? Where might we find it?

forming sensory impressions

Reading to form sensory impressions can bring out shades of meaning and appreciations, adding depth to a variety of topics and problems in the social studies. The reader gains a deeper understanding of the author's ideas and a deeper feeling for the people, places and events described. For example, the following expressions can stir impressions and feelings as they are read in different contexts: *the barren landscape, the dense tropical foliage, the whirling dancers at the fiesta, the grim look on the scout's face,* and *the waves crashing on the jagged shoreline.* Key abilities in forming sensory impressions are finding pictures and sketches that illustrate what is presented, making comparisons between one's own experiences and those described in reading material, visualizing or imagining as one reads, and comparing descriptions given in the selection to those in other sources.

Activities for Forming Sensory Impressions

Discuss the feelings, images, sounds, and other impressions evoked by the material.

See pictures, films, and other media that illustrate verbal descriptions in the selection.

Discuss the feelings evoked by sentences taken from the selection—for example, "The hard journey over the pass left them exhausted," and "There were shouts of joy as they approached the water hole."

Draw pictures, make murals, and give verbal descriptions of items presented in the selection, then compare them with descriptions given in the selection or related material.

Answer questions that focus attention on sensory impressions:

Have you ever seen a roaring river? Where? What was it like? How was it similar to the one in our story? How was it different?

Can you find a picture of a windswept plateau? A dense jungle?

How would you describe a gushing spring? A trickling spring?

How might we show grassy plains, golden wheat fields, or rolling hills in a drawing or a mural?

Developing Reading-Study Skills

No subject offers better opportunities to develop and apply reading-study skills than does the social studies. The following examples of activities and procedures not only sharpen basic reading-study skills but also improve learning in each unit.

Locating Information in Books

Learn the parts of social studies textbooks through such activities as these:

1. Examining the table of contents, guided by such questions as What are the main units or sections? What chapters are in the first unit? the second unit? . . . On what page is the glossary? On what page is the index?

2. Examining the list of maps, charts, diagrams and other aids: On what page is the map of Alaska? On what pages is the map that shows the population of the United States and Canada? On what page is the map that shows great circle air routes?
3. Using the index to locate specific topics and to clinch the learning that people are alphabetized by last name and places by first name: On what page can we find George Washington Carver? Is the first or last name of people placed first in the index? On what page can we find New York? Is the first or last word of a place given first?
4. Using the glossary to find the meaning, spelling, and pronunciation of terms
5. Assessing students' ability to locate information

Use study guides to familiarize students with textbook organization:

Which of the following should be used to locate the information noted below?

| A. Title | C. List of Maps | E. Glossary |
| B. Contents | D. List of Charts and Graphs | F. Index |

To find the pages on which deserts are described: _____

To find main parts or units in the book: _____

To find an illustration of a Corn Belt farm: _____

To find the pronunciation of a word: _____

To find the titles of chapters: _____

To find the location of major mining areas: _____

Using references

Use encyclopedias to find maps, tables, diagrams, pictures, graphs, and written material related to topics under study, with particular attention to such learnings as the following:

1. Articles are in alphabetical order by title, with articles beginning with *A* in volume 1, *B* in volume 2, *C–Ch* in volume 3, and so on.
2. Guide words at the top of pages tell what is presented on each page.
3. The last name of people is placed first.
4. The first names of places like Latin America and New York are placed first.
5. The index lists all articles and gives some facts not included in articles.
6. The index also lists maps, charts, pictures, tables, and graphs.
7. Study guides, questions to answer, articles to read, and related books to read are given for topics in our social studies units.

Use dictionaries to find a variety of information in addition to meaning, spelling, and pronunciation of terms, such as

Antonyms	Charts	Weights	Maps
Synonyms	Tables	Measures	Foreign terms
Word origins	Diagrams	Drawings	Abbreviations

Use other references and library materials to locate information on questions and topics in units of study:

The Card Catalog	Periodicals
City directories	*Readers' Guide to Periodical Literature*
Dictionaries	Telephone directories
Encyclopedias	*The Junior Book of Authors*
School atlases	*Who's Who in America*
Government directories	*World Almanac*
Guides, timetables, and folders	*Statesman's Yearbook*

Summarize on charts the skills involved in using library materials as shown in this example on using the card catalog prepared by sixth grade students:

1. Use the guide letters on each drawer to locate cards.
2. Cards are in alphabetical order by author(s), title, and subject.
3. Find the author card if you know the author's name.
4. Find the title card if you know the title.
5. Find the subject card if you do not know the author or title.
6. Note the call number on the upper left hand corner of the card.
7. Look for cross references, which are indicated by *see* and *see also.*

Skimming and Scanning

Use the ability to skim to preview and select material for further study, to get an overview, to find how a chapter is organized, or to decide if a selection can be used to answer a question, guided by such questions as the following:

Does the title tell what is included?

Do headings give clues to main ideas that are included?

Does the introductory paragraph give an overview?

Does the last section present a summary of main points?

Do the beginning sentences of paragraphs reveal main ideas?

Use the ability to scan to find a topic in an index; to find a name, date, or other specific item; or to find a particular map, chart, table, or diagram. Use questions such as the following to guide you:

Are you trying to find a date, a name, or the answer to a specific question?

Have you scanned the index or list of maps to locate it?

ORGANIZING INFORMATION FROM SEVERAL SOURCES

When students are expected to use several textbooks, reference materials, and other sources, they must be taught procedures for synthesizing the collected data. First, discuss the topic, question, or problem so that children know just what information is needed and can list specific questions for which data will be gathered. Next, have them locate the information in the available sources. For example, children in the early grades can check two or three classroom books to find information on the work of adults outside the home and work that family members do at home. They can then place a red slip of paper in each book to mark where the outside work of adults is discussed, a blue slip to mark the work of adults at home, and a yellow slip to mark the work of children. When children have developed writing skills they can label the slips of paper with words indicating topics. After the needed number concepts have been developed, children can note page numbers or the teacher may list page numbers on the chalkboard.

After information has been collected from several sources, it must next be pooled. One way to achieve this is to have students first study one source and summarize relevant data, then study the second source and add any new ideas. Students continue checking sources and adding new information, producing a final summary that includes relevant data from all of the sources. The note-taking and outlining skills previously discussed can be used by children in the middle and upper grades. In the early grades the teacher notes the information on the chalkboard as children report on each source.

Another procedure is to guide students as they prepare outlines that contain information taken from several sources. In the early grades the outline may consist of only two or three items such as (1) How Families Have Fun and (2) Summer Vacations. With these two topics as guides, the children find related information in two or three sources. The teacher notes their findings on the chalkboard as they are reported from each source. More detailed outlines are used in later grades as students find information in several sources and note details under each heading as shown in charts 11–1 and 11–2.

LEARNING HOW TO LEARN

If students are to become independent learners—a prime objective of schooling—teachers must introduce them to the techniques that teachers themselves use in their day-to-day instruction. Learning how to learn can and should

Arranging Notes from Several Sources in an Outline

1. Number each note that is taken from each source.
2. List the topics in outline form.
3. Write the number of each note under the topic related to it.
4. Use your outline as a basis for preparing a report.

Chart 11–1

An Outline of Notes on Production of Iron

A. Mining Iron Ore
   1. Note 1
   2. Note 4
B. Transporting the Ore
   1. Note 3
   2. Note 6
C. Processing the Ore
   1. Note 2
   2. (and so on)

Chart 11–2

Reading on Our Own

Concentrate on what you are reading.

Have a clear purpose or specific questions in mind.

Fit your speed of reading to your purpose and the material.

Get ideas from headings, pictures, maps, charts, tables, and graphs.

Figure out the meaning of each word.

Review the points related to your purpose or questions.

Chart 11–3

Concentrating as You Read

Focus your thinking on what you are reading.

Have note-taking and other needed materials ready for use.

Keep the purpose or question in mind and search for related ideas.

Use headings for clues to what is coming next.

Do not let noise or activity of others distract you.

Chart 11–4

Finding Purposes

Does the title suggest a purpose?

Do main headings suggest purposes?

Do you have questions of your own?

Are questions to guide reading listed?

Can questions listed during group discussions be answered?

Can you find purposes by skimming?

Chart 11–5

Finding Word Meaning

Look for
   Definitions
   Context clues
   Picture clues
Use
   The word box
   The glossary
   The dictionary
Ask
   When you have tried but cannot find the meaning

Chart 11–6

Speed of Reading

How does speed vary when reading:
   Main ideas?
   Specific details?
   Directions?
   Familiar ideas?
   Graphs? Tables?
   Flow charts?
   Definitions?
   Time lines?
   Maps? Diagrams?
   Stories?

Chart 11–7

Using Reading Aids in Books

Do you check headings to get an overview?
Do you use pictures to clarify words and ideas in the text?
Do you get the main ideas from graphs and tables?
Do you follow the steps in charts and diagrams?
Do you use the contents and the index to locate material?

Chart 11–8

Reviewing What You Have Read

Can you recall ideas related to your purpose for reading?
Can you recall ideas related to headings in the chapter?
Can you answer questions at the end of the chapter?
Can you answer questions listed during group discussion?
Can you think of questions about main ideas to ask others?

Chart 11–9

be taught; the reading and study skills essential to independent learning should be emphasized.

The skills that students must master to become independent learners are summarized in charts 11–3 through 11–9. The first chart, "Reading on Our Own," gives students specific pointers on how to read effectively; subsequent charts elaborate each point. "Concentrating as You Read" tells students how to develop effective study habits. "Finding Purposes for Reading" shows students how to find objectives. "Finding Word Meaning" lists techniques for developing the vocabulary used extensively in the social studies. "Speed of Reading" helps students discover when they should vary their rate of reading to fit their purpose and the type of material. "Using Reading Aids in Books" contains points on how to use headings, graphs, pictures, and other aids to improve comprehension. "Reviewing What You Have Read" suggests ways to clinch key ideas and engage in self-evaluation after completing a selection. All of the charts should be adapted to meet the special needs that arise in a particular class.

Questions, Activities, Evaluation

1. Examine a chapter in a social studies textbook and do the following:
   a. Note vocabulary that should be developed
   b. List activities for developing vocabulary, working from those suggested in the section on vocabulary development
2. Examine a chapter in a social studies textbook and make a plan for applying the comprehension skills discussed in this chapter.
3. Make a plan that shows how you might provide instruction that allows students to apply the reading-study skills discussed in this chapter.

references

Bond, Guy L., Miles A. Tinker, and Barbara B. Wasson, *Reading Difficulties.* Englewood Cliffs, N.J.: Prentice-Hall, 1979. Procedures for diagnosing and correcting reading difficulties.

Dallman, Martha, Roger L. Rouch, Lynette Y. C. Chang, and John J. DeBoer, *The Teaching of Reading* (4th ed.). New York: Holt, Rinehart & Winston, 1974. Practical techniques for improving reading skills.

Fry, Edward, *Elementary Reading Instruction.* New York: McGraw-Hill, 1977. Chapters on vocabulary, comprehension, and higher skills.

Lundstrom, John P., ed., "Improving Reading Skills," *Social Education,* 42 (January 1978), 10–31. Articles on vocabulary, critical reading, comprehension, and literature.

Turner, Thomas N., "Making the Social Studies Textbook a More Effective Tool for Less Able Readers," *Social Education,* 40 (January 1976), 38–41. Procedures and activities for use of textbooks.

Stewig, John W., and Sam L. Sebasta, eds., *Using Literature in the Elementary Classroom.* Urbana, Ill.: National Council for the Teachers of English, 1978. Using books to build vocabulary and teach fiction, poetry, and nonfiction.

DEVELOPING GLOBE AND MAP CONCEPTS AND SKILLS

12

How can globes and maps be used to improve learning in social studies?
What strategies and techniques can be used to develop globe and map concepts and skills?
What concepts and skills are taught at various grade levels? What techniques are helpful in map making?

Globes and maps are vital to the social studies program. They are used to locate places in the community, state, nation, and other lands, including parks, resources, products, ports, water bodies, historical sites, cities, transportation routes, mountain ranges, and population distribution, and to determine distance and time between places, along travel routes, and across areas. They are also used to determine direction from one place to another, to follow travel routes, to trace the flow of rivers and of migrations, and to compare selected regions with reference to area, population, resources, water bodies, landforms, products, occupations, and urban centers.

Globes and maps are also used to interpret the data needed to answer questions and test hypotheses; they are indispensable for discovering relationships and drawing inferences about climate and living conditions, industries and resources, terrain and travel routes, and location of cities in relation to topography. Maps can be made to synthesize data related to topics under study, showing the distribution of items in selected areas, associations between items, and interconnections within and between regions.

This chapter focuses on developing the skills and concepts essential to making effective use of globes and maps. It discusses the value of both commercial maps and maps made by students and teachers. Charts 12–1 and 12–2, directed to students, show how globes and maps may be used.

The Globe

The globe is the most accurate representation of the earth's surface; it should be referred to whenever questions arise about relative location, size, distance, direction, and shape of land masses and water bodies. Because the globe, like the earth, is a sphere, it has properties that cannot all be found on any one flat map. It shows (1) distance between places in correct proportion, (2) correct shape of land masses and water bodies, (3) areas in correct proportions, and (4) true directions. When a sphere is transferred to a flat surface, some distortion is inevitable; in many flat maps distortion is greatest at the outer edges.

The globe should be used in conjunction with maps whenever distortion creates problems and when misconceptions arise. Such misconceptions as the belief that Greenland is larger than South America (it is about one-eighth as large) or that the shortest distance from San Francisco to Moscow is across the Pacific (a polar route is shorter) can be avoided by referring to the globe. The relative position of continents, the shapes of land masses, and the size of various regions should be checked against a globe.

The globe is invaluable for developing fundamental concepts about the earth and its surface features. In the early grades the globe is used to develop concepts of the roundness of the earth, directions, the extent to which water covers the earth's surface (about three-fourths is water), differences in surface features from place to place, and size differences among major land masses and water bodies. In later grades, the globe is used to develop concepts related to night and day, time zones, changes in seasons, rotation and revolution, and high, middle, and low latitudes. These concepts are essential to the development of map-reading skills and are closely related to the development of major geographic concepts (see charts 12–3 through 12–8).

**Show These
on the Project Globe**

Main land masses and
water bodies

Names of the oceans, the
continents, and the islands

North Pole, South Pole,
equator

Tropic of Cancer, Tropic of
Capricorn

Arctic Circle and Antarctic
Circle

Prime meridian and inter-
national date line

Chart 12–3

**Find These
on the Globe**

Northern Hemisphere
Southern Hemisphere
Western Hemisphere
Eastern Hemisphere
Land hemisphere
Water hemisphere
Daylight hemisphere
Darkness hemisphere

Chart 12–4

**Use the Globe to Find
Distortions on Maps**

Compare Alaska on a world
map and on the globe.

Compare Greenland on a
world map and on the
globe.

Compare North America on
a world map and on the
globe.

Compare places on a polar
map and on the globe.

Chart 12–5

**Rotation and Time
on the Globe**

Demonstrate the cause of
day and night.

Show how to find time in
different places.

Locate the hour circles or
meridians and compare
them with time zones.

Show noon and midnight
by finding opposite
meridians.

Show how the calendar is
adjusted when crossing the
date line.

Chart 12–6

**Great Circles
on the Globe**

Show that a great circle
divides the earth into two
equal parts.

Show that the equator is a
great circle.

Show that the meridians are
great circles.

Show that parallels north
and south of the equator
are not great circles.

Show a great circle route
from New York to Bangkok.

Chart 12–7

**Revolution
and Seasons**

Show how the earth's axis
is tilted.

Show the orbit of the earth
as it goes around the sun.

Show the sun's rays during
the summer and winter
solstices.

Show the sun's rays during
the spring and fall
equinoxes.

Show the northern limit of
the sun's vertical rays.

Show the southern limit of
the sun's vertical rays.

Chart 12–8

Because the globe is such a valuable teaching device, each classroom should have at least one. In the primary grades, a raised relief globe that clearly shows land and water features helps give children the "feel" of the earth's surface. Raised relief globes are available in lightweight plastic that can be marked with crayon or chalk. These globes, which children can handle easily, can be used to develop initial concepts of the roundness of the earth, main land and water areas, and general nature of surface features.

A good globe for the next stage of instruction is the simplified merged-color beginner's globe. By comparing it with the raised-relief globe, children quickly grasp the meaning of the colors used to show relief. Also helpful is the markable project globe that simply shows major features in outline form with land clearly differentiated from water. This globe can be used in different grades to develop concepts of direction, to mark the location of places and special features, and to outline countries, regions, travel routes, and other items.

For middle and upper grades, a physical-political globe that clearly shows main surface features, yet is not cluttered with detailed printing, should be available in each classroom. A physical-political globe with a horizontal mounting that can be used to develop concepts of motion, time, distance, seasonal sun position, and the like is helpful in the seventh and eighth grades, and for advanced children in the fifth and sixth grades. Small desk globes (eight inches in diameter) for individual projects can be used to develop concepts and skills in all grades.

Maps

Maps are needed to show areas in large perspective. The globe is too small to show detail. The wide range of content shown on maps enables one to see at a glance many surface conditions and relationships that cannot otherwise be portrayed as clearly and as efficiently.

CONTENT

Maps may be classified according to content into such types as political, physical, physical-political, economic, historical, and special feature. The following list illustrates the diversity of the information shown on maps:

Political—boundaries, cities, states, countries, blocs of countries

Physical—mountains, lowlands, rivers, lakes, oceans

Climate—rainfall, temperature, winds

Population—distribution, change, migration

Economic—resources, crops, occupations, products

Physical-political—combinations of the above

Historical—explorations, events, territorial changes

Travel—trade routes, roads, railroads, air routes

Community—streets, buildings, agencies, harbors

Special—parks, monuments, literary works, religions

GUIDING PRINCIPLES

Because maps are symbolic representations, students must gradually be introduced to map language. First, simple maps with very little detail should be selected for the primary grades. More detailed maps may be used to meet the various problems that arise in later grades. The symbols, colors, and terms on the maps should be identified, learned, and used in reading and making maps. In general, each new symbol should be taught as it is needed. The legend should be analyzed and the symbols and colors contained in it located on the map and interpreted. Important terms should be learned and located on the map. Children should have opportunities to apply the terms as they write on slated globes and maps and as they complete desk and wall outline maps. Compass directions should be pointed out and reviewed as children change rooms, as new maps are introduced, and as questions arise. The scale of miles should be learned and used in measuring distances between places being studied in the unit. The different colors that show elevation should be explained and related to places of varying elevation visited by children in the class. Sizes of cities, distances between places, and types of climate should be associated with cities children already know, places they have visited, and places where they have lived. Experiences in making maps or models of familiar areas (classroom, school, neighborhood) should be provided to build concepts of distance, direction, scale, use of symbols, and functions of maps. Special attention should be given to the variety of maps in atlases and encyclopedias, as shown in charts 12–9 and 12–10.

Using Our World Atlas

BASIC MAPS

World maps	Asia
North America	Africa
South America	Australia
Europe	Polar regions

OTHER MAPS

Climate	Population
Temperature	Resources
Vegetation	Products

TABLES

| Rivers | Population |
| Mountains | Sea depths |

GLOSSARY

| Places | Map terms |

Using Maps in Our Encyclopedias

Location of cities, states, countries, continents, and water bodies

Maps of major cities that show famous landmarks

Physical relief maps that show surface features

Political maps showing cities, states, provinces, and countries

Regional maps of the United States, Central America, and other places

Historical maps of notable events

Interesting places such as parks and monuments

Comparison maps that show relative size of states and countries

Pictorial maps that show plants, animals, products, and resources

 Chart 12–9

 Chart 12–10

THE GRID

Maps and globes are made on grids that include reference lines—east-west lines (parallels) and north-south lines (meridians). The importance of these grid lines can be brought home to children in several ways. One widely used technique is to substitute a large ball for the globe and ask children to show the location of their community or another well-known place on it. The question of reference points and lines will immediately arise: Where should we mark the North Pole, the South Pole, and the equator? Do we need other lines? After checking the classroom globe, have the children mark reference lines on the ball with chalk and locate the given place on it.

A similar procedure can be used for locating surface features on a piece of paper. When children are asked to locate places in the neighborhood, they quickly discover that they must mark lines to show the different streets and then proceed to locate homes, the school, and other important places. In later grades, the same procedure can be used for locating states, countries, and other places, first drawing squares on the paper to serve as a grid, then sketching the places to be shown. Other helpful procedures are to review the grid lines on road maps, state maps, maps of the nation, wall maps of various continents, and the globe.

PREPARATION FOR MAP READING

Before children can use maps constructively, they must learn certain skills and understandings. Most important among these are directions, surface features, and concepts of the earth.

cardinal directions

The directions—north, south, east, and west—can be taught in terms of the specific locations known to the children. Ask them in which direction their houses face the school? What is the direction from home to school? To the grocery store? To other familiar places? What buildings are north? South? East? West?

Another technique is to have a group of children stand with their backs to the sun at noon. Explain that they are facing north, that south is in back of them, that east is to their right, and that west is to their left. Have them locate the same directions in the classroom. Then show them cards with the directions written on them and ask individual children to point in the direction shown Some teachers place labels showing directions on the appropriate walls of the classroom. Many teachers find it helpful to summarize key learnings about directions on the chalkboard or on charts, as shown in charts 12–11 and 12–12.

surface features

Children need specific experiences to develop an understanding of the surface features shown on maps and the terms used to express them. Both natural features (landforms, water bodies, and other concept clusters listed in chapter 5)

385

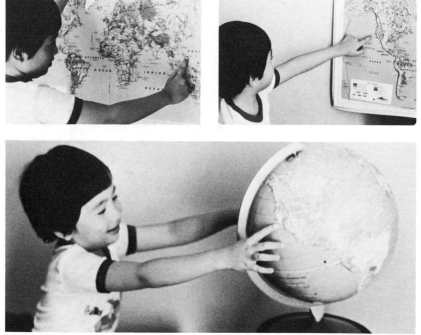

Walnut Creek, California

"We started here. Then we flew across the Pacific to San Francisco. I'll show you on the globe." The use of maps and the globe together helps to develop concepts and to improve skills.

Finding Directions at Noon

Stand with your back to the sun.
You are facing north.
East is to your right.
South is in back of you.
West is to your left.

Chart 12–11

The Sun and Directions

The sun rises in the east.
The sun sets in the west.
At noon the sun is south.
Our shadows are toward the north at noon.

Chart 12–12

and cultural features (highways, canals, and other things made by people) should be given attention. The objective is to develop a clear concept of the landscape features represented by symbols used on maps (see chart 12–13). Then students can bring meaning to map reading, as they should bring meaning to other kinds of reading.

Different surface features can be pointed out and discussed on short walks and study trips. This sharpens children's ability to observe, especially when they are encouraged to ask questions about what they see. Films, pictures, terrain models, and charts showing map terms should be discussed to clarify such specific concepts as plateau, bay, gulf, and harbor. Commercial or teacher-made charts and pictures of surface features with appropriate labels attached to them are especially helpful.

Encourage students to report on trips they have taken to mountains, beaches, lakes, valleys, canyons, parks, dams, and other places where various surface features could be seen; let them share and discuss postcards and photographs that show the features they are studying. Maps with raised relief can help them visualize mountains, valleys, winding rivers, and other surface features. In discussion, sketches and drawings made by students as well as those in textbooks should be used. When using textbooks, be sure to clarify new concepts through discussion, pictures, or films and filmstrips. Another helpful technique for intermediate grades, illustrated in chart 12–14, is to have students locate pictures or sketches that illustrate specific features. Then have them locate the same features on a map.

Can You Find Examples of These Concept Clusters on Maps?		
Natural Resources	*Major Landforms*	*Bodies of Water*
Soil	Plains	Rivers
Water	Hills	Lakes
Minerals	Plateaus	Gulfs
Wildlife	Mountains	Oceans

Chart 12–13

Find Pictures to Show Each of These Features
The rugged coastline of a fiord
Mountain land
A broad plateau
The hub of the highways
A long, winding river
A network of railways
Area of dense population
Desert as far as the eye can see

Chart 12–14

concepts of the earth
Specific concepts of the earth can be developed with a simplified globe. Begin by discussing the fact that the globe is a good representation (not a picture) of the earth. The surface is land and water, and where we live is one small part of the earth. Explain that the earth is shaped like a ball and that the globe shows the main land and water features. Introduce the term *sphere* and have children tell about objects they know that are shaped like a sphere or ball. Explain that the earth is a sphere, too. Teach the meaning of the term *hemisphere* by cutting an orange or ball of clay in half; point out that *hemisphere* means half of a ball. Hold the globe so that they can see the hemisphere on which they live.

Locate the North Pole and explain that this is the farthest point north. Next locate the South Pole and point out that we are farther from the South Pole than we are from the North Pole. Explain the term *equator;* locate it and point out that it is midway between the poles. Show the Northern and Southern hemispheres and have the group tell in which hemisphere we live.

Directions on the globe should be clarified. North is toward the North Pole; south is toward the South Pole. Never use the terms *up* and *down* to indicate north and south. Explain that *up* is away from the earth, and that *down* is toward the center of the earth (see charts 12–15 and 12–16). The diagrams in geography texts are helpful in this connection. Point out east and west and have students identify known places to the east and west of their state.

The major land and water bodies should be discussed. Begin with North America, explaining that this is the continent on which we live. Have students locate the Atlantic and Pacific oceans. Which states are between them? Which one is not? What countries to the north and south are between them? Show other continents, beginning with those that have been discussed in class. Point to one or two places on each continent that are familiar to children. Show the Indian Ocean, and point out that it is south of the equator and between the Atlantic and Pacific oceans. Have students compare the sizes of the continents and the oceans (see charts 12–17 and 12–18).

Do You Use These Terms Correctly? *North:* toward the North Pole, not up *South:* toward the South Pole, not down *Up:* away from the earth, higher *Down:* toward the center of the earth, lower	**Directions on the Globe** *North:* along meridians, toward the North Pole *South:* along meridians, toward the South Pole *East:* along parallels, toward the rising sun *West:* along parallels, toward the setting sun

Chart 12–15

Chart 12–16

The Continents How many major continents are there? On which continent is the United States? In what direction is each continent from our continent? Which continent is largest?	**Use the Globe** To find distance To find directions To find location To note distortion in flat maps To compare places To find shortest travel routes

Chart 12–17

Chart 12–18

SYMBOLS

Clear perception and meaningful association are involved in learning map symbols. To help children visualize the feature for which each symbol stands, use the following procedures:

1. Each map symbol should be visualized, and pictorial and semipictorial symbols should be introduced before nonpictorial symbols.
2. After a symbol has been taught, review it without a label so that children will learn the symbol and not rely on the label.
3. Be sure each child checks the legend before using a map. Discuss any new symbols or new uses of color. Review any symbols about which there is a question. Do this for textbook maps as well as for wall maps. Points to consider at different times are shown in charts 12–19 through 12–23.

Check the Legend

What is the scale of miles?

What do the colors mean?

What do the symbols mean?

Are other facts given?

Chart 12–19

Check the Key to the Map

What do the colors mean?

What do shadings mean?

Can you figure elevation?

Chart 12–20

Can You Find These on Our Maps?

Continent	Island	Plain
Desert	Isthmus	Tundra
Forest	Mountain	Valley
Hill	Peninsula	Volcano

Chart 12–21

How Are These Shown on Our Maps?

Airways	Population
Boundaries	Products
Capitals	Railways
Cities	Rainfall
Lowlands	Resources
Mountains	Rivers
Plains	Roads
Plateaus	Seaports

Chart 12–22

Symbols on Maps in Our Books

1. Straight lines show roads on level land.
2. Curved lines show roads on hilly land.
3. Black squares show houses.
4. A cluster of squares shows a town.
5. Lines winding between hills show rivers.
6. The winding line by the ocean is the coastline.

Chart 12–23

4. Compare the symbols on a new map with those used on a familiar map; be alert to changes in symbols.
5. Give specific attention to symbols for cities of different size, rivers, coastline, boundaries, canals, dams, and the like (see chart 12–24).

Map Symbols

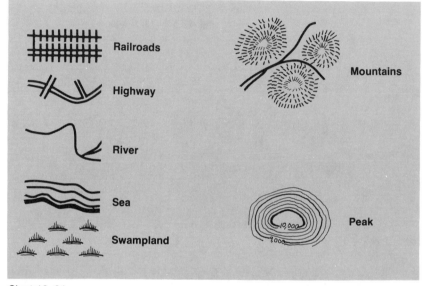

Chart 12–24

6. Explain and illustrate the uses of color to show elevation, countries or states, and vegetation (see chart 12–25). Point out that various lines or shadings of black and white may be used to show some of the same features (see chart 12–26). Have the group summarize what the colors and shadings represent.
7. Discuss the key on a map showing elevation. Explain that elevation is measured from sea level and that the colors show the elevation. Discuss profiles of mountains as illustrated in textbooks, and have the class make profiles showing elevation. Relate these to color maps showing elevation, explaining that the colors enable us to determine elevation. Summarize the colors and elevation represented by them, as shown in charts 12–27 and 12–28.

Maps can take on added meaning when they are used in conjunction with related study trips, pictures, filmstrips, motion pictures, the globe, reading, and discussion. For example, pictures of vegetation, landscapes, products, and types of shelter create in a child's mind impressions of the actual conditions in the area being studied. Aerial photographs should be compared with related sections of the map. Symbols used for canals and other cultural features be-

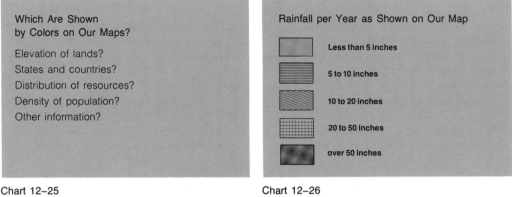

Which Are Shown
by Colors on Our Maps?

Elevation of lands?
States and countries?
Distribution of resources?
Density of population?
Other information?

Chart 12-25

Rainfall per Year as Shown on Our Map

Less than 5 inches

5 to 10 inches

10 to 20 inches

20 to 50 inches

over 50 inches

Chart 12-26

What Heights or Depth
Do These Colors Show?

Shades of red
Shades of brown
Shades of yellow
Shades of green
Shades of blue

Chart 12-27

Elevation on Our Wall мaps

Red	10,000 and up
Dark brown	5,000–10,000
Light brown	2,000–5,000
Yellow	1,000–2,000
Light green	500–1,000
Dark green	0–500
Grayish green	Below sea level

Chart 12-28

come more understandable after a child sees them in picture form. Use also should be made of photos of the earth made from outer space.*

LOCATING PLACES ON THE MAP

Early experiences in locating places should be carried out on floor layouts and maps of the community. The school, children's homes, and main buildings in the neighborhood should be located first. As the broader environment is studied, other places can be located on the map: the airport, railroad yards, nearby farms and dairies, and other places visited on study trips (see charts 12–29 and 12–30).

In state and regional studies, experiences may be provided in locating significant places on road maps. The grid on road maps—numbers and letters to designate east-west and north-south lines—is fairly easy to use. Call children's

*"Teaching Geography through Landsat Maps," *Social Education,* 41 (November–December 1977), 606–22.

391

attention to the index of places and guide them to find the point on the map where the given numbered and lettered lines meet.

Incidentally, the map inserts that show major cities can easily be projected with an opaque projector, allowing simple maps of the community to be made. This is an excellent procedure if the desired community is shown, because unnecessary detail can be eliminated, thereby securing a large map that can be used for many different purposes.

When introducing maps of the children's state or the United States, place them on a table so that children can be properly oriented and directions can be realistically noted. Have the children find where they live, then point out neighboring cities and states. This may be followed by locating places they have visited or read about. Discuss places being studied in the unit, pointing out direction and distance (in time as well as miles) from where they live.

The concept of relative location—location of a place in relation to other places or surface features—should include attention to such factors as accessibility, transportation facilities, and terrain. Some places may be nearby "as the crow flies," but because of some barrier, such as a mountain range, or because of the absence of transportation facilities, such as an airport or natural waterways, it may be difficult to reach.

Give specific attention to how mountain ranges, rivers, lakes, oceans, deserts, swamps, and jungles affect accessibility to given places. Discuss ways in which people change the environment and overcome barriers—such as building roads, canals, railways, and airports. Point out that relative distance and location change as improvements are made in transportation facilities. Modern air routes that follow great circles can be considered to bring home the importance of the area around the North Pole in travel from our country to Japan, Europe, and other places. The location of many cities near natural waterways and the availability of markets and resources to industrial centers should also be discussed.

As students gain a clear understanding of direction on maps and globes, they will grow in their ability to find and describe the location of places. Many fourth graders and most fifth graders can grasp the idea that lines of latitude are true east-west lines and that meridians are true north-south lines. At first the terms *east-west lines* and *north-south lines* may be used; the terms *latitude, parallels, meridians,* and *longitude* can be introduced later. *Degrees* as a concept of measure should be taught in relation to latitude and longitude and the location of main places. Guide students as they use lines of latitude to note places north or south of their city or state, and to find places nearer to or farther from the equator. Also show them that because parallels are true east-west lines, places on the same line of latitude, or parallel, are east or west of each other.

By checking meridians, students can identify places to the east or west of their city or state. For example, Los Angeles is east of San Francisco (it is even east of Reno), and South America is located east of most of the United States. They should also be shown that places on the same meridian are directly north or south of each other because meridians are true north-south lines.

Great circle routes, longitude, and a few of the commonly used map projections can be learned and used by many students in the upper grades. A great circle around the globe forms two hemispheres, and the shortest distance between any two points is along a great circle. The meridians and the equator are great circles; other great circles can be shown by stretching a tape measure or string tightly along the surface of the globe. A simple global ruler can be made for measuring great circle distances as follows: measure the circumference of the globe, divide 25,000 by the circumference, and you then know the number of miles per inch. Have students use a global ruler to find great circle distances between places.

Consideration of time zones should begin with those in the United States, followed by a consideration of time in Europe, beginning with time at the prime meridian and moving toward the United States and then on across Eurasia. A globe should be available for the discussion, and students should discover that meridians (on most globes) are spaced fifteen degrees apart, showing one hour of time ($360° \div 24 = 15°$). They should also check time zones in the United States to find deviations from meridians.

SCALE

Several points should be kept in mind in teaching the scale. The scale of miles or kilometers on maps may be expressed graphically by a line divided into segments labeled with miles or kilometers ($\underline{0 \quad 200 \quad 400}$), as a statement (one inch equals five hundred miles), or as a ratio (1:1,000,000). The graphic scale is relatively easy to use to compute distances between places. The inch-to-mile (or centimeter to kilometer) scale requires a child to measure accurately and then convert. Both these scales should be taught in the intermediate grades and reviewed in the upper grades. The ratio scale is the most difficult to understand because its use requires an understanding of fractions and ratio, and conversion to miles or kilometers requires the use of simple algebra. Since the scale on most maps and globes is expressed graphically or in terms of inches to miles, however, the ratio scale need not cause undue difficulty in the elementary school.

Several practical techniques can be used to help children understand distance as expressed by a scale. First, build specific concepts of distance by having students consider familiar distances, such as home to school and school to downtown or to neighboring towns and cities. Next find the same places on community maps and road maps. Community maps used in the primary grades should be drawn to scale by the teacher, although simple community maps furnished by business concerns could also be used. Many third and fourth graders can use road maps effectively if distance between known places is emphasized.

Many intermediate-grade teachers have found the following activities helpful in teaching scale:

Drawing a floor plan of the classroom to scale

Making neighborhood or community maps

Comparing two places shown on maps of different scale

Discussing distance and travel time between places the children have visited

Making maps of their state or region to scales of varying size

Discussing the use of small-scale maps to show a large area

Comparing outline maps (used by the children) with wall maps and noting the difference in scale

Discussing the scale used on textbook maps

Comparing distances between places being studied and familiar places (such as between New York and Chicago) and noting the scale

Comparing cities, states, and countries with respect to size.

Of key importance is the actual use of the scale on maps to answer questions that come up in daily classwork.

DISCOVERING ASSOCIATIONS
AND MAKING INFERENCES

The discovery of associations is a major objective of units in which geographic understandings are emphasized. Proper use of maps and the globe will contribute to this end. Their use should be combined with reading, viewing materials, and plenty of guided discussion, however, so that any stated association has a basis in fact. Caution also must be exercised in discussing cause-and-effect relationships; children should double-check their inferences by consulting other sources of information.

Among the important associations that children can be guided to infer are the following: (1) elevation and growing season, (2) elevation and density of population, (3) highlands and grazing, (4) lowlands and farming, (5) soil and farming, (6) mountains and rainfall, (7) growing season in relation to altitude and latitude, (8) natural vegetation in relation to rainfall, soil, and growing season, and (9) industry and natural resources.

How Do These Influence Climate?	How Are These Resources Used?	
California Current	Animals	Petroleum
Distance from equator	Coal	Silver
Elevation	Fish	Soil
Gulf Stream	Forests	Tin
Japan Current	Gold	Titanium
Mountain ranges	Iron	Uranium
Prevailing winds	Lead	Water

Chart 12–31   Chart 12–32

Systematic use should be made of globes and maps to help children discover associations such as those listed above. One technique is to have children compare two maps showing different facts about the same area. For example, after comparing a map of the United States showing population with one showing topography, children discover that few people live in high mountainous areas; they later find out if this relationship exists in other places. Or, by comparing a physical relief map and a map showing crops, children discover that much farming is done in lowlands. Another technique is to have children study a map and make inferences about conditions there on the basis of information they already have. For example, if a desert is shown, have them describe living conditions they might expect to find. If a rainfall map is being used, ask them to make inferences regarding areas where crops can be grown and areas that are too arid to support crops. (They may also discover something about soil in relation to rain and crops.) If a place of relatively low elevation is near the equator, ask what inferences they can make about climate. Have them make inferences about the effect of the ocean currents, winds, the Gulf Stream, and other factors on climate in various areas, as shown in chart 12–31. Still other inferences can be made after carefully studying symbols representing resources, industries, and similar items (guiding questions are shown in charts 12–31 and 12–32).

In discussing relationships between people and land and in making inferences about ways of living, avoid the erroneous ideas that human behavior is caused by the environment or that people must always do what they are doing at the present time. Rather, make it clear that custom, tradition, education, and the values of the people living in a particular area are also involved in the choices they make. As people's ideas and values change, their ways of living also change, and they may use resources differently.

DEVELOPING AWARENESS OF MAP PROJECTIONS

As noted earlier, the globe shows land masses and water bodies accurately in terms of area, shape, distance, and direction. When the surface of the globe is transferred to a flat map, distortion is introduced. Students in middle and upper grades should become aware of different projections that are used, distortions that exist, and the purposes for using different projections. This can be done, without getting into technical details, as follows:

Demonstrate how difficult it is to flatten a sphere by peeling an orange and flattening the peeling.

Place tissue paper on a globe and trace a small area such as the state of Colorado and a large area such as North America, then discuss how much more the paper is distorted when a large area is traced.

Examine and discuss diagrams in textbooks, encyclopedias, and other materials that show how distortion is introduced when the globe is flattened to make a map.

Compare selected areas on world maps with the same areas on the globe—for example, Alaska and Greenland on a Mercator projection and on the globe.

Compare the shape and area of North America or other continent as it is shown on different map projections, then discuss where the distortion is greatest in different projections.

Discuss different map projections and the purposes for using them as they are encountered in textbooks, atlases, and other sources—for example, showing accurate shape and area on interrupted and equal-area projections, which are used to compare places; showing shortest distance or great circle routes between places on polar projections, which are used to plan long flights; and showing accurate directions on a Mercator projection, which is used in navigation.

ACTIVITY CARDS BASED ON MAPS IN TEXTBOOKS

Recently published textbooks are replete with a variety of maps that may be used to develop concepts and skills. In addition to using suggestions in the accompanying teacher's guide, you may want to prepare activity cards or sheets for independent study, using the card shown in chart 12–33 as a model.

Map Activity Card

Directions: Open your textbook to page 197. Examine the map of the heartland of the United States. Write answers to these questions on a separate sheet of paper.

1. What states are shown on this map?
2. What symbols are used to show cities?
3. Which are the two largest cities on the map?
4. What symbol is used to show state capitals?
5. What is the capital of Illinois?
6. Which of the heartland states border Canada?
7. What states are in the southern part of the heartland area?
8. Do you think that *heartland* is a good name for these states? Give reasons for your answer.

Chart 12–33

Summary of Concepts and Skills by Grade Levels

The summary that follows is based on recently published courses of study, manuals that accompany social studies textbooks, handbooks on map and globe use, professional books for teachers, and recent studies of children's map-reading abilities.* The grade designations show the levels at which the concepts and skills are typically introduced and put to use in units of instruction. Grade placement should be flexible, with children moving ahead in terms of their abilities and backgrounds of experience.

KINDERGARTEN TO GRADE 2

In the beginning grades, concepts and skills are developed concretely in daily experiences of students. The following concepts and skills are introduced by the end of the second grade.

Directions: left, right; up, down; north, south, east, west; how to find directions by using a shadow stick, a compass, the sun

Orientation: within the classroom, on the playground, and in the neighborhood

Distance: blocks from school to the home, to the store, and to other places; relative distance to places on neighborhood and community maps; using distance between two well-known places as a basis for comparison

Time: in relation to distance from home to school and to main places in the community

Symbols: pictorial and semipictorial symbols; lines to show streets, roads, and boundaries; use of color for land and water

Legends: symbols used to represent items that are meaningful to children—for example, houses, school, stores in neighborhood

Globe: a model of the earth—it is round to represent the earth; how land and water are shown; how the earth makes one complete turn every day (cause of day and night); measuring the distance around the globe to show that it is the same in every direction

Comparisons: distance and time between familiar places; map symbols with what they actually represent and with pictures; large-scale maps with what they represent—classroom, school, neighborhood, community

Locations: principal's office, nurse's office, library, and other places in the school; lakes, parks, main streets, and other features on simple maps; land, water, community, state, nation, and continent on a globe

Map making: floor layouts and floor maps; sand table maps; pictorial symbols to show places on neighborhood community maps; simple maps related to study trips; a floor plan of the classroom; legends for own maps

Inferences: time in relation to distance to places in the community; directions to places (giving reasons for inferences)

*Grateful acknowledgement is made to Dr. Val Arnsdorf, University of Delaware, and to Dr. Haig Rushdoony, Stanislaus State College, California, for their comments and suggestions on this section.

Terminology: terms related to uses of maps and globe—for example, land, highway, road, street, freeway, hill, river, lake, ocean, mountain, county, city, town, bridge, tunnel, north, south, east, west

GRADES 3 AND 4

In these grades, concepts and skills are developed in community and regional studies at home and around the world. The following are introduced by the end of grade 4.

Review: concepts and skills introduced in earlier grades

Directions: relation to poles and equator; intermediate directions—northeast, northwest, southeast, southwest; grid lines on the globe and on maps as direction lines; direction of flow of rivers; upstream, downstream; use of compass

Orientation: of textbook, outline, highway, wall, and other maps; identification and use of north arrow on maps

Distance: blocks in miles and kilometers; miles and kilometers to places studied and to places discussed in current events

Time: in relation to distance to places; time of rotation and time of revolution of the earth

Symbols: identifying towns, cities, capitals; color; coastline; roads; boundaries; relating pictures and symbols; recognizing relief shown by shading; using the map symbols chart; noting how symbols may vary on different maps

Legends: checking before and while using maps

Scale: used in making maps—for example, one inch to a block, one inch to a mile, one centimeter to a kilometer; measuring distance to places studied; checking scale on textbook and classroom maps

Globe: a sphere that represents the earth; axis; poles; equator; Arctic and Antarctic circles; orbits of the moon and satellites

Comparisons: distances to places studied; relative sizes of oceans, lakes, rivers, cities, counties, states, countries, continents; areas on maps and the globe

Locations: resources; travel routes; rivers, canals; airports; cities, states, countries, continents; places on outline maps and the globe

Map making: pictorial maps; relief model maps; special maps on desk, outline maps, outline wall maps, and slated maps; legends for student-made maps

Inferences: general type of climate in relation to location and elevation; centers of population; major products

Terminology: sea, island, bay, delta, tributary, desert, plateau; climate, irrigation; harbor; continent, country, state. province, city, town, village; capital, capitol; hemisphere, region, poles, equator; coast, fiord

GRADES 5 AND 6

Concepts and skills developed earlier in the program are extended to include the following:

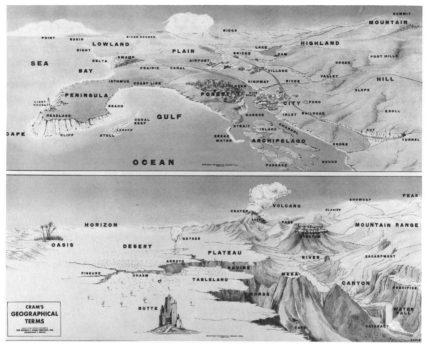

A chart on geographical terms should be available for frequent reference use. How might this chart be used to improve map-reading skills?

Review: concepts and skills presented in earlier grades

Directions: using lines of latitude and longitude to determine directions; east-west lines as lines of latitude or parallels; north-south lines as lines of longitude or meridians

Orientation: orienting the globe to show position of the earth in relation to the sun at different seasons of the year

Distance: using great circles to find distances between places on the globe; measuring distances north or south of the equator in degrees, miles, and kilometers

Time: time needed to travel by various means to places studied; time zones; time in relation to rotation of the earth; time in relation to longitude; prime meridian and international date line

Area: comparison of area of home state and other places; comparison of area of the United States and other places; distortion on different projections used in class; conversion of square miles to square kilometers and acres to hectares

Symbols: reading charts of map symbols; interpreting relief as shown by colors; visualizing steepness of slope from change in colors; interpreting contour lines

Legends: habit of checking before and while using maps

Scale: comparing maps of differing scales; using the scale to compare and to determine distances between places and to places by different routes

Globe: Tropic of Cancer as a line of latitude 23.5° north of the equator (the sun is directly over it about June 21); the Tropic of Capricorn as a line of latitude 23.5° south of the equator (the sun is directly over it about December 22); area between them referred to as the low latitudes. The Arctic Circle as a line of latitude 66.5° north of the equator, the Antarctic Circle as a line of latitude 66.5° south of the equator; the area between each circle and its corresponding pole as a polar region, these areas referred to as high latitudes. Lines of longitude, or meridians, as great circles that pass through the poles; the prime meridian (zero degrees) at Greenwich near London, longitude measured from 0° to 180° east or west of the prime meridian; longitude used to determine time, 15° equal one hour (360° ÷ 24), twenty-four time zones of 15° each; setting the clock ahead when traveling eastward through time zones; setting it back when traveling westward.

Comparisons: size, elevation, surface features, products, climate, and other characteristics of places studied; distances; early and modern maps; size of other places in relation to home state and the United States; surface features in areas studied—mountain ranges such as the Appalachians, Rockies, and Sierras; lakes, oceans, rivers; shipping routes to Europe

Locations: places studied by noting direction and distance from the United States; by using latitude and longitude; states, regions, and countries in relation to others; changes in boundaries—for example, expansion of the United States, formation of new nations

Map making: special feature maps on desk outline maps, outline wall maps, and slated wall maps; overlays on clear plastic for placement on physical, climatic, and other maps to show relationships to travel routes, population, products, and other features

Inferences: temperature at places near the equator and at high and low elevations; location of population centers and travel routes; types of industry in relation to resources and level of technology; climate in relation to location, elevation, ocean currents, and other factors; checking inferences by gathering and organizing related data

Terminology: mesa, peninsula, isthmus; reef, ocean currents, prevailing winds, wind currents; canal, strait, cape, gulf; upland, lowland, rapids, swamps, watershed, timber line; rotation, revolution, latitude, longitude, altitude, elevation, degrees

GRADES 7 AND 8

Considerable review and additional instruction are provided in these grades. By the end of the eighth grade, attention is given to the following:

Review: concepts and skills introduced in earlier grades

Directions: reading directions on different map projections; noting changes in direction on great circle routes

Orientation: systematic orientation of maps as they are used

Distance: using statute and nautical miles, kilometers; changing degrees of latitude and longitude to miles and kilometers

Time: international date line; showing where calendar time is changed and the new calendar day begins; associating longitude and time; determining time in major cities around the world

Area: square miles and kilometers; acres and hectares; distortion on maps; use of ratio in comparing relative size of states, countries, and other areas

Symbols: contour lines to show relief and elevation; hachures to show elevation and slope; international color scheme; isobars and isotherms

Legends: independence in determining the meaning of symbols by checking the legend

Scale: understanding of ratio scale and graduate scales

Globe: using the analemma to find the latitude at which the sun's rays are vertical at noon at a given time; using the ecliptic to find where the vertical rays of the sun strike the earth on any day during the year; understanding the equinoxes

Comparisons: changing frontiers; travel routes westward; early and modern routes; mountain ranges, great river valleys, and other surface features; metropolitan areas; map projections; old and modern world trade routes; ocean currents and their effects on countries

Locations: countries and continents in high, middle, and low latitudes; places by latitude and longitude; historical and current events; natural and cultural surface features

Map making: desk outline, slated, relief, and special-purpose maps

Inferences: climate; type of vegetation; products; population centers; travel routes; farming areas; industrial centers

Terminology: analemma, ecliptic; contour line, isobar, isotherm; continental shelf; equinox, solstice; archipelago, escarpment; topography, terrain

Map Making

In addition to using maps, students should have many opportunities to make them. Careful attention should be given to accuracy so that students form correct impressions rather than erroneous ideas of geographic conditions in places being studied. Have students check their maps against comparable commercial and textbook maps as well as against information secured from reading and from audiovisual materials. A good supply of outline maps should be available for use in both individual and group map-making activities. Where possible, follow standard practices in the use of colors and map symbols. The following list includes types of maps students can make:

Floor maps using blocks, boxes, and models or using chalk, tempera, and crayon on linoleum, paper, or oilcloth; simple line maps in the schoolyard

Pictorial maps of community buildings, harbors, products, types of housing, food, clothing, plant and animal life, minerals and other resources, birthplaces of famous people, arts and crafts, modes of travel, methods of communication, raw materials

Specimen maps using real items such as wheat, corn, cotton, and rocks

Relief maps of papier-mâché, salt and flour, plaster of Paris, clay, or moistened sand; large relief maps on a section of the schoolyard

Mural maps with strips of paper for streets, pictures or silhouettes for buildings, and so forth

Wall outline maps made by using an opaque projector or a pantograph

Jigsaw puzzle maps of states and countries

Slated maps and globes, or individual and wall outline maps, to show air routes, famous flights, early explorations, trade routes, physical features, boundaries, rivers, and so forth

Political and physical maps using symbols and colors to show various features

Transportation maps using various line and dot patterns to show railroad lines, airplane routes, steamship lines, and major highways

Communication maps using symbols to show telephone lines, cable crossings, radio networks and television networks

Special interest maps such as national parks, state parks, major imports, major cities, seaports, and river systems

Progressive or developmental maps of a region or topic such as the westward movement, colonization, or industrial America

Historical maps of the colonies, early travel routes, and early settlements

Transparent maps of resources, transportation networks, and other distributions to project and to place over other maps to show relationships

Certain techniques can be used to improve map making. Teachers should select, from the suggestions that follow, those most appropriate in terms of maturity of the students, available materials, and needs for maps. Chart 12–34 lists guidelines for making maps.

FIRST EXPERIENCES

In the early grades map-making experiences should be realisitic and concrete; they must be related to the children's immediate environment and based on concepts they understand. The following experiences are typical of those used by primary-grade teachers.

Use blocks or boxes to make a simple floor layout of the neighborhood around the school. Begin with the school and the main street in front of the school; add other items known to the children. Do not get involved in a long, drawn-out, detailed modeling project; keep to a few areas and structures familiar to children.

Make a simple drawing of the school and nearby places on a large strip of wrapping paper placed on the floor. A good time for such a project is after a study trip. Begin with the school, trace the route, put in key places seen, and mark the main streets clearly. Use colored paper cutouts or crayon drawings to show important places. A floor map of a farm can be made using objects made

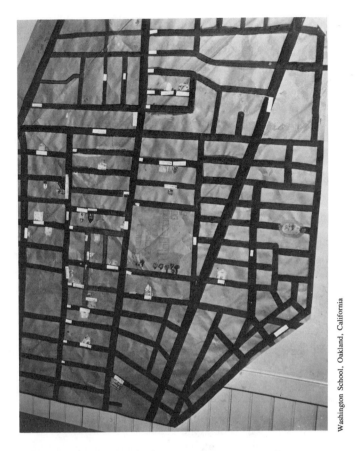

Black tape can be used to show streets on a community map.
If a change is needed, the tape can be lifted and moved.

by children—barn, fences, trees, animals, trucks, silo, and other buildings. A layout of the airport or the harbor can be made in the same way.

On a school district map that shows the school and streets, have children locate the school, their homes, and the more important buildings. Small pieces of colored paper can be used to show the children's homes. Use larger pieces of paper to show the school, stores, and other buildings.

Sand table maps can be made to show different features: farm layout, airport or harbor layout, a well-known park, a section of the community, the child's community, and neighboring towns. Line up the table so that it parallels a major street or road. Discuss the direction the road runs and where the sun rises and sets in relation to the table. Consider space between places, and locate major features accurately. Streets and roads should be laid out after a discussion of distances between places, thus providing readiness for later use of map scales. Use blocks, cutouts, or miniature buildings to locate places. Color hills, valleys, and bodies of water.

A flannel board can be used effectively to show different space arrangements. The layout of the school grounds, neighborhood, or a farm are examples of possible use.

Airplane-view maps can be made of a farm, airport, or the community. They may be made on a large piece of paper on the floor. One group, for example, after seeing an airport from the control tower, laid out the runways, hangars, beacons, nearby roads, and buildings as seen from above. Another group made a map of a section of their city after viewing it from a tall building. They also compared their map with aerial photos of the same section of the city.

Freehand drawing or sketching of maps is done in many classrooms after a trip, film, or discussion. This technique is used when a map of a small area is needed and when a map of the area is not available. If time permits, lay out the area first with blocks or in sand, so that the children get a realistic impression of the surface features.

MAKING MAP OUTLINES

Perhaps the simplest technique for making outline maps is to use the opaque projector to enlarge maps from textbooks, newspapers, magazines, or references, then trace outlines. Another method is to use slides; these may be traced onto a frosted glass placed over the desired map, or they may be purchased. A third technique is to project and trace maps contained in filmstrips or slides that present geographic content.

You can also use proportional squares to make enlargements. Draw small squares over the map to be enlarged, or trace a copy on tissue, then draw the squares. Draw the same number of large squares on butcher roll or tagboard. Mark the outline shown in each square on the matching large square.

Make chalkboard map stencils by punching small holes one inch apart on a large map outline. Hold this against the chalkboard and pat over the holes with an eraser containing chalk dust. Mark a heavy line over the dots to show the outline clearly. Or, using cardboard outlines as a pattern, trace maps on the chalkboard.

Small outline maps can be drawn on stencils for reproduction on duplicating machines; in some school systems, audiovisual departments furnish such outline maps on request. Printed desk maps can be secured inexpensively from commercial publishers.

Tracing paper or onionskin can be used to make maps if no projectors are available. If a large map is to be traced, use transparent tape to fasten individual sheets of tracing paper together. Place the tracing paper over the map to be copied and outline the desired features. Place carbon paper on the sheet to

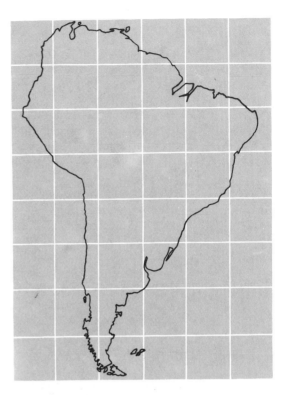

Proportional squares may be used to make enlargements of maps.

which the map is to be transferred, lay the tracing paper on it, use weights (books or blocks) to prevent slipping, and go over the map outline. Remove the tracing paper and carbons carefully to prevent smearing. (See charts 12–34 and 12–35 for a summary of guidelines.)

Making Maps
What is to be shown?
What facts are needed?
What size should the grid lines be?
What symbols should be used?
What colors should be used?
What would be a good title?
What should be in the legend?

Chart 12–34

Making Outline Maps
Project the slide on the mapping material.
Trace the boundaries and main features.
Locate other important items.
Mark basic symbols on it.
Label important places.
Color the parts according to plan.
Make a complete legend.
Print a clear title.

Chart 12–35

Materials for making flat maps should be selected with care. If tagboard or another slick-surfaced material is used, felt-tipped markers for printing and sketching are better than wax crayons or calcimine paint. Colored drawing pencils may also be used. On softer papers, such as bogus, newsprint, construction, mimeograph, manila, chipboard, and certain types of wrapping paper, wax crayons and tempera paint can be used successfully. Crayons and tempera can also be used on window shades, muslin, and percale.

In using colors for making physical maps, the standard international color plan should be used—blue for water, green for lowlands, and yellow, orange, and brown for higher altitudes. When color is used to show other features—states, countries, historical changes such as the frontiers during different periods—choose colors that contrast well and that do not decrease visibility of lettering. The finished map should be clear, sharp in color contrast, and easy to read.

If lines, dots, or shaded areas are used, be sure to plan for contrast and clear lettering. Some teachers have pupils print the lettering on white labels that can be placed over shaded areas and thus stand out. Lettering should be tried out ahead of time.

All lettering on maps should be clear and neat. Have students print difficult terms first on a piece of practice paper. Give attention to spacing, spelling, and proper use of abbreviations. Wherever possible, have all words printed parallel to each other. Encourage students to examine wall and textbook maps closely to discover effective ways to line up lettering on their maps.

Encourage students to add pictures and specimens to highlight ideas portrayed on maps. Use ribbon, yarn, or tape running from the picture (or specimen) to its location on the map.

Help the group to select symbols that effectively portray what is shown. Have them check other maps and identify symbols that seem to them to be appropriate. Consider the use of paper cutouts, hand-drawn symbols, colored symbols, and pins and colored bead heads. Symbols carved in pencil eraser heads or stick-prints can be reproduced easily by pressing them on an ink pad, then stamping on the map. Movable symbols may also be used.

Plan the legend that will be placed in a corner of the map. The title, symbols, colors, shading, scale, and other pertinent data should be shown clearly. A neat border around the legend sets it off clearly and adds to its appearance. Make the legend on a separate piece of paper so that the map is not ruined if a change must be made.

Give attention to directions on the map. Use arrows where necessary to show the flow of a river, wind currents, or ocean currents. Orientation of the map may be shown with arrows in one corner indicating the cardinal directions.

Puzzle maps (jigsaw maps) can be made from plywood, beaverwood, or

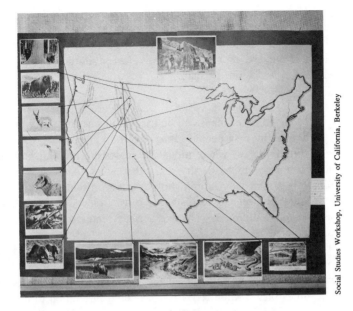

Social Studies Workshop, University of California, Berkeley

How might you plan for the use of a large outline map in combination with pictures to show specific locations?

heavy chipboard. Outline the map, trace in major features to be shown (states, regions, produce areas), and color in rivers, lakes, and other significant features. Saw into reasonable and logical sections with a jigsaw or coping saw. Fasten the border that remains to a whole piece of plywood; this can be used to hold the cutout pieces. On a map of the United States, the border can be labeled to show relative location of the Atlantic and Pacific oceans, and Canada and Mexico. Encourage students to make their own puzzle maps out of cardboard.

Another type of puzzle map can be made of felt. Secure a large piece of green felt for the base and several smaller pieces of felt in different colors to use as sections. Make a paper pattern of the desired region—for example, the United States. Cut this pattern from the large piece of green felt. Glue it to a piece of plywood, cardboard, or chipboard; this is the base map on which the smaller sections can be placed. Next, mark sections (New England states, Pacific states, and so forth) on the paper pattern and cut out each section; then cut each section from a piece of colored felt. The cutouts will adhere to the base map when placed on it. Other cutouts can be made to represent different regions and thus vary the use of the puzzle map.

Transparent maps for projection can be made by using special pencils and inks on plastic, by placing colored plastic cutouts on a plastic base map, and by making copies of maps in copying machines.

Hooked-rug maps are decorative and not difficult to make. Outline the map on a piece of burlap with chalk and tack it to a box or wooden frame. Use a hooked-rug needle to sew in heavy yarn. Select colors to show boundaries, states, provinces, or other features. Have children practice using the needle before they work on the map.

Modeled Relief Maps

Modeled relief maps can be used in discussing many problems. They can help show why people settle in certain places, why highways are built in certain places, where mountain passes are located, how mountain ranges cause certain areas to be dry and other areas to receive much rainfall, how climate is affected by terrain, how areas are drained by rivers, and a host of other questions related to distance, travel, elevation, and topography. Relief maps enable children to visualize surface features and conditions in the areas being studied.

Remember that the vertical scale on relief maps is different from the horizontal scale. For example, Pike's Peak, which may be prominent on a relief map, is only a tiny pinpoint on the earth's surface when its elevation (under three miles or 4.8 kilometers) is considered in relation to the circumference of the earth (25,000 miles, or 40,225 kilometers). Nevertheless, one child who has seen it said, "It was no pinpoint from where I saw it," thus indicating that relief on smaller areas stands out dramatically and realistically. By mapping a smaller area, less distortion is introduced. When large areas are mapped, however, considerable distortion is introduced and should be considered as children grow in their understanding of map scale. One technique is to draw a long line on the chalkboard to represent the distance across the area being mapped. Then draw vertical lines to show the relative height of mountains, plateaus, and other features to be shown. Thus, if a mountain approximately three miles high is located in an area three hundred miles long, the vertical line would be three inches while the base line would be three hundred inches. (Corresponding metric measurements would be mountain, 4.83 kilometers high; length of area, 483 kilometers; vertical line, 7.6 centimeters; and base line, 760 centimeters.) After such a demonstration, one fifth grader said, "That mountain isn't so high when you think of how long the ground is." When distortion exists, the teacher should explain that features are relatively higher than they should be to show them more clearly.

The outline on which the relief map is made should be carefully prepared. A wise procedure is to make two outline maps and to use the second one as a working guide while the modeling material is being placed on the relief map. Then, when one area is covered or one layer is on, the second outline map is available for easy reference. Make a list of the features that are to be shown, show pictures illustrating them (the jagged Rockies, long flat prairies, great valleys), and guide children to find them on physical maps, either wall maps or maps in atlases.

How might you use aerial views to improve map making and map reading in a unit you are planning?

Make the map outline by means of a projector or one of the other methods discussed under outline maps. Sketch in rivers, mountains, other features, and contour lines. After the outline is mounted on a base board, drive in brads and small nails to show relative height and position of peaks, mountain ranges, and hills; these serve as guides during the modeling process. Anticipate and discuss common errors, such as gross distortion of features (hills and mountains too large), omission of significant features (lakes, valleys, dams), inaccuracy of slope (rivers running uphill), and errors in relative location of features (Appalachians and Rockies same height). Plan for gradual inclines from plains to hills to mountains where appropriate. Some teachers also find it helpful to show and discuss relief maps made by classes of preceding years.

Many relief maps can be made and used without coloring them in any way. The features will stand out clearly and the surface will speak for itself as children use the map. In other instances, the surface can be painted to highlight features and to show contrasts. Tempera water paint works very well; the surface can be protected by shellacking after it has dried. Enamel can also be used if the surface is first shellacked. Another effective technique is to place sawdust in a can or jar of powdered paint and to shake thoroughly. After coating the areas to be colored with glue, sprinkle the sawdust on and allow the glue to dry. Brush off any loose particles. Clean sand can be used in a similar manner. Be sure to plan carefully for the use of different colors on appropriate sections

Clay Relief Maps	Papier-Mâché Maps
Have a map to guide modeling.	Have a map to guide modeling.
Mix clay or use ready-mixed clay.	Put one layer of papier-mâché on outline map.
Spread the clay over an outline map.	Add other layers as needed for hills and mountains.
Build up mountains, hills, and valleys.	Form valleys and river channels.
Trace rivers with a pencil.	Allow the map to dry.
Use tiny sticks to show trees and other items.	Paint with enamel or water paints.

Chart 12–36   Chart 12–37

of the map so that they will be clear in contrast and consistent with standard uses of color on maps. See charts 12–36 and 12–37 for guidelines.

RECIPES FOR MODELING MATERIAL

Several different materials can be used to model relief maps. If the maps will only be used for a short time, use simple and inexpensive recipes; finishing the surface with paint and shellac is unnecessary. If the maps are used often, they should be well made and shellacked to protect the surface.

paste and paper
Tear paper towels or newspapers into one-and-one-half-inch pieces. Put paste on one piece at a time, wad it or shape it with your fingers, and stick it on the map outline. Build up hills and mountains as desired. Paint with tempera paint after the paste has dried.

paper strips and paste
Begin with crumpled paper to build up terrain, holding it in place with string or masking tape. Dip half-inch strips of toweling into wheat paste and place them on the crumpled paper form. After two layers have been placed on the map, coat the entire surface with paste and allow it to dry; secure the base of the map so that it cannot buckle. After the map is dry, paint with calcimine paint.

sawdust and paste
Mix any sawdust, except redwood or cedar, with wheat paste (from wallpaper store); spoon paste into sawdust until it is well moistened and of good modeling consistency. Good proportions are five cups of sawdust to one cup of wheat paste. The mixture may be applied directly to wood or cardboard. Paint it after it is dry.

papier-mâché
This is one of the most popular modeling materials. Tear twenty to twenty-five newspaper sheets (or paper towels) into fine shreds and soak them for twenty-four hours. Pulverize the soaked paper by rubbing it over a washboard or by kneading it. Add wheat paste (or four cups of flour and two cups of salt) until

410

Social Studies Workshop, University of California, Berkeley

Arrange relief maps and globe for ready reference while students
make maps.

mixture is of the same consistency as modeling clay. Build up mountains,
plateaus, and hills by applying papier-mâché mixture to the surface. After three
to six days of drying, paint elevations, water, and other features.

salt and flour   Mix equal parts of salt and flour, using only enough water to hold the ingre-
dients together. Apply to map outline, modeling the terrain according to plan.
(Keep out of humid places because salt attracts moisture).

burlap   Finished results can be obtained by immersing burlap in patching plaster. Build
and patching   terrain on outlines by using crumpled paper and masking tape. Lay a piece of
plaster   burlap (or towel) over the outline and cut along edges to get a good fit. Remove
burlap and soak it thoroughly in spackling compound that has been mixed to the
consistency of pancake batter; knead the plaster mix in so that the burlap is well
soaked. Lay the soaked burlap over the outline, fitting it into hills, valleys, and
other features. After about thirty minutes and before the plaster is completely
dry, paint with calcimine paint. If it is completely dry, the paint may flake and
crack.

plaster   Because maps made of plaster are heavy, many teachers use this material only
for small maps. Mix five pounds of plaster with two handfuls of wheat paste.
Add water to get consistency of modeling clay. Build up layers, let dry for
three to six days, and paint.

411

plaster and sawdust

Mix one pint of plaster, one pint of sawdust, and a quarter pint of paste that has been dissolved in water. Knead and apply to map outline. Paint after the mixture has set for fifteen to thirty minutes.

plaster and papier-mâché

Add two pints of plaster, a quarter tablespoon of LePage's glue, and a half pint of water to prepared papier-mâché. Be sure that the mixture is of modeling consistency. Paint after mixture has set for thirty to forty-five minutes.

plastic starch and detergent

Mix one part plastic starch with four parts detergent. Beat mixture until it is fluffy and apply to map outline. Be careful of the surface because it crumbles easily.

Questions, Activities, Evaluation

1. Which of the examples of map and globe use presented in this chapter might you incorporate in a unit you are planning? Can you think of additional uses of maps and globes in the social studies program?
2. Study a recently published map and check the legend, the use of colors, and the information presented. Can you find related pictures to illustrate items on the map?
3. Prepare a list of questions you can use with children to direct their attention to items on the map. Review the summary of map and globe concepts and skills to identify specific points to include in your questions.
4. Study the charts presented in this chapter and note ways you can adapt them for use in a unit.
5. Examine two or three social studies textbooks that contain maps and notice how they are discussed in the text. Note questions that can be answered by children as they use the maps. Refer to the accompanying teacher's manual for suggestions. Make an activity card based on one of the maps.
6. Select one of the map-making activities and indicate how you might use it in a unit.
7. Make a plan for using one of the modeling recipes to construct a relief map.

references

BROWN, JAMES W., RICHARD B. LEWIS, AND FRED F. HARCLEROAD, *A-V Instruction: materials and Methods* (5th ed.). New York: McGraw-Hill, 1977. Section on maps and globes; list of sources.

HAWKINS, MICHAEL L., "Map and Globe Skills in Elementary School Textbooks," *Journal of Geography,* 76 (December 1977), 261–65. Identification of skills; recommendations for improving instruction.

HANNA, PAUL R., ROSE E. SABAROFF, GORDON F. DAVIES, AND CHARLES R. FARRAR, *Geography in the Teaching of the Social Studies*. Boston: Houghton-Mifflin Company, 1966. Basic concepts and skills; list of sources of materials in appendix A; map and globe symbols in appendix B.

HARRIS, RUBY M., *Map and Globe Usage*. Chicago, Ill.: Rand McNally & Company, 1967. A handbook of teaching suggestions for all grades.

KENNAMER, LORRIN, "Developing a Sense of Place and Space" in *Skill Development in the Social Studies* (33rd Yearbook), pp. 148–70. Washington, D.C.: National Council for the Social Studies, 1963. Concepts and skills involved in using maps and globes.

PRESTON, RALPH C., AND WAYNE L. HERMAN, JR., *Teaching Social Studies in the Elementary School*. New York: Holt, Rinehart & Winston, 1974. Chapter on maps and globes.

RUSHDOONY, HAIG A., ed., *Social Studies Review*, 17 (Winter 1978). Issue on geographic education; articles on using space photos, aerial photos, and product distribution maps.

DEVELOPING ATTITUDES, VALUES, VALUING PROCESSES, AND DEMOCRATIC BEHAVIOR

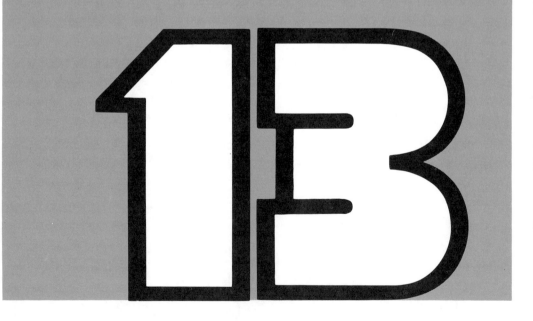

13

What strategies can be used to develop positive attitudes?
How can values education strategies be put to use in the social studies?
How can democratic values and behavior patterns be developed?

Strategies for achieving affective objectives of the social studies are presented in this chapter. Considered first is how attitudes are developed, with specific teaching strategies and examples given for units of instruction. Next, because values and valuing processes are so important not only in social studies instruction but also throughout the lives of students, they are examined in detail. The development of democratic values and behavior, a central goal of the social studies in particular and of education in general, is discussed in the final section.

Affective objectives are more difficult to achieve and assess than objectives centered on concepts, thinking processes, and skills. Outcomes are not readily observable, and as students mature they tend to exhibit attitudes and values that they believe to be important to their peers, members of their family, teachers, or members of other reference groups. In addition, some students may display what seems to be a positive attitude but in fact is not—for example, helping another student on a project may seem to be cooperative behavior when in fact the student wants to do something different. Furthermore, attitudes change slowly and values can take even longer to change. Although the change may be taking place, teachers may see little or no evidence of it. In spite of such difficulties, there are strategies that can and should be put to use in the social studies.

Development
of Attitudes

Whether we pay attention to their development or not, attitudes are inevitable outcomes of instruction. Too often in social studies, teachers give little thought to attitudes. Some assume that constructive attitudes develop "naturally" in the course of instruction. This may be true in *some* cases, but too much is at stake to leave attitude development to chance.

A DYNAMIC PROGRAM

Any instructional activity produces multiple learnings: concepts, appreciations, and attitudes do not emerge one by one. Students searching for necessary information in a study of pioneer life learn several things simultaneously: they will gather some new facts and learn how to locate information with greater skill; they should gain an appreciation of the hardships of the pioneers; they may discover how much easier it is to talk about needed information than it is to find it. Some outcomes may be more potent than those the teacher had planned. For example, the teacher's objective may be to improve study skills and student's grasp of certain ideas, but students *may* be developing poor attitudes toward the activity itself and even a dislike for the social studies program.

Because attitudes are rooted in feelings, activities in social studies should evoke positive emotional overtones. Positive attitudes and appreciations flourish in a dynamic learning situation. The two examples that follow highlight the importance of a dynamic program of instruction.

First, let us consider a group that is studying the westward movement in a rather dull, stultifying manner. Very little is being done to arouse the children emotionally, challenge their intellectual capabilities, or create motivation from within the context of their study. The objective of the lesson, in the teacher's plan at least, is to have the class find out how the pioneers obtained their food.

> *Teacher:* Today we are to study ways in which the pioneers secured their food. Our textbook contains information on how they got their food. Read pages 68 to 75 and keep a list of all the ways of getting food that you find in your reading. Raise your hand if you have a question.

Hardly a stimulating approach. Now look at another teaching situation. Here students and teacher are working together and attacking the same type of problem. Notice the difference in approach.

> *Teacher:* Yesterday as you dramatized life in Boonesboro, several of you raised questions about how food was secured. What were your questions?

Child A: Well, I was wondering how they got food outside of the stockade and how they brought it in.

Child B: Didn't they raise it right inside?

Child C: I was wondering how the women help to provide food.

Child D: I read that they had a hard time getting food in winter.

Child E: I think they ate nuts and berries and deer meat.

Teacher: Those are good suggestions. How do you think we could find some more information on their ways and means of securing food?

In the discussion that followed, the children themselves proposed many procedures for getting at this problem. The emotional response was especially gratifying. The group showed real interest as they proceeded to solve problems they found significant.

STRATEGIES FOR DEVELOPING CONSTRUCTIVE
ATTITUDES

Those who guide children must reflect positive attitudes. Teachers must be aware of their own attitudes. They must weigh their words carefully, and they must avoid facial grimaces, expressions of likes and dislikes, anecdotes and jokes, and any other evidences of negative attitudes, since children are quick to imitate and take on such behavior as their own. When children themselves exhibit negative attitudes toward others, they should be helped to find the reasons behind their behavior and to discover that their behavior is not consistent with such standards as fair play and respect for others. If a teacher accepts a child's negative behavior, it may lead other children to believe that the teacher approves of such behavior.

Knowledge and understanding properly learned and used, not just memorized, can lead to improvement in attitudes. All of us have heard someone say, "Had I known that, I would have acted differently." Or, "Is that so? Then we must do this." In using knowledge to improve attitudes, however, a common error is assuming that telling is teaching or that learning about something inevitably leads to a proper attitude toward it. This error can be avoided in part by centering the gathering of information on key problems as they arise, and by using this information to interpret the behavior of others and to solve emotionally charged problems. In addition, children should be guided to interpret facts in the light of fair play and other values. If any change in attitudes is to result, information must be put to use and interpreted in situations that have meaning to children.

Community activities are part of the attitude-building program. Children can participate in community activities; cooperation of parents and other adults can be elicited in developing positive attitudes; resource persons and community resources can be used in the school program. Festivals, pageants, holidays, and special events in which individuals of many different backgrounds participate are helpful. The spirit in which these activities are carried on and the skill with which children are made a part of them determine whether or not their contribution leads to changes in attitudes.

Symbolism and ceremony have long been used to develop values and attitudes. When approached in a way that develops clear insight into their significance, the following activities have been found to be helpful: flag ceremonies, observance of holidays, pageants, assemblies, musical programs that emphasize patriotism, exhibits, special television and radio programs, trips to historical shrines, anniversaries, films and filmstrips, and recordings. These contribute to the development of attitudes and ideals to the extent that children recognize their significance in their own lives and in the lives of others. Adults must also realize that the way they approach and participate in such activities greatly conditions the way children will react and learn.

As children mature, they tend to accept attitudes that are the result of their own thinking; hence, they need many opportunities to discover positive examples *on their own*. Discussion, group planning, group decision making, creative expressions, and actual participation in ceremonies and community activities may be used to help them make their own discoveries. Teachers should provide follow-up activities in which their discoveries can be applied, evaluated, and used again.

Experiences that kindle the imagination, create upbuilding emotional responses, and arouse positive feelings are also useful. Poetry, stories, drama, films, folk games, art, and music can all be used to create a *feeling tone* that promotes warmth, vitality, and other positive emotional reactions. Unless such feelings are developed, there will be no learning of a permanent nature. This is one of the major reasons why related experiences in art, music, and literature are so important in the social studies program.

Individual and group guidance techniques are sometimes needed to develop wholesome attitudes and to redirect behavior into more positive channels. Individual counseling and small-group discussion can be used as individual needs are discovered. Presentation of problem situations for group analysis and completion by the class of a story begun by the teacher are effective if related to problems that have arisen. Group standards and codes of behavior developed before study trips, interviews, and programs help to guide expression of attitudes in a positive way. Simple attitude inventories can be used as a basis for individual counseling and group discussion. Case conferences in which a particular child's difficulties are analyzed by the teacher and other school workers are helpful in unusual or extremely difficult cases. In some instances, specialists may be needed to assist in the development of a long-term program of therapy.

Role taking through dramatic activities and role playing give children opportunities to improve attitudes, release tension, identify with others, and find a positive role in group activities. In this way children may be guided to try *new* attitudes toward others, and as roles are played, they may gradually be helped to take on more positive attitudes or reject negative ones. An incident involving a negative attitude may be acted out, discussed, and reenacted in a positive way. After discussion of an incident, a positive portrayal of a solution may be tried. Through role playing, a problem situation may be dramatized creatively with a solution emerging as children portray what to them seems fair and reasonable. Children may act out roles in preparation for a situation they are about to face. Situations chosen to be dramatized will depend on the attitudes or problems needing emphasis. Meanwhile, the teacher tries to find clues to the children's feelings, needs, and values. These clues form the basis for discussion, planning, evaluation, and follow-up activities. A teaching strategy for role playing includes these steps:*

1. Warming up, in which the group clarifies the problem and interprets the problem story
2. Selecting participants, after describing or clarifying roles to play
3. Setting the stage by discussing use of space, order of action, and questions about roles
4. Preparing observers by assigning tasks and clarifying points to watch
5. Providing for role playing, with help as needed to begin and maintain it
6. Discussing and evaluating actions, ability to get inside the situation, and points made by observers, then considering proposed changes
7. Resumption of role playing, with emphasis on changes, next steps, and other points made by the group
8. Discussion and evaluation to make further changes
9. Sharing and generalizing, bringing in the similarity to experiences of students and values for use in future conduct

A child should not play the same role every time; roles should be rotated so that the feelings of others in given situations will become more real to each child. A child with one background can play the role of another, a leader can be a follower, or a child who finds himself or herself in one situation can take the part of a child in another. In selecting roles, however, a child should not be forced to take one for which he or she is unfitted or unwilling to try. Throughout, teachers should emphasize sincere expression of the roles being acted so that each child gets close to the feelings of the characters he or she portrays at different times. Once children grasp how others feel, they may begin to take on more positive attitudes toward them.

Direct instruction may be provided to get at attitudes underlying prejudice, to develop understanding of the nature of prejudice, and to eliminate it. The following example of a learning activity illustrates how this might be done.

*Fannie R. Shaftel and George Shaftel, *Role-Playing for Social Values: Decision Making in the Social Studies* (Englewood Cliffs, N.J.: Prentice-Hall, 1967).

Although it is presented in the form of an individual activity sheet, it can also be used as a small-group or a class activity.

Prejudice

Objective: To develop understanding of the nature of prejudice and ways to eliminate it

Focusing Questions: What is prejudice? How can it be eliminated?

Materials: dictionary; encyclopedia; textbook, *People in the Americas;* filmstrip, *Exploding Myths of Prejudice*

ACTIVITIES

Directions: Complete the following on a separate sheet of paper, not on this activity sheet.

1. Find and write the meaning of *prejudge,* as given in a dictionary.
2. Recall and list three prejudgments you have made of a person or thing in the past. For example, name one food that you prejudged before tasting it.
3. Find and write the meaning of *prejudice,* as given in a dictionary or an enyclopedia.
4. State how prejudging is a part of prejudice.
5. Find and write a definition of race prejudice, as given in the glossary of *People in the Americas.*
6. State how prejudging is a part of race prejudice.
7. After seeing *Exploding Myths of Prejudice,* complete the following:
   Examples of prejudging are _____.
   Myths about prejudice are _____.
8. List three things you can do to avoid prejudice:
9. You meet a person for the first time. Make a list of things you want to find out about this person while deciding whether or not to become friends. What prejudgments should you avoid? Why?
10. A person meets you for the first time. Make a list of things you want this person to find out about you while deciding whether or not to become your friend. What prejudgments do you want the person to avoid? Why?

Stereotypes also need to be considered as they are encountered in units of study, instructional materials, and experiences of students. Here are two examples of learning activities:

View a film such as *Stereotypes: African Girl Malabi* after listing students' responses to these questions:

What do you think Africans look like? What do they eat? How do they dress? What are their houses like?

Where did you get your ideas or mental pictures of Africans?

After showing the film, ask students to compare their responses to what they actually saw in the film.

Conclude by discussing how our mental pictures of others can lead to wrong ideas.

Evaluate statements that express stereotypes about a group in terms of fairness, equality, concern for others, or other defined criteria:

Which of the following statements are fair? Which are not fair? Why?

You cannot depend on members of *that* group.

All people are special in some ways.

Children should be seen and not heard when adults are around.

Housework should be done by girls.

People from that group are lazy.

Everyone knows that *they* are greedy by nature.

EXAMPLES IN UNITS OF INSTRUCTION

Every unit offers opportunities to develop wholesome attitudes toward others. Units on the home and family can be developed so that children discover many likenesses and common needs and at the same time understand differences among families in size, composition, type of home, roles of father and mother, religious affiliation, and the like. Children can be helped to understand that what seems natural to them may seem strange to others, and what is strange to them is natural to others. Each family wants to be respected and accepted by others, just as each child wants his or her own family to be accepted.

In units about the community, emphasis can be given to these understandings and appreciations: different types of work and services are essential; rules must be made and followed so that all may have justice and equality; differences among people should be respected, and all have a right to be themselves; positive attitudes toward others help to make a community a better place in which to live; and negative attitudes hurt others and reduce the effectiveness of those who hold them.

Units on state, region, or nation provide children with broader opportunities to discover contributions of others, common needs, examples of sharing, the great range of differences, and so on. Strength through diversity, power through teamwork, and unity through democratic values should be brought home realistically as reading materials, films, pictures, and other resources are used. A solid beginning can be made in developing appreciation of the contributions of individuals of different ethnic background, of interdependence among regions, of respect for the supreme worth of the individual, of the need for people with different abilities, and of the efforts of those who, from early days to the present, have tried to extend and preserve the rights of all people.

Appropriate attention should be given to ethnic and minority groups in units on community, state, or nation. The teacher can point out common misconceptions, stereotypes, and biases, and then discuss how they develop, why they should be eliminated, and how they work against attainment of basic democratic values. All students need opportunities to discover and take pride in the contributions of black Americans, Mexican-Americans, Puerto Ricans, Asian-Americans, native Americans, and others to our society. The abundance and variety of new materials make it possible to provide instruction leading to positive attitudes and basic understandings of lasting value.

Units on Africa, Mexico, Asian countries, and other areas may be developed to highlight the rich cultural heritages that exist in different parts of the world. All students, whether members of minority groups or not, need opportunities to develop appreciations of the creative ways in which very different societies have met and solved problems, interacted with other societies, and contributed to the growth of civilization.

*Strategies
for Developing
Values*

Many strategies have been proposed and used to develop, clarify, analyze, and act on values. They range from direct instruction (inculcation) and moral development to value analysis, value clarification, and action learning, as noted by Superka and others (see end-of-chapter references). Those most useful in the social studies program have been selected and adapted from the sources listed in the end-of-chapter references.

DIRECT INSTRUCTION

The most important direct approaches are modeling to set good examples, reasoned persuasion, and behavior modification. The following paragraphs present illustrative strategies for these direct approaches.

How does understanding of values help to explain human behavior in various cultures?

modeling to set examples

Models of valued behaviors are presented and discussed to provide good examples of honesty, fairness, cooperation, concern for others, and other values. The teacher, exemplary students, and others serve as models. Outstanding athletes, heroes and heroines in stories, film and television stars, great men and women, individuals from ethnic and minority groups, and other admired persons may be used as examples. Students are asked to find and share good examples and to criticize poor ones. High commendation is given to students who follow good examples and who set examples for others. At times, the teacher or another individual may play the role of devil's advocate and present a negative example for criticism.

reasoned persuasion

Sound reasons for accepting values and for behaving in accord with them are presented to students in a variety of ways. Individual conferences may be used, especially when problems and difficulties arise. Small-group discussions may be held to consider the common needs, concerns, and problems of a selected group of students. Large-group discussions may be used to emphasize the importance of values and related behavior. Episodes in films, stories, and other materials may be used to convince students of the value of accepting and living by democratic ideals.

behavior
modification

A variety of forms of behavior modification may be used to elicit and reward behavior that is consistent with desired values. In general, procedures such as the following are used:

1. *Specify behavioral objectives:* Demonstrate concern for others in discussion by taking turns, listening to others, and raising questions.
2. *State a criterion:* Janice will demonstrate the desired behavior 80 percent of the time in discussions during the coming week.
3. *Select a procedure:* Give Janice positive reinforcement through praise.
4. *Plan the environment:* Janice is to be moved from the rear of the room to the center.
5. *Carry out the procedure:* After discussing the situation, a contract is made and Janice participates in discussion according to plan. Praise Janice to reinforce desired behavior.
6. *Evaluate and repeat the procedure if necessary:* Provide for discussion with reinforcement and find out if Janice is meeting the criterion. If not, repeat the procedure or try a new one.

other direct
approaches

Emphasis on adherence to rules and regulations and the consequences of not following them are highlighted in all programs. Limiting choices in terms of maturity is used to aid students in analyzing issues and problems and in making decisions. Appeals to conscience and to adherence to the Golden Rule are used to get students to think more deeply about what is right and wrong in a given situation.

PLANNED QUESTIONING STRATEGIES

Three strategies that are closely directed by the teacher may be used to identify feelings, analyze problems, and identify values in events. The three strategies in charts 13–1 through 13–3 have been adapted from those developed in the Taba Curriculum Project (see Wallen and others in end-of-chapter references).

These strategies can be embedded in ongoing instruction and can be used in units all levels. They can be applied to stories, value-laden events and issues, problems faced by students and people under study, and incidents portrayed in films, case studies, or other materials. The strategy for clarifying feelings is helpful in getting students to identify with others, to project themselves into ''the other person's shoes.'' The strategy for analyzing problems helps to focus on what should be done to deal with a problem. The strategy for identifying values goes beneath the surface to find the values and reasons that underlie action in events.

A Strategy for Clarifying Feelings

Procedure	Focusing Questions	Illustrative Application
Recall and clarify the event.	→ What is the problem? What happened? What did they do?	→ What happened to Jim on the vacation trip?
Infer possible feelings.	→ How do you think they (he, she) felt? Why might they feel that way?	→ How must his parents have felt when he got lost? How do you think he felt? Why?
Infer other possible feelings.	→ What other feelings might have been involved? Why?	→ What other feelings might they have had? Why?
Infer the feelings of other persons.	→ How did others feel about it? The same? Differently? Why?	→ How did the ranger feel? The hikers? Why?
Relate to experiences of students.	→ Has something like that ever happened to you? How did you feel? Why?	→ Have you ever been lost? How would you feel in Jim's place? Why?

Chart 13–1

A Strategy for Analyzing Problems

Procedure	Focusing Questions	Illustrative Applications
Clarify the problem.	→ What is the problem? Issue? Difficulty?	→ Why is there so much litter around the school?
Identify alternative solutions and reasons for them.	→ What should be done? Why? What else might be done? Why?	→ What should be done about it? How can it be prevented? Are there other suggestions?
Identify strengths, weaknesses, and possible reactions.	→ Which is the best solution? What might the reaction be to each one?	→ Which proposals will work best? How might others react to them?
Relate to students' experiences.	→ Have you ever had a problem like this one? What did you do?	→ What has been done before? What did you do to help?
Identify reasons and related values.	→ As you look back, was that a reasonable thing to do? Why?	→ How did it work? Would you do it again?
Consider alternatives and reasons for them.	→ Is there anything you would do differently? Why?	→ What might be done differently this time? What might work better?

Chart 13–2

Procedure	Focusing Questions	Illustrative Applications
Clarify the facts.	→ What is the situation? What happened?	→ What did the story say was happening to the buffalo?
Identify main reasons.	→ Why did it happen? What reasons can you think of?	→ Why were they being killed? Are there other reasons?
Infer values from the reasons.	→ What do the reasons indicate is important to them?	→ What was most important to the hunters? The companies? The Indians?
Identify possible student action and reasons.	→ What would you do in the same situation? Why?	→ What do you think should have been done?
Identify student values from reasons.	→ How does this show what is important to you?	→ How does your view show what is important to you?

Chart 13–3

VALUE CLARIFICATION STRATEGIES

Value clarification strategies are designed to help students clarify their personal values. When clarifying values, provide an open atmosphere in which everyone's response is accepted, give students the right to pass if they wish, encourage honest and diverse responses and avoid questions or comments that inhibit thinking. A *value* is defined as something chosen, prized, and acted upon by the individual. The following processes are basic in the complete act of valuing:

1. *Choosing:* making choices freely, from among alternatives and after reflection
2. *Prizing:* cherishing the choice, being happy with it, and affirming it
3. *Acting:* acting on the value and doing so repeatedly

Many of the strategies proposed for clarification of personal values can be adapted for use in social studies units. The guiding principle is to use the strategies in connection with value-laden topics. The following examples have been adapted by the writer and teachers in workshops on valuing in social studies from strategies proposed by Raths, Simon, and associates (see end-of-chapter references).

clarifying responses — The values that underlie students' statements may be clarified by asking open questions that stimulate students to think through the values they hold and why they hold them. The teacher responds to comments about people, places, and activities under study by raising such nonjudgmental questions as these:

426

Is this what you mean? [The teacher restates a student's comment.]

Why do you feel (think, act) that way? How long have you felt that way?

Where did you get that idea? Are you glad you feel that way? Do others feel that way? Might some people feel differently about it?

Can you give an example of what you mean? Is that really what you feel (think, believe, value)?

What are some alternatives? Can you think of others?

value sheets   A value sheet is used with groups to provoke thinking about value–laden topics and issues: for example, neighborhood and community problems; state, national and international issues; civil liberties; treatment of ethnic groups; activities of individuals under study; and historical events. Value sheets are also used to stimulate thinking about friendship, courage, fairness, concern for others, and other value concepts in social studies materials.

An effective value sheet proposes a problem situation in a paragraph or two or even a single provocative statement. Sometimes pictures, cartoons, part of a film, or some other resource may be presented. As shown in the following examples, the presentation is followed by a few questions that focus on choosing, prizing, and acting.

Honesty

Recall the story of the pioneer boy who found the knife on the trail. What should he do about it? What would you have done? What does honesty mean to you? To your friends? In what ways do you show honesty? Your friends? How important do you think it is to be honest? If you plan to make any changes, what will they be?

The Future

"Change, change, change! People should expect even faster and greater changes in the next twenty-five years. Changes in homes, styles of living, friends, recreation, everything. And there will be changes in what we value." What do you think you will value most in twenty-five years? Which of the following will be most important? Least important? Rate each one from 1 to 5, with 1 indicating the most important, 2 the next, and so on.

Personal values: _____ health _____ wealth _____ hard work _____ liberty _____ intellect

Group values: _____ serving others _____ teamwork _____ respect for others _____ devotion to family _____ being generous

Social values: _____ education _____ welfare _____ law and order _____ patriotism _____ national freedom

Environmental values: _____ clear air _____ clean water _____ open space _____ use of energy _____ beautification projects

Might Makes Right!

What does this saying mean to you? What did it mean in the story we just read? In what situations should "might make right"? In what situations should it not? Why? How do you feel about using the idea in your relations with others?

voting   This simple and quick procedure for exploring values may be used as a springboard to discussion or study of a topic. The teacher poses the root question "How many of you . . . ?" in such forms as "How many of you think the city council should pass the new bicycle safety law?" "How many believe the schools should be open all year?" "How many of you would like to be a carpenter? A teacher? A nurse? A politician? An owner of a business?" Students in favor of a position raise their hands, students who are undecided fold their arms, and students who are opposed keep their hands down.

rank ordering   Students are presented with three or four alternatives and asked to place them in rank order:

Which are your first, second, and third choices for a career?
_____ health services _____ education _____ business _____ other
In what order of priority should these be placed?
_____ energy development _____ ecology _____ aid to the poor _____ school improvement
If you had been at the Alamo, how would you have ranked these?
_____ stay and fight _____ leave to save lives _____ leave but fight guerrilla warfare
Number in order five places that you would like to visit:
_____ China _____ England _____ Germany _____ Israel _____ France
_____ Japan _____ Russia

value surveys   Students are presented with a list of activities or values and are asked to check those they think are most important, or to rate them as to importance:

428

Imagine you are a legislator (or judge, merchant, and so on) and rate the following as to their importance, with 1 for most important, 2 next in importance, and 3 least important.

_____ honesty _____ fairness _____ wisdom _____ speaking ability
_____ cooperation _____ health _____ wealth _____ courage

Number the following in order of importance to you:
_____ happiness _____ health _____ wealth _____ education _____friendship
_____food _____ clothes _____family

Imagine you are an early settler in the West. Number the following in order of importance to settlers:
_____ happiness _____ health _____ wealth _____ education _____friendship
_____food _____ clothes _____family

position on a continuum
Students identify where they stand on an issue or problem by marking their position on a line at or between two extremes. A variation is to mark a line on the classroom floor and have students stand on the point indicative of their position. The following are examples:

Where do you stand on these issues?

Full freedom	Freedom in School	Strict rules
. . . .		

Always do it	Doing School Work	Forget it
. . . .		

Full control	Government Control of Energy Sources	No control
. . . .		

Completing unfinished statements
Several different forms of open-ended or incomplete statements may be used, as shown in the following examples:

I Wonder

After reading the story, I wonder _____.
After seeing the film on China, I wonder _____.
I wonder about _____.
I wonder why _____.
I wonder what would have happened if _____.

Feeling Best

I feel best in social studies when _____.

I feel best in discussion when _____.

A doctor must feel best when _____.

A child in colonial times must have felt best when_____.

Tucson, Arizona

How can completion of statements such as these improve the valuing process?

Feeling Proud

I am proud that I can_____.
I am proud of my schoolwork in_____.
A carpenter must feel proud when_____.
Teachers must feel proud when _____.

I Learned

In the unit on community workers, I learned that_____.
In the study of Martin Luther King, I learned that_____.
During the film on air pollution, I learned that_____.
From our guest speaker on energy, I learned that_____.
During the committee report on growth of our city, I learned that_____
_____.

I Was Surprised

While listening to the story about Helen Keller, I was surprised to find out
that _____.
In the unit on black history, I was surprised to find out that_____.
I was surprised that the president_____.
I didn't know that_____.

If I Were, or If I Had Been

If I were the mayor, I would _____.
If I were a union leader, I would_____.
If I were in charge of the schools, I would _____.
If I had been a city planner when our community was founded, I would have
_____.

If I had been an Indian when the colonists arrived, I would have _____
_____.

431

special diaries   Special diaries are focused on a single topic and may be an extension of several of the strategies noted above. For example, students may keep a diary from the beginning to the end of a unit. A series of valued ideas may be recorded and shared and discussed from time to time.

coat of arms   This strategy may be used to identify and record important traits, events, and contributions in the lives of individuals under study. Students are to find out and write the following on a shield divided into six spaces: (1) name of the individual, (2) field of work, (3) greatest contribution, (4) one quotation, (5) two wishes for today, and (6) a fitting motto.

weighing alternatives   Students evaluate alternatives related to issues or problems under study by listing and checking them, as shown below.

Check your position:

List alternatives	Should try it	Should study it	Should not consider it
1. _____	_____	_____	_____
2. _____	_____	_____	_____
3. _____	_____	_____	_____

either-or choices   Students are asked to choose between two alternatives. They may express their choices orally or in writing. Two students with opposing choices or views may pair off for discussion, or large-group discussion may be undertaken.

Should the city council increase or decrease spending on recreation?
Should ecology or jobs be given top priority in our community?
Should we increase or decrease contacts with Cuba?

Clarification strategies such as those presented above may be used as they best fit into lessons and units of study. They also may be used at appropriate

432

points in the strategies that follow—for example, to clarify issues, rank alternatives, put reasons for a position in order of importance, and assess consequences of actions.

MORAL DEVELOPMENT
THROUGH MORAL REASONING

Emphasis in this approach to values education is on stimulating students to develop progressively higher stages of moral reasoning (see end-of-chapter references by Kohlberg and Galbraith and Jones). The approach is based on Kohlberg's model of moral development, which includes these levels and stages:

Preconventional Level: reasoning based on consequences of action

Stage 1—punishment and obedient orientation; physical consequences determine goodness or badness

Stage 2—instrumental orientation; exchanging favors; helping each other

Conventional Level: reasoning based on conformity and loyalty

Stage 3—interpersonal concordance orientation; being a good boy or nice girl; conforming to get approval of others

Stage 4—law and order orientation; doing one's duty and showing respect for authority; loyalty to family and country

Postconventional Level: reasoning based on ethical principles

Stage 5—social contract, legalistic orientation; choosing right action in terms of standards or principles

Stage 6—universal ethical principle orientation; choosing right action in terms of universal principles of justice

Most elementary students are at the preconventional level, and most secondary students are at the preconventional and conventional levels; a few secondary students and some adults reach the postconventional level.

Philosophically, the program of moral development is rooted in a universally applicable conception of justice that is rational and cognitive. The view is held that moral principles are ultimately principles of justice and that central to justice are equality, reciprocity, and liberty. Concern for justice is evident at each stage of moral development, and one's conception of justice is reorganized at each higher stage. Justice, viewed as "an eye for an eye" at stage one, is restructured as equal exchange of goods and favors at stage two, followed by treating others in terms of group expectations at stage three and maintaining law and order at stage four. Justice as a social contract that protects equal rights of all is characteristic of stage five, followed by self-chosen principles of justice that embrace and respect equal rights for all at stage six.

teaching strategy The teaching strategy uses moral dilemmas that focus on such issues as authority, punishment, property, truth, civil liberties, conscience, property, contract, and social norms. Dilemmas may be presented orally or through a reading, filmstrip, or other medium (see *Values Education Sourcebook,* by Superka and others, listed in end-of-chapter references, for descriptions of materials). Students take positions on the dilemma, state reasons for positions, reflect on the reasons, consider consequences, and make a decision and defend it. Here is an example.

Should Alice Take Her Brother's Ball?

Betty was Alice's best friend. She had come to Alice's home to borrow a baseball. Betty had been chosen to play on a little league team and had promised to bring a ball, but didn't have enough money to buy one. She thought she could count on her best friend Alice to help her out. Alice didn't have a baseball, but her brother did. Alice liked Betty and wanted to keep her friendship. Yet she knew it was wrong to take something that belonged to someone else.

Should Alice take the baseball for her friend? _____ Yes _____ No
Why or why not? List your reasons below:

_____

_____

The teaching strategy for a dilemma such as this one includes these steps:

Moral Reasoning Strategy

1. *Present the dilemma:* Discuss it, define any unclear terms, and have students state it in their own words.
2. *Ask students to take positions:* Students take positions and give reasons for their positions.
3. *Present an alternative if there is little disagreement:* At least a 75/25 percent split of opinion is needed for good discussion. The following are possible alternatives or additions:
   a. If nearly all students believe Alice should take the baseball, state that Alice will have to buy a new one for her brother.

       b. If most believe Alice should not take the baseball, state that Betty will no longer be her friend.

4. *Provide small-group discussion:* Arrange groups of four to six students to identify and analyze reasons for each position and to prepare questions about reasons, both for and against, for presentation during class discussion. Circulate among groups, helping as needed and encouraging students to focus on reasons for positions.

5. *Guide class discussion:* Engage students in a critical examination of reasons, using such probe questions as the following:
       a. What are reasons for taking the ball? What are reasons for not taking it?
       b. What questions does each group have to put to the class?
       c. Which is more important, helping a friend or taking the ball? Why?
       d. What if Alice were in Betty's place? Should she expect Betty to take something for her? Why or why not?
       e. What might be the consequences if Alice took the ball? What if everyone took things to help friends?

6. *Provide follow-up activities:* Have students write a solution to the dilemma and list reasons for it, interview selected individuals to find other solutions and reasons, find related examples in social studies materials, or create a dilemma story that focuses on the same issue or another one.

guiding
discussion
    The teacher's role as discussion leader is basic to effective use of the strategy. Throughout the discussion of a dilemma emphasis must be given to what the central character or group *should* do. If students are asked what the person *would* do, the discussion shifts from moral reasoning to an analysis of the many factors involved in predicting behavior. The central objective is not to speculate about human behavior, but to sharpen moral reasoning.

    Student's reasoning can be improved by using probe questions such as these in group discussion:

    Perception-checking questions are used to clarify meaning, identify points of agreement and disagreement, and promote interaction among students:

       Are there any questions about what is happening in the story?
       What choice(s) does the person have?
       Can you state why that is important?
       Who can summarize the reasons given thus far?

    Issue-related questions focus students' attention on the particular issues involved in a dilemma:

       Should property rights be respected in this case? Why or why not?
       What obligation does she have to help a friend? Why?
       What punishment might she receive? Why do you think so?

Interissue questions focus attention on the conflicts between two or more moral values:

> Which is more important in this case, friendship or property rights? Why do you think so?
>
> Is it better to act on conscience or to help a friend? Why do you think so?

Role-switch questions encourage students to view issues from various points of view:

> From the point of view of Betty, what should she do? Why?
>
> Thinking in terms of what is best for her friend, what should Alice do? Why?

Universal consequences questions guide students to consider broader implications of their reasoning:

> Is it always important to do what a friend requests? Why or why not?
>
> What if everyone took this action? What might the consequences be? Why do you think so?

preparing
dilemmas

After several ready-made dilemmas have been analyzed, teachers and students may create ones related to topics under study. The following are steps in the procedure:

1. Identify a realistic issue in a unit, current event, or school activity:

> Should Jim join the John Brown's raid on Harper's Ferry? Why or why not?
>
> Should Mary tell on a friend who found ten dollars and does not want to turn it in to the school's lost-and-found office? Why or why not?
>
> Should Paul go along with the gang or obey school rules? Why?
>
> Should Mary follow her parent's advice or do as her friends suggest? Why?

2. Prepare an account to read aloud or to have students read that includes
   a. A central character or group facing conflicting choices such as telling the truth versus helping a friend, property rights versus human welfare, or freedom of speech versus maintaining the peace
   b. A concluding question that asks what the central character or group *should* do, then asks *why or why not* to get at reasons
3. Prepare alterations or additions to the dilemma to use if needed to get a division of opinion that will stimulate group analysis and discussion
4. Prepare probe questions to guide discussion and improve reasoning.

RATIONAL ANALYSIS

The central purpose of rational analysis approaches to values education is to develop students' ability to apply logical and scientific methods to issues and conflicts, in much the same way that they apply them to other topics in the social studies. The problem-solving model and the decision-making model previously discussed are quite similar to rational analysis models. One important difference is the deliberate testing or assessing of the value decision. This difference is illustrated in the following model that has been adapted from Metcalf (see end-of-chapter references).

Strategy for Analysis of Value-Laden Issues

1. *Clarify and define the value question or problem:* What is the problem? What issue or issues are involved? What terms need to be defined? What is to be judged?
2. *Gather purported facts:* What facts are available? Are others needed? Which are facts and which are opinions?
3. *Assess the facts:* How can the facts be checked? Which are supported by evidence? What do experts say?
4. *Clarify and select relevant facts:* Which facts are related to the issue or problem? Which are needed to make a value judgment or decision?
5. *Make a tentative judgment or decision:* What seems to be a reasonable judgment or decision? What are the reasons for it?
6. *Test the value principle inherent in the judgment or decision:* Does it apply to other cases? Is it consistent with other key values? Does it apply to everyone, including ourselves? What would the consequences be if it were adopted universally?

This model is especially useful in dealing with social issues and problems on which information can be obtained regarding the worth or goodness of solutions and proposals. As when using problem-solving and decision-making models, students gather and appraise information from a variety of sources. They sift out the critical facts and use them as the basis for a decision or value judgment. The final phase, testing the value principle by considering evidence and reasons, is of prime importance.

ACTION LEARNING

This approach provides opportunities for students to act on their values in the classroom, the school, and the community. The action projects selected should suit students' capabilities and level of maturity. Criteria such as those discussed in chapter 8, "Incorporating Current Affairs and Special Events," should be applied. The valuing strategies discussed in the preceding pages may be applied as the following strategy is used.

1. *Clarify the problem or issue:* What, if anything, should we do about the problem?
2. *Consider data and expert judgment, and take a position:* What are the facts? What do experts recommend? What is our position?
3. *Decide whether or not to act:* Should we get involved? What might we do? What are the actions we might take? What are the consequences?
4. *Plan and carry out action steps:* What steps should we take individually and as a group? Carry out the plan, making revisions as needed.
5. *Evaluate actions taken and project future steps:* Which actions were most effective? Which were least effective? What should we do in the future?

Notice that the action learning strategy is similar to the problem-solving and decision-making models discussed in earlier chapters. The main difference is that special emphasis is put on deciding whether or not to act, and if the decision is to act, *the action and evaluation follow.* Action learning is not limited to school and community projects; it can take place within the classroom as well.

Developing Democratic Values and Behavior

Renewed interest has been shown in developing attitudes and values through day-to-day activities in the classroom and in school.* The idea of a democratic school as a laboratory for learning, stressed by John Dewey decades ago, is currently viewed as a potent force in values education.

The school is the learning ground of democratic behavior, which is at the core of effective citizenship. The hidden curriculum, which includes learning acquired concurrently with the planned curriculum, is recognized as a potent force that can be used to achieve worthy objectives. The importance of making the classroom and the school a laboratory for learning democratic values and behavior has long been paid tribute in these two ageless bits of wisdom:

Actions speak louder than words.
We learn what we live.

The planned curriculum and the hidden curriculum must be brought together so that one does not counteract the other. Values taught in units of study should become a part of the daily living of students. The remainder of the chapter shows how this may be done.

*For example, see the article by Kohlberg (see end-of-chapter references) and Ronald S. Brandt, "On Moral/Civic Education: An Interview with Edwin Fenton," *Educational Leadership,* 34 (April 1977), 487–494.

Democracy is one of the most powerful ideas ever conceived. Its power and greatness stem from people's desire to govern themselves. It asks each individual to assume responsibilities; it emphasizes cooperation, not coercion; and it shows faith that with intelligence problems can be solved.

The democratic values and processes that are so important in our lives today constitute one of the richest parts of our cultural heritage. From the first concepts of democracy in the distant past to the great power of the democratic idea in the present, there has been a continuing struggle to win and extend human freedom and equality. If present and future generations are to extend that freedom and equality, they must thoroughly understand democratic values and processes:

Consent of the governed, equality of justice and opportunity, due process of law, general welfare

Use of intelligence and cooperative action to solve problems

Freedom of speech, press, assembly, religion, and inquiry

Individual rights, responsibility, creativity, and self-direction

Respect for majority rule, minority rights, and property

Faith in people's ability to improve conditions and solve problems

Open-mindedness, fair play, and respect for the views of others

Such values are part of instructional units in the social studies program. Units on family life, community living, our state, and the United States include much relevant material, and specific values are treated in depth in units on our American heritage, the Constitution, the Bill of Rights, and local, state, and national government. The conceptual foundations of values are developed by giving direct attention to the meaning of such concepts as consent of the governed, due process of law, and equality of opportunity. Both contemporary and historical events are considered to highlight the strength and enduring quality of basic values. As the outcome, students should appreciate the power of the democratic idea in the past and in the present. Instruction may be aimed at developing generalizations that can serve as guidelines for democratic living:

Government of a group is most effective if there is government by the group.
Human dignity is valued and each individual is accorded equal justice and opportunity.
Use of intelligence and freedom of inquiry are essential to the solution of problems.

STRATEGIES FOR MAKING APPLICATIONS

In addition to developing generalizations that include key values, students should have opportunities to practice democratic values and processes in daily activities. Participation and involvement give students a feeling for the self-discipline and individual and group responsibility, which are vital to democracy. The following examples illustrate how key values can be put to use.

Government of a group is most effective if there is government by the group. In classrooms where this value is applied, children have opportunities to develop group standards they can use in planning and working together. Individual and group work are evaluated in a way that helps each child grow in responsibility, self-control, and self-direction. Rules and regulations are viewed in the light of group welfare and individual rights and privileges. Changes are proposed and evaluated as new needs arise. Valuing strategies are used to analyze and evaluate problems that concern the group, as suggested later in this chapter. When such units as our community, our state, and our nation are studied, the class develops specific concepts that relate to government by the group. As children mature, they are given more opportunities to appreciate how their own contributions and those of others improve human affairs through government of, by, and for the people.

Each individual is respected and accorded equal justice and opportunity. Each child is respected as an individual who can make special contributions to group activities and who needs individualized learning experiences. Mutual respect among children is emphasized in an atmosphere that promotes individual and group effort, fair play, and concern for others. Children analyze contributions of men and women in their own and other ethnic groups and propose changes that should be made in the treatment of minority groups and women. Case studies of court decisions and selected events bring home the significance of due process and other rights. As the Constitution and its amendments are studied, students discover how it provides guidelines for extending equal justice and opportunity.

Freedom of inquiry and use of intelligence to solve problems are valued. Freedom of thought, speech, and belief are respected in the classroom, and emphasis is given to accuracy in reporting information, responsibility in checking its validity, analysis of various sides of issues and problems, and formulation of conclusions after careful study of the facts. Critical thinking and decision-making processes are put to use as students define issues and problems, clarify related values, consider alternative proposals, weigh consequences in light of values, and make decision or judgments on what should be done. Many units of study provide opportunities for students to discover that the efforts of individuals and groups to promote freedom of inquiry must be maintained and extended. The school and community serve as laboratories for making learning relevant and meaningful; they provide opportunities for students to participate in activities that call for freedom of inquiry and use of intelligence to solve problems.

DEMOCRATIC BEHAVIOR PATTERNS

Democratic values can be applied in other concrete and meaningful ways by giving attention to the development of democratic behavior patterns. The first step is to clarify inclusive categories of behavior consistent with the values and processes outlined above. The following behaviors are stressed in courses of study, instructional media, and units of study as key aspects of the American way of life.

responsibility   At the very center of the democratic idea is the concept that individuals can and will carry out responsibilities. Every right, privilege, decision, or plan of action carries related responsibilities. The success of democracy depends on people's accepting responsibility, both as individuals and as members of various groups.

Responsibility is developed in the social studies program as students plan, carry out, and evaluate learning activities. In the early grades they are taught responsibilities related to sharing and discussing ideas, using equipment and materials properly, and carrying out group work standards. The instructional program is extended in later grades to include a wide range of responsibilities in the classroom—planning group activities, preparing and giving reports, participating in discussion and other activities, keeping classroom morale high, and helping to improve the effectiveness of individual and group work. Concepts of responsibility are extended as students study the responsibilities carried out by members of the family, community workers, officials of government, great men and women of the past and present, and people in other lands.

concern   Individual development and group welfare are nurtured when concern for others
for others   is evident in all facets of living. Concern is often reflected in such expressions as "give them a break," "look out for others," and "lend a helping hand." Mutual respect, sensitivity to the needs of others, and a willingness to help are evident in the behavior of those who show concern for others.

Those who are developing concern for others rely on orderly methods of achieving purposes and consider the rights and responsibilities of others as well as their own. They begin to realize that respect is accorded others when differences in ethnicity, religion, status, and sex are considered, when common needs and similarities are recognized, and when differences are valued. They recognize the need for rules and duly constituted authority in the home, school, and community. As children mature, they begin to understand that in a democracy authority rests with the people and that maximum concern for others is secured only when the people give adequate time and thought to the problems of government.

open-mindedness   Critical thinking and problem solving, which are essential in a democracy, call for open-mindedness. Group action is most effective when all points of view are considered in planning and evaluation. Individual study and action can be improved when many ideas are considered and a critical selection is made of those that are most appropriate in a situation. Prejudice and superstition can be rooted out as differing points of view and authenticated facts are considered. As Jefferson put it, "Error of opinion may be tolerated where reason is left free to combat it."

Those who are developing open-mindedness consider and explore the value of the ideas of others as well as the value of their own. They are learning to be impartial, to report facts accurately, to analyze problems, and to appraise the validity of information. They consider facts and opinions in the light of the source from which they were obtained, their relationship to issues and problems, and their usefulness in solving problems. They seek better ways of doing things, establish reasons for making changes in ongoing activities, and support their beliefs with evidence and reason. They are growing in the ability to recognize the impact of feelings on their thinking and in the ability to curb emotions that lead to bias, prejudice, and erroneous conclusions. They are beginning to recognize the closed mind and the propaganda techniques used to instill distorted facts and ideas in the minds of susceptible individuals.

Units of work on the community, state, nation, and other settings reveal how open-mindedness has been a potent factor in clarifying issues and solving problems. The advantages of an open society in which problems are examined and discussed freely become even more evident when the disadvantages of a closed society in which selected doctrines must be followed are analyzed.

creativity   Much of America's greatness has come from the creativity of its people. Through the years Americans have found new ways of doing things as frontier after frontier has been reached and passed and new ones opened. America's children need opportunities to develop creative ways of doing things so that democratic living will be continually improved by a constant flow of new ideas.

Students show creativity through new or original responses to solving problems, organizing and expressing ideas, using materials, carrying out plans, and making improvements in individual and group work. Those who are growing in creativeness search for and use new ideas to solve problems and to express thoughts and feelings. They are sensitive to originality in others and are growing in their appreciation of the creative contributions made by individuals in the past and in the present. They are growing in the ability to express ideas clearly in oral and written form, as well as through various art media, and they are developing an appreciation of the ability of others to express ideas creatively. As they study various units, they are developing an understanding and appreciation of the value and importance of creativity in the lives of people at home and in other lands.

cooperation   Cooperation is essential to effective group action in a democratic society. The teamwork required in industry, education, science, government, and other significant fields illustrates this point. From the early days when neighbors worked together to raise the walls of a log cabin or to have a town meeting to the present time when a crew of workers erects a skyscraper or a group participates in a meeting of the city council, our progress has virtually depended on our ability to cooperate. Now cooperation among nations has become necessary not only for progress but also for survival itself.

Those who are developing cooperative behavior pool ideas, make plans, carry them through to completion, and evaluate the effectiveness of their work. When plans are changed on the basis of group decisions, they continue to work with others to achieve common goals. As they study various topics in social studies, they discover examples of cooperation in the home, school, community, state, and nation. As they mature and undertake more advanced studies, they gain insight into the need for teamwork in solving international problems, and they critically assess the actions of individuals and agencies working together to improve human welfare.

Strategies for Developing Democratic Behavior

Each social studies unit should help build the values that are at the base of democratic behavior; each unit should also help children to learn and practice the kind of behavior that demonstrates democratic values. Three interrelated strategies may be used. First, plans must be made for specific things that children can *do,* since democratic attitudes and behavior are best learned through active and reflective participation. Second, plans should be made for children to *observe* democratic behavior in action in the school and community. Third, plans must be made for children to *study* and *analyze* democratic behavior as portrayed in books, films, and other instructional resources. Notice the three levels of abstraction in the suggested planning: doing, observing, and studying. Although actual doing is essential, observing and studying should not be minimized, for they make it possible to extend and enrich the concept of democratic behavior. The two examples that follow illustrate the kind of planning that should be undertaken in each unit.

In a home and family living unit, cooperation among young children may be developed to higher levels through experiences such as the following:

Doing—planning and arranging a playhouse; sharing tools and materials, working together, and helping each other make furniture, home furnishings, dishes, table settings, dolls and doll clothes, pet cages, and scrapbooks; planning and participating in dramatic representation centered on home activities; making and carrying out standards to use on a study trip to see a home under construction; taking turns and sharing in a group discussion of unit activities

Observing—members of the family working together at home; children cooperating at home and at school; monitors and committees at work; men working together to build a house in the neighborhood; ways in which the janitor, teachers, and children in school work together to make the school a happy, clean place in which to work and play

Studying—pictures, filmstrips, and films showing members of a family gardening, cleaning the yard, shopping, and having fun together; picture and story books that portray cooperation among children, children and parents, and adults taking part in neighborhood activities; stories and poems that highlight teamwork in home and family living (Responsibility, creativeness, concern for others, and open-mindedness may be outlined in a similar manner for this unit of instruction.)

To illustrate ways to develop democratic behavior in upper grades, a unit on life in early America has been selected. Specific attention is given to ways in

which creativity may be developed; other categories of behavior may be analyzed in a similar manner.

> *Doing*—planning and using a variety of ways to organize information, for example,
> pictorial summaries, booklets, dioramas, and slides; creating songs and rhythms
> related to such activities as quilting, husking, hunting, weaving, and churning;
> making instruments to accompany songs and rhythms; drawing pictures and
> murals; making candles, dolls with authentic costumes, utensils, and other objects
> for use in creative dramatics, discussion, and reports
>
> *Observing*—individuals invited to school to demonstrate the use of spinning wheels,
> looms, and other objects; models, utensils, quilts, and other objects arranged in an
> exhibit or museum to highlight creative uses of materials in early times; authentic
> folk dances and songs performed by community or school groups; plays, pageants,
> and television programs to celebrate holidays and events of historical interest;
> creative contributions made by members of the class as the unit of work develops
>
> *Studying*—pictures, films, books, and other instructional materials that portray
> creativeness in the use of resources for food, shelter, and clothing; art, music, and
> literature of early times; contributions of great men and women during the early
> days of our country; explorers and ways in which they blazed trails and opened up
> new territories

These examples illustrate practical procedures that teachers have used to
develop democratic behavior. The point should be emphasized that examples on
the doing level can be found in nearly all activities in the social studies program
that involve group work; they can also be found in daily living and throughout
the school program. On the observing level, children can be guided to notice
examples in the classroom, elsewhere in the school, and in the community. As
historical units or units on faraway places are developed, the children can see
plays, festivals, pageants, and programs developed by school and community
groups and demonstrations by individuals invited to school. On the studying
level, books, films, filmstrips, and other resources offer many good examples
of democratic behavior. Television and radio programs should not be overlooked, particularly those related to topics in social studies. Finally, current
events are a good source of examples. Occasionally a bulletin board of pictures
and clippings can be arranged to emphasize concern for others, open-
mindedness, or one of the other categories of behavior. By giving systematic
attention to the development of democratic behavior in all these ways, a practical and realistic contribution to citizenship can be made in the elementary
school. Indeed, it is difficult to think of a more *basic* outcome of education!

 Questions, Activities, Evaluation

1. Examine a social studies textbook and note examples of each of the following: attitudes, prejudices, stereotypes, moral issues, social issues, democratic values, and democratic behavior.
2. How might you guide study and discussion of them? Which of the teaching
   strategies might you use? Make a plan to show how you would use them.

3. Prepare a list of ways in which democratic values and behavior might be developed in a unit you are planning to teach. Make a worksheet for each category of behavior—for example, responsibility:

Doing: _____

_____

Observing: _____

_____

Studying: _____

_____

Note specific examples in the appropriate spaces. Share and discuss your examples with others.

4. What is your position on the following? Check your position and discuss it with others.

Yes No ?

a. Values are personal, intimate, and private. The schools should take a hands-off policy and leave the teaching of values to the family and church. ___ ___ ___

b. The schools should make certain that students understand and adopt values that are basic in our society (for example, equality and justice). ___ ___ ___

c. The schools should not only develop an understanding of values but should also involve students in projects that apply and extend such values as equality and justice. ___ ___ ___

d. A reasonable position is to respect students' privacy but to help them think about feelings, actions, and conflicts in order to increase self-understanding and awareness of their values. ___ ___ ___

e. The schools should develop the skills and processes needed to deal with a variety of value-laden issues; they should not try to teach a selected set of values. ___ ___ ___

f. The schools should provide instruction that develops students' ability to engage in moral reasoning and thus attain the highest possible level of moral development. ___ ___ ___

g. There is some merit in all of the above, depending on the situation in which one finds oneself. ___ ___ ___

h. All of the above should be rejected. A better position is

_____.

references

BEYER, BARRY K., "Conducting Moral Discussion in the Classroom," *Social Education,* 40 (1976), 194–202. Procedures for guiding moral discussions.

FRAENKEL, JACK R., *How to Teach About Values: An Analytic Approach.* Englewood Cliffs, N.J.: Prentice-Hall, 1977. Emphasis on rational analysis; critiques of other approaches.

GALBRAITH, RONALD E., AND THOMAS M. JONES, *Moral Reasoning.* Minneapolis; Minn.: Greenhaven Press, 1976. A handbook with sample dilemmas and techniques for developing moral reasoning.

KOHLBERG, LAWRENCE, "Moral Education for a Society in Moral Transition," *Educational Leadership*, 33 (1975), 46–54. Outline of stages of moral development; argument for participatory democracy in a just community school.

METCALF, LAWRENCE E. ed., *Values Education* (41st yearbook). Washington, D.C.: National Council for the Social Studies, 1971. Rationale, strategies, and techniques for analysis of values.

RATHS, LOUIS E., MERRILL HARMIN, AND SYDNEY B. SIMON, *Values and Teaching*. Columbus, Ohio: Charles E. Merrill Publishing Company, 1966. Concrete suggestions for working with values in the classroom.

SIMON, SIDNEY B., LELAND W. HOWE, AND HOWARD KIRSCHENBAUM, *Values Clarification*. New York: Hart Publishing, 1972. Collection of practical strategies based on the Raths model.

SUPERKA, DOUGLAS, CHRISTINE AHRENS, AND JUDITH E. HEDSTROM, *Values Education Sourcebook*. Boulder, Colo.: Social Science Education Consortium, 1976. Chapters on approaches; reviews of materials for teachers and students.

WALLEN, NORMAN E., AND OTHERS, *Final Report: The Taba Curriculum Project in the Social Studies*. Menlo Park, Calif.: Addison-Wesley Publishing Co., 1969. Valuing strategies for analyzing feelings and problems.

EVALUATING STUDENTS' LEARNING

14

What guidelines should be used to evaluate learning? What devices and procedures are most useful?

How can self-evaluation by students be provided?

How can charts, checklists, and other devices be used in ongoing evaluation?

How can test items be constructed to fit instruction?

Students' learning is evaluated to determine the extent to which objectives have been achieved and to make decisions about needed program improvements. The evaluation process includes such phases as (1) stating objectives, (2) collecting, organizing, and interpreting evidence on the achievement of objectives, and (3) using interpretations to improve instruction and report pupil progress. Although the teacher plays a central role, students are also involved, through self-evaluation, and the principal and other school personnel provide assistance.

Evaluation has many functions in the social studies program. Objectives can be clarified and redefined as a result of the appraisal of children's learning. Through evaluation, teachers gain insights into children's progress—their problems, strengths, and weaknesses. Evaluative evidence is helpful in planning units, guiding learning activities, selecting materials of instruction, appraising methods of teaching, and revising the instructional program. Feelings of security for both the teacher and children can be enhanced if results are used constructively to strengthen the program. Finally, evaluation is essential in gathering evidence needed to interpret and report student progress and to carry out an accountability program.

Assessment may be done at the local, state, and national levels. Local assessment includes needs assessment to determine the discrepancy between the teacher's goals and students' achievement; it also includes the continuing appraisal of students' learning during each unit of instruction. Statewide assessment tends to emphasize achievement in reading and arithmetic. The National Assessment of Educational Progress, a project of the Education Commission of the States, includes the testing of nine-, thirteen-, and seventeen-year-olds in social studies, citizenship, and other areas. Available reports include data on male-female differences, regional differences, type of community, performance of blacks, and educational level of parents. The program's purpose is to provide baseline data on achievement and on progress in meeting objectives believed to be of nationwide importance.*

Guidelines to Effective Evaluation

Evaluation should be based on several guiding principles that serve as a framework for developing and using evaluative devices effectively in all aspects of appraisal. They may be used in guiding self-evaluation, in teacher appraisal of classroom experiences, and in appraising the overall effectiveness of the program.

POINT OF VIEW

A teacher's point of view serves as a lens to focus evaluation. For example, if a teacher places high value on the development of attitudes and values, then evaluation will focus on the extent to which students develop those attitudes and values stressed in instruction. If he or she values mastery of concepts and related information, then evaluation will focus on mastery of knowledge taught in a given unit of study. Ideally, the teacher will hold a comprehensive point of view, one that values all objectives of the social studies: knowledge, thinking processes, skills, and attitudes, values, and behavior patterns. Although some objectives may be given priority, none should be overlooked as learning is assessed.

INTEGRATING EVALUATION WITH INSTRUCTION

Evaluation should be an integral part of instruction. Effective teachers observe and note students' progress and needs; they make changes to improve instruction. Some of the most valuable assessment procedures—discussion, teacher observation, short tests, and checklists—provide immediate feedback, to the benefit of both teachers and students.

*National Assessment of Educational Progress, 700 Lincoln Tower, 1860 Lincoln, Denver, Colorado. *NAEP Newsletter* and list of reports available on request.

ONGOING APPRAISAL

Throughout the day, from day to day, and throughout the year, teachers should continually evaluate students and students should evaluate themselves. The teacher carries out diagnostic, formative, and summative evaluation. Diagnostic evaluation identifies individual and group needs. Formative evaluation provides evidence on daily learning and the effectiveness of instruction. Summative evaluation at the end of units provides evidence on the attainment of unit objectives. All three should be blended together as a part of instruction and used to improve teaching and learning.

COOPERATIVE PROCESS

Teachers, supervisors, administrators, parents, and students should work as a team to improve evaluation since all have a stake in the program. Teachers and students share in clarification of objectives and using techniques of appraisal. Group evaluation and self-evaluation are guided by the teacher and based on standards developed in cooperation with the students. Parents should be encouraged to discuss goals and achievements of their children. Supervisors and other school personnel should provide assistance and work with teachers to develop a balanced and effective evaluation program.

CLEAR OBJECTIVES

A central function of evaluation is to determine to what extent objectives are achieved. In any appraisal, whether by the teacher or children, objectives should be clear. Clarity may be achieved by stating objectives in performance or behavioral terms, as indicated in chapter 1. To give an example, responsibility may be appraised specifically and concretely when defined in terms of the student's ability to (1) state ways to carry out the tasks agreed upon in group planning, (2) state rules to follow in individual and group activities when little or no teacher supervision is provided, (3) describe and use a variety of data sources without help from others, and (4) describe improvements that can be made in group and individual work.

VARIETY OF SITUATIONS

Children's growth in attitudes, interests, concepts, and group-action skill can be appraised in group planning, discussion, sharing, reporting, and evaluation. How students behave in dramatic activities, construction, rhythms, and role playing reveals many evidences of growth. The ways they use materials, share materials with others, take and give suggestions, accept newcomers, and work together are of special importance. Students should be evaluated in these and other situations to determine whether key learnings are carrying over to their behavior.

Creative efforts also reveal evidence of learning. A teacher should be alert to new ideas; new ways of doing things; originality in construction, dramatic play, and artistic expression; and suggestions that arise in group discussion. These are excellent clues to cognitive and affective development.

VARIETY OF DEVICES

Many different instruments and techniques of assessment are needed to gather information on outcomes of instruction:

Observation	Teacher-made tests	Charts	Logs
Discussion	Published tests	Checklists	Diaries
Interview	Inventories	Pupil graphs	Anecdotal records
Case conference	Questionnaires	Rating scales	Behavior journals
Case study	Sociometric tests	Activity records	Evaluative criteria
Autobiography	Semantic differential	Samples of work	Cumulative record

Which assessment devices are selected depends on the objectives to be evaluated, the conditions under which children are working, and the type of behavior involved. If a teacher wants to gain insight into the *use* of concepts, attitudes, or group processes, the children should be observed in discussion, dramatic play, construction, or similar situations. The ways in which children use concepts and attitudes may be recorded in anecdotal records, a behavior journal, or a specially prepared recording form. If, on the other hand, a teacher must determine the *accuracy* of concepts or the attitudes of children toward certain objects or persons, tests or attitude questionnaires should be used.

Of course, the teacher should not use only one device to evaluate a given objective. Observation may be used continuously even though checklists, ratings, or tests are employed. A combination of devices is generally better than a single device. The important point is to decide on the kind of evidence needed, and then to select and use those devices that will secure it. For example, in a social studies workshop, one group proposed the following methods for evaluating particular outcomes:

Concepts and main ideas—observation, group discussion, tests, samples of work, individual and small-group interviews

Thinking processes—observation, group discussion, charts, checklists, interviews, samples of work

Basic skills—observation, tests, charts, checklists, group discussion, worksheets, rating devices

Attitudes, values, and behavior patterns—observation, questionnaires, checklists, rating devices, anecdotal records, recordings, discussion, interviews

As far as possible, assessment instruments selected for use in social studies should meet the criteria of validity, reliability, objectivity, practicality, applicability (curricular validity), usefulness, appropriateness, and descriptiveness. The instruments should measure what they purport to measure and should do so consistently and accurately. They should give similar results for different persons and be easy to administer, relatively inexpensive, and not too time-consuming. They should be related to the social studies program, contributing evidence that can be put to use. They must also be appropriate to the level of development of the group with which they will be used and fit into the overall program of evaluation, and the evidence they give should describe the behavior of children.

SELF-EVALUATION

Self-evaluation that promotes increasing self-direction is an essential aspect of evaluation in social studies. Through self-evaluation, children gain the ability to analyze their own skills, attitudes, behavior, strengths, needs, and success in achieving objectives. They develop feelings of personal responsibility as they appraise the effectiveness of individual and group efforts. They learn how to face squarely the competencies needed in various tasks and to assess their own potential and contributions. Their role in group processes can be clarified as they check themselves on cooperatively made criteria. Social learning is sharpened and enriched through self-evaluation because the child is participating more extensively in the learning process. The ability to appraise themselves is an ability that students will use throughout their lives.

If children are to be capable of self-evaluation, they must learn how to develop objectives to guide their evaluative efforts. This may be done through group discussion. Attention must also be given to the preparation of checklists, charts, and rating devices that children can use. The following devices are commonly used to promote self-evaluation:

> Group discussions and interviews
> Samples of the child's work gathered through the term
> Standards developed by the group and placed on charts
> Checklists made by the individual or group
> Scrapbooks made by each child
> Diaries or logs containing examples of ways the child has been cooperative, has shown concern for others, and so forth
> Recordings of discussion, reporting, singing, and so forth
> Achievement graphs kept by each child

ORGANIZATION FOR INTERPRETATION

Information should be summarized in a form that can be easily interpreted. If a picture of the status of children in a class is needed, a list may be prepared giving each pupil's name with related data summarized in tabular form. If information on a child's attitudes or interests is needed, a simple profile may be developed. In other instances, graphs, charts, summaries of anecdotes, sociograms, or a complete case study may be used.

In addition, a cumulative record should be kept for each child. The cumulative record gives a composite picture of growth. It should include space to record information about units of instruction the child has completed, growth in problem-solving ability, social attitudes, democratic behavior, skill in group work, interest in social studies, and strengths and weakness in various types of activities. Subsequent teachers can use such information to make more effective plans for the child's continued growth.

INDIVIDUAL INTERPRETATION

Each child has a unique rate of growth and development, personality, background, level of achievement, interests, problems, and needs. A child's growth to increasingly higher levels of behavior (not merely the child's status in the group or position with reference to national norms) should be the concern of each teacher. Setting arbitrary standards for all children is unrealistic and impractical.

Norms are helpful, however, as a frame of reference for considering the relative achievement of an individual or a group. If a bright child falls far below the average, the reason for the deviation should be studied. If a group "deviates from the norm," the reasons for the deviation should be investigated. After the reasons for the deviations are determined and the needs of the child or group are established, steps can be taken to provide learning experiences.

APPLICATION

Data gathered by the teacher or by the children through self-evaluation should be used to improve learning. Group evaluation in the classroom should reveal next steps, needs for materials, new sources of ideas, and improved standards of work. Overall evaluation of the effectiveness of the program should lead to clarification of objectives and better use of activities, materials, and evaluative techniques. Conferences with parents and interpretation of the program are other illustrative uses of evaluative data. Evaluation that does not lead to improvement is just another form of busywork.

THE ACCOUNTABILITY SYSTEM

One major use of evaluation data and procedures is in the accountability systems that have mushroomed in school districts throughout the country in recent years. Evaluation data on the social studies program are fed into the accountability system along with data from other subjects. The attainment of objectives set by teachers is appraised and the findings used to improve the

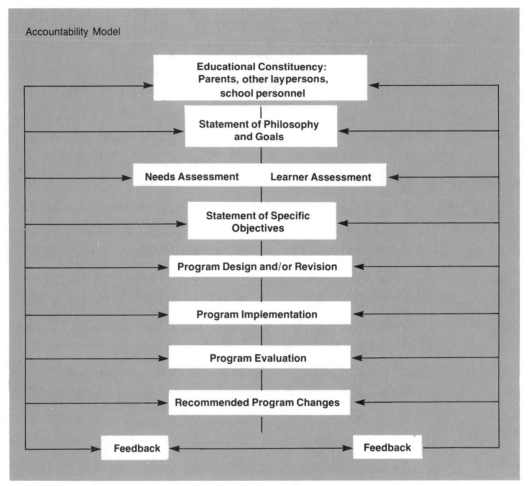

Accountability Model

Educational Constituency:
Parents, other laypersons,
school personnel

Statement of Philosophy
and Goals

Needs Assessment   Learner Assessment

Statement of Specific
Objectives

Program Design and/or Revision

Program Implementation

Program Evaluation

Recommended Program Changes

Feedback   Feedback

Chart 14–1

instructional program. The findings are also used as feedback to make changes in various components of the accountability system, as shown in chart 14–1.

Accountability systems include procedures for evaluation of the performance of teachers and other school personnel. Many systems use pupil progress toward the attainment of specified objectives as the basis for appraising the work of teachers. The teacher and evaluator should cooperatively determine the objectives to be assessed by completing initial planning sheets that identify terminal instructional objectives and specify related instructional objectives. Preassessment and postassessment measures are used to determine pupil progress. The teacher and evaluator cooperatively determine the means of assessment, which may include observation, checklists, test items, and other methods. The following examples illustrate this procedure at two different grade levels.

Accountability Assessment

GRADE 3

Terminal objective. To distinguish between rules and laws

Instructional objective. Given several examples, the student will state which are rules and which are laws

Preassessment. Write an *R* by each item below that is a rule; write an *L* by each item that is a law.

_____ Crossing streets at a signal

_____ Taking turns in a game

_____ Not running in the halls

Postassessment. Write an *R* by each item below that is a rule; write an *L* by each item that is a law.

_____ Not throwing rocks at passing cars

_____ Asking permission to leave the classroom.

_____ Not taking things belonging to others.

GRADE 5

Terminal objective. To identify contributions of Americans of different ethnic backgrounds to our culture

Instructional objective. Given a list of individuals, the student will write at least one contribution each has made

Preassessment. Write one contribution of each person listed below:

W. E. B. Du Bois _____

Susan B. Anthony _____

Edward R. Roybal _____

Postassessment. Write one contribution of each person listed below:

George Washington Carver _____

Harriet Tubman _____

César Chavez _____

A well-designed accountability system avoids such pitfalls as specifying easily attainable objectives, overemphasizing skill objectives at the expense of other objectives, making unwarranted comparisons between classes and schools, failing to interpret data in terms of background factors, scapegoating of teachers, and failing to give highest priority to instruction geared to individual differences. In short, the previously noted guiding principles should operate throughout the program, and accountability systems should contribute to, not detract from, the improvement of children's learning and the professional integrity of school personnel.

Assessment Techniques

OBSERVATION BY THE TEACHER

Day-to-day observation of children gives a developmental picture of growth that cannot be obtained in any other way. It is especially effective in social studies because of the variety of experiences the program provides. Children themselves create new and different situations (such as forming groups, meeting new problems, and locating new sources of information) in which learning may be observed. A teacher may create other situations in which specific concepts, attitudes, and skills may be observed; their carry-over to out-of-school enterprises may also be noted. The actual behavior of children in new situations—the goal of the experienced evaluator—thus becomes the focal point of evaluation.

The uses of observation for evaluative purposes are as varied and numerous as the types of experiences provided in the social studies program. A teacher may obtain evaluative data by listening to discussions, oral reading, dramatic play, comments about objects or persons, questions, and spontaneous expression during construction or on study trips. Watching children at work and at play provides data about interests, attitudes, concern for others, group processes, use of time and materials, use of skills, physical ability, emotional adjustment, attentiveness, persistence, ability to carry out directions, and acceptance of responsibility. For example, information on students' attitudes can be obtained by observing and noting:

1. Positive or negative statements made about an individual, group, object, organization, or activity
2. Number of times reference is made to the above in positive and negative terms
3. Willingness or unwillingness to work or play with an individual or group, or to defend or help others in time of need
4. Expressions of preferences, likes, dislikes, opinions, and reactions regarding individuals, groups, objects, and activities

In using observation as an evaluative device, teachers must recognize that similar types of behavior may reveal different kinds of learning. Different purposes, needs, and backgrounds produce different responses. Some children offer to help others because they are growing in cooperative skills; others offer help because they want to move in on another's activity. Some children may accept one responsibility eagerly to avoid another more important one, whereas some accept it because it is in line with objectives. A teacher can gain competence in recognizing and meeting these problems by knowing each child's background and by becoming a skillful observer.

Checklists are helpful guides to observation (and student self-evaluation). They should be specific, descriptive of desirable behavior, and easy to use. They may be used as overall guides in many situations, or they may be applied specifically to the child's behavior in planning, discussion, research, or construction. Checklists 14–1 and 14–2 are illustrative. Other checklists are presented in later sections of this chapter.

Checklist 14–1
Appraisal of Study Habits and Attitudes
during Research Period

	NAMES OF CHILDREN
BEHAVIOR TO BE OBSERVED	
Locates sources of information	
Uses the contents	
Uses the index	
Gets information from study aids— charts, tables, maps	
Uses encyclopedias effectively	
Uses dictionaries effectively	
Uses library facilities	
Takes notes related to topics under study	
Uses correct form in outlines	
Organizes information from several sources	
Arranges ideas in good order	
Selects illustrative material for reports	

Checklist 14–2
Concern for Others

Note: Check each child two or three times during the term to determine if growth has taken place.

Teacher _____
Date _____

	NAMES OF CHILDREN
BEHAVIOR TO BE OBSERVED	
Is sensitive to needs and problems of others	

Helps others meet needs and solve problems	
Willingly shares ideas and materials	
Accepts suggestions and help	
Makes constructive suggestions	
Sticks to group plans and decisions	
Works courteously and happily with others	
Gives encouragement to others	
Respects the property of others	
Enjoys group work	
Thanks others for help	
Commends others for contributions	

The kinds of charts, rating devices, and other assessment instruments that children can use in self-evaluation may be discovered through teacher observation. For example, after noting specific needs and problems in a discussion, one teacher guided the class in the development of a chart that listed these points: (1) stick to the topic; (2) be brief so that others may have a turn; (3) speak so all can hear; (4) give turns to others; and (5) listen to others.

The effectiveness of observation as an assessment device may be improved by following these guidelines:

1. Be alert to the uniqueness of each child and to creative contributions.
2. Look for constructive, improved behavior; avoid fault-finding.
3. Do not assume that similar expressions of behavior indicate the same learning for all students.
4. Be aware of your own feelings and attitudes toward students.
5. Be sensitive to the halo effect, since some characteristics may not be related to others.
6. Develop and use specific observational guides to appraise specific aspects of behavior.
7. Record what actually happened, not your reaction to it.
8. Use observation to secure evidence on many different types of learning, not on conduct alone.

GROUP DISCUSSION

Social studies programs rely extensively on group discussions in which children evaluate work periods, study skills, research activities, and specific problems as they arise. Each member of the group can participate, charts and checklists can be developed, attention can be given to problems as they arise, specific instances of behavior can be considered, and cooperative and continuous appraisal can be carried on.

Many teachers raise specific questions during discussion when various learnings are being evaluated. Questions should be directly related to the objectives of the unit currently underway. In the primary grades, for example, questions related to home, school, and community might include the following: How do we share at home? What jobs (responsibilities) do children, parents, and community workers have? Who helps us get library books? In later grades, when the teacher is appraising skills in problem solving, these questions might be used: Where can we find out about this? How shall we share what we find out? Why must all ideas be considered? How shall we put our ideas to use? Such questions reveal quickly and easily which children are grasping key ideas; they also indicate points that need additional emphasis. They make evaluation a part of the instructional program—*as it should be*.

Also helpful, particularly in small-group discussions, are questions that point to what comes next and what is missing. Such questions may be used to assess a child's ability to grasp the whole of a situation, to predict outcomes, to use ideas to solve problems, and to identify with others:

1. Cover part of a mural, map, picture, exhibit, chart, diagram, or collection and ask, "What is covered?" or "What is missing?"
2. Remove an object from an exhibit, a part of a jigsaw map, or a part of a model and ask, "What is missing?"
3. Give incomplete directions for making something, going somewhere, using something, conducting a meeting, or introducing someone, and ask, "What is missing?"
4. Cover part of a time line or give part of a demonstration and ask, "What comes next?"
5. Tell part of an incident or a story and ask, "What comes next?"
6. Show several pictures in sequence and ask, "What comes next?"

Another technique that may be used as part of discussion, or at least introduced during discussion, involves arranging objects or ideas in sequence or in proper order:

1. Show a set of pictures or cards with phrases or sentences, and have children arrange them in order.
2. Show pictures that belong in a scene (for example, airport, farm) and have children arrange them in relative position.
3. Have children put together, in proper position, parts of maps or large pictures that have been cut to show key ideas, such as relative location, relative size, and distance.
4. Have children arrange a floor layout of the community, a farm, or an airport.

Good sources of evaluation data are unstructured discussions in which children talk over problems and questions that come up spontaneously or with a minimum of teacher guidance. In such discussions children usually reveal attitudes toward others, concepts, erroneous ideas, reasoning ability, individual needs, and ability to participate in group work.

Charts are especially helpful in individual and group self-evaluation. They may be referred to by individuals, used in small-group activities, and used in group discussion to focus attention on specific items. Charts 14–2 through 14–13 may be used to assess the development of thinking processes. The charts presented in preceding chapters may also be used to evaluate as well as to guide students' learning.

Checklists are useful in assessing specific items related to study habits, participation in discussion, and other behavior of students in various situations. They are also useful in assessing reports, maps, and other products of students' work. Some checklists are designed for teacher use and others for student self-evaluation. Some are used in group work; others are used by individuals. The

Remembering

Is the problem clear?

What can you think of that is related to it?

How can you check what you recall?

Can you tell how it is related to the problem?

Chart 14–2

Observing

What did you observe?

How do your findings check with others?

How can you explain any differences?

Do we need to check our findings?

Was everyone looking for the same thing?

Chart 14–3

Interpreting

Can you state the meaning in your own words?

Can you state how some items are related?

Have you interpreted it as it is, not as you want it to be?

How does your interpretation compare with other interpretations?

Chart 14–4

Comparing/Contrasting

Have comparable features been identified?

Has each feature been defined?

Can you state how they are alike? Different?

Do we agree? If not, why?

Chart 14–5

Classifying

What is the objective for grouping?

What characteristics did you use to group the items?

Are the groups mutually exclusive?

Does each item fit into a group?

What other groups might be made? On what basis?

Chart 14–6

Generalizing

Did you identify the facts?

Did you find what is common in them?

Have you stated the central idea?

Have you checked your statement against the evidence?

Can you state the main idea and supporting details?

Chart 14–7

Inferring

Can you state the evidence or reason for your inference?

Does it make sense? Is it reasonable?

Does it follow from what is given or from the reason you used?

Does it make sense to others?

Chart 14–8

Hypothesizing

Can you state how it helps to explain the topic or problem?

Is it consistent with other ideas related to the topic?

Can it be tested by finding evidence?

Chart 14–9

Predicting

Can you state the factors or reasons you used?

What evidence did you use?

Have you double-checked to be sure you considered all factors or conditions?

Chart 14–10

Analyzing

Have you identified the main parts?

Can you describe each part? Tell why it is important?

Can you state how the parts are related?

Chart 14–11

Synthesizing

Did you bring together the most important items?

In what way is it a new or original presentation of ideas?

Can you state the organizing idea(s) that you used?

Are you satisfied with the form of presentation?

Chart 14–12

Evaluating

Was the focus of evaluation clearly defined?

Were standards of appraisal clearly defined?

Was related evidence gathered?

Can the judgment be supported by evidence or reasons?

Chart 14–13

teacher makes some checklists to meet specific group needs, and other checklists are planned cooperatively with the class. Checklists 14–3 through 14–5 illustrate practical devices that can be developed in social studies classes.

Checklist 14–3
Working Well with Others

Name: _____   Date: _____

School: _____   City: _____

How do you work with other students in making plans, discussing problems, making things, looking up ideas, and using materials? All of us need to check ourselves to see if we are doing those things that improve the work of the group. By checking

---

461

ourselves, we can learn things to do to improve group work. We need to know our good points and shortcomings and to consider things to do to improve. Read the statements below and place a check in the square that tells how often you do each item in the list.

HOW OFTEN DO YOU DO EACH ITEM LISTED BELOW?	ALWAYS	USUALLY	SOME-TIMES	NEVER	?
1. I stick to the job until it is finished.					
2. I take part in many different activities.					
3. I work with everyone in the class.					
4. I am eager to try out new ideas and to work on new problems.					
5. I share materials with others.					
6. I help set up plans and directions and follow them.					
7. I work happily without grumbling or losing my temper.					
8. I give in if my ideas conflict with the best interests of the group.					
9. I consider the rights of others.					
10. I am courteous and use good manners.					

Checklist 14–4
How Do I Work?

1. Do my own job	Yes	No
2. Finish each job	Yes	No
3. Follow directions	Yes	No
4. Listen attentively	Yes	No
5. Return materials	Yes	No
6. Clean up properly	Yes	No

Checklist 14–5
Am I Courteous?

1. Listen to others	Yes	No
2. Take turns	Yes	No
3. Share materials	Yes	No
4. Express thanks	Yes	No
5. Return materials	Yes	No
6. Work quietly	Yes	No

INTERVIEWS

Both formal and informal interviews are helpful in appraising learning. Informal interviews are helpful in talking over immediate problems, determining difficulties, and clarifying group standards and procedures. Formal interviews ordinarily involve checklists, lists of questions, or rating scales that have been planned ahead of time. In either type of interview, the teacher should aim to achieve and maintain rapport, be a good listener, guide the interview so that the purpose is achieved, and maintain a sympathetic attitude so that tensions are not created. Written records of interviews are helpful because they can be added to the child's cumulative record and thus give a more descriptive picture of growth.

LOGS AND DIARIES

Both individual and group diaries or logs are useful evaluation devices. The group-made log contains material dictated by the class, much of it growing out of group planning and evaluation. The individual log is a record of such activities as cooperation, acceptance of responsibility, work completed, or books read. Many teachers have group discussions regarding the items to be kept in individual logs and to share ideas as logs or diaries are written. Chart 14–14 shows a typical recording form.

Daily Learning Log

Name: _____ Unit: _____ Date: _____
Most interesting activity: _____
Least interesting activity: _____
Most valuable activity: _____
New concepts learned: _____
Other learning: _____

Chart 14–14

QUESTIONNAIRES AND INVENTORIES

Questionnaires and inventories can help determine interests, hobbies, attitudes, home background, and other items about individual children. Many teachers make and use informal inventories and questionnaires to meet specific needs as they arise in class. Checklists 14–6 and 14–7 illustrate those that teachers can make.

CHECK EACH OF THE FOLLOWING:	AGREE	DISAGREE	NOT SURE
1. People from Mexico are hard workers.			
2. It is fun to listen to Mexican music.			
3. Arts and crafts from Mexico are beautiful.			
4. Mexico is one of the first places a person should visit.			

Checklist 14–7
Interest in Transportation

DO YOU LIKE TO DO THE FOLLOWING?	LIKE	DO NOT LIKE	NOT SURE
1. Make model planes?			
2. Play with planes?			
3. Talk about planes with friends?			
4. Read stories about pilots?			
5. Visit the airport?			
6. Ride on planes?			
7. Make boats?			
8. Read stories about seamen?			

A variety of attitudes, values, feelings, and appreciations may be assessed by questionnaires or inventories based on five possible responses to an item. The responses range from strongly agree (or like, approve) to strongly disagree (or dislike, disapprove), as shown in chart 14–15. Students may respond directly on a rating scale or record their responses on a separate answer sheet.

SEMANTIC DIFFERENTIAL

The semantic differential is useful in measuring a generalized attitude toward almost any person, group, object, place, or event included in the social studies program (see Bloom, Hastings, and Madaus in the end-of-chapter references). Students check their position on a seven-point scale with bipolar objectives at each end, as shown in chart 14–16.

Rating Scale

1. We should try to understand the people of Russia better.

| Strongly agree | Agree | Uncertain | Disagree | Strongly disagree |

2. I like things that are made by the Japanese.

| Definitely like | Like | Uncertain | Dislike | Definitely dislike |

3. How do you feel about the decision to employ women on the police force?

| Very happy | Happy | Uncertain | Unhappy | Very unhappy |

4. What do you think about increasing trade with China?

| Strongly favor | Favor | Uncertain | Oppose | Strongly oppose |

5. We should have more units on black Americans, Chicanos, and native Americans.

| Strongly approve | Approve | Uncertain | Disapprove | Strongly disapprove |

6. How well did you like the city council's decision on bicycle safety?

| Really liked | Liked | Uncertain | Disliked | Really disliked |

Chart 14–15

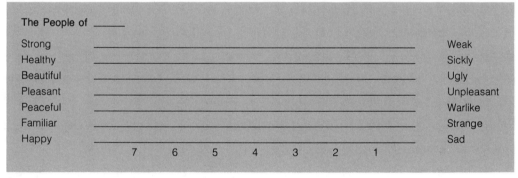

The People of _____

Strong		Weak
Healthy		Sickly
Beautiful		Ugly
Pleasant		Unpleasant
Peaceful		Warlike
Familiar		Strange
Happy		Sad

7   6   5   4   3   2   1

Chart 14–16

ANECDOTAL RECORDS

Anecdotal records are brief notes on specific instances of behavior as shown in the behavior journal in chart 14–17. Specific incidents and related teacher comments are noted separately for students in need of help in working with others. To conserve time and get maximum benefit from anecdotal records, some teachers simply use a page headed by the student's name and make entries during the day or after school. Others make notes as incidents occur for

465

later placement in the students' folder or cumulative record. Records should be limited to three or four aspects of behavior for which evidence of growth is needed, evidence that cannot be recorded in other ways. Anecdotes are most valuable when specific instances, such as those in chart 14–17 are recorded. General comments such as ''Paul cooperated with Mary'' or ''Peter was unkind in his manner'' are of little value.

Behavior Journal

Name: Walter D   Teacher: Miss Smith   Grade: 4

Date	Incidents	Comments
9–21	Did not share the picture with others.	Needs help in carrying out standards.
10–2	Helped to make rules for using materials, but did not share them with others.	Group chart may help. Individual conference is needed.
10–19	Discussed need for sharing with others.	Seems to understand reason for sharing; needs to work with one or two children.
11–2	Worked with David in preparing a report.	Growth in evidence; must place in a group of three or four as a next step.

Chart 14–17

CASE STUDIES AND CASE CONFERENCES

Some teachers make a case study of one or two children each year. Pertinent information on such items as home background and previous school experience, health records, anecdotal records, and data from tests are brought together and analyzed. Such a procedure gives a more complete understanding of a child's growth and has great value for guidance and teaching.

Case conferences are helpful in analyzing and interpreting the information regarding a child's development. In a case conference, all available evidence is considered by the child's teacher, former teacher or teachers, the principal, and guidance workers. The pooled judgment of several individuals is thereby brought to bear on specific questions and problems.

Making and Using Tests

Tests may be criterion-referenced or norm-referenced. Criterion-referenced tests are designed to show what a student actually knows or can do in a defined domain—for example, knowledge of ways to save energy or achievement of map skills. Norm-referenced tests provide comparative information on the relative achievement of an individual or class in the form of grade-equivalent, percentile, or other scores. Criterion-referenced tests are used with increasing frequency to identify what each student has achieved and to individualize instruction. They also provide information on the extent to which objectives set by the school system have been achieved, thus contributing to operation of the accountability system.

Schools with competence-based programs use criterion-referenced tests to assess the specific areas or domains of competence selected for emphasis. For example, map skills may be assessed by preparing items that assess the ability of students to interpret the map key, use the scale, identify directions, and locate specified places. The ability to use thinking processes may be assessed by preparing items that call for interpreting, analyzing, and generalizing, as illustrated by examples presented later in this chapter. The guiding principle is to define the domain of competence by specifying the specific competencies to be developed and to prepare items to assess each of them. (Superka and others describe tests, attitude inventories and other instruments for use in the social studies; Popham discusses procedures to construct criterion-referenced tests [see end-of-chapter references].)

TEACHER-MADE TESTS

Effective teacher-made tests are criterion-referenced. They reveal individual needs, facilitate grouping, and give teachers and students clues to progress, problems, strengths, and weaknesses. Conceptual, process, skill, and affective objectives may be evaluated. Situational or problem items should be included along with standard items. Pictures and graphics in textbooks and other media should be used to design some items. And items should be designed for assessing affective as well as cognitive objectives. The following paragraphs illustrate these points with examples.

situational items A valuable type of test for appraising students' ability to evaluate ideas, infer feelings, and handle problems is the situational, interpretive, or problem-solving test. A situation or problem is presented in a sentence, paragraph, or short selection and followed by appropriate items, as shown in the following examples.

A class was having a discussion on the duties of a committee chairperson. Listed below are suggestions as made by different children. Make a + mark beside the suggestions that you think are *good ones* for the chairperson to follow:

_____ Get ideas from all members.   _____ Urge everyone to do his or her best.

_____ Tell each person what to do.   _____ Ask members to stick to the topic.

_____ Ask others to accept the plan.   _____ Do most of the talking.

When making situational or interpretive tests, teachers should present problems that are realistic and challenging to the group. The kind of situation that could be used as a topic for discussion is usually satisfactory. By making notes on comments during discussion, the teacher can obtain leads to plausible answers or responses to include in the test.

items based on pictures and graphic materials

Special attention should be given to the construction of test items based on pictures, maps, charts, tables, and diagrams in textbooks and other instructional media. Here are some examples:

Look at the pictures on pages 38–39 that show the steps in the production of wheat. List the steps in order.

A. _____

B. _____

C. _____

D. _____

(*Objective:* To interpret pictures by listing the steps shown in sequence)

Look at the picture of the school on page 33.

How is it like our school? State two ways it is similar.

How is it different from our school? State two differences.

What regions are identified by the numerals? Write the numerals in
the spaces to identify each region:_____ Far Western
_____ Midwestern _____ Northeastern _____ Southeastern
_____ Southwestern.

(*Objective:* To compare and contrast by stating two similarities and two differences)

After studying the rainfall map on page 58, write the letter of the correct answer
to each of the following on your answer sheet.

(1) Average yearly rainfall in the reddish-brown area is
    A. 20 inches   B. 30 inches   C. 50 inches   D. 60 inches

(2) Average yearly rainfall in the orange area is
    A. 10 inches   B. 15 inches   C. 20 inches   D. 25 inches

(3) The city on the map that receives the most rainfall is
    A. Denver   B. Miami   C. Seattle   D. Chicago

(*Objective:* To interpret a rainfall map by stating the amount of rainfall in different regions, and to identify places with the most rainfall)

Study the table on population growth on page 111.

During what years was population growth highest? _____

During what years was population growth lowest? _____

What do you predict growth will be in the next ten years? _____

469

(*Objective:* To interpret data in a table by stating years of highest and lowest growth, and to make a prediction of growth by stating an estimate of increase during the next decade)

Look at the picture of the mural by Diego Rivera on page 98.

Which one of the values listed below is reflected in the mural?
A. Justice   B. Desire for freedom   C. Equal opportunity

(*Objective:* To infer the value emphasized by an artist by stating the dominant value reflected in one of the artist's works)

---

items
for affective
objectives
Consideration should be given to items designed to assess feelings, attitudes, and values because they are important and inevitable outcomes of instruction. The following examples may be adapted for use in a variety of units.

Importance of Pollution Problems

Mark the items below as follows: *A,* Very important; *B,* Important; *C,* Fairly important; *D,* Not important.

_____ 1. Air pollution   _____ 4. Noise pollution
_____ 2. Water pollution   _____ 5. Aesthetic pollution
_____ 3. Waste pollution   _____ 6. Soil pollution

(*Objective:* To demonstrate concern about the importance of pollution problems)

What Should You Do?
What Do You Do?

1. Everyone should put litter in trash cans.
   Strongly agree   Agree   Undecided   Disagree   Strongly disagree
2. I put litter in trash cans.
   Always   Most of the time   Sometimes   Seldom   Never
3. Everyone should pick up litter left by others.
   Strongly agree   Agree   Undecided   Disagree   Strongly disagree
4. I pick up litter left by others.
   Always   Most of the time   Sometimes   Seldom   Never

5. All students should pick up litter on the playground.
   Strongly agree   Agree   Undecided   Disagree   Strongly disagree
6. I pick up litter on the playground.
   Always   Most of the time   Sometimes   Seldom   Never

(*Objective:* To show positive attitudes toward ways of preventing waste pollution)

Working to Improve the Environment

What can you do to help improve the environment? Answer the items below as follows: *A,* I can do it; *B,* I am not sure; *C,* I cannot do it.

_____ 1. Urge other students to keep the playground clean.
_____ 2. Ask my friends to help clean up the neighborhood.
_____ 3. Give a list of ways to improve the environment to my neighbors.
_____ 4. Write a letter to the mayor on things that should be done.
_____ 5. Take cans and bottles to a recycling center.

(*Objective:* To demonstrate belief in one's ability to take action to improve the environment)

Many of the value clarification strategies discussed in chapter 13 may be used to assess values and attitudes. For example, the value-sheet strategy may be used as suggested for situational tests. The rank-order strategy, value survey, completion of unfinished sentences, position on a continuum, weighing alternatives, and either-or choices are good examples of devices that may be used to assess values. These and the other strategies should be reviewed at this point.

items
on thinking
processes

The following items show ways of assessing the intellectual processes emphasized in this text and in current instructional materials. They also illustrate assessment on different levels of cognition, ranging from observing, remembering, and interpreting to analyzing, synthesizing, and evaluating.

Observing

Look at the legend of the map on page 108 of our textbook. Mark an *X* by each of the following that is shown in the legend.

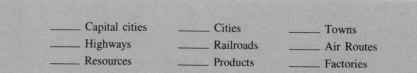

_____ Capital cities	_____ Cities	_____ Towns
_____ Highways	_____ Railroads	_____ Air Routes
_____ Resources	_____ Products	_____ Factories

Remembering

What concept is needed to complete the following concept clusters?

1. Major landforms: plains, hills, plateaus, _____
2. Natural resources: water, soils, animal life, plant life, _____

Interpreting

Which of the following statements best expresses the main idea in the reading selection, *Roger Williams' Colony?*

1. Members of all ethnic groups were welcome.
2. Members of all religious groups were welcome.
3. Quakers and Roman Catholics were welcome.
4. Dutch, British, and Spanish were welcome.

Comparing

Write *A* by each pair of workers that are in the same career family. Write *D* by each pair of workers that are in a different career family.

_____ Carpenter, plasterer	_____ Teacher, social worker
_____ Doctor, dentist	_____ Lawyer, judge
_____ Nurse, waiter	_____ Cook, store owner

Classifying

Mark a + by each of the following that is a natural resource. Mark an *O* by each of the following that is *not* a natural resource.

_____ Soil	_____ Water
_____ Iron ore	_____ Wheat
_____ Iron	_____ Forests
_____ Lumber	_____ Petroleum

Generalizing

Which of the following is the best generalization of the data presented in the table on page 125 of our textbook?

1. Unemployment is greatest for women.
2. Unemployment is greatest for black youth.
3. Unemployment is greatest for Mexican-American youth.
4. Unemployment is greatest for youth from Cuba.

Inferring

Which of the following do you think was the author's purpose in writing the article "Justice for Minority Groups"?

1. To report the facts
2. To arouse our interest
3. To stir readers to action
4. To show weaknesses in the law

Analyzing

Which of the following concepts are used to organize the reading selection on the Inca Empire?

_____ Location   _____ Size

_____ Communication   _____ Wealth

_____ Time period   _____ Travel

_____ Population   _____ Government

Synthesizing

Make a time line that includes the events listed below.

Cortez seized the Aztec capital in 1521.

Mexican soldiers won the battle of the Alamo in 1836.

French forces were defeated at Pueblo in 1862.

Mexico gained independence from Spain in 1821.

The Mexican revolution began in 1810.

The Treaty of Guadalupe Hidalgo was signed in 1848.

WRITING TEST ITEMS

Several basic guidelines should be kept in mind when preparing recall, completion, multiple-choice, matching, and binary-choice test items. Word each item clearly and write it on a level of difficulty appropriate to the group. Avoid textbook wording; otherwise, children will engage in rote memorization and will not learn to apply ideas and principles. Do not include items that provide answers to other questions. No clues or suggestions that can be used to figure out the correct answer to an item should be given. Avoid tricky questions and items that do not have definite answers. Give clear, concise directions and allow sufficient space for responses. Group items of the same type together in separate sections (completion, true-false, and the like). In addition, specific points must be kept in mind for each type of item most frequently used in the social studies program.

Simple recall items should measure a child's ability to recall an important name, place, concept, or date. A child must recall the appropriate response, not simply identify it from a list of possible answers. Questions or statements involving *who, when, where, what, how many,* and *how much* can be presented orally or in writing to measure a variety of specific learnings, as shown in the following examples:

> Who helps us check out library books? _____
> What should we say when someone helps us? _____
> Which airport worker tells planes when to land? _____
> What are the four major land forms? _____

Simple recall items should be short. Questions are usually easier to prepare than statements and are more meaningful to a child. Provide adequate space for answers, and write each question in such a way that allows only one correct response.

The completion test is another form of recall. It may be either a sentence or a paragraph with blanks to fill with words, numbers, or phrases that complete the meaning:

> The president during the War of 1812 was (1)   1. _____
> from the state of (2).   2. _____

Several points must be kept in mind if this type of item is to be used effectively in appraising learning in social studies:

1. Omit only key words, phrases, or dates, not minor details, common words, or everyday expressions. Do not write a statement such as "The pioneers ate much _____." Many different common words could be used here—food, meat, berries, and the like.
2. Use blanks of uniform size for all responses, since children interpret variations in size as clues to answers.
3. Avoid textbook phrases and sentences. Use definite statements with omissions that call for only one correct response; but if a student comes up with another response that is acceptable, give credit for it.
4. Avoid the use of *a* and *an* before a blank so that no clues will be given, for example, "Bill took an _____ from the fruit basket." *Apple* or *orange* are possibilities, but *banana, pears, plum,* or other fruit beginning with a consonant can be eliminated.
5. Do not omit several words in any one statement. If too many words are omitted, the meaning is obscured, as it is in this example: "Jamestown was _____ in the year _____ by _____." If used at all, this item should be written: "Jamestown was settled in the year _____."
6. Arrange the test so that answers can be written in spaces at the right, as shown in the example at the beginning of this section. This facilitates marking.

Professional test makers use this type of item more frequently than any other. It consists of a question or incomplete statement (called the stem) followed by a selection of possible responses. The correct or best one is the answer; the others are distractors. The usual procedure is to have children select the correct response from among three to five choices. This procedure can be varied by having students (1) select the best answer, (2) select the incorrect answer, and (3) select two or more correct answers. In the primary grades, children should be asked to underline the correct or best answer so that no difficulty will arise in marking letters or numbers that designate answers:

> *Directions.* Look at all four words and draw a line under the one word that makes the sentence true. (A variation: Draw a line through the incorrect words.)
> 1. Workers in sawmills make
>   nails   bricks   plaster   lumber

In later grades, numerals or letters may be marked, or machine-scorable answer sheets may be used successfully with most children.

> *Directions.* After each question there are four words that might be used to answer the question. Only one of the words is correct or better than any of the others. Make a circle around the letter in front of the word you think is best.
> 1. From which country did the United States purchase the Louisiana Territory?
>   A. England   B. Russia   C. Spain   D. France

If an answer column is provided, the directions should indicate the marking procedure:

> *Directions.* One of the four numbered answers is best for each exercise. Choose the one you think is best and write its number in the space at the left.
> _____ Which reference would you use to find the population of Illinois last year?
>   (1) An atlas   (3) An almanac
>   (2) An encyclopedia   (4) A geography

Keep the following suggestions in mind as you write multiple-choice items:

1. Use multiple-choice items to check recognition and discrimination. Use the simple recall form if the children should be expected to remember a given fact. Use the binary-choice form if there are only two possible answers.
2. Place the major portion of the statement in the introduction or stem, not in the possible answers. Make the stem clear and complete so that the student can determine the nature of the answer. Avoid negative statements in the stem whenever possible; they tend to be confusing.
3. Be sure all choices are plausible; children quickly eliminate absurd options. Word the incorrect responses as carefully as the correct ones; make some of them about the same length as the correct response if more than one word is involved.

4. Avoid clues such as words or phrases in the introduction that also appear in the correct answer, or placing *a* or *an* at the end of the introduction when the options do not all begin with a vowel or consonant. For example, "A pictogram is an A. illustration, B, narrative, C. tool, D. mural" can easily be answered by associating *an* with the option that begins with a vowel.

5. Phrase all choices so that they are grammatically correct when joined to the introduction. Avoid choices that overlap or include each other, as they do in this example: "Last year air travel increased A. less than 10 percent, B. less than 20 percent, C. more than 30 percent, D. more than 50 percent." Place choices at the end of the item, distribute them evenly among answer positions, include at least four chioces whenever possible, and keep all choices in the same category—that is, do not mix persons, places, and things.

6. Arrange the items in groups of five with a double space between groups. Group together items with the same number of choices—in other words, do not mix three-choice and four-choice items.

matching   Matching items are used to measure the ability to associate events and dates, events and persons, terms and definitions, principles and applications, tools and their uses, pictures and concepts, causes and effects, and the like. They should be used only when several pairs of items are sufficiently homogeneous to require a child to think critically in order to make proper associations.

Fairly simple matchings are used in the primary grades. Pictures of household objects such as a refrigerator, stove, or sweeper can be matched with words or phrases that describe each picture. Or parts of sentences or pairs of words can be matched, as shown in the following two examples:

1. Draw a line between the two parts in each sentence that belong together.

The farmer keeps baby chickens	in the coral.
The farmer keeps horses	in a pen.
The farmer keeps pigs	in a brooder.

2. Draw a line from each worker to the word that tells what he or she uses.

Carpenter	Cement
Electrician	Lumber
Mason	Pipe
Plumber	Wire

In later grades two basic varieties of matching are used: simple matching, as shown in the first example, and classification into categories, as shown in the second example.

1. In the space before each of the duties, write the letter of the official responsible for it.

Duty	Official
_____ 1. Collects taxes	A. Assessor
_____ 2. Determines the value of property	B. Clerk
_____ 3. Keep records	C. Judge
	D. Sheriff
	E. Treasurer

2. In the space before each of the responsibilities, write the letter of the branch of government that carries it out.

Responsibility	Branch
____ 1. Makes laws	A. Executive
____ 2. Interprets laws	B. Judicial
____ 3. Enforces laws	C. Legislative
____ 4. Appropriates money	
____ 5. Prepares the budget	

Guessing is minimized in the first example because of the number of names in the second column; it is minimized in the second example because some responses must be used more than once.

In another form of matching, maps, diagrams, or pictures are lettered to show significant features—for example, a map of the United States may be marked with large letters to show regions in which different types of production are carried on. The map is placed in the front of the room, and children are asked to study it and then write the letters in the spaces before matching questions such as the following:

____ 1. Which area is noted for steel production?
____ 2. Which area is noted for cotton production?

Keep the following suggestions in mind when preparing matching items:

1. Place related material in each matching exercise; do not mix people and events with other associations such as causes and effects.
2. Keep the number of items small (three to five); provide extra responses (two to three) in the second column, or permit certain responses to be used more than once in order to minimize guessing.
3. Arrange the items in the first column in random order; arrange those in the second column in alphabetical, chronological, or some other reasonable order.
4. Keep the columns close together and on the same page so that students will not become confused looking back and forth or turning the page to check matching pairs.
5. Use consistent form so that items in each column can be associated without difficulty. If parts of sentences are to be matched, be sure no grammatical clues are introduced.

alternative response (binary-choice) items Items in this category may be written in several forms: true-false, yes-no, right-wrong, correct-incorrect, and two-option multiple choice. They may be dictated or presented in written form. Carefully constructed two-choice items can be used to appraise interests and attitudes, detect misconceptions or superstitions, and test understanding of principles and generalizations. Use them when only two logical responses are possible, such as north or south, right or left, larger or smaller, and the like. Examples of several different forms follow.

1. [The true-false variety is simply a statement.] The area of Brazil is greater than the area of the United States.   T   F

2. [The yes-no variety consists of a question.] Do you have the right to break a rule made by your class if you did not vote for it?   Y   N

3. [The cluster variety is a statement with several completions.] Agriculture is profitable in the South because
   1. many workers are available.   T   F
   2. the land is mountainous.   T   F
   3. there are many forests.   T   F
   4. there is a long growing season.   T   F

Avoid items that could have more than two plausible responses, such as ''The pioneers came to Sutter's Fort on the Wilderness Trail.'' The multiple-choice form should be used in this instance because the Oregon Trail, Mohawk Trail, and California Trail could be used as other choices.

Alternative response items may be used in a variety of ways. Places on a map can be marked by letters or numbers and children can be asked to write T or F in response to statements regarding what is grown, what conditions exist, and the like. Comprehension of a topic can be appraised in a similar way after children have read a selection, heard a report, or seen a film. More than mere knowledge can be tested with items that require application of concepts:

If Iowa were in a mountainous region, its corn crop would be larger.   T   F

The ability to make comparisons can be tested by an item such as this one:

Make a + beside each of the items found in Mexico and California:
_____ Oil   _____ Forests
_____ Gold   _____ Coal

The ability to read and interpret maps can be measured by preparing items based on textbook or wall maps:

New York is farther from San Francisco than from Shannon.   T   F

The ability to describe conditions or activities can be measured by an item like this one:

Make a + beside each of the objects listed below that pioneers took on hunting trips:
_____ Blankets   _____ Canned foods
_____ Kettles   _____ Hatchets

Keep the following suggestions in mind when writing alternative response items:

1. Include an equal number of true and false statements, be sure the true statements are not consistently longer than the false statements, and arrange true and false items in random order.
2. Avoid specific determiners—for example, items containing *alone, all, no, none, never, always,* and the like are usually false, whereas items containing *generally, should, may,* and the like are usually true.
3. Make each statement definitely true or false; avoid ambiguous terms, such as *few, many,* and *important.* Place the crucial element of the statement in the main part of the sentence, not in a phrase or subordinate clause. Avoid double negatives.
4. Make each item short and specific. Avoid unfamiliar or figurative language.
5. Simplify the marking of correct responses (and scoring) by placing the answer column at the right, as shown in the previous examples. For scoring, make a stencil (with holes punched in the position for correct responses) to place over the answer column. If the items are dictated or no answer column has been provided, instruct the children to write + for true and 0 for false; these are easier to score than T or F or + and −.

essay tests Although not widely used in the elementary school, essay tests are helpful in the upper grades when students are mature enough to express themselves in this form. Essay items are useful in obtaining evidence on attitudes, problems, and issues and on such processes as synthesizing ideas, analyzing causes and other elements, evaluating decisions, and interpreting data. They are also used to assess skill in organizing and summarizing information, applying principles, and describing significant events, persons, and places. The element of free response frequently gives clues to learning that are not secured by objective tests. The particular questions should not be too broad in scope, nor should they be used to test information alone. Each question should be phrased so that students will know exactly what is expected of them. For example, the question ''How did the pioneers in Boonesboro live?'' is too general. A better question is ''How did the pioneers in Boonesboro obtain food?'' In general, essay questions should be used only when children will not experience undue difficulty in handling the writing, spelling, and composition skills involved in answering them. When students lack the necessary skills, essay questions can be answered in small group discussion or broken down into small units and objective test items prepared.

STANDARDIZED TESTS

Standardized tests are more widely used in reading and arithmetic than in the social studies. Because of diversity among programs of instruction, it is impossible to find a standardized test designed for nationwide use that fits each local program. Some general achievement tests include a short section on skills that are commonly taught in the social studies. The examples in chart 14–18 are typical of those found on standardized tests.

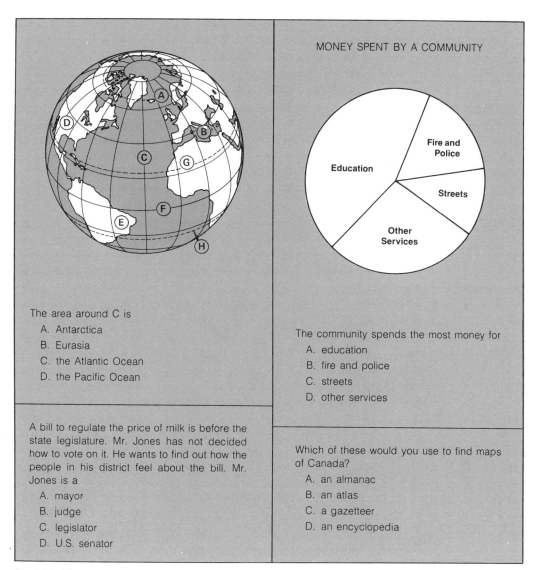

MONEY SPENT BY A COMMUNITY

Fire and Police

Education

Streets

Other Services

The area around C is
A. Antarctica
B. Eurasia
C. the Atlantic Ocean
D. the Pacific Ocean

The community spends the most money for
A. education
B. fire and police
C. streets
D. other services

A bill to regulate the price of milk is before the state legislature. Mr. Jones has not decided how to vote on it. He wants to find out how the people in his district feel about the bill. Mr. Jones is a
A. mayor
B. judge
C. legislator
D. U.S. senator

Which of these would you use to find maps of Canada?
A. an almanac
B. an atlas
C. a gazetteer
D. an encyclopedia

Chart 14–18

The following are illustrative of achievement tests that include a section on the social studies.

Comprehensive Tests of Basic Skills (McGraw-Hill)
Iowa Every-Pupil Test of Basic Skills (Houghton Mifflin Company)
Metropolitan Achievement Tests (Harcourt Brace Jovanovich, Inc.)

Sequential Tests of Educational Progress, (Addison-Wesley Publishing Co., Inc.)

SRA Achievement Series, (Science Research Associates)

Stanford Achievement Test (Harcourt Brace Jovanovich, Inc.)

See Buro's *Mental Measurement Yearbooks* and *Tests in Print* for descriptions of these and other tests. Examination copies may be found in local school district offices. See reference by Superka and others for descriptions of tests and other assessment instruments.

 Questions, Activities, Evaluation

1. Consider practical ways to use each of the basic guidelines to effective evaluation presented in the first section of this chapter. Which do you believe to be the most difficult to apply? Which do you believe now need greater emphasis?
2. In what ways can you provide for student self-evaluation in a unit you are planning?
3. Examine a cumulative record currently being used in a school system in your area. What provision is there for recording progress in social studies? What additional provisions, if any, are needed?
4. Note ways in which you might use each of the following in a unit of your choice: observation, examination of samples of work, interviews, discussion, charts, checklists, rating scales, and questionnaires.
5. Prepare several test items in each form discussed in this chapter. Plan items for assessing both affective and cognitive objectives.

references

BLOOM, BENJAMIN S., J. THOMAS HASTINGS, AND GEORGE F. MADAUS, *Handbook on Formative and Summative Evaluation of Student Learning.* New York: McGraw-Hill, 1971. Guidelines, sample items, and specifications for measures in the cognitive and affective domains.

BUROS, OSCAR K., *Social Studies Tests and Reviews.* Edison, N.J.: Gryphon Press, 1975. Selected by Buros from various yearbooks.

EBEL, ROBERT L., *Essentials of Educational Measurement* (2nd ed.). Englewood Cliffs, N.J.: Prentice-Hall, 1979. Chapters on construction of test items.

GRONLUND, NORMAN E., *Constructing Achievement Tests.* Englewood Cliffs, N.J.: Prentice-Hall, 1977. Suggestions for item construction.

HANNAH, LARRY S., AND JOHN U. MICHAELIS, *A Comprehensive Framework for Instructional Objectives.* Reading, Mass.: Addison-Wesley Publishing Co., 1977. Examples of test items and other evaluative devices for thinking processes, attitudes and values, and skills.

POPHAM, W. JAMES, *Criterion-Referenced Measurement.* Englewood Cliffs, N.J.: Prentice-Hall, 1978. Construction of items to assess performance in defined areas of learning.

"Revision of the NCSS Social Studies Curriculum Guidelines," *Social Education* 43 (April 1979), 261–73. Rationale, goals, and nine guidelines; followed by an example of how to use the guidelines for program assessment.

SUPERKA, DOUGLAS P., ALICE VIGLIANI, AND JUDITH E. HEDSTROM, *Social Studies Evaluation Sourcebook*. Boulder, Colo.: Social Science Education Consortium, 1978. Description of tests, inventories, and other instruments for use in the social studies.

APPENDIX: RESOURCE UNIT ON ENVIRONMENTAL PROBLEMS

To demonstrate understanding of environmental problems by identifying and describing:

1. Pollution and other problems in urban centers
2. The impact of population on quality of life
3. Urban renewal and steps that individuals and groups can take to improve quality of life

Initiation

This unit may be introduced in one of the following ways:

1. Arrange a display of pictures that show environmental problems in cities. Place the following question at the top of the display: *Which of These Problems Are in Our City?* Discuss the pictures and students' responses to the question, listing problems that are recognized as existing locally. Urge students to note other problems as the unit progresses.
2. Show a film or filmstrip available from the instructional media center that highlights environmental problems. Ask students to note the problems that exist locally. Follow this by asking if there are other local problems not shown in the film or filmstrip.
3. Invite an expert on environmental problems to make a presentation to the class, emphasizing problems that are critical in other cities as well as locally. After the presentation discuss the most critical local problems and answer specific questions raised by students.
4. Discuss environmental problems that students themselves have observed in the community or have learned about, posing such questions as

   What pollution and other environmental problems have you observed in our area?

   What problems have you seen on television programs? Discussed at home? Learned about in other ways?

   Which problems do you think are most serious? Why?

Development

A selection should be made from the activities presented in this section. Learning materials available locally should be noted and used as data sources for questions and activities suggested in the three main parts of this resource unit.

Pollution Problems

Focusing questions: What pollution problems are most serious? Air? Water? Noise? Aesthetic? Other? How can pollution be reduced?

ILLUSTRATIVE LEARNING ACTIVITIES

types of pollution   Organize committees to investigate different types of pollution and to contribute to the development of a retrieval chart:

Types of Pollution, Pollutants, Effects, Prevention

Types	Pollutants	Effects	Prevention
Air			
Water			
Soil			
Food			
Solid wastes			
Thermal			
Aesthetic			
Noise			

List and discuss ways in which recreational activities may contribute to pollution:

Type of Pollution

Activity	Air	Water	Soil	Noise	Waste
Camping	_____	_____	_____	_____	_____
Picnicking	_____	_____	_____	_____	_____
Hiking	_____	_____	_____	_____	_____
Boating	_____	_____	_____	_____	_____

air pollution   Investigate air pollution through such activities as

1. Identifying sources of air pollution in the community and surrounding area—motor vehicles, factories, burning dumps, power generating plants, and other sources
2. Inviting an expert to discuss causes and effects of air pollution, new techniques that are being developed to curb it, the economic costs, the human benefits, and current issues
3. Interpreting (and making) graphs of major sources of air pollution, such as

487

Social Studies Workshop, University of California, Berkeley

How can this kind of aesthetic pollution be stopped?

Major Sources of Air Pollution

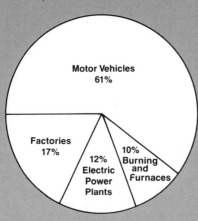

WHAT DOES THIS GRAPH SHOW?

What is the main source of air pollution?
What is the second main source?
What percentage do other sources contribute?
What main idea can be stated about sources?
What sources are not shown?
How can we find out about them?

4. Listing common air polluting activities such as smoking, burning trash and clippings, driving cars, using sprays, cooking outdoors, and burning oil and coal in furnaces, then discussing such questions as

Which activities are necessary? Which are not?

What substitutes might be used?

What habits should be changed? Why?

What habits probably will be changed? Why?

5. Completing a diagram that shows the causes and effects of air pollution, then discussing ways to remove the causes and minimize the effects:

Causes   Effects

```
——————————————╲                        ╱——————————————
——————————————————╲                 ╱——————————————————
                    ╲             ╱
——————————————————————  ┌──────────────┐  ——————————————————————
————————————————————————→│ Air Pollution │←————————————————————————
——————————————————————  └──────────────┘  ——————————————————————
                    ╱             ╲
——————————————————╱                 ╲——————————————————
——————————————╱                        ╲——————————————
```

waste pollution

Provide for individual and small-group investigation of waste pollution by

1. Identifying sources and causes of waste pollution by tracing the production of plastics, cans, bottles, or other items:

Name of product: _____

Raw materials used: _____
   How are raw materials produced? _____
   Good effects: _____
   Bad effects: _____

Steps in production: _____
   Good effects of each step: _____
   Bad effects of each step: _____

Uses of finished product: _____
   Good effects: _____
   Bad effects: _____

Steps in disposing of waste: _____
   Good effects: _____
   Bad effects: _____

2. Identifying common wastes and tracing the steps in disposing of them by completing such items as:

1. What waste is collected after a meal? _____
   List three steps in disposing of this waste.
   (1) _____

489

(2) _____

(3) _____

2. What waste is a part of gardening? _____

List three steps in disposing of this waste.

(1) _____

(2) _____

(3) _____

3. What waste results from mail? _____

List three steps in disposing of this waste.

(1) _____

(2) _____

(3) _____

3. Making a map of litter in one of the following: schoolyard, parking lot, playground in a park, picnic area, or construction site, with different symbols for paper, glass, wood, metal, cans, bottles, other litter, trash cans, walks, and entrances to buildings; then discussing the following questions:

Where is most litter found? Why?

Where might trash cans be relocated for ease of use?

How can attitudes be changed to reduce litter?

Why must each individual assume responsibility to reduce litter?

How can we stop littering in areas we use?

Evaluate students' attitudes toward litter by having them check their positions on such items as:

Litter prevention is	____ very important	____ important	____ not important
Playground litter is	____ a major problem	____ a minor problem	____ no problem
Litter at home is	____ a major problem	____ a minor problem	____ no problem
I litter when	____ no one is looking	____ no trash can is handy	____ in the country
People who litter	____ are just careless	____ are OK	____ are law-breakers

water pollution   Investigate sources of water pollution in the community and the surrounding area:

Interviewing public health officials and other experts on what is being done and what additional steps are needed

Interviewing individuals at power companies, paper mills, and other industries to find out what they are doing

Listing the most critical needs and proposing steps to be taken

Mapping the location of major sources of pollution

Social Studies Workshop, University of California, Berkeley

Are more dams needed for water supply and electric power?
What is their impact on the environment?

Identify the main sources of the local water supply and the care that is taken to provide safe water:

What are the main sources of our water supply? To what extent do we depend on other states for our water?

What methods are used to assure a clean supply of water?

Is any untreated sewage entering the system? If so, what steps are being taken to correct the situation?

Are industrial wastes or other pollutants entering the system? If so, what is being done?

What steps has our community taken to prevent discharge of pollutants? Could such steps be effective in other communities?

What is being done to assure an adequate supply of clean water now and in the future?

Analyze the costs and benefits of proposals for providing an adequate supply of water in the future:

What are the advantages and disadvantages of desalination? Getting water from icebergs? Building more dams? Cloud seeding? Recycling?

Why must ecological planning be a part of planning for water needs?

What damaging side effects may result from dams, desalination, and other sources if ecologically balanced plans are not made?

Make booklets, scrapbooks, and displays that show the causes and effects of water pollution, the costs and benefits of various ways of developing new sources of water, and ways to conserve water.

Make a list of what individuals can do to conserve water and to prevent pollution at home, in the community, and in recreation and vacation areas.

noise pollution Make a list of pleasant and unpleasant sounds to compare sounds heard in the city and in the country:

Which sounds in the country should be listed under pleasant? Under unpleasant?

Which sounds in the city should be listed under pleasant? Under unpleasant?

In general, where are more pleasant sounds heard?

Investigate noise pollution at home to answer such questions as

Which appliances used at home make the most noise? Vacuum cleaners? Dishwashers? Others?

What outside noises can be heard within our homes? Traffic? Airplanes? Sirens? Others?

What can each of us do at home to reduce noise?

Investigating noise pollution at school to answer such questions as

What are the main causes of noise in school?

What steps can be taken to reduce noise?

What responsibility does each student have?

What should be included in a plan to reduce noise?

Make maps that show the areas where noise is greatest in school, in the neighborhood, and in the community, then discuss reasons for the noise and steps that might be taken to reduce noise at critical places.

Investigate noise pollution in the community to answer such questions as

What regulations are included in the noise abatement program?

What steps are being taken to reduce noise from cars, jackhammers, and other noise makers?

What is being done about the use of noise insulation in buildings?

What are the most critical problems? What is being done to solve them?

Summarize ways to reduce noise at home, in school, and in the community, guided by such questions as

Which noises are necessary? Which are not?

How can unnecessary noise be reduced or eliminated?

How can we reduce noises we make that bother adults but do not bother us?

What should be done when individuals continue to make noise that disturbs others? Why?

Population Change

Focusing questions: How has population of our community changed during the past three decades? How has it changed in urban areas of the United States? In other parts of the world? What has been the impact on housing, health care, services, and the environment?

ILLUSTRATIVE LEARNING ACTIVITIES

Investigate changes in school and community population and related changes in school facilities, housing, and provision of public services by

1. Interviewing school officials, urban planners, and city officials
2. Making charts, graphs, or tables of past and predicted changes
3. Identifying changes in school facilities, housing, fire, police, water, utilities, and other services
4. Describing how density, traffic, and mix of population in terms of ethnic groups vary in different zones of the city, in high-rise apartments and single-dwelling subdivisions, and in ethnic enclaves
5. Comparing changes in our community and other communities
6. Identifying and analyzing proposals for the future that will take account of anticipated population changes

Investigate population growth in our country and other countries, and relationships to the supply of food, environmental problems, use of energy, urban problems, and related topics through such activities as

1. Comparing population data on our country and other countries, using the World Almanac, encyclopedias, and other sources to answer such questions as

   What has been the growth of population in our country over the past 30 years? What percentage of the growth has been in cities? What has been the growth in Latin America? In Japan? In India? In China? What percentage of the growth has been in cities? In what areas has the rate of increase been greatest? Why? What are the predictions for the year 2000? What proposals have been made to meet problems caused by overpopulation?

2. Collecting and arranging pictures, charts, graphs, maps and clippings that highlight population growth and related problems, using such organizing themes as changes in our community, growth of our country, major population growth areas of the world, predictions for the year 2000, and proposals for meeting overpopulation problems

Clarify the meaning of population figures by

1. Measuring the space needed for 35 students standing close together
2. Projecting the space needed for 100, 1,000, 10,000, and so on
3. Comparing the number of classrooms in a school for 500 students with one for 2,500 students
4. Comparing figures on density of population for states, our country, and other countries

Analyze population distribution and density in different areas:

1. distribution and density in our state and nation
2. distribution and density in the four great population areas of the world: China, India, Western Europe, and the eastern United States

Develop the meaning of *rapid growth of population* as follows:

1. Give each student a half sheet of paper on which six two-inch squares have been dittoed.
2. Ask students to place two beans in each square, then four, then eight, and to continue doubling the number until each square is filled.
3. Relate the rapid growth to population growth and predictions in selected areas.
4. Discuss implications for food, housing, health care, schools, environmental problems, water, and utilities.

Urban Renewal and Planning

Focusing questions: What urban renewal projects are underway in our city? How have new towns been created to overcome current problems? How would an ideal city be designed?

ILLUSTRATIVE LEARNING ACTIVITIES

Investigate urban renewal plans and projects through such activities as

1. Inviting a member of the urban renewal commission to present information on plans for renewing inner city areas and on projects underway:

   What are the plans for malls, plazas, and green spaces?

   What are the plans for walkways, landscaping, and lighting?

   What historic buildings are being restored and preserved?

   How will the central business district be changed?

   How will transportation be improved?

Social Studies Workshop, University of California, Berkeley

Are more freeways the answer to traffic problems?
What are the alternatives?

2. Inviting an urban planner or a person who has visited "new towns" in England or planned communities in our country to show slides and describe what has been done to solve critical problems and improve the quality of community life
3. Designing an ideal city of the future, using boxes, blocks, construction paper, and other materials to create a table-top or floor layout with planning guided by such questions as

What major zones should we have: residential, business, industry, or other? How should they be arranged? How should open space be used within them and between them?

How large should the city population be? How much area will be needed to provide for the stated population?

How can traffic, housing, pollution, and other urban problems of today be avoided? How will transportation be provided? What kinds of dwellings will be needed? How will wastes be handled?

What provision will be made for services? Education? Health care? Recreation? Fire and police protection? Welfare? Other?

What other provisions should be made?

Conclusion

Activities such as the following may be used to conclude this unit:

1. Ask students to generalize by stating a main idea in response to these questions:

    In general, what are the main environmental problems in urban areas?

    How has population change contributed to environmental problems?

    How can individuals and groups work to improve the environment?

2. Have students make and illustrate booklets or scrapbooks on environmental problems, including material on how to improve the environment as well as material on pollution and other problems.

3. Have students present reports or panel discussions on various problems and steps that can be taken to solve them.

4. Arrange for groups of four or five students to make murals that highlight problems believed to be of critical importance in their own urban and suburban area.

5. Have students plan and present a program, skit, or dramatization that focuses on selected problems.

Sources of Materials

FOR STUDENTS

Kit of materials from the instructional media center.

Classroom and school library resources.

FOR TEACHERS

ERIC/SMEAC Information Reference Center. Columbus, Ohio: Ohio State University, College of Education. Bibliographies on environmental education.

Fowler, John M., *Energy Environment Source Book*. Washington, D.C.: National Science Teachers Association, 1979. Reference book on energy and environmental topics.

AGENCIES AND ORGANIZATIONS

Conservation Foundation, 1250 Connecticut Avenue, Washington, D.C. 20036

Environmental Science Center, 5400 Glenwood Avenue, Minneapolis, Minnesota 55422

Garden Club of America, 598 Madison Avenue, New York, New York 10022

Izaak Walton League of America, 31 North State Street, Chicago, Illinois 60610

Keep America Beautiful, 99 Park Avenue, New York, New York 10016

League of Women Voters of the United States, 1730 M Street, N.W., Washington, D.C. 20036

National Audubon Society, 950 Third Avenue, New York, New York 10022

National Coal Association, Southern Building, 15 and H Streets, Washington, D.C. 20036

National Wildlife Federation, 232 Carol Street N.W., Washington, D.C. 20036

Public Affairs Committee, 381 Park Avenue South, New York, New York 10016

Scientists' Institute for Public Information, 355 Lexington Avenue, New York, New York 10021

Sierra Club, 1050 Mills Tower, San Francisco, California 94104

Society of American Foresters, 1010 16 Street N.W., Washington, D.C. 20036

Superintendent of Documents, Government Printing Office, Washington, D.C. 20402

U.S. Department of Agriculture, Conservation Service and Forest Service, Washington, D.C. 20025

U.S. Department of Energy, Information Service, P.O. Box 62, Oak Ridge, Tennessee 37830

U.S. Department of the Interior, Bureau of Reclamation, Fish and Wildlife Service, National Park Service, Water Pollution Control Administration, Washington, D.C. 20025

Wild Flower Preservation Society, 3740 Oliver Street N.W., Washington, D.C. 20015

INDEX
OF
AUTHORS

INDEX
OF
SUBJECTS